SHOOTING FOR CHANGE

SHOOTING

JUNG JOON LEE

FOR CHANGE

Korean Photography after the War

DUKE UNIVERSITY PRESS
Durham and London
2024

Printed in the United States of America on acid-free paper ∞
Project Editor: Michael Trudeau
Designed by A. Mattson Gallagher
Typeset in Minion Pro, National 2 Narrow, and SMMyunjo Std by Westchester Publishing Services

Library of Congress Cataloging-in-Publication Data
Names: Lee, Jung Joon, author.
Title: Shooting for change : Korean photography after the war / Jung Joon Lee.
Description: Durham : Duke University Press, 2024. | Includes bibliographical references and index.
Identifiers: LCCN 2023040694 (print)
LCCN 2023040695 (ebook)
ISBN 9781478025993 (paperback)
ISBN 9781478019923 (hardcover)
ISBN 9781478059202 (ebook)
Subjects: LCSH: Photography—Korea (South)—History—20th century. | Photography—Political aspects—Korea (South) | Photography—Social aspects—Korea (South) | Korean War, 1950–1953—Photography. | Korean diaspora in art. | Postcolonialism and the arts—Korea (South) | Nationalism in art.
Classification: LCC TR106.5 .L44 2024 (print) | LCC TR106.5 (ebook) | DDC 770.9519509/045—DC23/ENG/20231212
LC record available at https://lccn.loc.gov/2023040694
LC ebook record available at https://lccn.loc.gov/2023040695

Cover art: Yong Suk Kang, from *Maehyangni P'unggyŏng*, Maehyang-ri, 1999, gelatin silver print. Courtesy of the artist.

We are grateful to the Association for Asian Studies (AAS)—www.asianstudies.org—for providing financial assistance toward publication of this book with an award through its First Book Subvention Program.

For the people appearing in this book
whose names I do not know

CONTENTS

ILLUSTRATIONS

Plates

Figures

NOTE ON TRANSLITERATION

I use the McCune-Reischauer Romanization for Korean transliteration except with regard to (1) the names of artists and scholars who have previously exhibited or published their work outside of South Korea with the current Romanization; (2) the official Romanization of cities and towns in the Revised Romanization of Korean except in transliterated captions and titles; and (3) the names of institutions, companies, and businesses that have their own Romanization known to the author. The names of Northeast Asian origin are presented as family name first, given name second, excepting names otherwise familiar from widely published Romanized transliterations. Unless otherwise noted, all translations are my own.

ACKNOWLEDGMENTS

As this project comes close to an end, I am more than ever aware that an academic monograph is truly a collaborative project. So many people have taught, supported, and pushed me to pursue not just knowledge but also collective enrichment and care for the communities that I became part of. The least I can do here is express my profound gratitude to the artists, photographers, visionary thinkers, teachers, friends, activists, colleagues, librarians, archivists, curators, and students who have contributed to this work. I must note that this is necessarily an incomplete list of all the people I want to thank. Nonetheless, these acknowledgments are for them as well.

I began research for this book in 2007 at the CUNY Graduate Center, and it began to take shape as photographs of candlelight vigils in South Korea started to spread online in June 2008. I could not have looked so closely into the sea of images and listened carefully to the circulating photographs without the mentoring and advice of Geoffrey Batchen, Anna Chave, and Peter Hitchcock. I am thankful for their encouragement and sustained support. I am indebted to John Tagg, who encouraged me to delve deeper into the conceptual grounds of a project framed by nationhood, which has resonated throughout the process of writing.

My thanks go to the then director David Harvey and other folks at the CUNY Center for Place, Culture, and Politics, where I was a doctoral fellow.

These seminars helped me delve further into issues of urbanity in relation to photographic practices as civic resistance. In particular, Karen Strassler offered strong support for my work. She also handed me a copy of her first book on vernacular photography in Java in anticipation of my publication. I hope she knows what that meant to a graduate student struggling to keep afloat in New York City.

I also send my warm thanks to my students and former colleagues in the Department of Art and Design at Queensborough Community College, where I began full-time collegiate teaching. CUNY is truly a transformative place, and I am grateful to my students for teaching me what higher education can and needs to do.

I am thankful for the support of my colleagues at Rhode Island School of Design (RISD), especially Professor Emerita Mary Bergstein for her continued encouragement. It was a pleasure to work on the manuscript in conversation with Namita Vijay Dharia, whose strength and vigor in the final stages of completing her own book also provided inspiration. I thank all my colleagues with whom I engaged in enriching discussions about decolonial approaches to teaching and research as part of the Decolonial Teaching in Action faculty seminar offered by the Center for Social Equity and Inclusion. These conversations helped me look deeper into my own desire for decolonializing research and writing. My research for the book has also been supported by RISD's Professional Development Fund and Humanities Fund.

In addition to those mentioned above, several colleagues and friends have read my manuscript and provided thoughtful commentary at various stages of my writing. Rebekka Gold has provided priceless editorial suggestions and comments on this project. The Clark Institute Colloquium, led by Margaret Olin and Amos Morris-Reich, provided an opportunity to workshop an early version of my camptown portrait chapter. I am grateful to the organizers and participants of this event, including Shawn Michelle Smith, who returned thoughtful comments and warm encouragement. My deep appreciation to Erina Duganne, Heather Diack, Ann Murray, Sophie Jung, Midori Yamamura, Yu-Chieh Li, Jie Guo, Jae Won Edward Chung, and Bridget Martin for inviting me to work with them on photography and art and share my work. Eleana Kim's comments on the chapter on artworks and photographs of the DMZ and US military base sites helped me think further about the anticipation and need for change in these areas; Carla Hung, Kevin Duong, and Tamta Khalvashi also read parts of this chapter closely and provided invaluable comments, and it has been a joy to work and think with them.

I appreciate the opportunities to present versions of the book chapters at several institutions, courtesy of Caitlin Beach and Asato Ikeda at Fordham University; Amy Chin at Vassar College; Iftikhar Dadi at Cornell University; Nayun Jang at Sogang University; Youngju Ryu, Se-Mi Oh, and Kaeun Park at the University of Michigan; Paul Gladston and Minerva Inwald at the University of New South Wales; and Yu-Chieh Li at Lingnan University. From across College Hill, Samuel Perry has shared parts of his manuscript for his volume on queer Korean literature, which I am grateful for. I also thank Jie-Hyun Lim and Nayun Jang at the Critical Global Studies Institute at Sogang University for their support and anticipation.

I thank Ken Wissoker of Duke University Press for his consistent support for my project, which became an anchor for me to rely on and continue to believe in this book. I am also thankful to Ryan Kendall for her assistance and support and to the production, design, and marketing teams at Duke University Press. I have immense gratitude for the anonymous readers of my manuscript and their comments, which enriched and sharpened my arguments.

The early stages of my research were supported by the Joan and Stanford Alexander Award at the Museum of Fine Arts, Houston. I am grateful to Anne Tucker and Yasufumi Nakamori, who were then the museum's department of photography curators. Funding from the CUNY Graduate Center made possible my research at various archives and institutions, including the 4.19 Revolution Library and the War Memorial of Korea.

My research for this project was enriched by comraderies and friendships: Forged at the GC, my friendships with Ananda Cohen-Aponte and Maya Jiménez continue to bring me comfort and security. It has been a pleasure to work with Hosu Kim and Yeong Ran Kim, and I look forward to our continued collaboration on the projects we have embarked on. I greatly miss friends who are now based in Asia: Meebae Lee, Chu-Chiun Wei, Sachiko Onuma, and Yuko Fujii—I seek chances to visit and look forward to seeing you whenever I make the trip. My special thanks to Sung Hee Yook, for her kindness and hospitality at her Seoul home, especially in the early days of my research. I am also thankful for the lively dialogues I had with participants of various conferences. A wonderful colleagueship began in Binghamton many years ago with Hye-ri Oh.

Many of the photographers and artists whose work I discuss in this book have met or conversed with me by email with generosity, excitement, and kindness. I am especially grateful to Yong Suk Kang, Oksun Kim, siren eun young jung, Sunmin Lee, Agnès Dherbeys, Hwangbo Kangja, Yeondoo Jung, and Suntag Noh; special thanks as well to Cheon Chin Soon, Pak Lisa, and Kyungsook Yoon for kindly sharing their photographs.

I could not have completed this book without the support of scholars, curators, editors, and archivists at various institutions across the world: I thank chief curator Youngju Son and curator Sunyoung Kim at Museum Hanmi; the staff at the Still Pictures Research Room of the National Archives in College Park, Maryland; and the photography collection archivists at the Imperial Museum of War, London. Noonbit Publishing's editor Kyu Sang Lee has provided continued support throughout my research. I am also thankful to Professor Ju Suk Park at Myongji University for sharing his insights and knowledge.

In Korea and New York, my family has given me limitless support and love. I thank my parents Chung Ai Oh and Kwang Yong Lee and my late grandmothers Hyun Sook Lee and Ju Hee Lee for their unwavering encouragement and pride. I also thank Jiyoung Kim and Jisoo Kim for always being there for me.

And to Agustin Chung, who has stood by me throughout this incredible (and at times strange) journey, you have been the kindest partner, friend, and comrade. This one is for you.

INTRODUCTION

The Time of Korean Photography

Notes on National Photography and Temporality

Immiscible times—the temporal disquietude provoked by supernaturalisms that are never entirely enfolded or assimilated into the ever-accelerating, preemptive forward push of chronology and capital—are indexical signs of strain, stress-fissures in homogenizing, deracinating translations.
Bliss Cua Lim, *Translating Time*

Reconstituting the discourse of cultural difference demands more than a simple change of cultural contents and symbols, for a replacement within the same representational time frame is never adequate. This reconstitution requires a radical revision of the social temporality *in which emergent histories may be written.*
Homi K. Bhabha, "Freedom's Basis in the Indeterminate"

Shooting for Change is a book on postwar Korean photography and the discursive ways in which photography makes meaning. The project was a long time in the making; its development has been motivated in part by the necessity of finding adequate and appropriate ways to write about photography broadly and a history of Korean photography specifically. In this endeavor, I was confronted with two major issues. First, the more I wrote about photography in and of Korea, the more questions arose about the seeming futility of approaching this body of work using those historico-authorial frameworks considered foundational in the discipline of art history for any serious photography scholarship. Furthermore, there seemed a constant demand that this history strive to define what is uniquely or comparatively "Korean" about Korean photography. I began to see a way forward by exploring transdisciplinary approaches to photographic topics. Engaging with lively dialogues on the postcoloniality of East Asia (both north and south) and its stubbornly irreducible relationship with the United States, I stopped seeing the transnationality of Korean photography as inhibiting. Instead, transdisciplinary discussions on photography, East Asian postcoloniality, American imperialism, and diaspora allowed me to think critically about the desire for a history of Korean photography as an epistemologically decolonizing practice.

Shooting for Change is therefore also a book about grappling with so-called national photography, and I start the book by probing photography's "nationality" as an ontological identificatory index. This probing also necessitates an investigation of what such questions demand of a study of photography in order for it to become legible in the academy. For this purpose, I treat temporality as a key onto-epistemic framework in producing knowledge of photography while paying close attention to the potentiality photography enables when we engage with the medium in multisensorial ways.

To expand on the discussion of temporality and national photography, I revisit photography's assumed temporal coevalness through a critique of modern temporality in the introduction. This critique is followed by a discussion on photography's contingency and catachrony, exploring how they may unravel incommensurable temporalities of national, nonwhite photography against the homogenizing temporality of modernity in knowledge production. Hence, through the work of thinkers in postcoloniality and feminist scholars in and outside of Asia and North America, I offer a temporal critique of national photography.

My critique of temporality does not seek to lay out the irreconcilable differences between the temporality of Euro-American photography and the "belatedness" of nonwhite photography in a homogenous temporal map of global photography. Rather, I hope to recoup—despite the continuing impact of the temporality of modernity—national photography's potentiality to disrupt, per Walter Benjamin, "homogenous, empty time" perpetuated in the racialized economy of academic knowledge, and to challenge the treatment of national photography (and the even more broadly defined global photography) as evidencing the diversification of the history of photography.[1]

At the same time, I note that this project is not aimed at securing a counterposition of modern temporality in photography studies. To do so, I feel, would be to repeat the homological production of knowledge on photography that is tailored to those who find comfort in seeing things only through the framework they already know. This study on Korean photography does not exist to prove that the center-periphery of the geography of photo history can be overturned. The project rather refutes the logic of center-periphery (or ubiquitous centers), regardless of who would attain the central position through adherence to the temporality of modernity and a historicism based on it.

The specificity and criticality of the term *subaltern*, first used by Antonio Gramsci in his *Prison Notebooks* in the 1930s and taken up by Ranajit Guha in the 1980s for studies of South Asian subalterns, has its epistemic anchor in the work of the Subaltern Studies Group, through which postcolonial studies gained their criticality in the academy. Running the risk of dislocating and despecifying subalternity from that scholarly history, my own analyses of the onto-epistemology of nonwhite, non-Western photography are greatly indebted to the work of postcolonial studies scholars. After probing the temporality of national photography, I interrogate the "nation" as a category of cultural containment to be kept uncontaminated from non-Korean concepts and practices through authenticated Korean discourses and reimagine the place of the Korean diaspora in Korean photography. Finally, I provide a brief discussion on the Korean War and militarism as a broad backdrop in the context of rupturing identarian logics, complicating the spatiotemporal categorization of nationality.[2] The introduction thereby provides the context, background, and methodology by which this book addresses Korean photography.

The normalization of militarism, especially in the wake of the Korean War, is central to the context and content of *Shooting for Change*. One of the most striking impacts of war is its everydayness, its ability to become mundane and unnoticeable, its pervasiveness in life. My use of the term *militarism* in this book is about this pervasiveness, rather than referring to the military force, installations, and politics involved in it. Korean militarism—its modern formation, expansion through the colonial period, and normalization through the Korean War and postwar military regimes—is transnational, both making and riding the geopolitical currents of northeast Asia and crossing the Pacific Ocean to the United States. The rigid formality of rank, usually according to seniority (by age or time in position), is present in any group of two or more, even in casual settings. Although this is commonly recognized as Confucian tradition in South Korea, it traces back specifically to the militarized colonial education since the early twentieth century. The phenomenon is neither obsolete nor bound by generation or location: seeing students from South Korea on my Rhode Island campus play such roles outside of the classroom, even if jokingly, I am struck by how militaristic "Ǒptryŏppŏtch'yŏ!" is, and how entrenched it remains despite its irrelevance to art school life.[3]

To examine the history of Korean photography therefore entails an investigation of photography vis-à-vis the making of the militarized nation, and what it means to practice photography in the normalized conditions of transnational militarism. *Shooting for Change* treats the transnational militarism of Korea not as a unique subject of Korean photography, but as a lens through which we may probe the officially and culturally sanctioned readings of images when returning to them at different times. To examine this relationship between militarism and photography, three key approaches are explored: treating photography as (1) a multitemporal event (being experienced in heterogeneous time); (2) a multisensorial encounter (the affect of photography); and (3) a medium of plural performativity (the becoming of a political subject). In this examination, a critique of the gendered historicization of photography in South Korea, parallel to militarism, offers a thread connecting the approaches. As such, the book owes a profound debt to studies on the gendered underpinnings of various photographic practices across the world, exposing the gendered violence of colonialism and imperialism in the writing of photo history itself. As with other parts of the book, this critique also has been inspired by recent feminist and LGBTQ+ movements and cultural productions in South Korea.

Time: An Onto-epistemic Query

"What makes these photographs uniquely Korean?" Repeatedly expected to produce knowledge addressing the medium's difference from an imagined neutral state—aestheticism free from national (and thereby cultural, ethnic, social, etc.) context—it seems that a country's photography cannot have its meaning, or name, until it is identified as constituting a national photography. The body of photographic work is expected to represent the nation, even as the images are called upon to constitute a national photography.[4] At the same time, it must also avoid becoming yet another photography of the Other, whose identity is addressed only by virtue of its deviation from (or similarities, however behind the curve, to) European and Anglo (white) American photography.[5] To define photographs of-in-about-from Korea as Korean photography is therefore to write a history of the medium epistemologically framed by nationhood—with its culture treated as content filling that frame—and in turn to produce knowledge based on and about those differences that define the "Koreanness" of the medium.

This "national" is not merely or exactly referring to an official, or fully representative, Korean photography, but becomes an identitarian boundary of photography.[6] National in this sense is not just an index of difference but a process of Othering-as-subjectivizing, through which photography gains its identity.[7] This process, when writing a history of national photography, also establishes *the* history of photography as a priori, a core from which any less broad history of photography extends, and an acceptance of it. To wit: the point of origin for the history of photography is reckoned as the invention and development of the camera in France and England, and later from vernacular to artistic developments in Euro-America; all "other" studies are founded on this understanding, to the extent that I have heard a photo historian at a globally renowned art college call histories of photographic practices outside the West "the alternative history of photography." Such a singularized history casts any history outside of it as national, separate from yet subordinate to the core—the role of any imperialist subject.[8]

It seems, however, that the criticality of probing national photography has faded, partly in the desire to move on from the pains of identity politics, and partly as the critique of global photography has come to carry more weight. Still, the issues of locating photography are conjoined with issues of temporality—and that of modernity in particular. Before assuming this book's position in any kind of theoretical framework, it is thus necessary to understand why the temporality of photography's location is still bound to a modern temporality, which valorizes nominated difference, in order for this photography to become a subject of knowledge—and as such, it is necessary to investigate photography's onto-epistemology: the interrelatedness of the ontological and epistemological becoming.

Rey Chow explains why nonwhite culture is bound in white culture by an impossible task to become a subject of knowledge, and why shifting the research focus or frame may not resolve those issues: "To put it in very simple terms, non-white culture, in order to 'be' or to 'speak,' must: 1) seek legitimacy/recognition from white culture, which has denied the reality of the 'other' cultures all along; 2) use the language of white culture (since it is the dominant one) to produce itself (so that it could be recognized and thus legitimized); *and yet* 3) resist complete normativization by white culture."[9] Following Chow's points, even if a project examining a non-Western photo practice sets out to complicate the location of national photography—say, by focusing on global networks and circulations, or the itineracy of photography—the photography of the nonwhite culture must seek legitimacy/recognition from white culture (what academy training entails).[10] Furthermore, the researcher is required to deal with the fatigue of being expected to seek this legitimacy/recognition in the language of the singular history of photography, carrying on its obsession with identifying variants of modernism in nonwhite photography. Most importantly, while doing this diligent work, the researcher is expected to resist the history's normativization and maintain its position of difference. To add to Chow, the act of resistance against normativization ends up serving the liberal humanities enterprise—capitalizing on diversity and inclusion—that subsumes difference as an identitarian index.[11]

Hence, it is essential to approach the rise of national photography studies in the 1990s and 2000s (of which I am part) in the context of "a genealogy of colonial divisions of humanity," which Lisa Lowe discusses in *The Intimacies of Four Continents*: "The genealogy of modern liberalism is thus a genealogy of modern race; racial differences and distinctions designate the boundaries of the human and endure as remainders attesting to the violence of liberal universality. To observe that the genealogy of modern liberalism is simultaneously a genealogy of colonial divisions of humanity is a project of tracking the ways in which race, geography, nation, caste, religion, gender, sexuality and other social differences become elaborated as normative categories for governance under the rubrics of liberty and sovereignty."[12] As such, before launching a study of national photography, or "cultural" photography even, the normativization of nation as an episteme of photography needs to be called to task.[13]

Jasbir Puar joins Chow and Lowe in probing what feels like an epistemological gridlock. Quoting Chow, Puar argues, "'Difference' produces new subjects of inquiry that then infinitely multiply exclusion in order to promote inclusion. Difference now precedes and defines identity. Part of Chow's concern is that poststructuralist efforts to attend to the specificity of Others has become a universalizing project that is always beholden to the self-preferentiality of the 'center,' ironically given that intersectionality functions as a call for and a form of antiessentialism."[14] Therefore, how the "national" in national photography is defined may differ among studies as they attend to the specificity of Others and potentially call upon the intersectionality provided by various other studies. Yet the query itself is predicated on "the self-referentiality" of a Euro-American approach to what requires definition, and for whom the definition is aimed. Sometimes the question leads to nuanced analyses. Other times, nationality is treated as inherent.

"What does photography tell us about Korea?" The question presupposes that research on photographs produces knowledge fulfilling the "aboutness" in the question—in this case, *about* ethnographic indexes of Korea, made identifiable, and definable, in photographs.[15] Approaching the subject of knowledge production not from a critique of "difference as an episteme" but from the epistemology of "aboutness," Kandice Chuh notes the impoverishing effect of studying that "aboutness" as a measure of relevance and means for gatekeeping: "Aboutness functions as an assessment of relevance and, within the racialized economy of academic knowledge[,] preserves the (racist) epistemologies of (neo)liberalism through a reproductive logic that is utterly unqueer."[16] Chuh sees that "the determination of what something (a novel, a field of study, a lecture) is 'about' often is conducted as a way of avoiding engagement with 'difference,' and especially with racialized difference"; and, often, this avoidance ends up being masked by a focus on the difference, not an engagement with.[17]

While I acknowledge that this assessment may appear critical of the inquisitive nature of ethnographic scholarship, Chuh is not referring merely to the legitimacy of academic inquiries, but to the epistemic violence it bears on subjects that may only gain its legitimacy through its (acceptable) difference and relevance (e.g., "national" photography's relationship to modernity showcasing variations and relevance). Thus, the nationalizing of photography, borrowing from Chuh, is a way to "compartmentalize knowledge" in order to normativize what may be unruly and prickly—by sweeping it under the rug of *the* history of photography and pulling it out when difference needs to be showcased to uphold and solidify the ever-expanding field. The discipline of aboutness determines "what counts as knowledge, expertise and specialization" and is "taken up as and into the structures of the university in an architectural and intensified way."[18] Moreover, given the normativizing effect of the question *about* Korea, we must also ask what it means to produce a history of Korean photography that is also part of the so-called global history of art, when much of the effort (sometimes its entirety) has to be dedicated to a critique of, as Lisa Yoneyama puts it, "the homogenizing myths of nationalist epistemology."[19]

How, then, can this project of writing *about* Korean photography sustain its onto-epistemic reason? Can epistemological correctives undo "the (racist) epistemologies of (neo)liberalism" in the humanities studies of photography? Navigating through the possibilities and limits of difference and aboutness, I am mindful of the fact that "epistemological correctives cannot apprehend ontological becomings; the complexity of process is continually mistaken for a resultant product," as Puar writes.[20] Accordingly, I do not attempt epistemological correctives by prescribing a methodology for national photography. Indeed, such epistemological correctives cannot apprehend or account for the process of ontological becomings—here, the becoming of Korean photography. Hence, the probing of the onto-epistemic in the *writing* of Korean photography is itself part of the becoming of Korean photography, and it is not a curative for the national methodology.

Puar's onto-epistemic query helps in rethinking the political applicability of representation. Working through Gilles Deleuze and Félix Guattari's theory of assemblage, Puar states the recognized subjects of representation—based on identificatory categories of differences for intersectionality to be enacted—are assumed to be "the dominant, primary, or more efficacious platform of political intervention"; on the other hand, assemblage, "a Deleuzian nonrepresentational, non-subject-oriented politics is deemed impossible." The identification of the subject, a priori of intersectionality, appears to assure the possibility of political transformation; however, unlike intersectionality, assemblage is based on disidentification of concrete representational categories, through "lines of flight, movements of deterritorialization and destratification."[21]

This exposes the frictional relationship between assemblage and intersectionality. Though not oppositional, they are irreconcilable. Treating the affect of both assemblage and intersectionality not as incompatible concepts or fallouts but as frictional praxes in my studies of photography, I engage with the (im)possibilities of national photography through this friction, irreconcilability, and incommensurability: not just in terms of location but the equally critical issue of temporalities in the writing of photography. The analysis of temporality as an onto-epistemological investigation of photography reveals how the writing of photography arranges the irreconcilability of temporalities (between Western and the non-Western, or nonwhite, photography) in the homogenizing time of modernity so that they can be seen from the represented location of a normative position. Through the analysis, I propose a becoming of Korean photography, its onto-epistemology, not despite but for its potentiality in friction.

The Location of Enunciation

In the writing of national photography, modernity has been a constant episteme. Fundamentally, modern constructs are at the forefront of the very term "national photography." Beyond the relative youth of the medium, present understandings of nation and nationhood are grounded in modern (and Eurocentric) political concepts and denominations of (current) power structures.[22] A potential virtue of modernity as episteme is its normative position from which different times are called upon, and certainly, a history of photography that champions all national histories of photography is more easily realized if national photographies are charted according to a standard time. How a national photography is defined then depends on how one situates national traits commensurate to this global time—that is, the subjects of a national photography are identified from the standpoint of modern temporality, even though their national contexts (of different times) are provided as a distinguishing backdrop. In this reading, where a national photography embodies temporal incommensurability, modernity as episteme works to reconcile with this incommensurability by continuously expanding, while focusing on "aboutness" which ultimately evades the processes of the onto-epistemic becoming of differences—the systemic workings of (neoliberal) inclusion and diversity in the academy. This temporality, although in plain sight, is often overlooked, as photography is theorized and widely accepted to be inherently multitemporal. The reading of multitemporal events through a photograph risks being glossed over as an epistemic work of multitemporalities when, in fact, epistemic projects are often in friction with the "homogenous, empty time" of the normativizing location.[23]

One reason why the temporality of modernity has successfully championed all temporalities is its reading of different times, which, in fact, cannot be done without modernity's "ex-nominating" power. Addressing a persistent failure in photo studies, scholars such as Christopher Pinney problematize a focus on the global, which ends up centering Europe and North America as photography's location yet again. Pinney questions why "global" has only referred to the medium's travel between Europe and Anglo (white) America and the rest of the world, eliding travel between Europe and Anglo (white) America—a practice of differentiation rather than difference. Following Roland Barthes's notion of "ex-nomination" in the bourgeoisie erasure of its appellation in the political arena as avoiding being named, "undergo[ing] a real *ex-nominating* operation," Pinney espouses the term to describe how certain photography gets freed from its location and others do not: "The space of 'Euro-America' is 'ex-nominated,' rendered un-marked and un-located . . . [as] the ex-nominated heartland."[24]

The itineracy of photography should be dealt with more critically, he continues, which will then "help erode the localizing and territorial boundaries which certain approaches to photography in its nominated forms have sought to establish."[25] He hopes that a method comparing "differently-located practices of photography"—what he calls "a parallel itineracy of method" for studying a "World System Photography"—will transcend the current model of nomination, and eventually denominate all practices of photography. While this proposal addresses the issues of locating photography in the ever-expanding field of photo studies, and I find the concept of "nomination" and "ex-nomination" effective (and refer to it throughout this chapter), I do not wish to rush toward the "System" as a way of connecting dots. Primarily, such a focus on "parallels" returns to the question of difference, determining how a located practice comparatively differs from one another. Inevitably, photographies compete with each other from their location in this "World System," fighting through postcolonial entanglements in hopes of being denominated one day.[26]

Significantly, Barthes finds the temporality of death—conjured and permanently suspended in his widely admired book *Camera Lucida*—a denominating essence of photography; however, the experience of death, both as "real" and suspended, is expected to differ by culture, society, locality, economy, and individual, as Barthes himself once had discussed many years before the book in his critique of the *Family of Man* exhibition and rejects the exhibition's conflation and its universalizing effect.[27] While by no means refuting Barthes's evocative work on the essence of photography on the grounds of diversity,[28] I want to pay attention to how his multitenses and multispaces become unequivocally commensurable, without ever being required to either be nominated or ex-nominated, or, conversely, to "provincialize" each place and time—to use Dipesh Chakrabarty's proposition in rethinking the place of knowledge production in the context of historicism and subalternity. The multimoments and places, in fact, can be summoned without, for example, the provincialization of Barthes's Paris at his present; on the road to "Beith Lehem" near Jerusalem in August Salzmann's photograph—that is, taking on Salzmann's place and time represented in the photograph; and the time of Jesus, as Salzmann's time conjures it up in Barthes at his present. According to Barthes, his consciousness gets dizzy in these three tenses, even without having to locate each time: "my present, the time of Jesus, and that of the photographer."[29]

While the temporalities Barthes presents to us are not unusual (one's own time, the time of the photographed event, and those of other related historical moments), I am reminded by Chakrabarty's, Bhabha's, and Chow's examinations of modern and postcolonial subjectivization and exemption. The dizzying of Barthes's consciousness is caused by him looking at Salzmann's photograph and conjuring the times and locations of Salzmann's photo taking, and of Jesus. But following Chakrabarty, the French poststructuralist and his chosen subjects are indeed exempt from the "provincialization" (including the explicated specification) of their historical and political context tied to their spatiotemporality in a process that constantly haunts non-Western, nonwhite photography.

After all, who needs to nominate Jesus and his spatiotemporality (or Barthes's and thus Salzmann's) when it is indeed predicated on the Gregorian temporality of the Christian world synchronizing the times of the rest of the world?[30] But even without acknowledging that, the place of Barthes's enunciation, ironically, ex-nominates them; and the parahistorical connections formed between the tenses are welcome. Apparent to those who are, consistently and relentlessly, nominated within the discourse of globalism, it is, indeed, the force of whitewashing, the "ghostly matters" of hauntology appearing in non-Western, nonwhite photography.[31] At this point, it is important to remember a critique, twenty-some years earlier, of the *Family of Man* exhibition, in which Barthes cynically questioned why the exhibition organizers did not ask Emmett Till's parents what they thought about the exhibition, and posited the homogenization of death (of mankind) he saw there as "everyone dies, though differently, therefore we are one people." The discussion in *Camera Lucida* is a welcome redaction of his position that, "however universal, they are the signs of an historical writing," but his initial approaches cannot be forgotten by perpetually nominated subjects.[32]

Scholarly attention to race, repression, and reproduction has helped unravel the paradoxes laden in the essence of photography (e.g., the temporality of death in photography) and the repression of multisensorial experiences of the medium for privileging visuality. Notably, Fred Moten has pointed out Barthes's universalizing shift from his essay on the *Family of Man* exhibition to *Camera Lucida*; Moten unpacks what is at stake with the performance of modernity in Barthes's "regressive return to 'that-has-been' and/or to where-you-been[,] the staging area for the performance of that violent and ruptural collision that is both the dramatic life of blackness and the opening of what is called modernity."[33] Moten (and most notably Tina Campt) unravels photography's sonic, haptic, and somatic qualities in Black life that unsettle the vision-privileging poststructuralist regime of senses. According to him, the sound of photography, the reverberating sonority of the photographic encounter, is "vulgar" and "shouty" for Barthes because it distracts from the visuality of the photograph and its ability to prick: "Wounding photography is absolutely visual; that is the only way you can love it."[34] Moten observes that the repression of phonic substance in semiotics is applied to the semiotics of photography in *Camera Lucida*: "That the semiotic desire for universality, which excludes the difference of accent by excluding sound in the search for a universal language and a universal science of language, is manifest in Barthes as the exclusion of the sound/shout of the photograph; and, in the fundamental methodological move of what-has-been-called enlightenment, we see the invocation of a silenced difference, a silent black materiality, in order to justify a suppression of difference in the name of (a false) universality."[35]

Working through Moten's critique, the interconnectedness of temporality and sensoriality is irreducible. The universalizing appeal of modern temporality silences the foreign sound of the photograph, be it animalesque howl (analogized as the sound of crying Korean mothers who lost their children by Western journalists) or "mo(ur)nin(g)" of Black visuality (through Emmett Till's photograph).[36] The shout of the historicality of Emmett Till's photograph should not and cannot be muted in the temporality of universal humanism. Hence, to attend to the multisensoriality of photography is to reconsider its onto-epistemology and intersectionality, "to listen to (and touch, taste, and smell) a photograph, or a performance, . . . to attune oneself to a moan or shout that animates the photograph with an intentionality of the outside."[37]

Furthermore, Shawn Michelle Smith reveals how Barthes's punctum and studium are conflated in the process of objectifying the subject of the photograph and in order to evade his own objectification, especially in his writing on the portraits of Black people in *Camera Lucida*—namely William Casby, with whom he sees "the essence of slavery laid bare," and James Van Der Zee's aunts and uncle, whose deductive racialized identification, interestingly, leads him to remember his own white aunt.[38] Smith examines the ways in which Barthes deals with his own anxiety about race and reproduction (as well as death), and, as Moten has also noted, about universalizing the Black subject via studium (turned punctum) and ultimately making all photographs self-referential, to the effect that all photographs are about him and of him.[39] In closing the chapter on race and reproduction, Smith then graciously turns the pointer to herself to enact what Barthes has done to photographs by picking up a photograph of Barthes and finding that she "can meet Barthes part way," forming kinship through this image he left behind, thereby performing the very act of seeing oneself in Others, a kind of homage to the melancholy Barthes invokes via family photographs.[40] The affective work of individuating the universality of *Camera Lucida*, nevertheless, "does not give over as easily to a history of subalternity," as David Eng notes; as Smith aptly examines, that uneasiness exposes Barthes's ex-nomination of his place of enunciation in universalizing photography and its arrested subjects.[41]

Barthes unquestionably paved the road for affective engagement with photography on a profoundly intimate level. A critique of canonic works often puts the critic of far less significance in the risky position of being seen as not understanding the point or even being merely reactionary. But as Moten, Smith, Puar, Chow, and Chakrabarty demonstrate, perceiving an approach that ex-nominates even as it claims the opposite is common enough. Indeed, it is an issue that is obvious to the Other even as it feels impossible but necessary, per Spivak, to tackle time and again.[42]

Photography's Contingency and the Disjuncture of History

And contingency as the *signifying time* of counterhegemonic strategies is not a celebration of "lack" or "excess" or a self-perpetuating series of negative ontologies. Such "indeterminism" is the mark of the conflictual yet productive space in which the arbitrariness of the sign of cultural signification emerges within the regulated boundaries of social discourse.

Homi Bhabha, "Freedom's Basis in the Indeterminate"

As commonly understood today, (national) photography reflects, among other things, the urgency and desire to remember events and how that urgency and desire translates an event by reproducing and re-viewing the image in other times and spaces. Collective memory and commemorative photographs are a case in point: for memories and postmemories of events to be conjured by photography, the ritualistic repetition of time and encounters (e.g., annual commemorations) is a must. Commemorative events, for example, typically deploy photography to affectively associate the events with certain groups of people. For nationally shared events, photographs of the event are used to create postmemories for the people who did not directly experience it.[43] This conjuring of memories and postmemories can even determine who becomes a national subject—who shares this memory when called upon, and who does not.

In this context, the reproduction of images articulates a desire to not only remember an event in specific ways, but to designate the timing for conjuring up those memories, and doing so unites the remembering subjects by synchronizing their time. The time of modernity hence aids national photography in establishing a boundary that defines what the national is and how this national is accepted as an empirical practice of, in this case, photography. Remembering events that frame a history of a nation through photography is therefore also a practice of nation making. And for nation-states such as the Republic of Korea that grapple with volatile geopolitical positioning, this means of nation making has been both invisible and overwhelming.

National photography becoming a product of the temporality of modernity haunts the history of Korean photography. There is the constant demand, or claim, that Korean photography's Koreanness distinguishes itself from other histories, that in the seeming act of reclaiming its history, it must *become* legitimate, a subject identifiable, and thus written in normativizing language of *the* history of photography, while resisting being completely normativized. To claim its national identity on this plane is therefore to accept the force of the homogenizing time and participate fully in the epistemological project of modernity, but nonetheless remain as its transcendental Other.

Given that this participation is often acknowledged, and indeed celebrated, as producing a much-needed history, is writing a history that problematizes the very framework of the national even desirable for photo studies? What is a way out of this conundrum, or is looking for a "solution" likewise problematic? Demanding a fast solution to what fundamentally requires decolonial praxes may overlook the struggle many photographers and photo studies scholars deal with and ignore the work they have already been doing.

Rather than looking for such a solution elsewhere, it may begin when we stop trying to manage the temporal disjuncture of photography, and instead seize it as the position from which to write the medium's history against identitarian logic.[44] Temporal disjuncture as an epistemic event is close to how I understand Walter Benjamin's "contingency" of photography:[45] a way of distinguishing between the remembering of multiple moments through photographs and the persistent disobedience of different times in photography.[46] In "Little History of Photography" (1931), Benjamin writes, "No matter how artful the photographer, no matter how carefully posed his subject, the beholder feels an irresistible urge to search such a picture for the tiny spark of contingency, of the here and now, with which reality has (so to speak) seared the subject, to find the inconspicuous spot where in the immediacy of that long-forgotten moment the future nests so eloquently that we, looking back, may rediscover it."[47] The critical point of Benjamin's contingency, which we recognize in our time (of the past about the future), does not lie in the fact that these multitenses are conjured up when looking at a photograph, but rather in the fact that the spark has been in our unconscious and we now come to arrest it, "that we should seize hold of this memory."[48]

Blasting open homogenous, empty time, the spark of contingency is what photography allows us to do with history, with our own political agency: to arrest it, to write it (appropriating a memory), and to make history. The blast-opening of the continuum of homogenous temporality is a step toward taking ownership of and making visible or sensible the temporality, agency, and (even) incommensurability of national photography. Hence, the political potentiality in seizing "the inconspicuous spot" in photography opens a possibility to do away with the need for methodology turning differences into identitarian indexes.

Likewise, Chakrabarty sees potential in "minor" history beyond writing "good" minority history, provided "we stay with heterogeneities without seeking to reduce them to any overarching principle that speaks for an already given whole."[49] Chakrabarty here warns about the routinization of innovation, in that "successfully incorporated 'minority histories' may then be likened to yesterday's revolutionaries who become today's gentlemen."[50] In that sense, to write about the difficulties of national photography is to work through "minor" methods, rather than to write a minority history of modernity, which uses a majoritarian framework.[51] One way to work through such methods is to let what Avery Gordon terms "the primitive of the past" take us with its unruliness:[52] We need not be frightened when social life, "fraught with ghosts, does not obey our rules of method and our disciplinary organization of it."[53] We need not be frightened to view "the disjointed nature of any particular 'now' one may inhabit."[54] And we need to let photography touch us to sense the disjointed nature of the particular "now," for "a plurality of time existing together, a disjuncture of the present with itself."[55]

Siegfried Kracauer, however, while sharply critiquing the hollowness of history as chronology, brings attention to what he sees as the dialectical nature of time—as period (shaped time) and as chronology—and acknowledges that Benjamin overlooks this dialectic as he "drives home the nonentity of chronological time without manifesting the slightest concern over the other side of the picture."[56] In fact, for Kracauer, the incommensurability of time does not mean different times cannot exist coevally but that both "the incoherent series of shaped times and chronological time as a homogenous flow" exist as a dialectic.

At this point, I am reminded, by Kracauer and Homi Bhabha, that the space of temporality and the discursiveness of modernity has not yet been questioned. Bhabha asks, "What is this 'now' of modernity? Who defines this present from which we speak? This leads to a more challenging question: *What is the desire of this repeated demand to modernize? Why does it insist, so compulsively, on its contemporaneous reality, its spatial dimension, its spectatorial distance*?"[57]

Modernity, Bhabha contends, is "about the historical construction of a specific position of historical enunciation and address."[58] This position, which I take as the foundation of one's positionality as a speaking self (a modernist subjectivization), is treated as a temporal break: "the *time-lag* between the Great Event and its circulation as a historical sign of the 'people' or an 'epoch,' that constitutes the memory and the moral of the event as a *narrative*, a disposition to cultural communality, a form of social and psychic identification."[59] The privileged distance from the event, required for "bearing witness" or being "subjected," is what he calls historical "belatedness." Bhabha's time-lag (via Frantz Fanon's thoughts on "the signifying time-lag of cultural difference"[60]) does not signify a perpetual state of the subaltern's belatedness to modernity, but enables "a representative position through the spatial distance, . . . a specific position of historical enunciation and address."[61]

If the contingency of photography can be taken as a resistance against the temporal alignment to partake in homogenous, empty time, Bhabha's notion of postcolonial "belatedness" bespeaks this refusal. The time-lag is a place from which one makes perceptible the incommensurability of time in the enunciation of events—and, for my purpose, in the writing of a history of photography. I find a prickliness in the time-lag's refusal to "catch up" and synchronize with the temporality of modernity, its refusal to desire a place in its globality. The refusal insists that the time-lag of postcoloniality not be discarded simply as a colonial signification of Western superiority, but instead be reckoned with to make visible and sensible where liberal historicism fails—for example, in the ex-nomination of the dominant theory of the social. In that regard, Bhabha sees "the ethnocentric limitations of Michel Foucault's spatial sign of modernity" and explains how Foucault arrives at a "'correlative,' overlapping temporality" with the example of the French Revolution:

> Through Kant, Foucault traces "the ontology of the present" to the exemplary event of the French Revolution and it is there that he stages his sign of modernity. But it is the spatial dimension of "distance"—*the perspectival distance from which the spectacle is seen*—that installs a cultural homogeneity into the sign of modernity; a Eurocentric perspective at the point at which modernity installs a "moral disposition in mankind." The eurocentricity of Foucault's theory of cultural difference is revealed in his insistent spatializing of the time of modernity. Avoiding the problems of the sovereign subject and linear causality, he nonetheless falls prey to the notion of the "cultural" as a social formation whose discursive doubleness—the transcendental and empirical dialectic—are contained in a temporal frame that makes differences repetitively "contemporaneous," regimes of sense-as-synchronous. It is a kind of cultural "contradictoriness" that always presupposes a correlative spacing. Foucault's *spatial distancing* seals the sign of modernity in 1789 into a "correlative," overlapping temporality.[62]

In line with Bhabha and Chakrabarty, Bliss Cua Lim problematizes the closing-in of the time-lag and synchronizing the time of differences in the cinematic language of time in the horror genre, especially in Asian films as adopted (translated) by Hollywood. Bringing the analysis of historical temporality to the cinema of the fantastic, Lim offers a temporal critique of cinema through which the ghostly return of history, writ large with colonial violence and contemporary exploitations, haunts our present. According to Lim, "Modern time is thus projected in every direction to include even what exists outside of or prior to its minting as a concept, entertaining an 'ideal of objectivity,' a belief that its conception of history is the 'overarching language,' the universal narrative to which all specific instances can be subsumed."[63] To put the modern world on this plane, the camera, for instance, is expected to represent a simultaneity of that moment of the shutter clicking and the event unfolding before the camera.

The expected simultaneity between the click and the event is (like a clock) a "spatialized misconstrual of time, . . . the familiar-but-false sense of correspondence or synchronicity between the inner duration of consciousness and the homogeneous time of the clock"—the regimes of sense-as-synchronous.[64] This simultaneity between the camera and the event is therefore an imagined one: the viewer "sees" this "moment" as part of the universally shared time that can be measured with and against all other spaces by virtue of being in the same time. Moreover, in practice, the viewing and reading of a photograph hardly ever stops at seeing it as an instant. As if the photographed event is part of a process or progression, context is almost always conjured up (sometimes by the photograph, other times by the curator, viewer, author, etc.) to connect the imagined moments within those processes and progressions. The modern temporality of the camera highlights the different times a photograph summons on the lineal map of temporality, while the place from which the summoning occurs remains critical to the concept of ex-nomination.[65]

Even so, the image produced as an impression of the very moment that the clock is punched does not merely tell the time of the photo making. All the actions involved with the experience of a photograph are part of the photograph itself as an event, rather than of the event captured in the photograph, as Ariella Aïsha Azoulay puts it.[66] Adding to Azoulay, I argue that the photographed event cannot be actualized as such ever again, because the event of photography undoes the homogenizing instant framed by the photographer, rupturing the near-universal faith one might have that an image forever captures a moment of the past. The event of photography is indeed an Event, in that it defies historicization as a representation of a particular moment in the past. Rather, it encompasses many more "time-lags" and in-betweens and the distance of the temporality through which one makes photographic meaning, including in the hands of the photographer or the viewer, on computer screens, in galleries, on social media, and in protests—

and even when the images await re-viewing in archives, as part of the Event. So, if the camera is a clock, we should ask an image: "What time is it there?"[67]

The concept of "time-lag" relates deeply to what Lisa Yoneyama calls "catachrony" and "temporal discombobulation," a glitch to the regimes of sense-as-synchronous. Yoneyama examines catachrony as a kind of temporal catachresis in reference to a moment when a Japanese politician, commenting on the controversy over the relocation of Futenma base in Okinawa, "remember[s] the wrong things at a wrong moment," in this case, by referring to a novel set in the time of the Meiji government on the annexation of Okinawa, rather than the US military-colonial settlement. Yoneyama points out how bringing up the Ryukyu Disposition in the context of what was largely seen as an issue of US military imperialism brought attention to the impossibility of considering the histories of pre–World War II Japanese empire and postwar US empire in Okinawa separately, even as they do not align coevally. Catachronies, therefore, can "generate an *unlearning* that critically unsettles the way we believe we know our history."[68]

The concept of catachrony is critical to examining teleology in national photography, in that defining photography within a national frame is a project of modern temporality which obscures temporal discombobulation and conflates multiple spatiotemporalities in homogenous, empty time through epistemic labor—labor provided in particular by researchers of color, whose race and ethnicity are counted on for the practice of diversity within the academy, which then expects them to produce the scholarship of diversity. By catching the moment of catachrony in and outside of the photographs discussed in this book, we too have the opportunity to *unlearn* the way we believe we know our history.[69] As Chakrabarty puts it, "what underlies our capacity to historicize is our capacity not to."[70] Accordingly, this book aims not to be *about* the "Koreanness" of photography in the modern time but a query on an onto-epistemology of Korean photography's history in the making.

Unfixing National Photography

Writing in 2002, as the field of photo history was culturally diversifying, Rey Chow criticized how "culture" came to function "as a shield that hides the positivism, essentialism, and nativism—and with them the continual acts of hierarchization, subordination, and marginalization—that have persistently accompanied the pedagogical practices of area studies."[71] The phenomenon is relevant to not only pedagogical practices in area studies in the United States but also to a seeming counterhegemonic project of photo history a year earlier. A small circle of photo historians in South Korea, associated with the Research Institute of the History of Photography (RIHP), published an anthology of essays in celebration of the sixtieth birthday of the late Ch'oe Injin, the founder of the institute.[72] The topics of these essays range from Korea's first contact with photography in the nineteenth century to the practice of ethnographic photography during colonial rule. Among them is an essay critiquing the state of the history of photography in Korea, positing that the history of Korean photography must find a new methodology distinct from the "Western" mode determined by "Western art history."[73]

The essay argues that until 2001, study of the history of Korean photography had adopted the methodology of Western art history without giving it much thought and as a result, produced poorly examined studies. It contends that photo historians considering Korean photographs must avoid applying "Western categorizations" of photography—"art photography, media photography, commercial photography, landscape photography, portrait photography, fashion photography, and documentary photography"[74]—as these categories merely reflect "Western ways of thinking, governed by Western tradition, institutions, and mentality"[75] and fail to take into consideration the particular sociopolitical conditions affecting the aesthetics of photography in Korea. It concludes by suggesting that early photography in Korea is conceptually and aesthetically closer to traditional Korean ink painting than to photographic works outside Korea—and that, therefore, photography in Korea, especially early photographs, should be studied within the context of the artwork of traditional Korean media.[76]

The essay's call for a uniquely Korean methodology for a history of photography may appeal strongly to anyone interested in non-Western subjects. While positioning a Korean methodology against a Western mode (assuming there is one single methodology that applies to all studies of art history in "the West," and a respective one in Korea) aptly addresses what may have been overlooked in the study of photography in Korea, it also echoes a purist approach rooted in the perception of "authenticity"—ironically applying the homogenous, sovereign notion of time in Western modernity.[77] The founding of the United Nations in 1945, the writing of the Universal Declaration of Human Rights in 1948, and the drafting of Geneva Conventions in 1949, as Monica Kim lays out, contributed to the conception of the South Korean nation-state as having the sovereign power to contain its people and culture (and their behaviors), which cultivated the liberal democratic view of the world as a "family of nations."[78]

Other issues arise from the desire for uniquely Korean studies of photography. If photography is a medium used by people throughout the world, and if this use reflects certain traditions and conventions established by different peoples in different parts of the world, how should one argue that photography automatically becomes a medium contained within the modern concept of the Korean nation, which is, already, based on "the very notion of nation we use today [which] is modern and Western in its origins, largely having to do with the rise of the world system of nation-state"?[79] And, what about the changing perceptions of nation and citizenship, closely related to issues of gender and race, which result in the realpolitik of citizenship and national belonging that are often overlooked in defining the Korean nation-state?

Then, what kind of an authentically Korean methodology could identify an authentically Korean photograph?[80] Granted the possibility of applying an authentic, non-Western methodology in examining a work of Korean photography, could it produce a kind of history separate from the hegemonic expectation that cultures outside of Euro-America be "pure," uncontaminated by the political, sociocultural, intellectual, and aesthetic productions of the West? The desire for purity and authenticity in cultures outside of the European and Anglo-American is equally troubling.

Indeed, the essay pleads for the "feeling of nationality" against the imperialist subject (the West) that taints the authenticity of Korean photography.[81] Naoki Sakai problematizes this feeling as he traces the systematic introduction of nation and nationalism by Fukuzawa Yukichi in East Asia in the nineteenth century, and the ways that Fukuzawa aimed at modernizing Japan through "the creation of the institutional conditions for the feeling of nationality."[82] Sakai points out that this "feeling of nationality" permeates "knowledge production in the humanities, particularly in area studies," and "refuse[s] to view nationality as something given," reversing the order from national to transnational.[83]

This reversal of the order of priority ("while never rejecting our struggle with colonial modernity") is key to Sakai's interrogation of how the "transnational" is defined in subordination of the "national." He argues "that nationality is a restricted derivative of transnationality, and [the] guiding question is how the transnational, the foundational modality of sociality, is delimited, regulated, and restricted by the rules of the international world."[84] Likewise, for RIHP to work toward an anticolonial methodology for Korean photography, rethinking the order of priority in national photography could be useful; as such, the "national" or "Western" categories of photography do not define Korean photography, but Korean photography defines the new categories of, and for, a history of photography as a praxis of anticolonial knowledge production.

Moreover, looking for a methodological antithesis would not so much undo as replicate, in a supposedly authentic form, the problems of "Western" approaches that RIHP tries to avoid—by reproducing what modernity casts as the unique cultural essences of non-Western Others to be preserved within state boundaries and the feeling of nationality. Per Lydia Liu, "Universalism thrives on difference. It does not negate difference so much as absorb it into its familiar orbit of antithesis and dialectic. The situated articulation of cultural difference has been embedded in the universalizing processes of past and present all along, and it is these processes that determine what counts as difference and why it should matter."[85] This universalism, which in photo studies can be applied to the "global" of global photography, complicates and expands on the comparativeness of location.

The "national" in Korean photography is inescapably relational—relational in its onto-epistemology and in its incommensurable yet shared time. Consequently, an epistemological shift from "Western" to "authentically" Korean will fail to decolonize its history of photography unless we work out its interrelatedness with ontology. To propose a different ontology, as Lim puts it, "is to conceive time precisely as a relation: *a profoundly plural relation with difference*,"[86] to imagine and embrace "the contours of a temporal coexistence with otherness that is both prior to every encounter but not pregiven or foreclosed[,] a shared time around which we ford differences, when the very fording—not overcoming, but precisely wading through otherness—discloses the variegation of the present."[87]

As such, *Shooting for Change* does not equate "transnational" with "international," "global," or any entity that does not fit well in the "national" framework, but, following Bhabha, critically explores what enables the location (and the time-lag) of its enunciation. If the "national" in Korean photography is at stake, what is at stake in the transnationality of Korean photography? Or, by contrast, what makes this transnationality a stable episteme of Korean photography? To explore these questions, I locate the time-lag, or spatiotemporal distance, of the Korean diaspora—which enables the positionality of the addressing self—in the transnational Korea. Korean nationality and its effect (and affect) on photography is thus unfixed from a limited, parochial state of being.

Chapter Summaries

The main body of the book is organized thematically into three parts, following photographic practices from vernacular and art to documentary and archival, while treating the formative periods in nation building and transnational militarization as backdrop and cultivator for photographic works.

The first part of the book explores, through the concept of catachrony, the ways in which photography both creates and ruptures the rhetoric of the tripartite national relationship—comprised of the family, *minjok* (ethnonational subjects of Korea), and nation-state—and their collective memory. Chapter 1 examines how Korean War–era photographs of war orphans—especially those including UN service members, focusing on their relational dynamics—come to frame contemporary memory making of the war, particularly as the photographs are remediated in contemporary Korean War commemorative events. The narrative of victimhood became a common literary and visual rhetorical device in the decades following the Korean War, and its symbolism continues to dictate popular Korean War imagery. Using examples from American and British archives, the chapter problematizes the remembering of the Korean War through war orphan imagery, as it perpetuates, for example, an infantilization of the nation—one that demands regrowth and remasculinization through a patriarchal ideology shaped by transnational militarism. This rhetoric has also affected Korean diasporic communities outside of Korea emerging from the Korean War, such as those involving interracial adoption.

Continuing the theme of photographic family narratives through catachrony, chapter 2 discusses family photographic portraits through a dual lens: photography's capacity to convey the changing family narrative through portraiture and how family pictures embody the desire under the *kukka* (nation-state, here more specifically the military regime) to transform Korean society from colonial and war-ridden to modern and industrial. The chapter analyzes the changing styles of family photo-portraiture and their entanglement with familial vis-à-vis state interests in the twentieth century. This examination exposes how the photographic portraiture of family has embodied and mediated the patriarchal, developmentalist ideology of the Korean military regime, inseparable from the colonial elites' desire for personal and nationwide transformation.

Photography has been a key medium for documenting civilian protests. The second part of the book focuses on the ways that three major moments of public protests—in 1960, 1987, and 2008—converge as a multitemporal event of photography and continue to resonate, as in the weekly candlelight vigils against President Park Geun-hye leading to her impeachment in March 2017. Iconic reportage photographs first emerged from South Korea in 1960, ultimately igniting a nationwide democratization movement against the military government in 1987, and the civic response to these images transformed the relationship between photography and political movements in South Korea. Chapter 3 examines the politics of photography in South Korea from the years of the military government's censorship of media and cultural production through the dramatic changes in the 1980s as bloodshed peaked with the democratization movements led by students and labor activists against the regime.

In less than two decades, online viewing and sharing of photographs became ubiquitous, as evident during the 2002 and 2008 candlelight vigils that swept South Korea; this is photography manifested as part of political activism. Exploring the event of photography as performativity in plurality, chapter 4 examines how the photography of the 2008 events was also about the making of what I call a photo public, the plural performativity of new political subjectivity. Through this exploration, the chapter reconsiders the relationship between polity, performativity, and the political event, as photography becomes the site/sight of the event's political potentiality.

The third and final part of the book, composed of chapters 5 and 6, probes the visualization of the spaces of transnational militarism—namely, the Demilitarized Zone (DMZ) and US military camptowns in South Korea. US military camps and installations continue to occupy territories that are, for most Korean civilians, imagined spaces—fiercely protected and in practice kept utterly separate from them—residing beyond the sovereignty of South Korea in the name of peacekeeping. Adjacent to the military base camps, camptowns became a zone between the nonmilitary civilian land and the territory of the state of exception according to the US-Korea Status of Forces Agreement. The photographic works in question are those of United States Forces Korea base camptowns and towns adjacent to the DMZ. The final section of the book teases out what may become possible when we begin to explore affective possibilities beyond looking and identifying the subject of camptowns via photographic representations. The works of photography presented throughout this book engage with endlessly intriguing questions of nation, militarism, and memory. Looking forward to the pleasures and pains of delving into these photographs, I hope the readers of *Shooting for*

Change continue to encounter the medium through a series of questions asked here—partly to unsettle the easy identitarian borders made for the sake of securing its place in Eurocentric epistemologies—and continue to explore the relationships that photography mediates between us.

That being said, there is one profound nation-centric limitation to this exploration to be addressed. By now, the reader must have noticed a glaring lacuna in the discussion of Korean photography: the absence of North Korea, the Democratic People's Republic of Korea (DPRK). It is easy enough to find photographs of DPRK by photographers (not all but mostly Western) emphasizing the conditions of the totalitarian state, such as mass games and mobilized crowds for state events, often in stereotyping and Orientalizing ways. There are occasional exceptions, including the work of Chris Marker in 1957, from a time when foreign photographers were invited to (and still had the flexibility to wander off the streets of) Pyongyang and elsewhere, but these are few and far between.[88] Aside from the fact that I, as a Republic of Korea national, do not have on-site research access—another legacy of the Korean War—I have no interest in including, and exploiting, photographs of DPRK to produce an index of North Korean ethnography that hinges on a sense of liberal superiority. There is a future for such a focus: some South Korean artists have made photographs of the Korean Demilitarized Zone from the South Korean side, or juxtaposed photographs of Arirang Mass Games with those of South Korean rallies against North Korean military activities.[89] Although it is not within the scope of this book, I have learned from thoughtful analyses on the geopolitical entanglement of history, representation, and aesthetics of North Korean photographs by scholars of Korean photography and look forward to more work being done in that arena.[90] For now, I hope that the troubling absence of North Korea in my project makes conspicuous the place from which the history of Korean photography is being enounced, experienced, and anticipated. This absence is where the book aches. It is the hauntology of Korean photography after the war.

PART I

FAMILY CATACHRONY

1

War and the Image of an Orphan Nation

Light hits an elderly white man's cheek, revealing with great intensity the crosshatched wrinkles and creases across his face. The light bounces off and through his silvery, unruly eyebrows. The man's mouth is firmly closed, his eyes vacuously staring, likely out the window through which the light shines in. Except for the golden chain around his neck hanging down his chest to where it's cropped out of the frame, and the gray fabric clothes he wears, inanimate objects are absent from the photograph. Darkness wraps the rest of the room in which the man sits. The details of his face, such as the age spots on his forehead, become more noticeable with extended viewing. Perhaps because of the extremely close-up view, intimacy arises despite the lack of acquaintance between him and the viewer. While it is difficult to know what he is staring at or how he feels, he seems both tired and aloof, yet also somehow adamant. Despite a search for hints, the photograph remains impenetrable. It wouldn't feel strange if he moved and disappeared into the blurry darkness to go about his day.

This is a portrait of Mr. Robert Dherbeys, who lives in Romans-sur-Isère in southeast France (plate 1). An odd beginning for a book on Korean photography, but this face, and its unlikely intimacy, has been a "catachrony" for my multifaceted project on Korean War photography and memories. Catachrony, as Lisa Yoneyama puts it, means "remembering the wrong things at a wrong moment," which may generate an unlearning of a temporality that has ordained the way one remembers historical events, popularly through photographs shaping the memory and postmemory of the Korean War in South Korea and the Korean diaspora.[1] As discussed in the introduction, an incident of catachrony—such as when the Japanese politician was asked to comment on the relocation of Okinawa's Futenma base and "mistakenly" remembered a novel set in the time of the Meiji government on the annexation of Okinawa, rather than the US military colonial settlement—sheds light on the repression of knowledge production based on "the *ability* to make connections, to perceive affinities and convergence of geohistorical elements that have worked together to constitute mid-twentieth-century violence."[2]

The mid-twentieth-century violence pervading this chapter is the Korean War (1950–53). Following Korea's independence from Japanese colonial rule at the end of World War II, in September 1945, the Soviet Union occupied the peninsula north of the 38th parallel and the United States occupied the south. The North and South Korean leaders failed to agree upon holding a free presidential election for (re)forming a single nation. As a result, the Republic of Korea (ROK) was founded in 1948 in the south, and the Democratic People's Republic of Korea (DPRK) was established the same year in the north. Over the next two years, tensions between the north and south escalated, eventually pitting South Korea and the United Nations against North Korea, which had military support from Communist China and material support from the Soviet Union.[3] The Korean War resulted in the deaths of over 1.3 million Korean civilians and soldiers, with an additional 184,000 Chinese soldiers and 36,000 UN soldiers, of whom the majority were Americans. This was the first combat operation of the Cold War era, shaping the course of US-Soviet, US-China, and Soviet-China relations, not to mention those between each party and the ROK and DPRK, for the next several decades, as well as initiating the militarization policy that has governed US global engagement into the current century.[4]

The visual catachresis within Robert Dherbeys's portrait involves the personal history of the French photographer Agnès Dherbeys (b. 1976). Agnès was adopted by Robert and Jacqueline Dherbeys from South Korea at the age of five and a half months. Agnès's portrait of her adoptive father, Robert, is part of her photo series *Retired* (2013–15), a counterpart to her portrait series of birth parents titled *Omone* (*Mother*, 2013). *Omone*, which Agnès made in South Korea working with the then Museum of Photography, Seoul (MoPS, renamed Museum Hanmi in 2022), partnered with narrative texts, oral histories from birth parents recalling their experiences of sending off their children for adoption. Agnès began *Retired* after returning from South Korea. According to her, she had no intent of juxtaposing the two series in the beginning, but the curators of MoPS encouraged her to. While it may thus appear that the striking juxtaposition was not designed specifically by the artist, she herself chose to return to Romans-sur-Isère upon her return from South Korea, to photograph her distant father, and to again position herself outside of the frame. These choices are as decisive as the curators' choice, which amplifies the view of the two series as independent yet interconnected projects.

Dherbeys's series, indeed, enable a temporal and spatial convergence of history, people, and affect. The remembering of an aging man in a small city in France during the course of a study on photography and the memory of the Korean War offers a trial run for exploring the possibility of connecting disparate times and places of history as a way of unraveling a temporality that shepherds war memories through a peculiar photographic subject: images of war orphans, as will be explored in this chapter. The photograph of Mr. Dherbeys presents a catachrony which cracks open the temporality of advancement—of Korea's progress from war-ridden nation to global leader, an entrapment that drives the desire to remember the war with the imagery of orphans. The face of Robert Dherbeys demands an exploration of the connections between the history of transnational and interracial adoption and the constant, indulgent use of orphan imagery in remembering the war.[5]

That the faces we do not see in Dherbeys's photo series are those of "orphan-turned-adoptees," their exclusion was, of course, a deliberate choice, made to avoid yet another indexing of adoptee subjects. But the absence of the adoptees within her work is loud, calling out for a profound reconsideration of the popular use of the faces of orphan children to remember the history of twentieth-century violence. Similarly, the juxtaposition of aging faces from other sides of the globe, the contrast between the birth parents—some reunited with their children, but most not—and the ennui of Robert's days as he grapples with ongoing insomnia and feeling of emptiness, complicates the feel-good trajectory expected of transnational adoption stories.[6] And the trajectory of the story increasingly told today, that of the grown-up adoptees' journeys back to birth places and birth parents. This misalignment of times and places positions transnational adoption as the afterlife of the war; more broadly, the catachrony reveals the neoliberal temporality of reparation and reconciliation, baring the violence inherent in the production of Cold War temporality as defined by cause and effect, alliance and hostility, and advancement and closure.

This chapter presents an effort to unlearn imperialist readings of Korean orphan photographs by examining how Korean War photographs become transtemporal and transnational, as the dynamics among the photographic subjects—in the following discussion, between war orphans and UN military service members—continue to frame the contemporary remembering of the war in South Korea and the Korean diaspora. The chapter considers these photographs of war orphans (used interchangeably with "orphan photographs" and "orphan images") as embodying the desire to fix a symbolic identity onto the children: as orphans, and thus as war tropes.[7] These images come from photo books, exhibitions, catalogues, brochures, posters, and websites; and, most importantly, from photography archives classifying the images under "subject" titles referring to orphans, principally the photography collections at the United States National Archives (NARA) in College Park, Maryland, and the Imperial War Museum (IWM) in London. Occasionally, I have also considered photographs not clearly identified as images of orphans, but whose subjects, grouped together without clear presence of parents or other relatives, allude to the context of and are encouraged to be seen as orphan photographs.

To this end, the chapter scrutinizes photographs of Korean War orphans from these archives and photographs reproduced in Korean War commemorative events in South Korea and among the Korean diaspora, namely for a photography exhibition in Dallas in 2012. For the past two decades, I have observed the repeated use of orphan photographs in memorial events and venues. Commemorative events of the Korean War and the media continually reproduce the orphan-subject as symbols of the victim nation and its plea for universal sympathy. In turn, the images serve to provide contrast to the understood current economic and cultural standing of South Korea as an "advanced nation (*sŏnjin'guk*)"—an affect designed to intensify the dramatic contrast between then and now. This multitemporality, I argue, calls for questioning the symbolism of orphanhood in the national narrative of the Korean War and delving into the economy of affect.

Furthermore, illuminating the role of the archival subject classification of "Orphans" in the context of the Cold War in the Asia-Pacific—as marking the geopolitical relations between South Korea and the United States (symbolizing the West)—I call into question photographic encounters affectively reproducing the dynamics of these relations. To what end does this orphan-subject classification fulfill a multilateral imperative to remember the war in ways that safeguard the Asia-Pacific geopolitical power dynamics in which the United States maintains its centrality? How do South Korea and its diaspora take control of, if not contribute to, maintaining this geopolitical map, in this case through the memory making and memory renewing of the Korean War? And how might the photographs direct us to new possibilities for unlearning, relearning, and remembering the Korean War?

Korean War Orphan Photographs in War Archives

A photograph in the collection of the IWM shows Australian Private Gordon Mosey bathing a Korean orphan, called Pak, on a sunny day during the Korean War (figure 1.1). Taken by Phillip Hobson (b. 1922–d. 2006), the official photographer to the Australian forces in Korea during the war, the image shows what appears to be a rather peaceful day despite the war. Pak was a houseboy, one of many taken in by military units as "mascots." He balances himself in a water-filled tub, a metal drum cut in vertical half, as it tilts slightly to his right. Private Mosey holds Pak's neck tightly as white foam drips down his face. Pak's frowning eyes try to focus on the camera lens. Placed behind them is another drum, possibly working as a furnace. The child in this shot appears to be in much better condition than, for instance, the Korean photographer Im Ŭngsik's photograph of a war orphan in the center of war-torn Seoul (figure 1.2), indicating that, with the care of soldiers, these children are bathed, fed, and protected.

The boys in these photographs are just two of many, orphans having been a major subject for "atrocity pictures" since World War II. During the Korean War, orphans were a frequent—and easily accessed—target for war photographers, as over a hundred thousand Korean children were orphaned by 1951, and about ten thousand orphans lived on the streets when the armistice was signed in 1953.[8] The archives of the IWM and NARA contain boxes upon boxes of photographs—easily hundreds, if not thousands, of individual images—of Korean War orphans living in institutions established to accommodate the rapidly growing street population during and after the armistice. Some photographs depict orphan boys "adopted" by military units

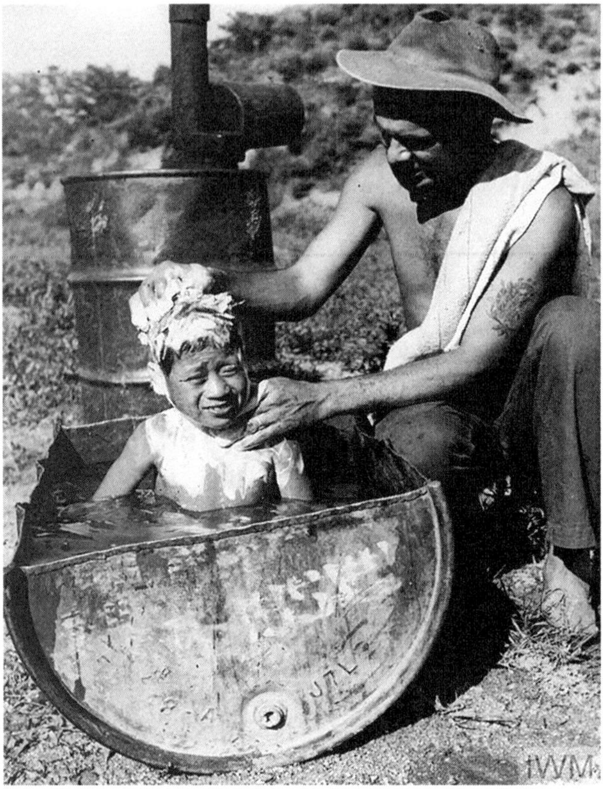

FIGURE 1.1 Phillip Hobson, "Private Gordon Mosey, of Australian Fik Visitors Section, bathes 'Pak,' a Korean orphan his unit adopted," undated (c. 1951–52). MH 32858 Central Office of Information Korean War Official Collection, Imperial War Museum, London.

to live with the servicemen at their bases. Others were taken in orphanages funded, if not directly operated, by overseas Christian charity groups and military units, such as the Pohang orphanage "adopted" by the US Marine Corps.[9] Many of these photographs were taken to record, and publicize, interactions between orphans and GIs. Hundreds of similar photographs in the archives depict GIs holding, embracing, watching, helping, and offering things to orphan children.

Such war orphan images come to allegorize nations as victims and saviors, especially when they represent the experience of war in commemorative settings. The relationship between these allegorized subjects likewise presents the enduring geopolitical asymmetry, thereby continuing to inscribe meanings to orphan imagery globally. While there are reasons for why some images become clichés (although clichés, bypassing scrutiny, can be powerful producers of collective imagining), photographs of orphans cannot be

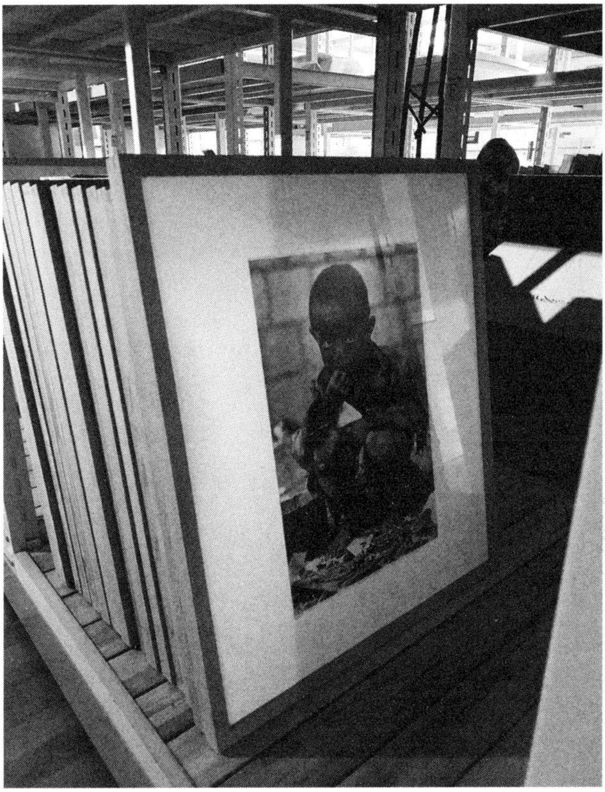

FIGURE 1.2 Digital photograph of Im Ŭngsik's *A War Orphan, T'aep'yŏngno*, 1950. Framed gelatin silver print. National Museum of Modern and Contemporary Art, Cheongju, 2022. Photograph by author. The black-and-white photograph depicts a barefoot boy covered in dirt and wearing ragged clothes, in a squatting position, looking directly into the camera lens as he brings something to his mouth, possibly food. Next to him is a round container or can-like object. What appear to be paper scraps and garbage surround him. The grid pattern of a stone wall provides an out-of-focus background. The tonal contrast of the photograph accentuates the lighter background and his dirt-covered body and face, as well as the white of his eyes, the wrinkles on his forehead, and the scar on his knee.

dismissed as merely tropes without contextual purpose. The subject does not simply appear in photographs because wars create orphans, but because of its ability to provide a particular narrative for commemorative events, sharing a certain affectivity in memory making.[10] Critically, "collective" memories are maintained through selecting which subjects will be remembered (and which forgotten) and when these images are used to refresh the memories of war.

The first step toward a different futurity for the photographs' subjects—moving beyond their perpetual consignment to the narrative of orphanhood—is to reexamine the technology of representation in signifying and subsequently remembering the war through the photographs of Korean war orphans. Exploring the possibilities for knowing and remembering these lives differently requires an undoing of the prescriptive reproduction of the subject as rescued victims. From there, a new, more critically considered approach might be possible: For instance, what if we relied less on the symbolism of orphan images for war memories, such as in upholding the ethno-national collective memory of the Korean War, and more, to repeat Yoneyama, on varying senses and affects for making connections and perceiving affinities and convergence of geohistorical elements?

Indeed, alongside a rising interest in photography's affect, various scholarly and artistic projects have argued for paying closer attention to the "touch," "feel," and "sound" of photography.[11] For example, Tina Campt argues that the reverberating touch of photography (in archives) is necessarily transtemporal and ontologically haptic: "The haptic temporalities of the archive in question are composed of moments of contact when photographs touch us and animate reflections and responses. These temporalities include, but are in no way limited to, the moments of photographic capture; the temporality of the photographic re/production of material objects; their assembly and reconfiguration as nodes of state, social, and cultural formation; and the present and future temporalities of their interactions with researchers, archivists, and the broader community."[12] Following Campt, a shift of focus from the indexicality of ethnography to the haptic qualities of photographic encounters can help to change the ways in which we *know* orphan imagery. Rather than confine the subjects of the photographs in orphanhood (even outside of the labeled archival boxes) to reproduce national allegory, we need to radically reimagine them, to let them break free and grow old, as everything outside the boxes has: as human beings, as people.

Exhibiting *Abandoned Children*

Understanding how the framing of orphans as a national war trope dominates contemporary war memorialization requires more than looking at or imagining war orphan photographs differently. This is especially true of exhibitions, where the tight narrative structure of the curation, location-limited accessibility, and strictly designated space engineers the ways orphan photographs frame the war and vice versa. This section examines how a commemorative exhibition employed orphan photographs in re-viewing the war through the binary of victims and saviors, and what that does to the remembering of the Korean War—especially for, and as, a diasporic community in the United States.

A cross-Pacific perspective on the legacy of the Korean War was on display in Dallas, Texas, in 2012. To commemorate the Korean War, Dallas-based media company News Korea Inc., with support from the Korean Association–North Texas and the Korean product supermarket chain H Mart, organized a photography exhibition titled *Han'guk chŏnjaeng yuksibijunyŏn t'ŭkpyŏlchŏn chŏnjaengŭi sangch'ŏ, kŭrigo hŭimangŭi kirok (Korean War: Scars of War and the History of Hope, 1950).*[13] From June 18 to 30, photographs of the Korean War, including some on loan from the Korean War Veterans Association (KWVA), were on view at the H Mart community center located inside the supermarket (figure 1.3).[14] In the style of *Family of Man*, the 1955 blockbuster photography exhibition at New York's Museum of Modern Art, the black-and-white photographs were installed on the gallery walls and larger ones were hung in the center of the room. The exhibition was divided into four sections: "During the War," "Post-war American Occupation by Jerry Kasten," "Changes in Seoul," and "Children of the War." The last section, subtitled *Pŏryŏjin Aidŭl* (*Abandoned Children*),[15] included photographs of orphans in war-torn landscapes, some of them with GIs.

The exhibition was a commemorative event for the Korean American community in Dallas. Older community members stated that they recalled their war and postwar experiences through the photographs, according to the staff writer Kim Kungsŏn,[16] while the younger generation felt they were able to indirectly experience the war through the photographs "transparently project[ing] the brutality of the war."[17] The testimonies of Korean American viewers emphasize how a victim-savior analogy dominated the exhibition's narrative: the Korean nation (or nation to be), rescued by soldiers standing

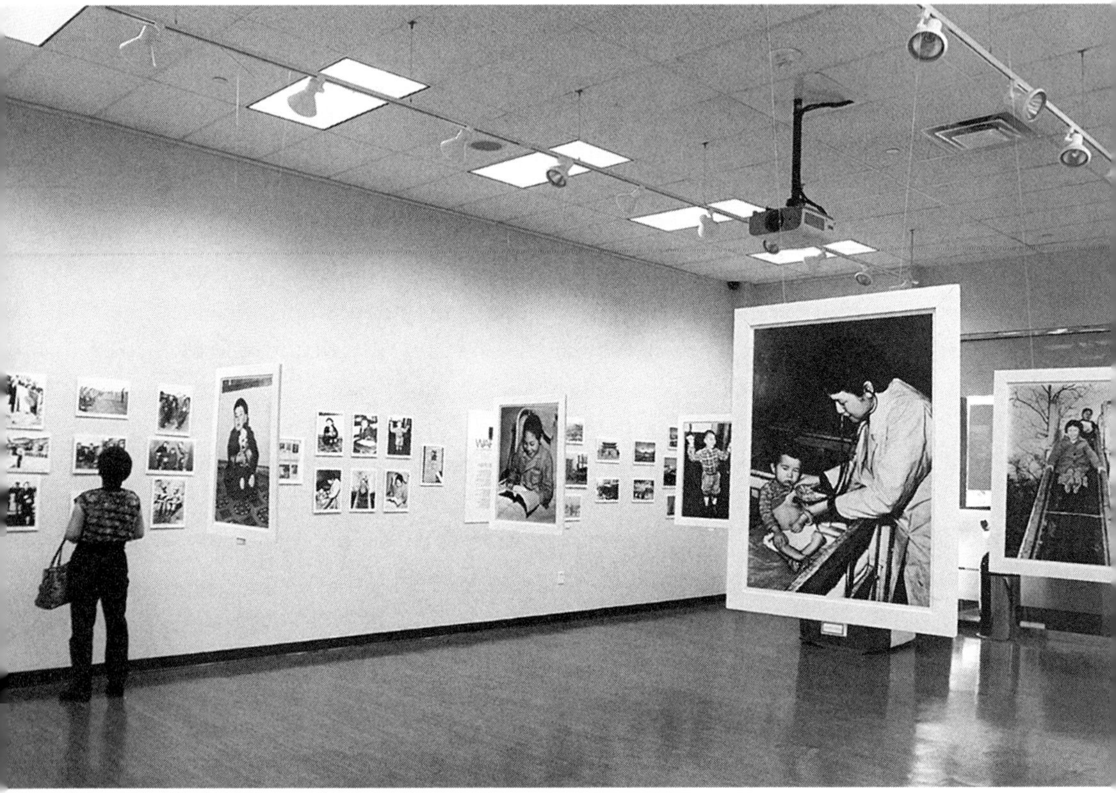

FIGURE 1.3. Jerry Kasten, installation view, *Han'guk chŏnjaeng yuksibijunyŏn t'ŭkpyŏlchŏn chŏnjaengŭi sangch'ŏ, kŭrigo hŭimangŭi kirok (Korean War: Scars of War and the History of Hope, 1950)*, Dallas, June 2012.

in for the United States. This narrative also establishes a subject-victim and photographer-savior relation. In South Korea and the diaspora, the rhetoric of suffering and victimhood, especially during the colonial Japanese occupation and existential calamity of the Korean War, leads postwar-generation Korean viewers to understand its subjective history as casualties—and, in the case of Korean Americans, to subjectivize themselves in transnational, diasporic postmemory.[18]

Moreover, the visualization of the victim-savior narrative is closely related to the identitarian categorization of Asian Americans based on "a shared sense of embodied vulnerability," according to Thy Phu.[19] This sense of embodied vulnerability in diasporic communities requires intergenerational encounters that mediate and pass on war memories, and commemorative events are often a place of such encounters; for the Dallas exhibition, the rhetoric of reunion was emphasized by the exhibition organizers' decision to invite the US Army veteran and Dallas resident Jerry Kasten (b. 1932–d. 2021) to exhibit his photographs of war orphans taken as a staff photographer in Korea between 1955–1958. With Kasten's photographs of orphans, the dynamics of the Dallas exhibition inevitably became entangled with Korea-US relations, which themselves are often represented in the dichotomies of subject-photographer, victim-savior, and occupied-occupier.[20]

As discussed earlier, the young Dallas audience felt photography projected "transparently" the brutality of war. For the young audience, the exhibition constructed a war-ridden Korea through its incessant creation of analogies of (and the power dynamics inherent in) subject versus photographer, Korea versus the United States, civilians versus service members, the Korean American community versus (non-Korean) American veterans of the Korean War. The young audience's expectation of the medium's "transparency" is thus particularly disquieting, as, with such expected transparency, the photographs conveniently affirm the power dynamics of the analogous relationships and identifications with geohistorical, ethno-national subjects.

Becoming a Global Family in the Aesthetics of *Sunansa*

Photographs of orphans in recent publications and exhibitions continue to be an icon of the Korean War and are themselves a commemorative medium. For those using orphan imagery for war commemoration, photography is a favorite medium through which the affective workings of sympathy—what Amit Rai calls the "rule of sympathy"—claim victimhood.[21] Rai argues that "sympathy always needs an object of pathos, and in abolitionist discourse the spectacle of the slave's suffering body, or the lamentable state of her mind would be that horrid but ideal object."[22] Examining the epistemic practice of "the rule of sympathy" and *sunansa*—the history of suffering, where one's individual (and familial) history of suffering represents the national history of suffering—in the making of war memories furthers an unlearning of perpetual orphanhood as a national war trope.

As with other militarized conflicts, orphan photographs became an ideal object of such pathos in Korean War memorialization. Zahid Chaudhary explains that this "sympathetic feeling is a replication of the other that is indissociable from an affirmation of the self."[23] For non-Koreans, the imagined standpoint of the other (the orphans) for American (NARA, Dallas) or European (IWM) viewers is "indispensable to our moral formation as subjects even if its nature is necessarily imaginary."[24] The affect of sympathy thus facilitates the articulation of power relations—in the Dallas case, between Korea and the United States. Therefore, as Rai puts it, sympathy is "a mechanism of differentiation and normalization," which in this case does not just apply to Koreans versus non-Koreans, but also among Koreans and the Korean diaspora.[25] This mechanism becomes fully active when an image—such as Im Ŭngsik's orphan photograph—is represented as a symbol of war.

South Korean postwar cultural production took full advantage of the affective workings of sympathy through the differentiation and normalization of bodily suffering, with literature and visual art widely invoking the metaphor of an individual's suffering to represent the nation's recent, violent past. Kwŏn Myŏnga argues that, in literature, narrating the recent experience of the war through the national fate of *sunansa* was crucial to reimagining and reconstructing the Korean subject after the Korean War.[26] Those narratives often involve physical injury, rape, traumatization, and collective shaming, which must eventually be either overcome or severed from one's life, just as the nation needs to recover from war and colonial trauma. Frequently, and pointedly, this physical suffering is gendered. Kwŏn notes that postwar literature becomes also invested in an "organic reconstruction" of a healthy family.[27] This narrative relies on the analogy of *minjok*, people of the same ancestry and heritage, representing the Korean nation. Although it is debatable whether this vision of the family existed under Japanese colonial rule (1910–45) and US military occupation (1945–48),[28] the analogy dominates postwar rhetoric and was "naturalized" through postwar literature.

In Korean postwar cultural production, the patriarchal desire for the reconstruction of the family and nation engendered the rise of South Korea's ethno-nationalist-masculinist culture—and was compounded by the ideology of anti-communism and the resistance against it during successive postwar military regimes. The military junta of Park Chung Hee in the 1960s and '70s was driven largely by industrialization and subsequent national significance in the global market. As discussed in more detail in chapter 2, a new family ideal, visualized in propagandistic posters, commercials, and tabloid features, focused on the transformation of the traditional extended family into a nuclear family: mobile and readily available for rapid industrialization. Not coincidentally, in cultural production this ideal family is remasculated by the strong patriarch.[29] The signification of the triad relation—family-*minjok*-nation—

turns the gendered body and family into a seeming natural, organic entity, engineered for transforming the nation.[30]

In this allegory of family and nation, orphan photographs can be reframed as an effective representation of the destroyed family, situating the subject in convenient, convincing narratives of suffering and helplessness. When reproduced in the context of war commemoration, orphan photographs, and images of other victims in the Korean War, are reframed as *minjok sunanja*, which translates to national/ethnic sufferers.[31] Photographs such as that of Pak and Private Mosey thus fulfill the desire to reconstruct the family: many of the service members in the photographs cared for and supported the orphaned children, often "adopting" them into their bases, and even in some cases adopting them into their own families in the United States. As Tobias Hübinette has argued, the orphaned war victim, as allegory of the victim nation, is now embraced in the paternal care of the United States[32]—perhaps not so organically, but strategically a safe choice given South Korea's geopolitical situation.

This reverberates distinctly in the rhetoric used in the Dallas exhibition and the positioning of South Korea in the exhibition. The postwar positioning of South Korea has been that of the ultimate victim: the ex-colonial subject, the target of war making, and the object of imperialist competition between the United States, China, and Russia disguised as capitalist democracy versus communism. The habitual self-deprecation through identifying the nation as "a trash depository of the superpowers" is closely related to a self-degradation that leads to, according to Kwŏn, "the negation of one's own past, which does not bequeath the existential foundation for one's own subject formation, and thus conjuring a constant desire for entirely new subjectivity."[33]

Photography which renews the memory of the Korean War from the position of a victim encourages new generations to acquire this memory of the Korean War. But this overpowering narrative of victimhood and rescue hinders other possible ways of seeing orphan photographs and making sense out of them—forestalling and even confiscating the power of the image, and the subject, to break the binary. The desire for an entirely new subjectivity collapses memories between the war and now, leading to the tireless use of orphan photographs as the symbolic representation of the state of South Korea after the war. In turn, the transtemporal identification of the orphan today signifies the continued "negation" of what came between the two moments of photo making and photo viewing. In this negation, South Korea—given the continued geopolitical conflict—remains the orphan in the picture.

In the Dallas exhibition, the flip side of "the rule of sympathy" coin is identification: differentiation of subjects by way of identifying with the subject of the orphan imagery. This enables the Korean and Korean American viewers to feel "a sense of belonging in a benevolent nation."[34] The victim narrative also enables Korean and Korean American viewers to see themselves and others as "abandoned children" despite their temporal and spatial distance from the war. By grouping the photographs of children by themselves or being "saved" by the service members under the title *Abandoned Children*, the Dallas exhibition recapitulates the history of *sunansa*, this time mainly for and via Korean expatriates and Korean War veterans. Thus the exhibition is also about the diasporic community and their positionality in their "adopted" country. The *sunansa* allegory in turn reinscribes the notion of pan-global Koreanness in an attempt to unite the diasporic communities and South Korea through the rule of sympathy.

With its focus on Korean War orphans, the Dallas exhibition emphasizes the narrative of victimhood to reimagine *minjok*, inviting Korean Americans to see themselves as part of this all-embracing global Korean family. The diasporic Korean viewers are now encouraged to join the narrative of *sunansa*. As such, the orphan photographs are no longer merely images of the past, but a powerful visual tool for retelling the story of US-Korea relations.

The American Gaze, Transnational Adoption, and Victimhood Nationalism

Speaking at the Dallas exhibition opening, Kasten spoke of his wish to find the orphans who were the subjects of his photographs, strongly suggesting that he expected at least some of his orphan subjects to be in the United States, and thus invoking the history of Korea-US adoption.[35] In fact, the curator of the exhibition, Im Jiŭn, chose to emphasize the subject of orphans in the exhibition upon learning of Kasten's interest.[36] This adds another layer of identificatory frame to the exhibition: that of victims cum orphans cum adoptees.

Kasten's stated intention also intimates the profound, and precarious, relationship between photography and subjectivity. In Dallas, the metaphor of South Korea as orphans is reactivated almost sixty years later by an American veteran calling upon those orphans to be identified and brought before him. The orphans, and symbolically the orphaned nation, remain as such until they have been found and named by the American who "captured" them in images.

The interest in commemorating the Korean War through the work of American photographers in and outside of South Korea thus reflects a desire to see the Korean War through the "eyes" of Americans, and under the auspices of American interests.[37] Photography books and exhibitions of photographs taken by Americans in South Korea become products that valorize the photographer's gaze. Yet through this gaze the experience of war is neutralized, becoming a merely memorable past. This is not a coincidence. The American gaze reaffirms and reinstates the narrative of victimhood, as witnessed from a legitimate, "rational" viewpoint. In addition, an American gaze such as Kasten's comes full circle to fulfill a Korean desire—such as that which General Paik Sun Yup articulated in John Rich's *Korean War in Color*—for American affirmation and self-victimization, what Jie-Hyun Lim calls victimhood nationalism.[38]

According to Lim, the collective dichotomy of victims and perpetrators is foregrounded in nationalism's transnationality, and this nationalism becomes "complete when victimhood becomes hereditary in the national historical imagination."[39] The collective dichotomy created in the Dallas exhibition relies on the transnational relationship between Korea and the United States and on the rhetoric of hereditary collective suffering in the Korean diaspora. The victimhood narrative also enables the patriarchal reform of the family, turning orphans into subjects of repatriation into the family-*minjok*-nation. In this process, the perpetrator is always identified as an outside force, be it communist North Korea, imperialist United States, or colonialist Japan.

As such, the role of the Korean state in making Korean War orphans the face of the war's official memory is quite ironic: through the visualization of the Korean War with war orphans—vis-à-vis victimhood nationalism—the victimizer takes on the protective coloring of the collective victim.[40] The orphan images in commemorative events help those responsible for postwar victimization hide behind the crying faces of orphans. Indeed, Kwŏn notes that the identification of *minjok* as *sunanja* became the prevailing narrative of historical writing during the Park Chung Hee regime.[41] The orphan imagery thereby functions as "the memory wall of national victimhood,"[42] inhibiting other ways to remember the war while, for example, folding the time of the military regime. The orphan image leaps the time of the regime, of brutal oppression and collective self-sacrifice for the sake of the family-*minjok*-nation, and arrives directly at the present moment of remembering. It is the military state—the military and state congealed during the Park regime—that metamorphosizes into the collective victim.[43]

On the other hand, analyzing the dynamics of children and adults as represented in transnational adoption, Eleana Kim states that "the benevolent American soldier stood in as a parental figure, thereby crossing racial and cultural moats of confusion by taking on a parental role to provide for and clothe the needy third world child."[44] By contrast, photographs of Korean adults helping orphans are hardly ever seen in archives, publications, and exhibitions, despite the many orphanages founded and managed by Koreans. Images depicting Korean relatives—if they exist at all—do not tell the story of victim and savior preferred by publications or exhibitions.

Kim's analysis echoes powerfully as I flip through the photo cards in the archival boxes of the NARA and the albums at the IWA and click through the digitized versions depicting "adopted" children in the UN military bases and the servicemen—their "adoptive" fathers—such as Private Mosey and Pak, or Sergeant Tyler and an orphan girl (figure 1.4). The Korean adults in the photographs, with no captions about them, appear to be representatives or employees of orphanages facilitating the patriarchal role of the UN servicemen.

The narrative of Korean children being saved by UN service members, mostly white American men, was fully exploited by adoption agencies following the armistice of the Korean War, upon which large-scale South Korean international adoption began. Following various individual and institutional campaigns for international adoption in the United States, Child Placement Services was established by the presidential order of 1954. The Holt Adoption Agency was established the following year "as a private sectarian agency to provide intercountry adoption services for available children,"[45] and by 1958, South Korea became the largest single contributor to foreign adoptions in the United States.[46] Between 1955 and 1992, more than 120,000 Korean children were adopted by foreign families, 60 percent of the adopting families being US citizens.[47] Yet while international adoption soon became a significant issue in Korean society, open discussion and evaluation of adoption policies were not publicly available until the 1990s.[48] In this context, images of orphans become an effective medium of sympathetic mimesis, through which potential American and European adoptive families become "a virtuous citizen-subject; sympathy as a technology of the self perfects that self's assimilation into the fold of (Christianized) citizenship."[49] As American adoption advertisements and campaigns took advantage of orphan photographs, the act of seeing orphan imagery engendered the potentiality of adoption, a potentiality for assimilating into the fold of benevolent citizenry.[50] The shift from orphan-subject to citizen-subject in this sympathetic mimesis is notable.

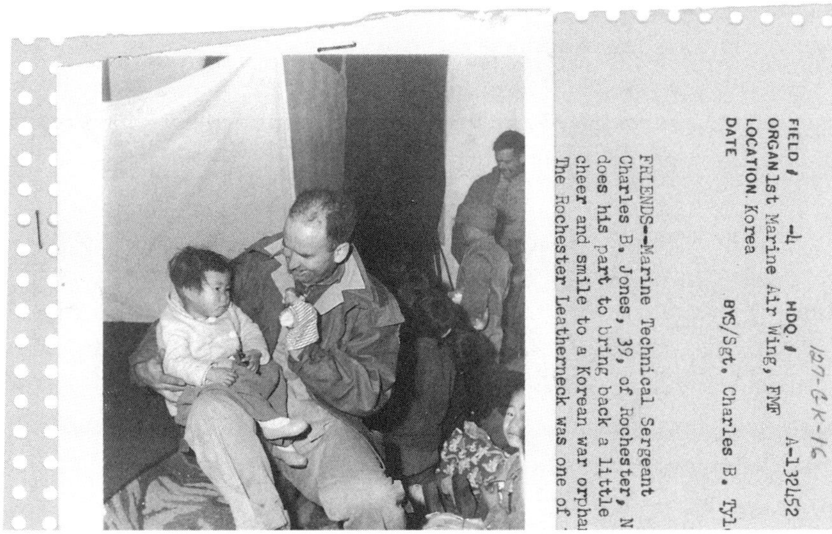

FIGURE 1.4 Sergeant Charles B. Tyler, "FRIENDS," undated (c. 1951), gelatin silver print. Field # -4 HDQ # 127-GK-16-A132452. Collection of National Archives and Records Administration, College Park, MD. The black-and-white photograph is stapled to a small yellow sheet of paper perforated around the edges of two sides with descriptions identifying the image and Sergeant Tyler's activities. The photograph shows Sergeant Tyler, a white male service member, using his right leg and arm to hold a Korean girl with short hair. Her face exhibits no enthusiasm, although Tyler tries to entertain her with a hand puppet in his left hand. Other small Korean children and a serviceman are in the room.

Thy Phu and SooJin Pate offer insightful assessments of this American gaze. Critiquing the ways that child victim images are used to define and control identities, Phu argues that images can conjure a "civilian gaze" through which transpacific altruism as humanitarian initiatives take place. This altruism, what she calls "transpacifism," binds Asian sites to the United States and is valorized "as a means of symbolic reconciliation."[51] In the case of the Korean War, rather than a reconciliation between the United States and South Korea—they are and were allies—a paternalistic, debtor-creditor bond was established. Yet this gesture of transpacifism is still the lens through which military photographs of orphans are read in the United States. The US occupation of South Korea following Japan's surrender in 1945, the villages that were wiped out, and the civilians that were killed during the war were not personal and did not cater to the interests of the benevolent citizenry of the United States;[52] war orphans on the street, however, provide a comforting, self-aggrandizing reason for desiring civility in war. With perverse irony, the military gaze at orphans is thus neutralized to become a civilian gaze. It is the rhetoric of this civilian, and civil, gaze that sees and seizes orphans in the pictures, as potential adoptees, and subsequently, adoptee-citizens of the United States.

That being said, Pate contends that the "militaristic gaze" of the US empire is what captures orphans in the photographs taken by service members. Examining mostly film stills (treated as photographs) from the NARA archives, Pate considers the politics of orphan images and international adoption through the dichotomy of orphans and American militarism. Conspicuously leaving out Korea as a subject—whether as Korean militarism or birth parents—Pate's analysis finds that the militaristic gaze "fashioned [orphan boys] into American soldiers and Korean girls were constructed in the image of camptown sex worker."[53] According to Pate, the gendering and sexualizing of orphans is at the heart of Cold War Orientalism, making the NARA materials documents of the neocolonial relationship between the United States and South Korea—a gendered, symbolic representation.[54]

The militaristic gaze resonates with the affective workings of sympathetic mimesis and subject formation. Crucially, however, this gaze holds force in the South Korean state as well, to legitimize and maintain victimhood nationalism through photography. The complete absence in Pate's analysis of Korean (adult male) subjectivity, particularly within the Korean military, servicemen, brothel managers, birth fathers, and so on, and their relationships with the US military thus safeguards the Korean ethno-nationalist-masculinist rationalization for postwar remasculinization. In this reading of archival imagery, the Korea represented as houseboys and orphan girls is trapped perpetually as a sexually violated victim[55]—just as in victimhood nationalism, despite Pate's assumed intention.

Unlearning the Temporality of an Orphan Nation

Orphan photographs from the Korean War demonstrate how individual photographs can be effective material in keeping up the collective memory of war, as they undergo symbolization and thus become a medium of the collective memory of suffering. However, they do not merely evoke empathy for universal suffering, but show how Koreans and Korean diasporic communities turn themselves into "national/ethnic sufferers" by identifying (and transfiguring) themselves as war orphans through the "civilian" and "militaristic" gaze.[56]

The state has been central to this project. At the same time, discussion of other children of the war, such as mixed-race children and war orphans of GIs and Korean women and war orphans adopted both within Korea and internationally (by non-Koreans), was suppressed in South Korea.[57] It is thus significant that while the affect of pan-Koreanness was important to the curation of the Dallas exhibition, it minimized the significance of mixed-race children of American GIs and Korean women, particularly those "abandoned" soon after the war. Many foreign soldiers in Korea left behind mixed-race children, and the single mothers of these children struggled to support themselves in a society even more hostile to mixed-race children than fatherless but "fully Korean" children.[58]

Photographs of mixed-race children—indeed, the mixed-race children themselves—would disrupt the masculinist-unitary *minjok* paradigm, not to mention photographs made for and about adoption. Tobias Hübinette has found this exploitation of selective pan-Koreanness rampant in his examination of popular media such as films and Korean pop song lyrics that deal with the subject of Korean adoptees. His examples present the argument that Korean children adopted by non-Koreans became a threat to the patriarchal values of Korea.[59] To be cleansed of the impurity of adoption and non-Koreanness, popular media has depicted the nation, imagined as a female or child's effeminate body, as requiring rescue and defense through nationalist ideology—the ideology of the nation (and the members of Korean diasporic communities, who must never forget their Koreanness) as a unified family.

In this pan-Korean familial memory making, Hübinette claims that Korean adoptees' subjectivities must be considered subaltern. Many adoptees and their birth mothers have had their situation used against their long-term reclamation of agency. Although recent adoptee movements and activism have brought changes in many aspects of interracial and transnational adoption and its ramifications, adoptees and birth mothers have long been silenced, spoken for by adoption agencies or adoptive parents. Hübinette contends that "nationalist feelings of shame and dishonor" resulted in "invisibility and unspeakability": "The adopted Koreans simply cannot speak for themselves as they are already represented as mute physical bonds by supplying and receiving governments, as grateful rescue objects by adoption agencies and adoptive parents, and model adoptees by adoption researchers."[60]

War orphan imagery that functions as the symbolic representation of the nation re-creates this frustrating silencing, ironically doing so as a means to commemorate the war.

While this chapter by no means argues for an iconoclasm of Korean War orphan images, it does call for a critical assessment of the repeated use of orphan photographs as icons of perpetuated victimhood. In her book *Adopted Territory*, Kim notes that the planning committee of the 2004 Gathering, an international convention of Korean adoptees organized by the International Korean Adoptee Associations, decided to eschew war orphan imagery in their literature, conference materials, programs, and signage.[61] As orphan imagery has consistently been in the Korean government's official rhetoric of adoption and even more conspicuously dominated Korean media reports, the committee's decision reflects an understanding of the damaging conflation of orphan images and the subject of adoptees with the symbolic link between Korea and adoptees as the motherland and children.[62] Kim argues that the use of orphan images ends up erasing "the historical specificity and political realities of adoptees," which she sees as a representational violence operating under "a nationalist logic and an inalienable ethnic identification on what is a much more complex and ambivalent relationship."[63]

Kim's examination illuminates how the use of Korean War orphan photographs creates a double bind for the subjectivity of adoptees in the modern history of Korea: they cannot exist beyond the framework of *sunansa* that sutures them with their birthplaces. Similarly, Hübinette suggests that repeated reconstruction of Korean War experiences through the figure of orphans infantilizes all individual experiences of the war.[64] The orphan figure effects the narrative of victimhood, which in turn helps legitimize the history of South Korea's international adoption practice.

Whereas the representational, teleological, and identitarian indexing of orphan-turned-adoptee subjects has become commonplace, the work of Agnès Dherbeys challenges such indexing and defies the logic of victimology and the neoliberal and sanguine narrative of repair. Converging in the geopolitics of affect, the catachrony of *Retired* becomes ever so critical at this point: it disrupts the binary, symbolic representation of the figure of the patriarchal, white, Western "savior" and the Korean orphan turned adoptee. Robert Dherbeys, as photographed by Agnès Dherbeys, in no way fits the narrative of a benevolent white patriarch who saved the orphaned Korean girl, much less made her the fierce photographer whose work during the violent days of the political protests in Thailand won her the prestigious Robert

Capa Gold Medal Award in 2010. In showing her retired, widowed, and unexpressive adoptive father,[65] Agnès documents uneventful days in an uneventful town.[66] The photographs, however, convey the sensation of a quiet yet revealing reunion between father and daughter—which is particularly striking given the absence in her South Korean counterpart photo series, *Omone* (*Mother*), of socially conditioned scenes of cathartic reunion occasionally appearing in morning TV shows.

To the South Korean viewer, transnational adoption—in this case represented by birth and adoptive parents—is the embarrassing result of (past) poverty and ignorance. As national development and enlightenment continues in the shadow of the militarized past and present, the state (and other interested parties) seeks to curtail criticism on transnational adoption by perpetuating the public rhetoric of victimhood: a story of children abandoned due to war and poverty and the ignorance and low morale of birth parents. In the process of remembering the Korean War and the struggle for postwar recovery through the imagery of orphans, the affect of shame in sending children for adoption to "advanced nations" transforms into acceptance and hope. In the tradition of constant development and progress as a nation, the viewer sees that the advancement of the country remains the most critical aim, and that the history of transnational adoption was deeply unfortunate but ultimately inevitable (especially since most returnees are adults and presented as belonging to both their adoptive and birth countries). This narrative presents the ongoing, if greatly lessened, practice of transnational adoption as terminable only through even more economic and cultural advancement, as befitting a neoliberal temporality of unrestricted and overwhelming growth. This self-legitimization continues to allow the adoption agencies—and the state that promoted their growth—to do their work without public scrutiny.[67]

The small French city of Romans-sur-Isère and the small towns that Agnès visited in South Korea to meet the subjects of *Omone* provide pairings and similarities that reinforce the multispatiality of transnational adoption, rather than the binary of the "benevolent First World" nation versus the "unfortunate Third World" nation. Despite the viewer's unfamiliarity with these places, the towns' declining economies and aging populations can be inferred. The adoptive parents get older as the birth parents get older. Mr. Dherbeys's days appear empty, like the emptied-out family store that he is about to exit for the last time (plate 2). Although the number of residents slowly increased over the years, many young people, like Agnès back then, have gone elsewhere in search of opportunities, and more conspicuously so in the small towns she visited in South Korea. The feeling of loss is prevalent in the photographs of birth parents and sustained in the photographs of the adoptive parent, differently yet equally intensely. In Agnès's photographs, the sense of personal loss expands and permeates the landscape as well, and further. In this way, *Omone* and *Retired* tie in with the GI-orphan photographs from the archives as part of the larger context of the Cold War in the absence of adoptee images.

As such, although Agnès's photo series bring to mind points of comparison between South Korea and France, they do not create the expected binary between the distinct worlds of her birth and her upbringing. This is crucial, given the ways in which transnational adoptee identity is typically represented. Kim Park Nelson finds that the field of transnational adoption studies has traditionally forced adoptees to subjectivize themselves between their native and adopted homes.[68] In this process of subjectivization, what is made visible is not the postcolonial geopolitics that seeps through the global state of imperialist capitalism or the face of the receiving countries, but the subjectivity of successfully grown adoptees returning to their "roots"—or of tormented adoptees to be belatedly nurtured by their birth country. The juxtaposition of Robert's face with those of the birth parents Agnès met with (in some ways a visual catachresis itself) performs a salient critique of the temporality of an orphan nation, which promises reparation—a false promise from both economic advancement and ethno-nationalism.

Since shortly before the sixtieth anniversary of the Korean War, the Korean news media has repeatedly boasted of discoveries of "never-before-seen" war photographs, including those of orphans in South Korea. Although commemorative events including publicities with photo-articles were much more modest due to the COVID-19 pandemic, the seventieth anniversary of the Korean War in 2020 was publicized with film footage and stills of civilians, including children. Orphan images almost always make the cover of commemorative exhibition catalogs and programs, representing the desire to remember the Korean War through the figure and metaphor of an orphan nation and the narrative of *sunansa*. These images and their deployment will therefore perpetuate the imperialist and patriarchal historicization of the Korean War unless they are exhaustively examined in relation to the politicization of visual culture in the postwar era. For one, Agnès Dherbeys defies the narrative of transformative subjectivization—as a legacy of the Korean War—of an adoptee in the Western world returning for a closure and rekindling. Her photo series offer different ways to envision transnational adoption and imagine different futurity of, and with, Korean War orphan photographs.

2

The Place of Women in Family Photography

Photography has used the subjects of victimized children and women to symbolize mid-twentieth-century Korean history. At the same time, vernacular practices of photography, namely family portraits, reassert individual family members' places and roles in the patriarchal social structure. As such, family photo-portraits, from studio portraits to social media posts, serve as a symbol and indicator of a kyriarchal status quo.[1] In South Korea, remembrance of the past and postwar practices of photographic portraiture come together in the economic-developmentalist curation of memories. The result is the construction of a national subject that constantly strives toward infinite advancement—to become a better representative of the Korean people and nation. As with remembering the Korean War through orphan imagery, visualizing the *minjok*—ethno-nation—through the ideal family stems from a desire to transform the destructive past into a productive, or at least meaningful, present and future.

As in many other cultures, portraiture has been possibly the single most popular genre of photography in Korea since its introduction. Portraits are composed to present a certain vision. Korean photographic portraiture—of babies on the hundredth day after birth and their first birthday, and of families in general—developed in part as a response to the need to construct an instantly accessible, modern identity. The success of that endeavor is proven by the manner in which such portraits have not only reflected changes in the Korean family but also contributed to them. While the growth of the photographic industry, coinciding with South Korea's rapid economic development, encouraged the popularization of baby and family portraits, it also reveals a deep-seated need to define the immediate family according to gender and seniority, and the state as a larger cultural family.

During the late Chosŏn period in the nineteenth century, photo-portraits were made for the royal family and the elite class, the *sataepu* (scholar-official). As with portrait painting, portrait photography was first the province of the upper class, who encountered the medium from foreign sources.[2] Early photographic portraits resemble the Chosŏn traditional portrait paintings—likewise made exclusively for the royal family and ranked members of the court—but now with Western-style tables and chairs. For example, the composition, sitter's pose, and emphasis on detail in a nineteenth-century portrait of a court lady are comparable to the *ŏchin*-style royal portrait paintings (figure 2.1).[3] The sense of nobility thus created typifies the early aesthetic approach to photo-portraiture.[4]

Photography studios opened, and multiplied, throughout Korea in the late nineteenth century, with the *yangban* and *chungin* classes having first access to photo-portraits made in these studios.[5] In 1895, Emperor Kochong ordered the *tanballyŏng* decreeing that men cut their *sangt'u* (hair bun), a traditional sign of men's status. According to Ch'oe Injin, with hair and headdresses no longer immediately indicating hereditary social status, this *tanballyŏng* led to the rise of new bourgeoisie, originally from a lower social class.[6] The making of individual, group, and family portraits in the new medium offered a new way to represent personal modernity and wealth.

A weathered gelatin silver print taken by the Kukchŏnsajin'gwan (Kukchŏn Photography Studio) in the first decade of the 1900s shows an early style of family portrait (figure 2.2).[7] A short-haired man with a mustache sits on a chair next to a small table atop which sits a flower arrangement. He wears a tailored suit, the chain of his pocket watch visible against his vest. At the far

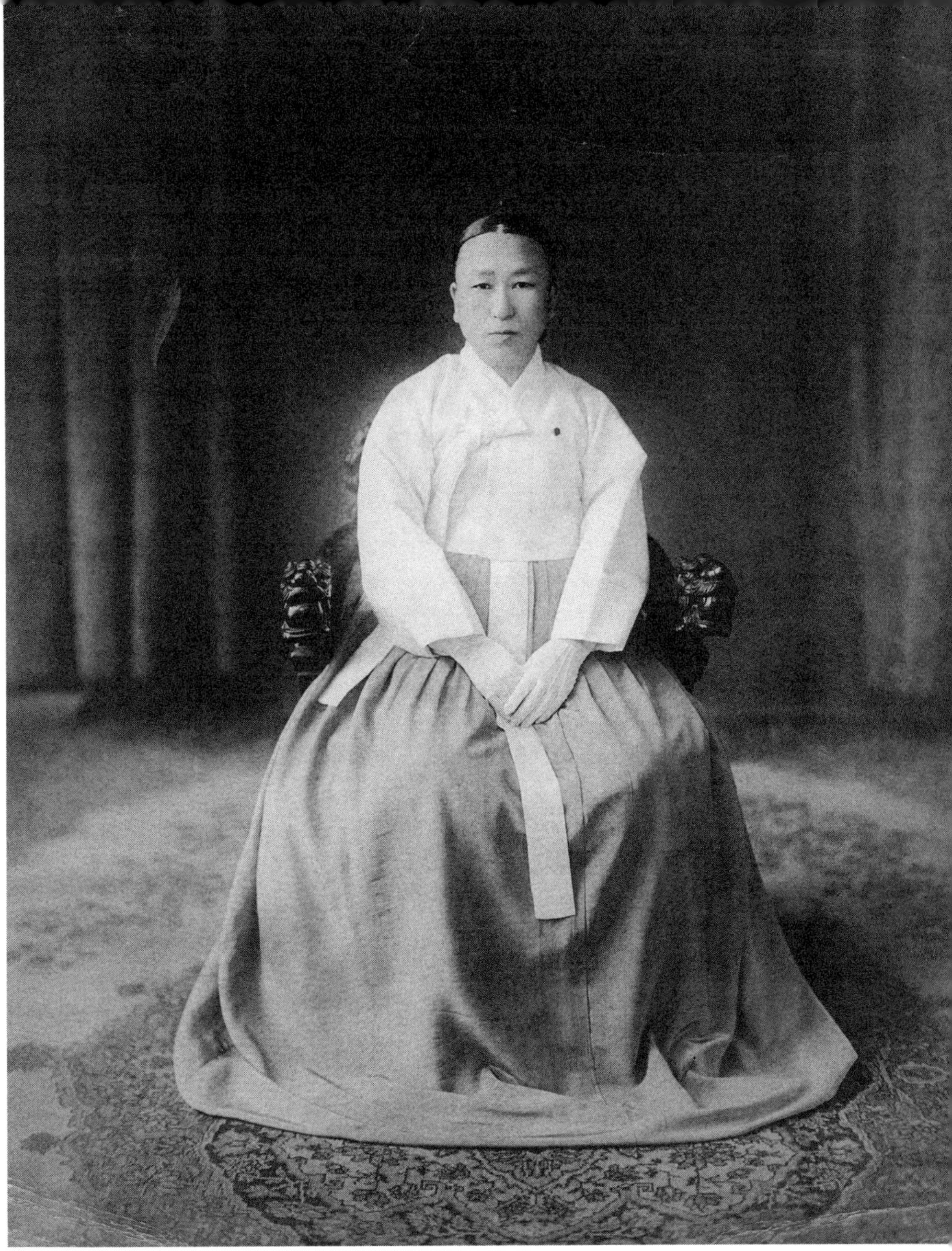

FIGURE 2.1 Photographer once known, *Chŏnggyŏngbuin Kimssi* (*Lady of Chŏnggyŏng*), c. 1930s, gelatin silver print. Courtesy of Museum Hanmi. In a black-and-white photograph, a middle-aged woman in Korean traditional dress and wearing white gloves sits on a chair with her hands clasped on her legs, looking directly at the camera (in the middle of the room). Her manner and dress, as well as the decorative chair arms and delicate patterns on the carpet, indicate her high status.

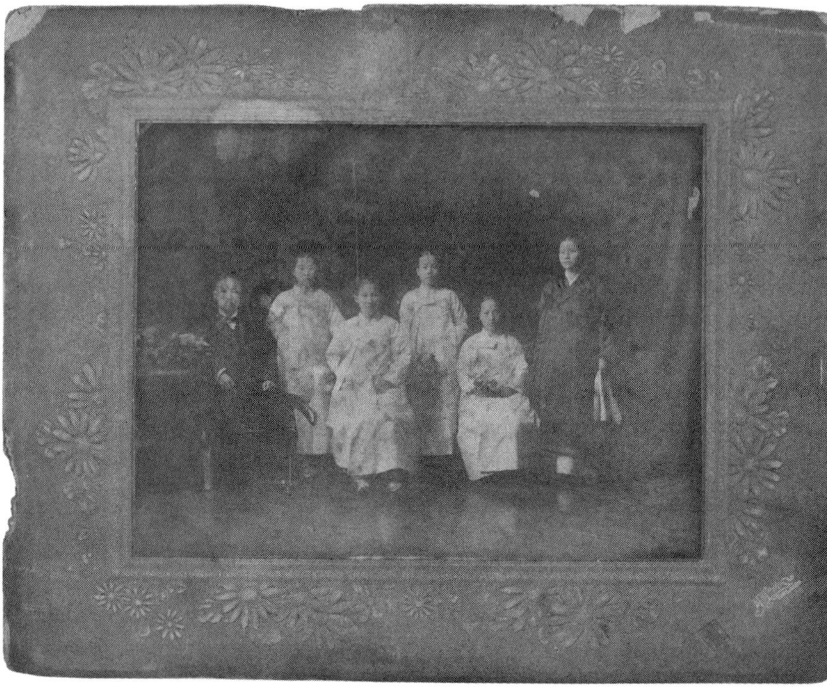

FIGURE 2.2 Kukchŏnsajin'gwan (Kukchŏn Photography Studio), *Portrait of a Family in the First Decade of the 1900s*, gelatin silver print, 20.8 × 26.8 cm. Courtesy of Museum Hanmi.

right of the photograph is a woman wearing a dark coat over a white dress, holding a scarf. Between the man and woman are four women in a style of dress commonly worn until the mid-twentieth century. Two of them sit; the other two stand behind them alternately. While the photograph is described as a family portrait by the Museum of Photography, Seoul (now Museum Hanmi), it is uncertain what the relationships between the people are: the man and woman on each side may be the parents of the four women between them, or perhaps, given that polygamy was common during the Chosŏn period, the four women are not, or not all, siblings.[8] In any case, the attire, studio setting, and the frame, decorated with floral patterns, testify to the work as a portrait made for an elite family or group to be displayed in their home.

The European concept of the family, defined as "an autonomous group—a state, a spiritual unit, a bond of nurturance," was consolidated and visualized during the social upheaval of the Renaissance.[9] In the Enlightenment period of the seventeenth and eighteenth centuries, the European aristocratic cultural intelligentsia promoted further changes in cultural values by emphasizing the power of reason as a means of reforming society.[10] This period established the concept and structure of the modern family. Central to the role of this modern family is the modernizing capacity of the family-as-concept, and this turn is closely related to the concept of patriarchy as the protector of society. As Pak Yŏngt'aek states, in eighteenth-century Europe, monarchs were portrayed as kind but powerful father figures; if one defied the power of a monarch, it was treated as if equivalent to disobeying a father.[11]

Likewise, family portraits have long embodied and symbolized values that are crucial to the upholding of patriarchy in various cultural contexts. According to Julia Hirsch, in Europe, the tradition of family portraits represented three ancient patriarchal principles: the family as a state, rooted in property; the father symbolizing a spiritual assembly based on ethics; and the mother symbolizing an affective bond based on instinct and passion. More broadly, Hirsch finds the precursor of the family photograph in the Renaissance family portrait. This portraiture depicts the family as a self-contained unit, the most significant aspect of which is that the family is shown emancipated from church and manor, a system of agricultural estates to which peasants provided labor and, in return, lords provided protection to peasants.[12]

These significations have, of course, undergone transformation alongside the definition of "family" in the succeeding centuries. Yet they retain striking relevance to the contemporary practices of family photographs. Bonglim Choi, for example, finds that family photo-portrait practice remained more or less unchanged in Korea during the second half of the twentieth century, comparable to "crafts that depend on the tradition of formality"; more drastic changes in the concept of the family were recorded by artists at the turn of the twenty-first century. Without drawing on specific South Korean sociopolitical contexts (other than changes in familial patriarchy), he argues that the formal settings and fashion of studio family portrait practice remained uniform because "the concept of the family embraced by the general public rarely changed, and the photography studio, photographer, and the family all depend on this uniformity."[13]

A standardized visualization of a model family, signified by styles, objects, and manners, is a central function of family photo-portrait making. The early practice of family photo-portraits in Korea also envisioned a sense of transformation—both familial and individual. Visually representing this transformation became the most critical role of the family photo-portrait in the twentieth century; the transformation of the family in modern Korea, from its members to their occupying space, is closely related to the fall of the Chosŏn, the subsequent periods of colonization and war, endemic militarization, and post–Korean War nation-(re)building efforts.

Crucially, in the second half of the twentieth century, the developmentalist ideology of the military regime became entangled in the practices of family photo-portraits. What might appear to be an innocently uniform representation of a nuclear family was in fact a visual affirmation and valorization of self-improvement—a key virtue in the post–Korean War military regime, which emphasized the continued betterment of the family-*minjok*-nation as national ideology. The visual rhetoric of self-improvement articulated in the practice of family photo-portraits has shifted through its changing (and sometimes unchanging) modes, styles, and tropes. In particular, family photo-portraits both reveal and designate the place of women in Korean family and society, a place which women artists' work on family photo-portraits began to challenge at the turn of the twenty-first century.

Using examples of vernacular family photo-portraits and portrait series by artists spanning a century, this chapter examines the ways that the photographic family portraiture has embodied and mediated the twentieth-century transformation of the Korean family as the crux of the nation-state's modernization, and thus propagated the patriarchal, developmentalist ideology of the military state. The subjects include an early twentieth-century family portrait; studio and snap family portraits; family portraits made by Korean women photographers; and portraits of ethnic minority families in and outside of Korea. Analyses of these photo-portraits reveal the ways that the place of women in family portraiture is constructed by patriarchy and challenged, refused, and replaced by women themselves, as subject, photographers, and viewers.

The chapter begins with a survey of the development and current state of family portrait practices, departing from a study of the family portrait of Yi Kwangsu, an elite writer of the colonial period who called for changes in family structure and relations. Yi's portrait, like many others, was a performative production of an ideal family. Central to my discussion of the rise of the vernacular practices of family photo-portraits is national pressure on the family unit to maintain rigid social and gender roles during a time of considerable changes in household structures and an increase in gender sensitivities. Entrenched in the practice of primogeniture, family photo-portraits visualize the gender-designated position of family members, starting from the hundredth-day baby portraits to family portraits with adult children in the second half of the twentieth century. The chapter will examine the patriarchal implications of studio photo-portraits made during this period, while interrogating the validity of this status quo as the only lens through which the Korean family can be photographed.

Exploring family portraits by two Korean women artists, Sunmin Lee and Oksun Kim, the chapter traces a later shift in focus from traditional familial relationships to women and nonnormative family members, respectively. The works of Lee and Kim are not antithetical to the practice of family and baby photo-portraits in Korea despite touching on the meaning of family, issues of patriarchy, gendered labor, race, and sexuality in contemporary South Korean society. Rather, they subvert the photo practice by including objects and styles that have been part of, and have been the fallout from, that traditional practice, in turn revealing the mundanity of family life during off-camera moments and outside of photo studios.[14] At times making the familiar frame of heteronormativity and mono-ethnicity particularly conspicuous, the works of Lee and Kim also problematize the contradictions within the rhetoric of family in the midst of racist, misogynist, and ableist campaigns against families that do not fit into the portrait of the family carved out by militarized ethno-nationalism.

Finally, the paradoxically (or conveniently) effective *tamunhwa* (multiculturalism) and ethno-nationalism attributed to the pan-Korean family is demonstrably unsettled in family portraits collected and shared by members of the Zainichi Korean activist collective Mirinae. Since 2006, the government has officially endorsed *tamunhwa chŏngch'aek* (multicultural policy) to promote public awareness of racial, ethnic, and cultural diversity and support international and interracial families. Grounded in neoliberal technocratism, the official effort has met with criticism and backlash across the mainstream political spectrum. At the same time, *tamunhwa* seems to be promoted within South Korea only, while ethno-nationalism is emphasized in diasporic Korean communities as needed. As such, the state promotes tolerance to multiculturalism and Koreanization of non-Koreans within the country and long-distance nationalism (pan-Koreanness) outside of it.

To explore the affect of Mirinae's family photo-portraits of marginalized women and make connections between these and Kim's and Lee's works is to join the collective effort of (re)writing the history of women as recorded by family portraiture. In this effort, *listening* to images is to, first, resist the historicization of the photographs as an epistemologically disciplining practice of writing the history of photography (of Others), and, second, to tend to the different "frequencies" of the images that can be found when acknowledging that many photo archives of women, especially marginalized ones, do not fit into institutional and disciplinary practices.[15]

Family Photo-Portraits: Modernity's Recto

Participation in the new cultural practice of family portraiture in photography studios implied a family's affluence in the first half of the twentieth century. Crucially, such families were willing and eager to become part of a new class representing modernity in colonial Korea. Modernization, in whatever manifestations it occurred and was promoted by colonial power and its local supporters, therefore, is irrevocably steeped in colonial desire to make Koreans the subjects of Japan—*hwangminhwa*. Consequently, the cultural production of many well-known elites of the colonial period is entangled in controversy over their procolonist work and colonial collaboration.

Among these elites is the prominent Korean writer Yi Kwangsu. Although he once lived in Manchu working with independence activists, Yi later turned colonial collaborator and was an advocate of the modernization of the Korean people, placing a heavy emphasis on marriage and family as a vehicle for that modernization.[16] Yi's widely reproduced family photo-portrait of circa 1928 showcases several of the contemporary changes within family relationships that he propagated (plate 3). Interestingly, the family photo-portrait of Yi expands on the family unit to include a friendship: the photograph shows Yi, his second wife, Hŏ Yŏngsuk, their first baby, Ponggŭn, and an American friend, whose identity has not been recorded.[17] Their son, holding a wooden toy pigeon, is the central figure in the picture, centered and elevated to the height of the adults in a reflection of the rising importance of children among Korean elites.[18] In addition, by including his American friend, the portrait articulates how Yi valued association with "the West" through an individual representing the modern man.[19]

The outstanding distinction between Yi's family photo-portrait and the Kukchŏn Photo Studio family portrait is formalistic. Where a full shot at the Kukchŏn Photo Studio includes the floor and props such as tables, flowers, and curtains, the focus in Yi's family portrait is on the sitters' upper bodies. Props have been eliminated and the background is completely dark.

In the Kukchŏn portrait, the family members sit and stand in alternate rows without any physical contact. In Yi's family portrait, the light and dark contrast between the background and the sitters emphasizes their facial features, creating a much more intimate atmosphere of warmth and intimacy between the father, mother, child, and family friend.[20]

Such formal differences are rooted in Yi Kwangsu's arguments for the modernization of the nation. One of the first shifts in modernizing peasants and those of the lower classes was the "nuclearization" of the Korean family. Korean families in the early colonial period were typically extended, some still practicing polygamy. Writers such as Yi Kwangsu, Chu Sikyŏng, Yi Injik, and Mun Sangu emphasized the importance of children having prospects for a better life than their parents and argued that this required adult children to become more independent.[21] These writers also considered the practice of *chohon*, underage marriage, primitive. They further extended the risk beyond that of familial health, arguing that such family structures could destabilize the nation.[22] Many nationalist and independence activist intellectuals likewise believed that the stability of the individual led to the stability of the nation—and that this stability was to be found in the nuclear family, freed from uncivilized customs and traditions maintained within extended families. Yi's portrait of a compact and generationally clear-cut family—parents and young child—suggests what a modern family should look, even as the inclusion of a foreign friend indicates a new direction for familial "extension." (More on Yi's portraits later.)

Perhaps unsurprisingly, participation in the modernization movements initiated by organizations and institutions began under the control of the governor-general of Japan in Korea and was initially a product of upper-class aspirations. The changing space of the home, for example, reflected economic divisions. Objects such as pianos, gramophones, art catalogs, and Western-style furniture became choice decorations for the home, signaling wealth and comfort even as the general public experienced poverty.[23]

Interest in this standard of living naturally crossed class lines. *Kachŏng-pangnamhoe*, an exposition modeled after the Exposition of Family held in Japan in March 1915, is a case in point. *Maeilsinbo* (*Daily Times*), a newspaper company founded and operated by the governor-general, organized the exposition, which opened in September 1915. It functioned as an educational exhibition showcasing the "new family," detailing where they lived, how they lived, what they did, and what they wore.[24] A great success—unexpectedly high turnout led the organizers to extend viewing hours and dates to accommodate demand—the exhibition in essence suggested an ideal way to live as (middle-class) members of the "new family" in a colonial Korea modeled after Japan.[25] Accordingly, it also conveyed a colonial desire to reform the nation in the colonizer's image, which in the 1920s appeared less aggressive by virtue of implementation in so-called cultural rule / cultural politics (*bunka seiji* in Japanese; *munhwa chŏngch'i* in Korean).[26] This was partly aimed at suppressing uprisings and legitimizing the exploitation of resources and labor force under the motto of reform. At the same time, the popularity of the exposition reflected the yearning of Korean elites for the modernity they believed they experienced on visits to Japan.[27]

Such yearning was not, in fact, in opposition to the desire to claim national subjectivity. According to Jung-ha Kim, Korean colonial subjects emulated the hanging of photo-portraits in Japanese colonialists' homes in Korea; instead of hanging the emperor's portrait, they hung the *ŏchin* of Kojong and Sunjong.[28] Making, acquiring, hanging, and viewing photo-portraits in daily environments therefore became a cultural activity through which elites openly participated in reformation, with all the signification of their modernist identification from their props to fashions and mannerisms, and to modernized familial relations.

Family portraits of upper-middle-class families taken for specific events—the hundredth day after birth (*paegil*), the first birthday (*tol*), and the sixtieth birthday—began appearing in the early twentieth century. A family portrait taken at a sixtieth birthday in the 1920s shows an elaborately prepared birthday table and the gathering of extended family members for the occasion (figure 2.3). The emblem on the lower right corner of the paper frame marks the photograph as taken at the Choil Photography Studio in Gongju.[29] The lavish table and Western attire of some of the men and boys indicate the high social and economic status of at least part of the family.

Family portraits taken in larger cities in the 1930s and 1940s reflect a major shift in the middle-class Korean family. A family portrait photograph made at Ch'ŏnyŏndang Photo Studio in Kyŏngsŏng, the colonial name for the administrative district of present-day Seoul, in the 1930s shows parents with two children (figure 2.4). The man wears *yangbok* (Western attire/suit) while the woman wears a simplified and modernized Korean dress.[30] The older child wears a striped shirt and sits on his father's lap; the baby sits on their mother's lap toward the center of the photograph. The plain, monochrome backdrop of the portrait is highlighted, creating a vignette, which frames and encloses the family within. The tight composition, cutting below

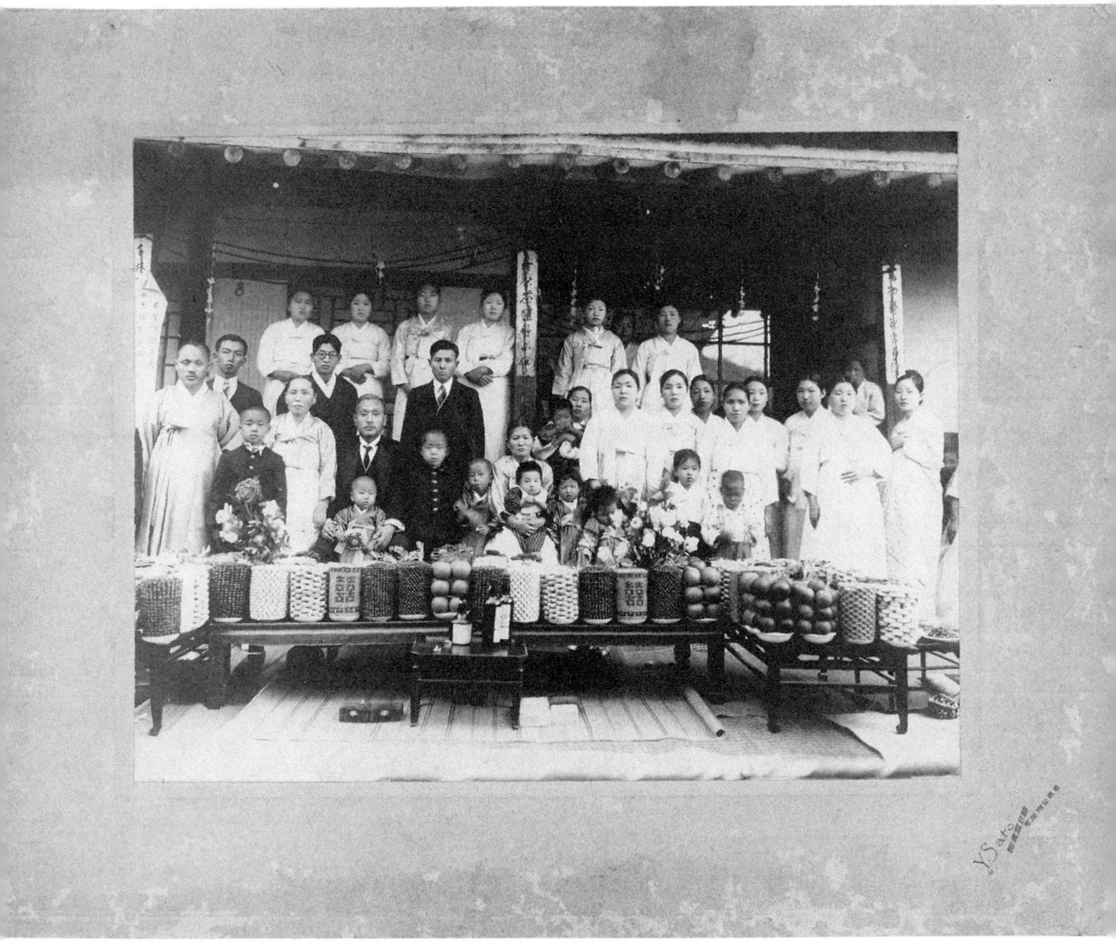

FIGURE 2.3 Choilsajin'gwan (Choil Photography Studio), *Portrait of a Family Taken at a Sixtieth Birthday Banquet*, c. 1920s, gelatin silver print. Courtesy of Museum Hanmi.

the sitters' waist, emphasizes the closeness of the family members and places the children in equally central positions. As in Yi Kwangsu's family photo-portrait, this implies the importance of children and accentuates the role of parents as child-rearers: the parents will enable the children to become this modernizing force rather than looking to them as contributing to family-community labor. The children will thus grow up as modernized Koreans, enlightening the nation and eventually, hopefully, bringing independence from colonial rule. In this way, the photo-portrait functions as a visual

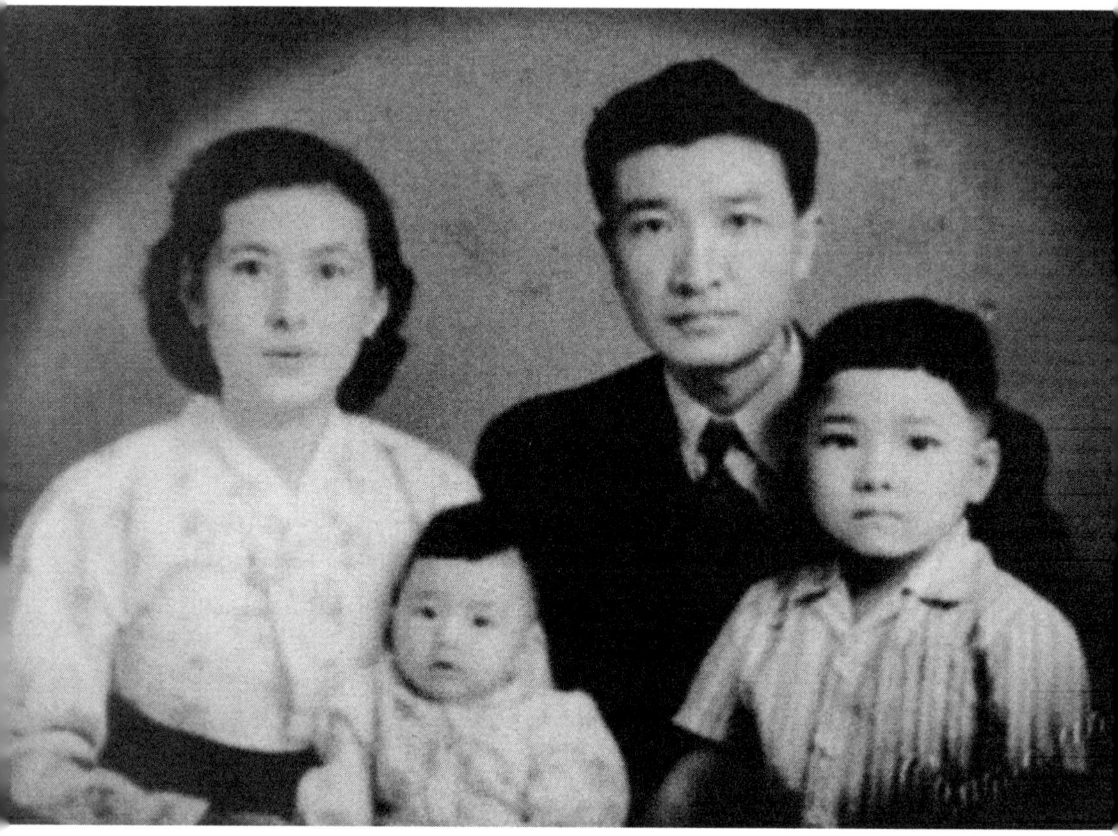

FIGURE 2.4 Ch'ŏnyŏndangsajin'gwan (Ch'ŏnyŏndang Photography Studio), *Portrait of a Family*, c. 1930s, gelatin silver print. Courtesy of Pak Yŏngt'aek and Patach'ulp'ansa.

affirmation of familial transformation and an anticipation of children's future in the uncertain times under the colonial rule.

This emphasis on imagining and representing children as symbols of a family's—and a nation's—future is even more prominent in the popular conventions of portraits taken on the hundredth day after birth (*paegilsajin*) and the first birthday (*tolsajin*).[31] While taking baby pictures is common across the world, a specifically Korean practice of photographing the hundredth day after birth, and the first birthday complete with a specially prepared banquet, emerged in the early twentieth century. This became widely practiced in Korea by the 1960s, as more people could afford these portraits following the Korean War, and more photo studios, photographers, and cameras made their production possible.[32] As baby portraits reflected a desire to bring up a child as a modernized citizen, the practice of photo-portraiture on the hundredth day after birth and the first birthday suggests how the modernization and industrialization of Korea involved reforming the place of the child within the household and the nation. Furthermore, the portraits also signified the gender-differentiated place of the child in one's home and nation: in the hundredth-day photo-portraits, the phalli of male children were exposed and female children were dressed fully in white. The male child, his sex made central to the viewer, embodies the hope of bringing affluence to the family, and thus of transforming the poverty-stricken, war-torn nation into an industrialized power.[33]

Indeed, although the Korean War and the socioeconomic devastation that followed slowed the expansion of vernacular family photography, it returned as the favored medium depicting the Korean family in the 1960s. This decade also opened with a dramatic political upheaval: Park Chung Hee's coup d'état in May 1961, which successfully upended the civilian administration, making him the de facto leader of the military regime. In 1963, he was elected the third president of the Republic of Korea and upheld his position until his assassination in October 1979. During this time, the portrait of an ideal nation and the citizenry that would contribute to the nation's economic and cultural advancement was painted by the regime, realized in photo studios, and upheld on the walls of the family home.

Park's militarization of the nation has been examined in relation to his own ambitious militarization as part of Japan's Manchuoko Imperial Army in the early 1940s. Similarly, his approach to transforming Korean families and individuals as contributing subjects to the nation's development resembles that of *hwangminhwa*.[34] The junta's emphasis on the good citizen, constantly striving toward the nation's betterment, was earlier the rhetoric of colonial governance, and, as discussed, internalized by Korean intellectuals during that period. For example, Yi Kwangsu called what he considered the "malaise" of uneducated Koreans "stepchildren traits." The Korean masses were metaphorized as children—as with the rhetoric of war orphans discussed in chapter 1—with the insinuation that they must be put under guardianship.[35] For Yi, such "innate" Korean traits cannot be eliminated, but, as colonial subjects, Koreans could work hard to become "good Japanese people" (by becoming good subjects of the emperor)—in short, *hwangminhwa*.[36] This required the colonial subject to constantly prove their potential, an extension of political and social antagonism against colonial subjects into their personal and psychological sense of self.[37] The ideology of the family as a basic national unit that bears, grows, and educates the male born into a *sanŏmnilkkun*—the industrious worker (literally the worker of the industry) of the military regime—follows directly from the ideology of *hwangminhwa*.

Picturing the Place of Woman: In Her Own Body, Family, and Nation

Although the nuclearization of the traditionally extended family was initiated and promoted by Korean elites at the start of the twentieth century as a way to modernize Korea and thus enable it to regain independence, it was not until the Park regime that official measures were implemented to bring women's bodies under the biopolitics of state-encouraged or state-sanctioned birth control, abortion, and involuntary sterilization.[38] The Park regime considered the significant increase in population after the Korean War a threat to the desired rapid growth in the gross national product. To control population growth—and thereby accelerate both the transformation of the family and economic growth—the government inaugurated the Family Planning Measure (*Kajokkyeheoksaŏp*), implemented in conjunction with the first Five-Year Development Plan in 1962.[39] This was followed by the Mother and Child Health Act (*Mochapokŏnpŏp*) in 1973, under the Yushin Constitution, which was Park's emergency measure that gave him executive power over administration, legislature, and jurisdiction, and gave him the power to retain this executive status for his lifetime.[40] Among other tactics, the act legalized abortion. In fact, as Eunjung Kim states, the act ushered in a new wave of eugenics (the first being during the colonial period in the 1920s) to "achieve economic prosperity and to empower an independent capitalist nation-state."[41] Under this act, parents with hereditary and infectious diseases, along with parents in low-income households, were subjected to involuntary sterilization.[42]

The government also tried to lower the birthrate through various educational campaigns conducted by the newly established Ministry of Health and Society and the Association of Taehan Family Planning. For these campaigns, the institutions took advantage of visual materials, especially in the form of posters—the government's favorite means to educate the public.[43] The poster-calendar of 1968 produced by the Ministry of Health and Society and the Association of Taehan Family Planning shows an illustration of a mother with a son and a daughter (figure 2.5). On the bottom of the poster-

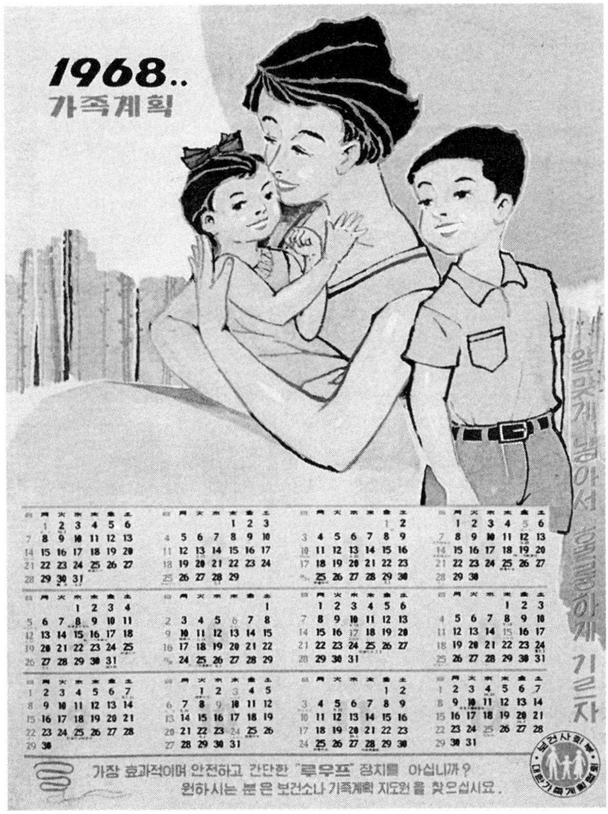

FIGURE 2.5 Family Planning Campaign Poster Calendar of 1968. Planned Parenthood Federation of Korea.

calendar, a sentence encourages the use of female contraceptives. By only including the figure of the mother and not the father, and only encouraging the use of female contraceptives, the poster emphasizes women's responsibility for planning families, underscoring the gender-differentiated roles through which the modernization process was organizing itself.[44]

The regime's propagandistic imagery promoted the diligent, patriotic nuclear family willing to submit to the various campaigns of the military government—principally to provide flexibility for maximizing the labor force and remain easier to govern—and relied heavily on division of family roles by gender. For example, *kakyepussŭkiundong* (bookkeeping campaign) encouraged wives to be more concerned with their expenses and savings by placing them in charge of household bookkeeping.[45]

Family nuclearization was further entrenched in the early 1970s, under the third Five-Year Economic Development Plan implemented by President

Park. Anticipating a large-scale migration, the Park government carried out the mass development of apartment housing in the largely unused or agricultural land south of the Han River in Seoul.[46] Most of the new housing was designed to accommodate nuclear families, and many of the units were two- and three-bedroom apartments.[47] Meanwhile, labor policies were vastly changed in favor of employers at the expense of unions. During Park's Yushin policies, workers endured excruciating hours, while other family members also endured the absence of spouses or parents. These moves, however, assured families' devotion to the nationalistic cause of modernization.

Examinations of family photo-portraits from the early twentieth century to the present have focused on the appearance of socioeconomic sophistication and familial harmony based on patriarchal lineage (figure 2.6). Nuclearization continued to be a prominent feature of these portraits. In the 1980s, family photo-portraits largely become uniform in style and composition, changing primarily according to popular trends over time. The portraits thereby showcase the new norms of the nuclearization of the family and the ways in which familial harmony and happiness are represented (plates 4 and 5). To visualize this harmony, the physical and psychological place of each family member and together as a whole became crucial.

More recently, the significance of representing happiness and harmony has extended to family portraits with adult children. In a family portrait made in the 2000s, the father sits in an armchair wearing a formal dress suit, while the mother in a white dress sits on a stool holding a bouquet of white flowers (figure 2.7). The late-adolescent male child stands behind the mother in three-quarter view, wearing a black suit that resembles his father's. The daughter, who looks slightly older, is at the center of the photograph, standing with her left hand resting on the back of the father's chair and her right hand on her hip, so that her body is positioned diagonally between the parents. She smiles, her mouth open. The background of the portrait appears to be painted, giving an illusion of a study with a large painting hung on the wall. The chiaroscuro effect of the backdrop yields a soft, dreamy impression. Overall, the photograph appears highly composed, and was likely retouched by the photographer; most studios digitally manipulate portrait photographs. The dress, pose, composition, and backdrop of recent family portraits show that "harmony," "luxury," and "sophistication" are some of the key themes families wish to convey through their portraits. These characteristics suggest in turn that this portrayal is a matter of role-playing, rather than a reflection of reality.

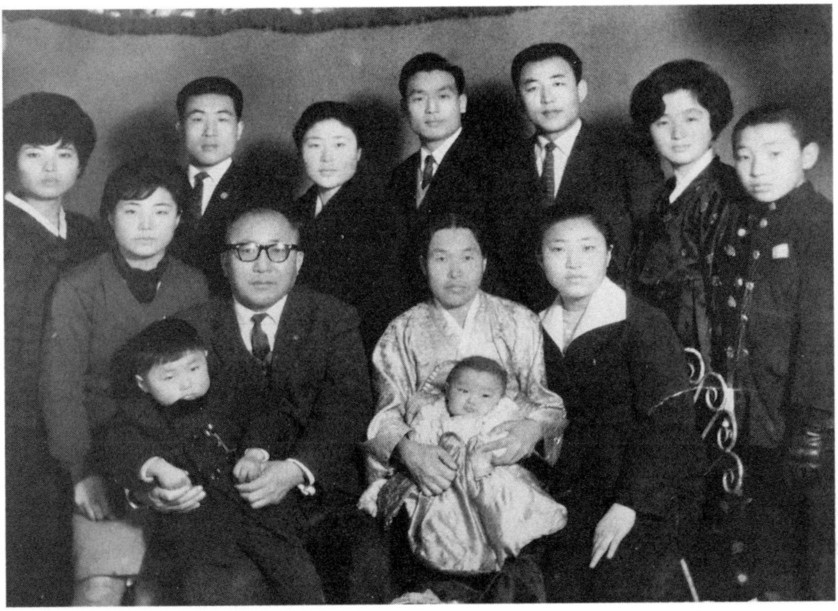

FIGURE 2.6 Studio family portrait, gelatin silver print, 1968. Courtesy of Cheon Chin Soon. This black-and-white thirteen-person family portrait, possibly for the baby's *paegil* (hundredth day), shows four men, six women, a schoolboy in a uniform, and a small boy, sitting and standing in two rows. The men wear suits with ties and women wear either Korean traditional dress or jackets. In front of them, an older man wearing a pair of glasses sits with a boy on his lap, holding the boy's hands. To his left—at the center of the group—is an older woman with a baby, both wearing light-colored Korean dress *hanbok*; to her left is a woman in her school uniform. The older man and woman sitting in the center seem to be the parents, parents-in-law, and grandparents of the younger group surrounding them.

While contemporary *tol* portraits are likewise expressions of young families' hopes and expectations through the performance of a fantasy, presented by dressing their children and themselves in special garments emulating those of imagined royal families (Western or Chosŏn), this family portrait with grown-up children also appears to convey what they perceive as an ideal: a happily united nuclear family with elements showing wealth and sophistication. The portrait becomes a kind of totem of the yearning for *hwamokhan kajŏng*—harmonious home/household/family—and a successful fulfillment of that potential symbolized in baby portraits of *paegil* and *tol*. Crucially,

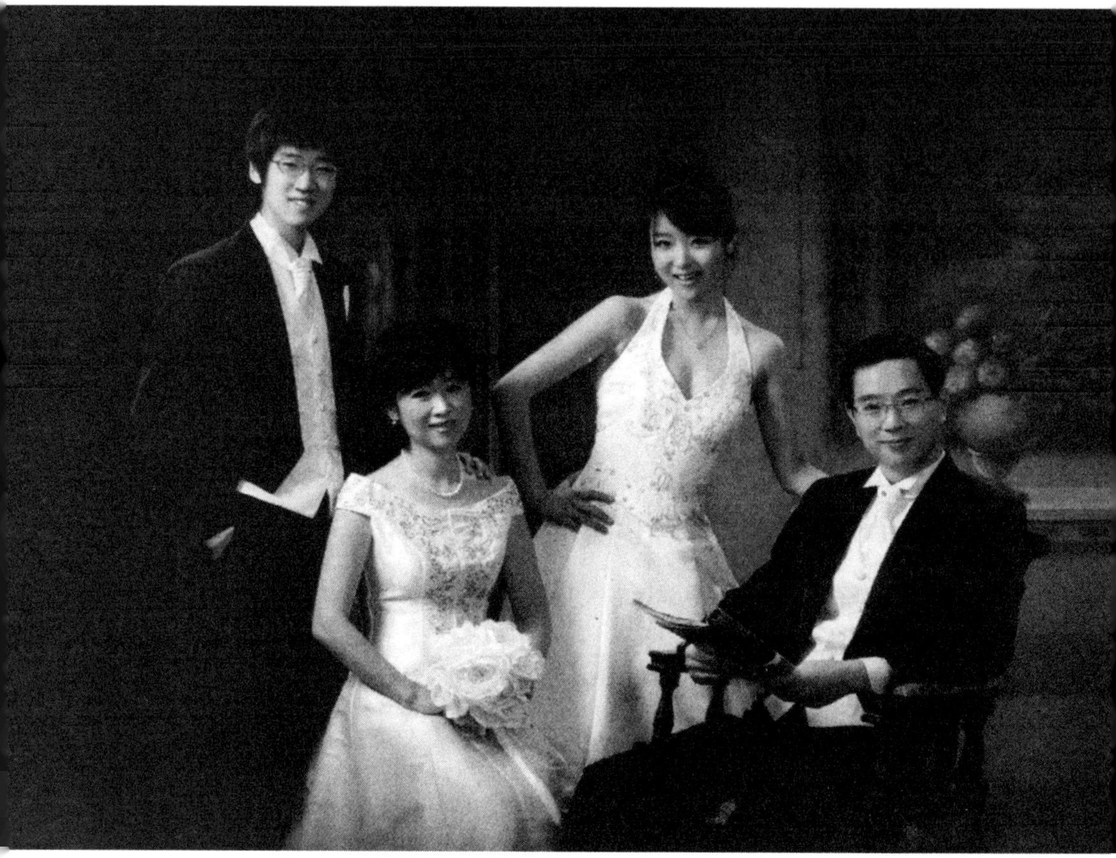

FIGURE 2.7 Acrovista Studio, Seoul, *Portrait of a Family*, c. 2000s, c-print. Courtesy of Oh Hyŏnju and Noonbit.

however, the desire to present the harmonious family now extends beyond the portraits including very young children.

This is related to a particular stage of the lifetime of the family. Parents wish to make family portraits before the child leaves their home for either mandatory military service or marriage.[48] However, the practice also positions the mother in a specific place of affect, and in some cases, "hysteria." In research conducted on family portraits as a practicing studio photographer, Kim Miae states that mothers expressed the most enthusiasm during the photo shoots. Kim posits that, for the mother of the family, portraits exhibiting her harmonious household celebrates her role as a wise, nurturing mother with well-raised children.[49] Hence, from gender-differentiating baby portraits to elaborate

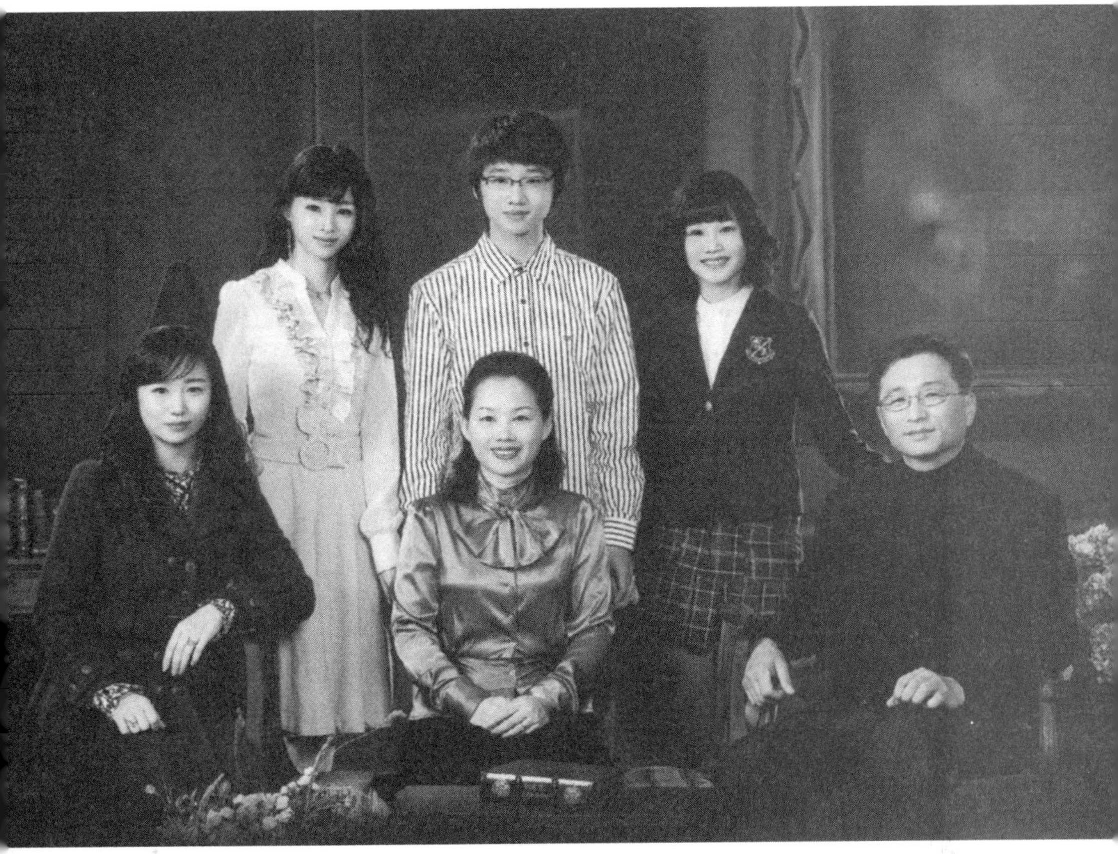

FIGURE 2.8 Gaya Studio, Gongju, *Portrait of a Family*, c. 2000s, c-print. Courtesy of Oh Hyŏnju and Noonbit.

studio portraits with adult children, family portraiture continues to pin the designation for women (and thus men as well) within familial relationships.

In a portrait of a family consisting of parents, three grown-up daughters, and a grown-up son, the mother sits in the center of the photograph (figure 2.8). As in the previous example, the background of the photograph is painted, giving the illusion of a luxuriously decorated house. Three family members sit in the front row and three stand behind them; the father sits on an armchair to the mother's left, and to her right sits a daughter. The son stands directly behind the mother and the two daughters stand on either side of him. While the father's position in the armchair may symbolize his familial authority, the mother is read as the central figure of the family.

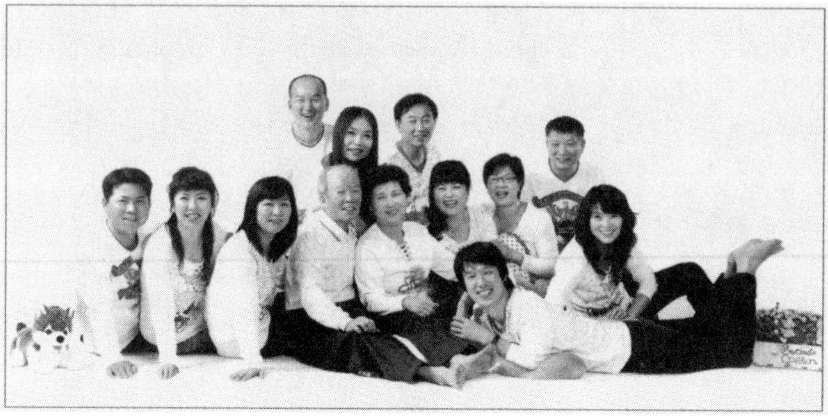

FIGURE 2.9 Studio Photo 21, Ulsan, *Portrait of a Family*, c. 2000s, c-print. Courtesy of Oh Hyŏnju and Noonbit.

Kim argues that this photograph, hung in the living room, may function as a response "to the confused psychological/emotional state of the middle-aged mother,"[50] and at the same time provide affirmation of her success as a wife and mother. While such a reading is fundamentally sexist and essentialist, encounters with individuals and media caricaturizing middle-age (menopausal or not) women as irrational and ill-mannered are commonplace. Such a reading hypothesizes that even when the woman of the household is in the center, it is not because she and the family opted for the particular composition (or variations on it), but because the family, and specifically the patriarch, is kind enough to do the aging woman this favorable gesture of allowing her to sit in the center. It indicates that there is a designated space for women in the patriarchal order articulated in family portraits.

Families also choose to make more relaxed and less ornamental family photographic portraits, articulating different aesthetic preferences than those I have so far examined. One example shows a family of thirteen; a set of older parents and adult children with their spouses, likely gathered for the parents' anniversary or a sixtieth or seventieth birthday (figure 2.9). Plain white replaces the dark, painted backdrops, providing a brighter mood. The family members are dressed much more casually, in coordinated white T-shirts and dark pants. All the family members smile with their teeth showing, something rarely witnessed in the more formal portraits discussed above. The group is seated closely together in an elliptical shape that conveys a sense of stability and harmony.

However, this family portrait, and others like it, were made in photography studios and thus still greatly affected by the photographer's vision. In fact, the studio owner and photographer of the family photo-portrait states that his unique marketing strategy—he encourages his clients to make family portraits annually on the parents' anniversary—has helped his studio grow in a competitive market.[51] While such photo-portraits may appear to have an alternative aesthetic, it is also about marketing more than a fundamental shift in outcome. The elements of such studio portraits still portray the family harmony cherished throughout the twentieth century.[52] In Choi's contention, the stylized, formulaic aesthetics of earlier familial performance in photography is incapable of generating critical discourses in the way that art photography is (as discussed in the following section). Yet the very desire to maintain the formulaic aesthetics of family portraits (despite stylistic variations and updates) and the unchanging gendered positioning of family members speaks loudly and clearly as to what a family should look like, even in one of the most rapidly "advancing" cultures in the world.

Yŏchaŭi Chip (Woman's House)

The gendered realities of everyday life during the rapidly industrializing decades under the military regime left deep impressions on family gender dynamics that continue to surface in various aspects of contemporary Korean life. Since the 1990s, Korean women artists and photographers have regularly explored the gender dynamic of family in the transformative Korean society. This is the central theme of Sunmin Lee's photographic series, *Yŏchaŭi Chip* (*Woman's House*, 2002–2010), in which she photographed the everyday life of numerous families in situ. Unlike traditionally idealized representations of the Korean family as a social unit, Lee's photographs capture families in their homes while they conduct the most mundane activities, such as eating meals and cleaning while attending to children.

Lee's work offers an unromantic portrait of a family in which the men and women fulfill their duties in this gendered tradition. A photograph of Sunja Lee's family from *Yisunjaŭi Chip* (*Sunja Lee's House*, 2004) shows an annual ancestral ritual, in which the descendants pay homage to their ancestors who in turn look after them (plate 6). Three women are outside the room where the ritual is taking place. Two of them are peeking inside, while a third one is sitting on the floor with her face turned from the room. Inside the room, typical dishes for an ancestral ritual are placed on a table, to which a man bows. Other members of the family, including children, stand by the bowing man. The photograph shows a typical scene of an ancestral ritual. Only men are allowed to conduct and attend the ritual, even though women spend days preparing the special dishes (plate 7). It is uncertain which of the three women outside the room is Sunja Lee. But as they all are equally excluded from participating in the ritual, despite their significant contribution, the name Sunja Lee itself becomes a synonym for "woman," in the same way as the title of Lee's series *Woman's House* encompasses the many titles of its constituent photographs.

The figure of the mother is a perpetual synonym for sacrificial love across cultures and time. In Korean cultural production, the mother (*Ŏmŏni*) is often symbolized as incessantly giving to her children despite being overworked and exploited, with serious health problems (just think of Player 456's dying mother, performed by Kim Yŏngok, in the 2021 global hit Netflix series *Squid Game*). Kwŏn Myŏnga finds an impulse in this sociocultural narrative to undermine the anxiety of being in proximity to Others.[53] Indeed, "the sadness arising from the narrative of sacrificial love" is exploited to mask over or push aside the evident presence of difference and otherness. The reason why the "crisis" in society is continually framed as a crisis in the family, Kwŏn states, is because the family is considered the most basic unit of reproduction.[54] Hence, the emphasis on an eternally giving motherhood (or sisterhood or daughterhood) is part of the patriarchal desire to exclude different forms of "family" from the basic unit positioned as essential to the family-*minjok*-nation.

Yŏchaŭi Chip questions the valorization of mother's sacrificial love and her affective distance from the rest of the "House." The tired and disengaged expressions seen in the series' portraits of young mothers—women confined to the relentlessness of housework and child-rearing—are a symbolic antithesis to the public faces of the incessantly hardworking mother that reappear during, for example, presidential election campaigns. The mothers of unyielding love and labor, often represented by old women in outdoor markets in campaign commercials, mythologize the Park Chung Hee–style developmentalist economy, in which these mothers sacrificed the main part of their lives to educate their children and thus contribute to the betterment of the nation. The perseverance of these sacrificial mothers is often symbolized in the old-fashioned and unkempt appearance and brusque mannerism of older women. For instance, an elderly market soup vendor was made famous by a campaign commercial of the Unified Party candidate, Lee Myung-bak, for the 2007 presidential election. Fast forward a decade and a half, this sacrificial love still pressures young women in many ways, as familial affect needed for upkeeping a family in the hypercompetitive, cutthroat labor market in which gender equality is seen as a threat to male employees' wages, benefits, and success. Issues regarding unevenly gendered household workloads, especially in young child-rearing families, are a key factor affecting the declining (heteronormative) first marriage and birth rates, not to mention the wage gap.

The expected role of the mother as family caretaker allows society to praise her sacrificial work while, as Pak Yŏngt'aek puts it, degrading the true value of her labor: "Here the ideology of family is used to create gendered labor and make women become economically dependent on men."[55] Kwŏn warns that the return to the myth of sacrificial mothers is not only a reflection of a collective drive for the family-*minjok*-nation's betterment (i.e., continued economic development and the global acknowledgment of it), but it also underscores the dismay and tiredness over the era following the 1997 and 2008 economic crises that have failed them.[56]

If the studio portrait of the family centering a middle-aged mother was an effort to paper over a kind of family crisis, Sunmin Lee's work lets the crisis part of ordinary family life become apparent. Together, the studio portrait and Lee's portrait reveal what is at stake for contemporary Korean families: the daily practice of gendered labor and familial rituals of patriarchal lineage and the treatment of women's discontent as something shameful to be covered up. In contrast to the studio portrait, in which the mother is the central figure of the family, Sunmin Lee's photograph of Sunja Lee's family illustrates a familial event where women are excluded from participating but required to provide their labor for the ritual. Yet in both photographs, while the women of the family have fulfilled their roles as the actual preparer of the event, their expressions show hints of unhappiness, exhaustion, and detachment.

The simultaneous reliance on women's labor and exclusion of women's presence shown in *Sunja Lee's House* has increasingly been acknowledged by Korean society as unfair, but is still regarded as necessary and inevitably normal. Nonetheless, the legal organization of the family has undergone some changes in South Korea in the 2000s. The eradication of *hochuche*, the civil registration of family members under male heads, began in 2008.[57] Under *hochuche*, a modified practice of primogeniture, women were legally subject to male kin: when the husband died, the wife was required to register under the eldest son, or the next closest male kin. Likewise, in the matter of inheritance, male children were ranked above female children, as well as the mother, as beneficiary to the family estate. The patriarchal nature of *hochuche* was not simply a matter of civil law; it grounded relations between male and female family members and among heteronormative gendering systems in general.

The activity of taking family portraits has long been a confirmation of this patriarchal—with the implications of proper and *yangban*-bourgeois—family order, especially for those who desired to obtain and visualize that status. Therefore, despite the recent legal changes, the baby photo-portraits displayed at Sunja Lee's house continue to visualize the desire and affirmation of the family's future via patriarchal lineage—only those of sons and grandsons hang above the door to the room. Two of these portraits show the babies in the costume of the king of Chosŏn and are hung where the portraits of the elders or ancestors are traditionally situated, and where *ŏchin* was hung. The picture of Sunja Lee's home thus illustrates the familial lineage of ancestors, parents, children, and grandchildren—but one that connects only the male members of the family. But it would not be surprising if Sunja Lee herself hung the portraits of her grandsons on that wall. Traditionally (and heteronormatively), it is usually the husband's parents, notably his mother, who vociferously expresses a preference for male descendants. The "family portrait" of Sunja Lee thus shows how the patriarchal ideology of family becomes self-perpetuating through the combined practices of ancestral ritual and modern baby portraiture. And in turn, despite the (probable) discontent of being excluded, the patriarchal ideology is internalized as Sunja Lee willingly places her grandsons' portraits up above her.

Happy Together: *Tamunhwa* and Selective Ethno-nationalism

Sunmin Lee's photo series address issues in the idealized Korean families whose lineages have continued through the bearing of male children and through women's domestic, as well as affective, labor—labor that is taken for granted by the patriarchal society. This family's role in *minjokchuŭi*, which translates as "nationalism" in South Korea, is reciprocal, but also potentially undermined by the changing definitions of what the Korean family is.[58] As much as the traditional Korean family emphasizes primogeniture and its lineage, the contemporary conditions of neoliberal globalization have raised significant challenges to its perpetuation. Among other scapegoats for the declining birthrate are an increasing number of single adult households, and the rise in the average age of people entering a first marriage.

Tamunhwa, in many ways, was expected to compensate for these issues, as policy makers expected that higher awareness of multiculturalism would reduce sociocultural concerns related to international marriages and, in turn, increase their numbers. Under government encouragement, *tamunhwa* became a commonly used term to refer to relationships between, primarily, Korean men and non-Korean women.[59] The number of international marriages between Korean men and non-Korean women began to rise after South Korea reestablished diplomatic relations with China in 1992. They took place largely among unmarried men in rural areas of Korea where there was a significant shortage of eligible women.[60]

International and interracial marriages and their domestic spaces are the subjects of the artist Oksun Kim's photo series *Happy Together*. As with Sunmin Lee's photographs, Kim's work allows the viewer to peer into the domestic, intimate space. But Kim's families are not so typical in South Korea.[61] Terms such as *kukchekyŏrhon* (international marriage) have been used indicating how marriages between Koreans and non-Koreans have been differentiated from "usual" (*pot'ong*) marriages between Koreans.[62] Kim's work zooms in on the mundane, familial space of living, its foreignness signified only by the subject's body and an air of stage-like psychological intensity.

From this series, *Candie and Ray* (2002) depicts an interracial couple in their living room. The Korean woman, Candie, a bar owner, wearing embroidered *kyeryanghanbok* (modernized traditional Korean dress) of vivid red, looks directly into the camera, while the white man, Ray, an English teacher, stands by the corner of the room looking at an oblique angle away from the camera (plate 8).[63] The living room of Candie and Ray contains standard items found within South Korean family homes: a cabinet displaying bottles of whiskey and Korean wine, a potted orchard, floral-patterned curtains, and a faux-exotic carpet.

In this mundane domestic space, the couple stand awkwardly away from each other, lending an ironic edge to the title of Kim's series. The sight/site of that distance, or disjuncture, relates back to the family-*minjok*-nation narrative. In a nation whose establishment was based upon the legitimacy of *tanilminjok* (ethnocentricity), enshrined in the foundation of the Republic of Korea by Syngman Rhee's emphasis on *ilminjuŭi* ("One People Principle" or "united-citizenry"), international marriages were treated as taboo,[64] and a threat to national stability following the Korean War.[65] Though the South Korean media emphasizes recent positive changes in line with the government's campaigns on *tamunhwa*—for instance, in TV shows focusing on non-Korean residents and naturalized citizens of South Korea, the attitude toward international and interracial marriage in Korean society remains less than welcoming in cases where the spouse is not white, heteronormative, and able-bodied.[66]

Personal experience with this kind of bias drives Oksun Kim's examination of it. Kim's work was initially conceived as an exploration of her own experiences in an international marriage, which entails issues from the technical—such as visa status—to major differences in language, customs, and traditions.[67] In *Oksun and Ralf* (2002), Kim and her German husband sit in their living room (plate 9). Unlike the studio portraits of an idealized Korean family, the couple's lethargic poses and expressions imply the mundaneness of the everyday life of a married heteronormative couple in South Korea—regardless of race and ethnicity. This sense of ordinariness and boredom is highlighted by the domesticity of the space they inhabit: the intercom system with a small monitor above Ralf, old-fashioned but typical of South Korean apartment units; the unleveled frames hanging behind Kim; and the seemingly insignificant items sprawled on the traditional Korean tea-table between them.

Today, the term *tamunhwa* equally carries negative connotations of racism, ethnocentrism, and a threat to national security, especially accompanied by the fear of terrorism and treason. In this multivalent meaning, it exemplifies anxiety over the necessarily unpatriotic Other, tainting not just the pure bloodline of the *tanilminjok* but, more importantly, the advanced status and reputation of the ROK's economy and culture. While examining the correlation of the two is not within the scope of my research, prejudice against interracial marriages certainly has a long history in South Korea, especially in its association with marriages between Korean women and American service members. The photographs of those families could never present an ideal, as they were symbols of national trauma.[68]

In South Korea, the storefront windows of photography studios exhibit photographs that represent their ideal oeuvre.[69] As well as portraits of famous residents of the neighborhood, such as TV personalities or politicians, the studios often hang family and baby portraits. These almost always present ethnically Korean and (seemingly) heterosexual family units, unless the sitter is famous and/or white—for instance, the Korean singer Patti Kim, who rose to unprecedented stardom in the 1960s and 1970s, whose family portrait including her white husband and their biracial daughter, as well as a daughter from her previous marriage, was hung in the main show window of the Ran Photography Studio in July 2019 (figure 2.10).[70] Portraits of queer couples

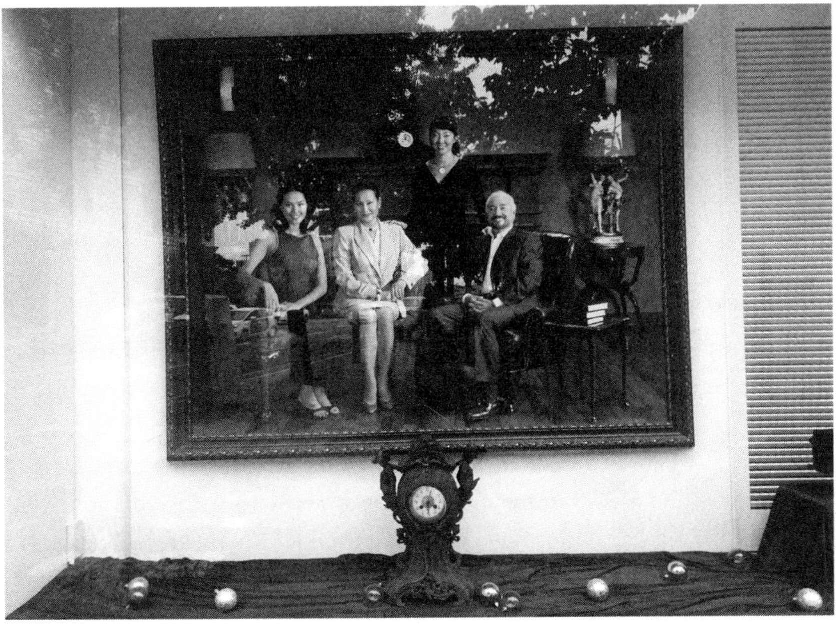

FIGURE 2.10 *Family Portrait of Patti Kim*, Ran Photography Studio storefront, Seoul, July 2019. Photograph by author.

and families almost never grace show windows, even in cases of celebrity.[71] Because photo-portraits of nonheterosexual families and *tamunhwa* families consisting of nonwhite family members do not usually receive spots for public display,[72] public displays of portraits reproduce sexual normativity, racial inheritance, and, except for Koreanness, preference of whiteness over others.[73] This is directly related to the marketing of photo studios in a society that finds ethno-nationalism an antidote to global capitalism, neoliberalism, and national security and continues to valorize the patriarchy of family-*minjok*-nation.

Portraits of the Unusual Days: Women, Kinship, Diaspora, and *Pot'ongi Anin Naldŭl* (*Days That Are Not Usual*)

In these conflicting nationalist approaches, militarized patriarchy vis-à-vis neoliberal technocratism has also kept out the voices of marginalized communities in the Korean diaspora. The *tamunhwa* campaign does not align well with Korean diasporic communities, of which members are generally considered *tongp'o* (compatriots), but culturally and politically also treated as less-Korean, not-Korean, or even defectors. For example, Zainichi Koreans (Korean descents living in Japan), although sometimes considered *tongp'o*, have occupied ambiguous categories for the South Korean state and media partly due to their factional alliance with North Korea, such as that of the Choch'ongryŏn (Chaeilbonchosŏninch'ongyŏnhaphoe).[74] The concept of *tamunhwa*, therefore, only applies to ethnically non-Korean Koreans and residents and their children within South Korea.

The respective series by Sunmin Lee and Oksun Kim depict, among other things, women's immobility within the mundanity of the everyday life in ethnocentric and heteronormative society. While this immobility has been exacerbated by, for example, experiences of daily fatigue in the caretaking of the family—considered unfortunate but ordinary—their photographs render these moments not normal: "*pot'ongi anin naldŭl*," "the days that are not usual," in direct translation. The harmonious family is envisioned in a studio portrait, which places every member of the family in their designated, gendered position within the heteronormative middle-class household—as an ideal Korean family, which *should* be the normal version of the family. By showing *pot'ongi anin naldŭl*, their works expose the cracks within the days forced to be *pot'ong* (normal or usual) for the sake of keeping the fantasy of the harmonious family.

Pot'ongi Anin Naldŭl (*Days That Are Not Usual*, Korean edition, 2019) is in fact the title of the Korean edition of a book about the lives of women of ethnically or socioeconomically marginalized groups in Japan: Zainichi Korean;[75] descendants of *burakumin*,[76] Ainu, Okinawan, Filipina, and Vietnamese women. First published in Japan in Japanese in 2016, stories and photographs of twenty-two minority women between the ages of twenty and seventy were collected and shared by members of the activist organization Mirinae (originally Chaeilchosŏnin yŏsŏngdŭrŭi moim, the Gathering of Chosŏn Women in Japan).[77] By exhibiting family photo-portraits in conjunction with personal stories, the book makes visible the ways in which pan-Koreanism aligns with the history of imperial violence and the marginalization of ethnic minority women living in Japan—imprinting not only the faces and voices of Zainichi women past and present, but also those of other ethnic minority groups and socioeconomic outcasts on the history of collective movements against imperialism in Asia and the Pacific. The photographs from these women's family albums become placeholders for the cherished, often painful memories of the difficulties they endured as minorities in twentieth and twenty-first century Japan and, more broadly, of marginalized, diasporic experiences.

The photography project also traces the importance of making family photo-portraits, as they were the only means of showing themselves to the family members back home before the internet. Indeed, many of the photographs collected by Mirinae were taken to be sent to relatives in Korea to show how well they have adapted to Japan and, for other minority women from *buraku*, Okinawa, and Hokkaido, to depict days that are special, not *pot'ong*. This is not unlike the stories of other diasporas across the world, where these photographs had the responsibility to show the families back home how well the relocated family members are doing. And even here, imperialist power dynamics were internalized in the process of self-identification and self-representation. For example, looking "Americanized" was important for the Korean diaspora in the United States, as the appearance symbolized well-adjusted middle-class American life—the American dream. At the same time, for other Korean diasporas, such as those in South America and Southeast Asia, to look like contemporary Koreans was more appropriate, since the families back home did not privilege the culture of these places.

Ŏm Miok, a South Korean scholar writing about the women in *Pot'ongi Anin Naldŭl*, states that "the first- and second-generation minority women of the lowest socio-economic class, because they lack education, accept the fate of woman in their internalized and embodied culture of patriarchy. These women expose the state of diaspora, in which the multivalence of ethnicity, class, and gender have been sutured together."[78] The multigenerational women of the community, the daughters, mothers, and grandmothers together, thus write about the transtemporality of their marginalized womanhood. Their multigenerational experiences, for sure, cannot be summed up in a couple of family pictures. However, the photographs become a medium through which the women's individual stories relate to one another and reveal their intersecting concerns. Gender discrimination in the diaspora, and the patriarchal culture of the home country re-created in the settlement communities, put even more pressure on these women as they face racism and class discrimination.

Sharing family photographs, perhaps some of the most intimate and personal images of their own family and their history, also helped the women come to terms with family secrecy and shame that intensified with the experience of racism and discrimination (figure 2.11). Adding to Ŏm's point,

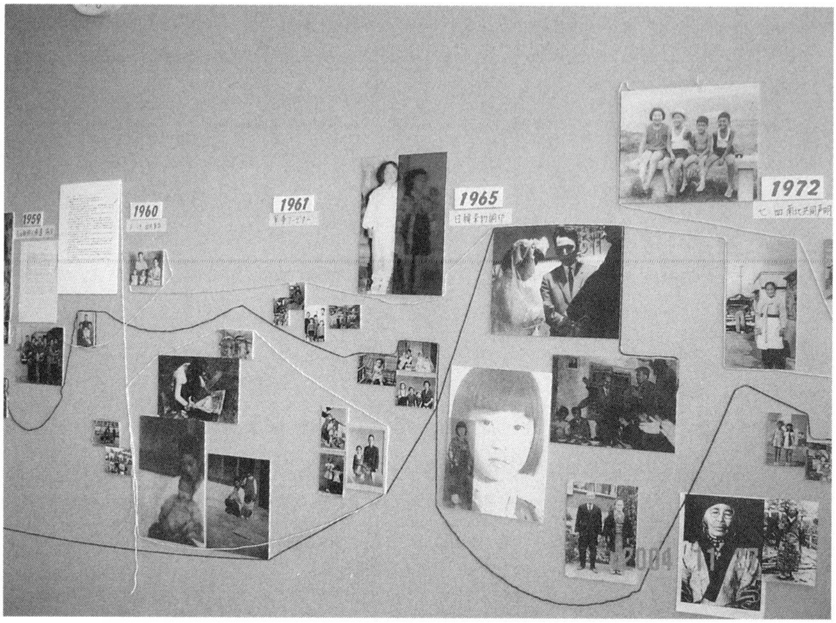

FIGURE 2.11 Hwangbo Kangja, installation view, *Zainichi Kajoksajin* (*Zainichi Family Photographs*), Korean Diaspora Art Exhibition, Tokyo Keizai University, 2004. Courtesy of Hwangbo Kangja. The photograph shows an installation view of Mirinae's exhibition, *Zainichi Family Photographs*. Photographs varying in sizes, styles, and subjects are mounted on the wall. Labels reading "1960," "1961," "1965," and "1972" indicate important dates for the families appearing in the photographs, which are arranged below the labels. Threads of different colors (tones in this black-and-white version) connect photographs across the chronological arrangements.

Hwangbo Kangja, the key organizer of Mirinae and the family photograph projects, and many other participants of the book write in their essays about the process of choosing family photographs: looking for family photographs and selecting one of them led to remember and rewrite the history of their families; to listen to the unheard voices of their grandmothers and mothers; and to understand, share, and accept the pains and joys in their lives—to honor these women (figure 2.12). In this collaborative work of affect, photographs are one of the many elements of their history writing, and a means of recollecting memories of enduring marginalization and discrimination while activating solidarity.

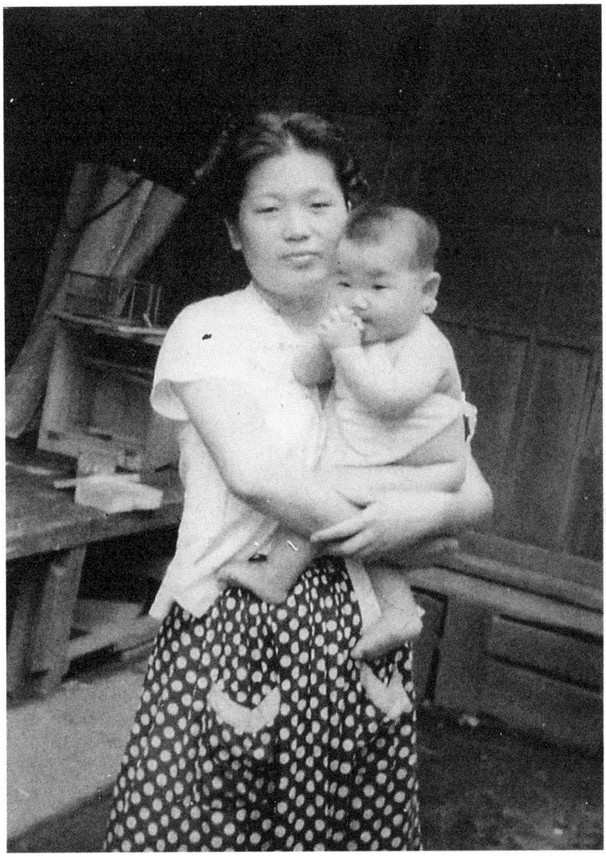

FIGURE 2.12
Hwangbo Kangja's mother holding her by their rented room in their relatives' house, Osaka, 1957, gelatin silver print. Courtesy of Hwangbo Kangja.

The family photographs appear to be *pot'ong*, yet their individual stories of marginalized communities are not. Even wearing *ch'imachŏkori*, the black and white Korean dress for the Zainichi women (not worn in general by South Korean women, as for them it is outdated and resembles North Korean attire for public occasions), was a drastically consequential act of self-declaration and self-affirmation of their Korean ethnicity. For example, Pak Lisa traces her realization of her Korean identity shortly after she turned four in 1978, recalling a conversation with her Korean mother.[79] It was her first time trying on a multicolored traditional Korean dress for young girls (plate 10). Her mother told her they were Korean for the first time, and while Pak wished to wear the dress in front of her Japanese friends in kimono, her mother did not let her. Without explicit descriptions of the circumstances, Pak's portrait of her wearing colorful children's *hanbok* and the dialogues between her and her mother let the reader imagine the painful withholding of the family's cultural signs of Korean identity, as Pak's mother desperately wanted to prevent her daughter from experiencing the same discrimination she has.

At the end of her essay, Pak writes that she now wears *ch'imachŏkori* when she teaches: Pak is a *minjokkangsa* (*minjok* lecturer) in Sakai, just south of Osaka. Her statement that she can now wear the dress whenever and wherever she wants hints at her pride even when she is confronted by people who make faces and ask her why she insists on wearing the dress in class while she wears *pot'ong* attire outside.[80] Pak's answer to them is simple: because she is *chosŏnin*—a term many Zainich Koreans choose to refer themselves to, a term that points to the Korea before the colonization and subsequent partition, but also used as a racial slur by the Japanese. Her use of the term to identify herself as *chosŏnin* is a cathartic reclamation of it.

As with Pak, dress choice is discussed by several of the participating authors as once-traumatizing but now a symbol of their ethnic pride. The photographs depicting women wearing traditional Korean dress, therefore, show the days that are not *pot'ong* for them. By wearing the dress, they celebrate even the sacrifice they have made to wear it, to be who they are, and to continue to take up the weight of this history.

Especially intriguing is their refusal to be *pot'ong*. Although it may not have been relevant to the authors, it recalls a book, *Kŭkhi pot'ongin chaeilhan'gukin* (*Extremely Normal Korean in Japan*, 1987), written by the Zainich Korean Kang Sinja.[81] This book won the 1988 Asahi Journal Prize in nonfiction. According to Kim Pŏmsu, Kang's interviews where she referred to herself as neither Japanese nor Korean but in-between, when published in South Korea, greatly influenced a shift in the representation of Zainichi Koreans.[82] Mirinae's book claims the opposite: that while their experience of marginalization in Japanese society has been normalized, the writing of women's history through family photographs make their lives special, not normal. Moreover, by establishing solidarity and coalition with women of other marginalized groups in Japan, Mirinae also reaches out to the women in Korea, to look for their own family photographs, and to rewrite their history of women in the photographs.

This work of feminist solidarity is not merely a recovery of absent women's voices; as Homi K. Bhabha puts it, "To write or speak from the place of absence extends the recognition of difference to a performative right to differ across, and within, the realms of intellectual work and political work—to elaborate a feminism without guarantees."[83] The multigenerational, multiethnic, and transnational work of Mirinae claims their own unprescribed cartographies of kinship and belonging, undoing ethno-national and patriarchal denials of their places. They "strike out in a direction of their own."[84]

Photo-Portraiture and a Family Scandal: Modernity's Verso

Photo-portraits of the Korean family from the colonial period to the present day express a complex desire for modernization and economic advancement while upholding patriarchy in the family and the state. These portraits display not only the changes in photographic practices but also the ways in which familial desire has been cultivated by the colonial government (via the elites) and later the military government, through the rhetoric of affective genealogy both surrounding and upheld by the population. Today, photographic portraits of babies and families express the desire to display a harmonious and affluent (monoethnic) heterosexual family that resembles the high society of the imagined "First World," the fantasy of which is performed at *tol* banquets and photography studios. The vernacular practices of baby and family portraiture have shown how such familial desires have been tied to the state's desire during the military regime and have continued its oppressive definition of what a family is—that is (photographically represented as), heteronormative, child-rearing, middle class, and ethnocentric (non-Chinese Korean, unless lawfully providing cheaper labor as belated *sanŏmnilkkun*, and non-brown or Black). This context only heightens the importance of approaches outside the cultural norms, such as those explored by artists including Sunmin Lee and Oksun Kim, and the Mirinae collective looking into the real *pot'ong* days of the Korean and diasporic family rarely presented in studio photographic portraiture. The family pictures of Lee and Kim, especially, express what is at stake for the early twenty-first-century Korean family—the heritage of patriarchal lineage, gendered labor, sexuality, *tamunhwa*, and its future in South Korea.

Here, I come back to the family photo-portrait of Yi Kwangsu. Some of the earliest cultural changes in the family and familial intimacy in the early twentieth century were captured in this family photo-portrait. First, there is the American friend: while he may have signified modernity and advancement for Yi, the inclusion of a foreign friend is also telling of the family's understanding of what familial intimacy is. This seems provocative even by the contemporary understanding of what a family photo-portrait should include and exclude. Indeed, a cropped version of the portrait, excluding the friend, has been used in various recent literature on Yi.[85]

More complicated, however, is the seemingly straightforward presentation of a man and his wife, for it is Yi's second wife, Hŏ Yŏngsuk, in the portrait. Hŏ herself was prominent in the history of medicine and journalism in early twentieth-century Korea, being the first Korean woman to have passed the Japanese medical licensing exam. She met Yi while completing her residency in Tokyo. Their affair led to Yi's divorce from his first wife and subsequent move back to Korea to start a new family. Hŏ became the first gynecologist in Kyŏsŏng, where she opened her own practice. In addition, she became a staff writer and the first woman editor of literary arts (*hagye pujang*) for *Dong-a Ilbo*, succeeding her husband in 1925.

Both Yi and Hŏ's careers epitomized the aspirations of modern elites in colonial Korea, and their family portrait appears to perfectly capture what it means, and looks like, to be a modern family. At the same time, the context of the family photo-portrait begs the question of how we envision modernity via such a portrait and what this modernity really entails in "modern Korea." Yi's second marriage was already a scandalous event, and Hŏ has been blamed for his departure from the independence movement and his pledge to become a loyal colonial subject of the Japanese emperor. But more than that departure, the queer relationships that Yi and Hŏ individually engaged in before and after their marriage challenge the imagined ideal of the family portrait.[86] Yi's 1918 short story, *Yun Kwangho*, is considered among the earliest "transcultural queer literature" published in East Asia,[87] and relates to a same-sex relationship he had with a young man named Sim T'aesŏp.[88] Hŏ also wrote about "having secret tryst with girls in the chapel and how her 'older sister' implored her to seek permission from her parents to move into the dormitory so they could sleep together," and allegedly continued to have same-sex affairs during her life.[89]

How does this contribute to Yi and Hŏ's family portrait and the visualization of new, ideal, and seemingly heterosexual colonial elites? The yearning for a fit, literate, and productive family, a symbol of positive and productive national transformation and betterment, has been one of the major driving forces for the continued family portrait practice. Through this desire, the military state also framed the ideal Korean family. By contrast, Yi's photo-portrait is a presentation of one of the most scandalous relationships of colonial Korea, with betrayal, extramarital affairs, same-sex love, and finally a divorce in 1946—four years before Yi was taken to North Korea and died mysteriously.

Nonetheless, the most critical aspect of this iconic family photo-portrait is not the sensational life story of the couple, but the historicization through which the nonconformist (and queer) relationships in their work and life are suppressed and diverted—just as the Korean media has cropped out Yi's American friend from the family photo-portrait. Korean critics have treated the queerness within their relationship as a colonial aberration, a symbol of subversive colonial subjectivization;[90] the militarized developmentalist framing of the family has ruled out what would not fit the ideal family portrait of transformative betterment. To perpetuate the family-*minjok*-nation trinity, the ideal family portrait must embody the futurity of betterment, one that fulfills the developmentalist (more recently, neoliberal), heteronormative, and patriarchal desire of the state, military or postmilitary. While Yi's photograph has been charged with, most significantly, his betrayal to the Korean independence and nation-to-be, this family photo-portrait also serves as a transtemporal object, one that begs for continual reexamination of the Korean family narrative and its photographic visualization.

Yi's portrait thus becomes a visual catachresis testing our ability to bring together disparate times and places and "to perceive affinities and convergence of geohistorical elements that have worked together to constitute mid-twentieth-century [gendered] violence."[91] That catachrony in turn calls for rethinking the stakes of gendered places in contemporary Korean photo-portraits, including those of the Korean diaspora in Japan. In this way, we can seek to unlearn the designated place of women (and other gendered and racialized bodies) in and outside of photo-portraiture.[92]

PART II

PERFORMING MULTITEMPORALITY

3

Shooting Social Movements

As film photography became readily accessible, even ubiquitous, in the second half of the twentieth century, the affective power of the medium began to concern the military regime. While photography was often used in state propaganda, it was also feared by the state for its capacity to stir the public's opinion on antiregime protest. And rightfully so: although years of strict censorship followed, what catalyzed widespread public support of activism was the vicarious experience of the movement—especially of its human casualties—through (photographic) representations, especially toward the end of the military state.

While even the most iconic protest photograph cannot tell the whole truth, it inevitably produces truth-seekers. The truth-seeking social movements against the regime in South Korea, led mostly by prodemocratization groups, university students, and labor activists from the 1960s through the 1980s, were pivotal to the dramatic changes in the political system of the nation-state and future social movements. In this context, photographs of protest events not only informed the public of relevant facts but became a battleground upon which the movements' legitimacy and effectiveness were judged by Korean communities, both in and outside of Korea. For Koreans, this photography offered, and offers, a mediated way of experiencing social movements.

A common approach to iconic photographs of social movements uses them as a touchstone for recounting the history of those movements. The sociopolitical history is entered through, and accentuated by, the photographic record. But once again, submitting photography to an onto-epistemologically subordinate representation, although intended to strengthen the position from which knowledge is produced, says more about limitations of a teleological approach to the experience of photography. The chapters in this part concern the temporality of photography in the experience and memory of democratization movements, explicating the ways in which photography enables multitemporal engagements with iconic, and later collective, images of public dissents, and their affect in the continued meaning and memory making of the events.

In this chapter, I reconsider iconic photographs of the two key democratization movements of South Korea in the twentieth century—the 4.19 Revolution of 1960 and the 1987 June Uprising—with a focus on the multitemporality of the event of photography. Between these signal events, extreme censorship hindered the practice of photography as a political tool for the citizenry. Nonetheless, the rise of the photography movement Saenghwaljuŭi realism, shortly before and during the early days of the military regime, demonstrates the engagement of photographers with the everydayness of postwar struggle through their aestheticization of that struggle.

The Postmortem Photograph of Kim Chuyŏl

The Korean War transformed the methods, subjects, and discourses of photography, while photography's sociopolitical significance expanded enormously. One of the most critical events of photography since the Korean War occurred in April 1960, following the exposure, through photographs, of a young student protester. As dramatic and even overblown as it may sound, this is a story of a photograph that led to a revolution.

By the mid-1950s, the Korean populace had become profoundly discontent with the corrupt Syngman Rhee government. Even prior to the Korean

War, the crash of the agriculture-based economy initiated a flight to urban areas;[1] the end of the war saw the unemployment rate skyrocket.[2] Although Rhee had been a leading figure of the independence movement since the 1910s, his cooperation with and official promotions of former collaborators (with imperial Japan) turned anti-communists was extensive, causing widespread resentment.[3] Furthermore, numerous incidents of violence against political opposition and civic groups, incited by mobs hired by Rhee's government, were common occurrences—and common knowledge—in the late 1950s. By 1960, seven years after the end of the Korean War and fifteen years since independence, Rhee had served three consecutive terms and hoped to serve another. His repeated amendments to the constitution extending his presidency in particular were heavily opposed by students.[4]

Less than a month before the election, Rhee secured victory when his only opposition candidate died of an illness, and the election was further orchestrated by the government to install Yi Kibung, a loyalist and political heir of Rhee, as vice president. On March 15, 1960, the government declared that Rhee and Yi had been elected with 100 percent and 79 percent of the vote, respectively.[5] This was, however. the result of various fraudulent actions taken by the government: campaigning by the opposition Democratic Party was violently disturbed by mobs hired by the leading Liberal Party. A quarter of the votes were cast before election day, while voters were forced to cast ballots openly in groups of three to five; and ballot boxes were swapped with fixed boxes brought by government mobs.[6] Fed up with the blatantly illegal actions, citizens came out into the streets of cities across the country to protest. Such collective expressions of discontent were unprecedented. Even middle and high school students gathered in Cheongju, Daegu, and Busan to protest.[7] The threat to the government by student activity led the Rhee administration to close schools for several days and set a curfew starting at 5 p.m.[8]

The most consequential attack against student protesters occurred on election day in the city of Masan in the southeast of Korea, where hundreds of middle and high school students marched peacefully. Despite the nonviolent protest action, the police force fired teargas grenades and guns to break up the march. Eight people were killed, over eighty people were seriously injured, and an unknown number went missing.[9] The subsequent coverage by journalists from Seoul, Busan, and Daegu, as well as from overseas, led to further protests against the Rhee government. Nonetheless, for weeks the only official response was intensified government silence and suppression. Then, on April 11, a body was found floating in the sea near the central pier (*chungangpudu*) of Masan by fishermen. The body was of one of the missing students from the Masan march: Kim Chuyŏl, from the city of Namwon.[10]

Kim's body was stark proof of police brutality: a police teargas canister was embedded in his face, having pierced his brain through his left eye. Stones had been tied to his ankles by police in an attempt to sink his body in the sea off Masan. Hŏ Chong, a photographer for the Busan-based newspaper, *Busan Ilbo*, photographed Kim's floating body before it was taken out of the water (figure 3.1). On April 12, 1960, Hŏ's photograph of Kim ran in newspapers, including on *Busan Ilbo*'s front page and in *Dong-a Ilbo*.

While other, more forensic photographs show Kim's corpse after it was taken out of the water (figure 3.2), the photograph of the semisubmerged body was chosen for the news report. Hŏ's photograph abstracted the mutilated and bloated corpse to an acceptable degree for publication but nonetheless effectively conveyed the violent response of the Rhee government in the face of public protest.[11] The photograph shows an indistinct dark matter (i.e., seawater) surrounding a figure, of which only the head, shoulders, and arms are recognizably human. Kim's head shows the crew-cut hairstyle typical of male students at the time. As did other high school students, Kim had worn the high-collared, colonial-style school uniform, which would have had his name embroidered on the left chest.[12] The most striking aspect is Kim's face: his features are entirely indistinguishable, with a blurry, grayish substance protruding from where his eyes should be. Except for his head and arms, the dark water hides his body.

The shocking, eerie photograph of the upright floating body revealed the brutality of the police force not only in their attack on Kim but also in their attempt to cover up the murder. Its publication led to an eruption of protests and counteractions.[13] Over and over, opposition met by retaliation was documented by photographers, leading to further protests and suppression. Demonstrations from April 11 to 13 in Masan were dispersed when the police opened fire on protesters. In Seoul, massive gatherings consisting mostly of university students were met with government-supported gang violence.

The cycle culminated with a demonstration by Korea University students on April 18, 1960, which was attacked by the Anti-Communist Youth Group, another set of gang members hired by the Rhee government. Chŏng Pŏmt'ae, a photographer working for *Chosun Ilbo* at the time, photographed the streets where Korea University students were shot in Seoul. His photos were immediately published in *Chosun Ilbo*.[14] In one of the photographs, dead and wounded students lie in the street in front of the Ch'ŏnil Department

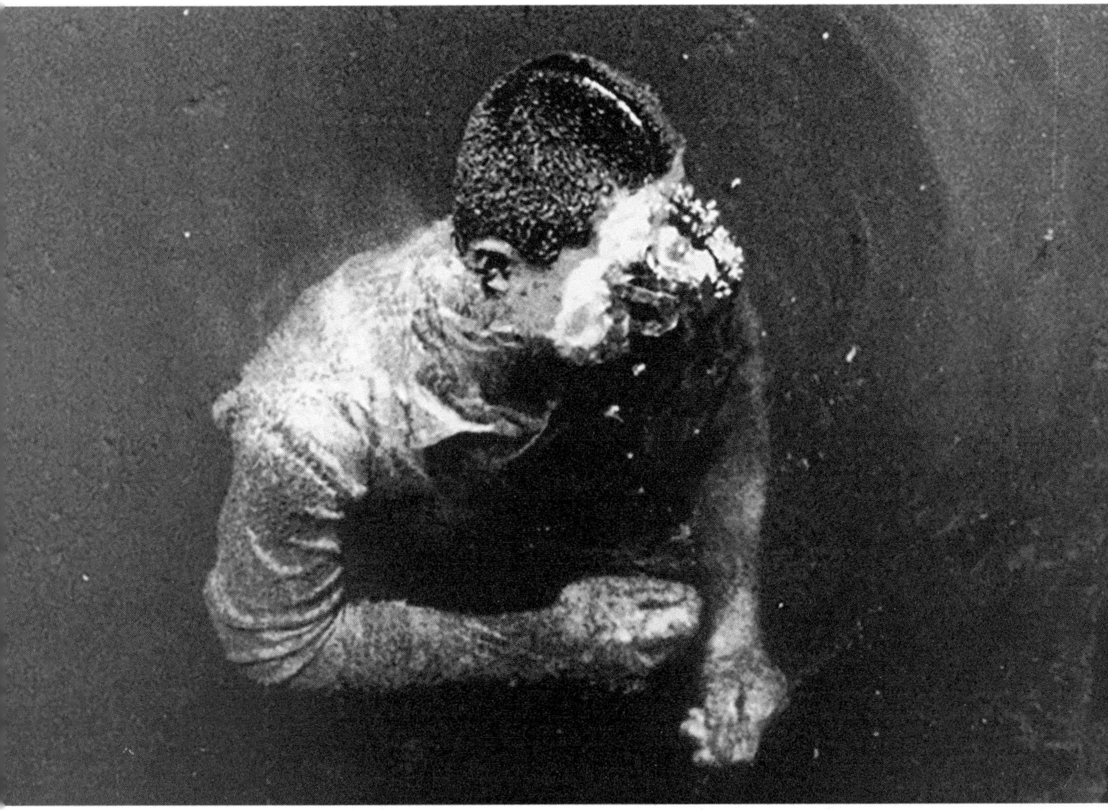

FIGURE 3.1 Hŏ Chong, *Kim Chuyŏl's Floating Body by the Central Pier of Masan*, April 11, 1960.

Store (figure 3.3). Next to them is a military jeep with a man, most likely a member of the Anti-Communist Youth Group, in the driver's seat. Fearing further attacks by armed forces, passersby do not seek medical attention for the severely wounded. This protest, retaliation, and documentation in turn led to a march the next day, April 19, by thousands of university students from the Congress Hall to *Kyŏngmudae*, the old Office of the President of the Republic of Korea. This march too was broken up by the police, firing directly at students.[15] The demonstration ended in a massacre of over 125 students, an event remembered as the Bloody Tuesday of the Democratic Revolution, but more generally referred to as the 4.19 Revolution.[16]

The impact of the photographs of protest and retaliation, their ability to catalyze mobilization of the public against the government—especially the

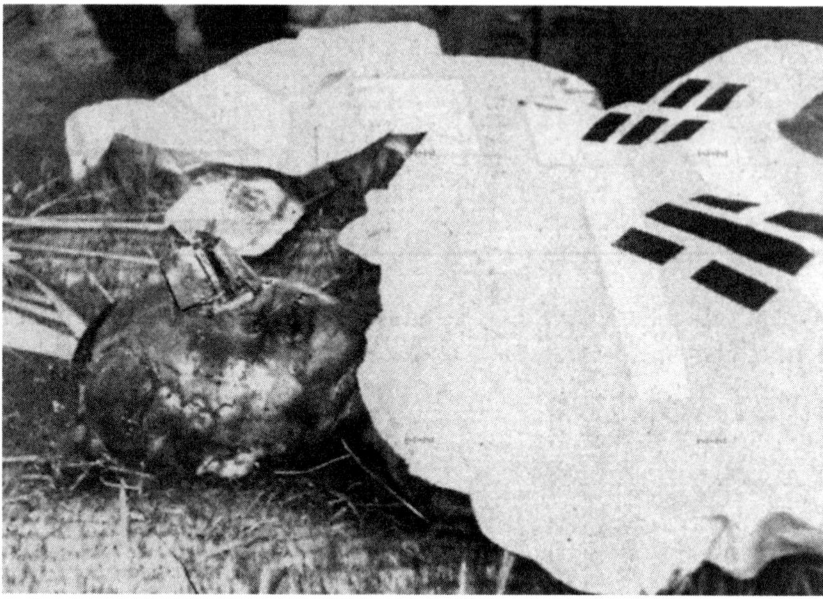

FIGURE 3.2 Photographer once known, *Kim Chuyŏl Wrapped in a Korean Flag before Autopsy*, *Dong-a Ilbo*, April 14, 1960.

shock reverberating from Hŏ's photograph of Kim—alarmed the Rhee administration. Fearing more public outcry of the sort that exploded with Kim's photograph, the government prohibited photographs of the student protests from running on the pages of major newspapers. The martial law, in effect from April 20, censored reports on the Bloody Tuesday events, although some newspapers, such as *Chosun Ilbo*, published reports on April 21 without photographs.[17]

The student marches coinciding in various cities across the nation were an unprecedented act of solidarity of the postwar era, and their consequences continued to move the public despite media censorship. University professors organized a demonstration on April 25 involving more than three hundred professors from twenty-seven universities, declaring a national emergency and calling for the impeachment of President Rhee.[18] The demonstration was supported, and joined, by other citizens.[19] The group also protested the false government accusation that their students were communists, and demanded the prosecution of the people involved in the fraudulent election.[20]

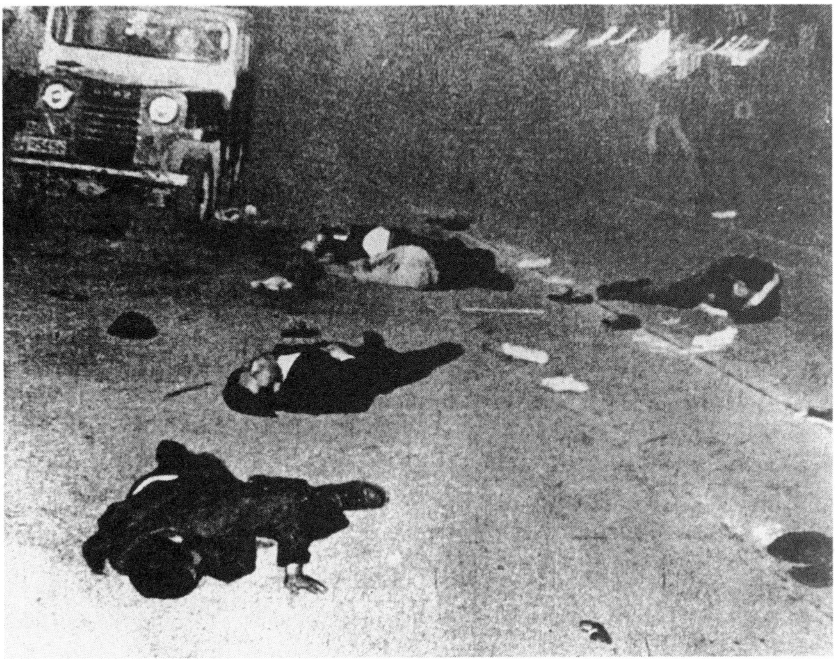

FIGURE 3.3 Chŏng Pŏmt'ae, *Injured and Dying Korea University Students in front of Ch'ŏnil Department Store*, Seoul, April 19, 1960. Courtesy of Noonbit.

As more and more civilians joined the marches, the chief martial law administrator, Song Yoch'an, ordered the army to stop firing at demonstrators and organized a meeting between student representatives and Rhee.[21] Having lost the support of the elite class, military officials such as Song, and the US embassy, Rhee was pressured by the Congress to step down, which he did on April 26.[22] The vice president, Chang Myŏn, took over the government as prime minister, and Yun Posŏn became president, although this was to change shortly.[23] The 4.19 Revolution thus brought the first republic and the era of Rhee and his followers to an end—ironically fueled by the attempts at suppressing dissent through which Rhee intended to ensure his power.

As a metonym for the social uprising and consequent government response, the ghastly image of Kim Chuyŏl's body drove public response to full-scale revolt. Critics believe that the photograph of Kim was the single most powerful catalyst for the 4.19 Revolution, eclipsing, for example, news reports detailing the series of demonstrations against the rigged election or the death toll.[24] During the turmoil of the postwar nation-building period, photography was therefore not merely a record of civic movements and state reaction but a catalytic *event* for such movements. This event of photography did not end at the moment Hŏ pressed the shutter button, or the moment the photograph was developed in the darkroom, or when it was printed halftone on the front page of the newspaper. The event of that photograph continued throughout April 1960, reminding the protesters of their cause and motivating the collective body to march on.

And that event has continued. A photograph seemingly concludes an event—the resulting product is intended for memory, capturing what happened in the immediate past; yet Ariella Aïsha Azoulay holds that the further act of "see[ing] the photograph—or the knowledge that a photograph has been produced—[is] an additional factor in the unfolding of the event of photography (not of the photographed event). The encounter with the photograph continues the event of photography that happened elsewhere."[25] Not only elsewhere, but at other times: since the 1990s, Hŏ's photograph of Kim's floating body has reappeared in books, articles, online news portals, and blogs, especially in commemorations of the student movements that led to the 4.19 Revolution. Placed side by side with Kim's school portrait photograph, and photographs of his body laid on the ground and covered with the Korean flag, Hŏ's photograph affectively conjures up Kim's short life and violent end, extending the event of photography and summoning the past and future of the subject.[26] These continued encounters with the photograph reassert the explosive power of the image and its ability to galvanize a mass movement and ultimately drive a society to revolution.

Today, Hŏ's photograph of Kim is cast on a memorial plaque installed at the tip of Chungangbudu, the site where Kim's body was found floating (plate 11). The plaque introduces the historical significance of the location, stating that "Kim Ju Yeol [Chuyŏl] sprang up as the beacon of the April 19 Revolution in this sea" and describing the site as "Where the 4.19 Revolution Began."[27] The cast image details the bloated, flesh-torn surface of Kim's dead face and the embedded canister, while the shiny, solid metallic sheen of the relief highlights the bloated hands decomposing in seawater. This tactility brings back Kim's body in a very different way than the black-and-white photograph. The haptic quality of the cast image blurs the line between what it feels to be "looking" at the past versus sensing the reverberation of history, thus disturbing the sense of present.

Taking Shawn Michelle Smith's words literally, the cast photograph is "the conduit through which the horrific past touches the present."[28] It both attracts and repels, the surface inviting touch while the relief sculpture of the mutilated corpse makes that touch nauseating. Here, temporality is nonexistent without the bodily sensing of it. The event of sensorial encounters with photography begets the time of photography, not the other way round. The reverberation of 4.19 thus unfolds in the push and pull of the horrific past.

Saenghwaljuŭi Realism, Photojournalism, and Censorship during the Junta

Photography movements during the junta were deeply affected by the Korean War and the postwar political turmoil. The governments succeeding Rhee's administration learned their lesson from the affective potential of the 4.19 photographs: henceforth, photography, especially photojournalism, entered a dark age under strict censorship by Park Chung Hee and the subsequent military government. It was twenty-seven years before another iconic photographic event like that of Kim's photograph occurred.[29] This censorship correlates to a breakdown of a polity during the junta, yet also to significant steps in the art world toward a major democratization movement; despite the seeming constriction of photography communities during the junta, it was in fact an active period of networking, organizing, and institutionalizing the study and practice of photography. Once regarded as amateurish, the medium became the basis for photography programs in institutions of higher education and museum exhibitions.

Although the 4.19 Revolution toppled the Rhee presidency, a counter-revolutionary military coup on May 16, 1961, led by Lieutenant General Park Chung Hee, subsumed the movements toward democracy. Park officially became president through an election in 1963, and his rule lasted until his assassination in 1979. Military rule then continued for another decade after Park. The coup reached deeply into South Korean life. As Kwŏn Myŏnga explains, it reversed the subjectivization of the new revolutionary citizen of the 4.19 Revolution, impounding even the possibility of existing as a social being, a citizenry. This was, according to Kwŏn, "a politics of death."[30] At the same time, those who value Park's legacy have emphasized the rapid industrialization and economic development during the regime, arguing that it fed and nourished the people—as long as they aligned themselves with the regime's ideal of citizenry, committing themselves to lifting their families out of poverty and to national advancement.[31] It is this aspect that Saenghwaljuŭi realists turned their camera toward.

Nevertheless, the politics of death quickly loomed over photography, and all other areas of cultural and creative production. To suppress public discontent and the growth of oppositional power, the military government imposed censorship on social, cultural, and political outputs.[32] Under the regime, photographers had to submit to strict rules for publication and exhibition. Photographers, particularly photojournalists, also had to self-censor their works to avoid the notorious Korean Central Intelligence Agency (KCIA) interrogations.[33] Beginning on May 16, 1961, all press materials fell under the martial law (Military Revolution Tribunal Law), which issued an edict that controlled the activities of journalists.[34] Article III of the martial law ordered all press (*ŏllon*), publications (*ch'ulp'an*), and reports (*podo*) to undergo state preinspection (*sachŏn'gŏmyŏl*) and to self-censor contents that were critical about the coup; the article specifies news articles (*kisa*), editorials (*nonsŏl*), cartoons (*manhwa*), and photography (*sajin*) as subject to censorship.[35]

Many weekly or fortnightly photography magazines and journal publishers had to endure temporary shutdowns.[36] Photographs of the Masan uprising and 4.19 Revolution, including that of Kim Chuyŏl, were too provocative for reproduction in mass media, even though the Park regime also opposed the Rhee administration as incompetent.[37] The potential for another resistance event following the impact of Kim's photograph was specifically preempted by, for example, the imposition of martial law in June 1964, due to which photographs of student protests against the establishment of official diplomatic relations between South Korea and Japan in 1965 were banned from publication.[38] Because the fixed type blocks of newspaper pages meant taking out the whole type block of censored material, the space was left empty. This was referred to as printing "bricks," and censored newspaper photographs, called brick photographs (*pyŏkttolsajin*), would run as black, or blank, rectangles in newspapers.[39]

Although, as noted by Ju Suk Park, magazines in the style of *Life* such as *Monthly JoongAng* (*Wŏlganjungang*) flourished and boosted mass interest in photography, state censorship on publication continued in the following decade.[40] The Yushin Constitution Emergency Measure Decree No. 1 of 1972 again mandated preinspection of articles, reports, editorials, cartoons, and photographs by military officials before they went out to the press. Yet despite these hardships, photographers continued with their work, making suitable adjustments. Exploring what it meant to practice photography in heavily censored postwar South Korea, the following decades saw the growth of networks of photographers, such as Kangrŭngsauhoe, while many photographers who practiced *ssalonsajin* (salon photography) gravitated toward new artistic movements.

The dominant style of photography in South Korea in the 1950s and early 1960s, Saenghwaljuŭi realism (translated as Everyday Life realism, Life realism, or Life-ism)[41] was led by photographers including Im Ŭngsik (Limb Eung Sik), Chŏng Pŏmt'ae, and Yi Hyŏngnok.[42] "Aesthetic humanism" was a major interest for followers of Saenghwaljuŭi realism;[43] in depicting the hardships of everyday life after the war, often involving children in the images (figure 3.4), adherents treated photography as a medium for portraying the reality of postwar South Korea, as "a record that describes historical contents concretely to express things in view of their reality in time and in space."[44] The movement therefore emphasized the indexical power of the photographic medium, while at the same time prizing the medium's capacity to conjure up humanistic emotions such as sympathy and familial love.

Im's belief that Saenghwaljuŭi realism offered "an opportunity to confirm a social impact of photography" was proven in the events of 1960.[45] As an artistic movement, however, it needed to seek beyond the function and aesthetics of reportage photography. The term *realism* implies that its followers do not merely show real objects, people, or things, but that their depictions encompass the larger scene of the everyday that can symbolize life during the (postwar) period. Unsurprisingly, the favorite subject of the Saenghwaljuŭi realists was the everyday struggle of the people affected most harshly by the Korean War. While the photographers of the movement aspired to the style of so-called straight photography, the preference for subjects that evoked sentimental (mostly sympathetic) values was apparent.[46]

The photographers of the loosely grouped movement became important figures in photographic circles, publishing their own monographs and later teaching at the newly established photography departments in colleges during the military regime.[47] Works associated with Saenghwaljuŭi realism tended to be approached as contrasting with the styles dubbed *yesulsajin* (art photography) and *ssalongsajin* (roughly equated with Pictorialist and composed photographs). The historians of photography Pak P'yŏngjong and Yi Kyŏngmin argue that these terms were in fact used mainly by

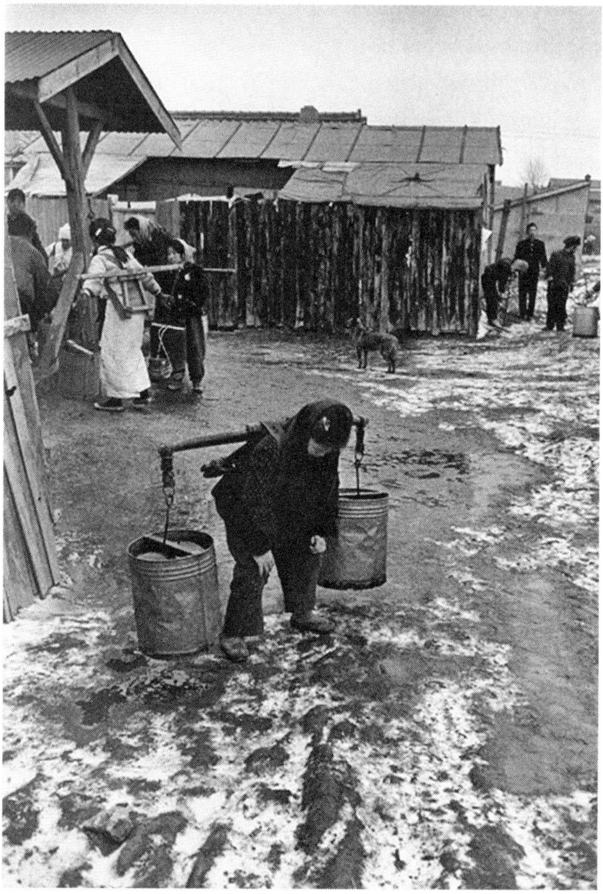

FIGURE 3.4 Chŏng Pŏmt'ae, *Water Carrier Girl*, Hyeonjeo-dong, Seodaemun-gu, Seoul, 1960, gelatin silver print. Courtesy of Noonbit.

Saenghwaljuŭi realists to differentiate their work from the established academic and amateurish genres.[48] Indeed, by generalizing—and trivializing—the work of photographers outside the movement, Saenghwaljuŭi realists simplified and deintellectualized *ssalongsajin* while asserting their status as one of the first true Korean (postwar) photography movements.[49] Photography in South Korea was thus dichotomized in the discourse as realism versus salonism. Yet Saenghwaljuŭi realism—though emphasizing their "straight" approach to the everydayness of their subjects as opposed to formal—was also an aestheticizing movement.[50] By merging such an aestheticized, humanist approach with a documentary one, Saenghwaljuŭi realism held a critical appeal for photographers and audiences alike and became a prominent artistic style for photography in South Korea.

Even as the everyday-ism of Saenghwaljuŭi realism was about photographing the everyday life of a people finding their way out of the rubble of war while coping with the dramatic political turnover of the 1950s and early 1960s, the realist movement adjusted to find ways of continuing despite the censorship. As pointed out by historian of Korean photography Cho Usŏk, Im modified "realism" with "Saenghwaljuŭi" to avoid possible association with socialist realism,[51] as the state, and later the military regime, severely persecuted anybody purported to have communist or socialist connections.[52] For instance, the photographer Ch'oe Minsik, although not officially accepted by Saenhwaljuŭi realists, tells stories of his numerous arrests by undercover police officers during the military regime due to his efforts to photograph poor neighborhoods in Busan, where he was based. Any cultural production that brought poverty and other types of inequality visible to the wider public was attacked by the military government.[53] The Saenghwaljuŭi realists were thoroughly aware of their difficult positions as the revealers of what the government sought to control and conceal. And this awareness affected their approach to realism—in particular, it accounted for the focus on overtly sentimental aspects of humanism as demonstrated through images of familial relations and children.[54]

One of Ch'oe's widely produced black-and-white photographs depicts a mother (or grandmother) and child, presumably at an open market in Ŏnyang in 1965 (figure 3.5).[55] The close shot shows the woman feeding the child, who is strapped to her back. She turns her head to put noodles in the child's mouth with chopsticks while her other hand holds a bowl. Her headscarf and long sleeves, as well as the steam coming from the lower right of the picture, indicate that the photograph was taken in winter. The scene implies that the woman cannot afford to let the child free from her back even for feeding. By cropping out anything that may distract from the desperation of the scene, Ch'oe emphasizes the virtues of sacrifice and love during recovery from war, rather than highlighting a state of poverty which might incense the military government.

A more politically pointed photograph by Chŏng Pŏmt'ae—a mother-child photograph at the Kyŏnggikotŭnggunbŏpchaep'anso (Gyeonggi Military Supreme Court, 1961)—depicts the trial of a group of political prisoners convicted of criminal activities associated with communism, which was a regular feature of the years following Park's coup d'état (figure 3.6). The photograph was taken from the front of the courtroom, facing the attendees and a group of defendants. In the foreground of the image is a woman with

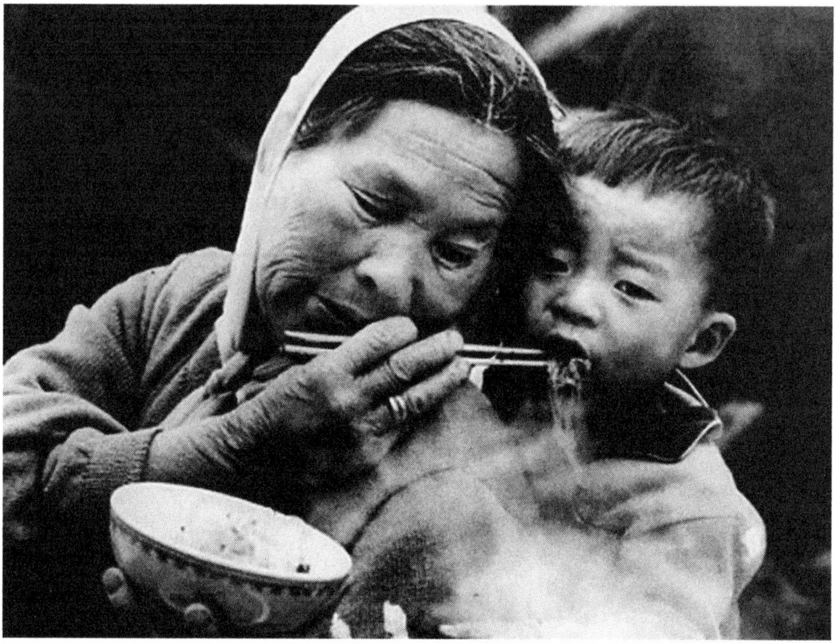

FIGURE 3.5 Ch'oe Minsik, *Ŏnyang Market*, Kyeongsangnamdo, 1965, gelatin silver print. Courtesy of Noonbit.

her head down, wearing a convict's uniform. A seating area for a stenographer surrounded by wooden panels occupies the space between the woman and a group of male defendants. The only person who looks directly at the camera in the photograph is a toddler holding onto the woman's uniform. The innocence of the child contrasts with the presumably shameful lowering of the woman's head, yet highlights the connection between the mother and child rather than the specificity of the ideologically fueled event. Thus, while Chŏng's photograph depicts a particular political event specific to the military regime, details of the event are suppressed in favor of the symbolization of the universally sympathetic love between mother and child, and the innocence of the child versus the omniscience suggested by the judicial setting.

The situation of the Saenghwaljuŭi realists is comparable to that of the Photo League in the United States during the height of McCarthyism. The House Un-American Activities Committee (HUAC, 1938–75), an investigative committee of the United States House of Representatives, targeted individuals and organizations suspected of communist intent or influence. The Photo

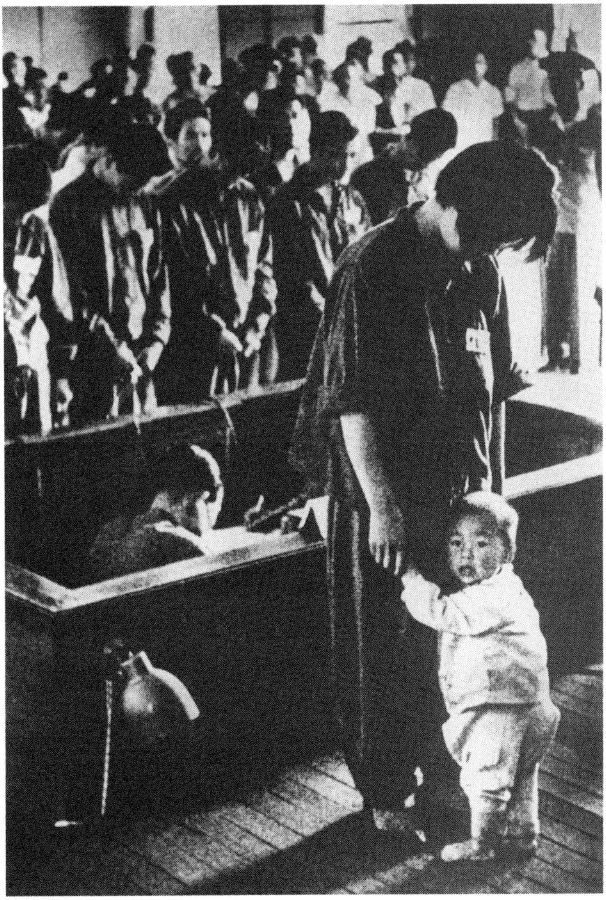

FIGURE 3.6
Chŏng Pŏmt'ae, *Kyŏnggikotŭnggunbŏpchaep'anso*, 1961, gelatin silver print. Courtesy of Noonbit.

League, added to the attorney general's list of "subversive organizations" as early as 1947, was "vulnerable because of its dedication to documentary photography."[56] The league was disbanded in 1951, as the stigma led to a substantial reduction in its membership.[57] Unlike the Photo League, however, Saenghwajuŭi realism was not an organization but a movement and loose terminological association regarding an aesthetic approach to the medium. By accentuating their humanistic and artistic values, rather than the critical and social aspects crucial to documentary photography, the movement avoided the military government's possible persecution. Nonetheless, the movement declined by the mid-1960s and became obsolete by the 1970s, ironically just as underground democracy movements began to reemerge.

Photojournalism, on the other hand, was targeted by military censorship to a far greater degree. A later example is the ban on photographs concerning the May 18 Gwangju Democratic Uprising in 1980. The civic uprising, against the military coup of General Chun Doo-hwan (less than two months after the assassination of Park), ended in the massacre of over two hundred civilians by military forces.[58] The martial law troops, specifically trained for riot control, began marching into Gwangju by the afternoon of the 18th, blocking all major road entrances to the city. The troops began to open fire at protesters as well as passersby, initiating the "containment" of the civic movement which lasted until May 27. Few photojournalists from Gwangju, or from other countries, were able to report on what they initially thought were student demonstrations,[59] while the military regime sent intelligence agents to each newspaper company to censor what was to be published about the uprising and its suppression.[60] Reproduction of photographs of the Gwangju Uprising was banned except for those depicting violent (counter)actions on the part of the protesters. Thus, available public imagery cast the event as an unruly riot by citizens of Gwangju against the rest of the nation—a misconception which prevailed until the 1990s.[61]

Korean photographers certainly understood the danger of photographing the uprising. Sin Pokchin, a Gwangju-based photojournalist, risked his life photographing the violence from windows in the building where he hid. One photograph shows troops marching on Kŭmnamno, a major road in downtown Gwangju (figure 3.7). On the other side of the road, sequestered by the military vehicles, protesters, captured and stripped by the troops, run with their hands on their heads. Another photograph shows masked people examining the corpses of casualties as they lie in plywood coffins in a large room (figure 3.8). Possessing film that could reveal facts about the ten-day massacre placed Sin in great danger. To avoid confiscation, Sin hid the film cassettes in an earthenware pot and buried it.[62] Only in June 1988, eight years after the uprising, was one of his photographs published on the front page of the first issue of the Gwangju-based newspaper *Jeonnam Ilbo*.[63]

Censorship was also a major obstacle to the creation of illustrated news magazines along the lines of *Newsweek* or *Life* during the military regime. Under the martial law of 1980, the Chun government annulled the registration of 172 periodicals in July, including *Ch'angjakkwa pip'yŏng* and *Ppurikipŭnnamu*, and closed down 617 publishing companies in August. By the end of November, the government consolidated all presses (*ŏllonsa*

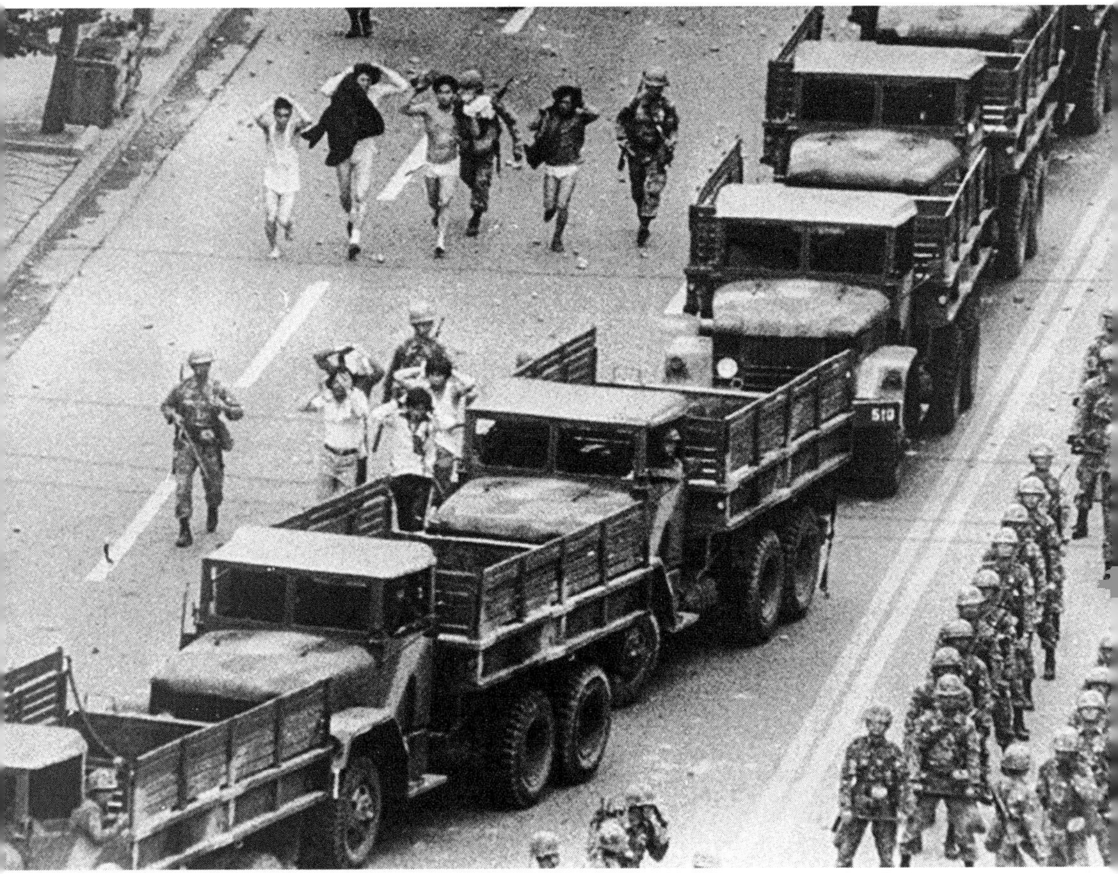

FIGURE 3.7 Sin Pokchin, *Kŭmnamno, Kwangju*, May 1980, gelatin silver print. Courtesy of Noonbit.

t'ongp'yehap) and legislated Ŏllon'giponpŏp (Basic Law of the Press), a de facto dismantling of the role and power of journalism.[64]

This contributed to the broader absence of discourse on documentary photography during the period. Indeed, photo historians such as Ju Suk Park find that Saenghwaljuŭi realism should not be discussed through the discourse of the documentary. Certainly, photographers during this period—sensibly enough, given the risks—identified their approach with realism rather than documentary, as did critics and historians. While the will of the photographer to create the body of documentary work focusing on particular

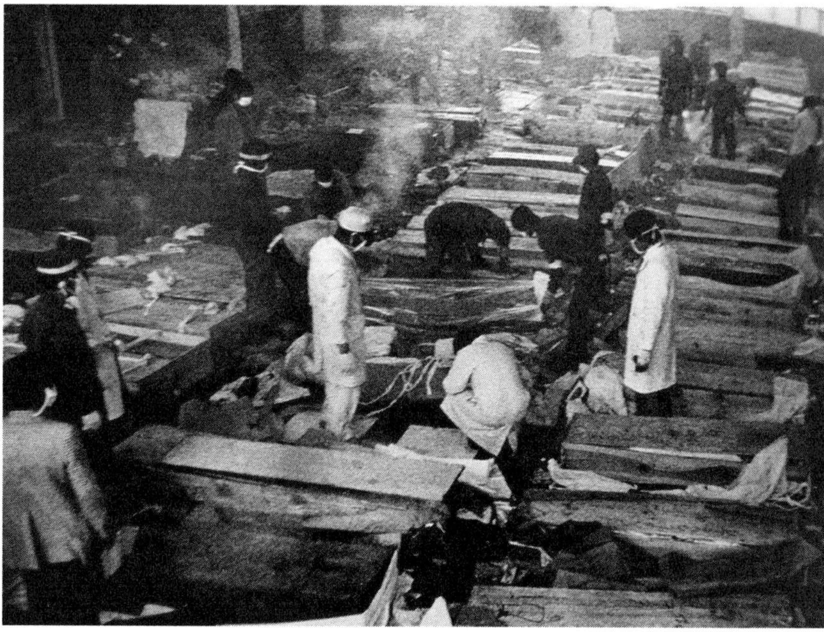

FIGURE 3.8 Sin Pokchin, *Kwangju*, May 1980, gelatin silver print. Courtesy of Noonbit.

issues and topics could be easily targeted as based on ideology, realism, especially Saenghwaljuŭi, could be argued as neutral by virtue of coming straight off the streets—closer to how the term *straight photography* is generally used in Western contexts.

The censorship of the Gwangju Uprising photographs and the years of the images being buried, both literally and metaphorically, does more than hold back the images from the public view: it is part of the event's transtemporal meaning making. According to Young Chae Seo, the coverup and distortion of the history of the uprising in the following years made "the problem of Gwangju [become] properly problematic."[65] In other words, the violence that came after the violent event of 1980 that silenced the uprising intensified "the problem of Gwangju," becoming in and of itself atrocious. The 1980s is often described as the decade of national "guilt"; Seo focuses on the guilt that a generation of people felt as they were unable to properly address, let alone join, the uprising during and immediately following the event. The affect of guilt originated in "the temporal gap that separated the actual event and its official recognition, [as] complex structures of feeling emerged."[66] But guilt here is also an affect that privileges identitarian subjectivization, especially in reference to age, education, and gender, in defining who has access to and is able to own guilt vis-à-vis their participation in the history of the 1980s. Indeed, Seo focuses on the experiences of men—and only men—who were either college students in the 1980s or had local ties.[67]

Notwithstanding generational (in)accessibility to such affect (or the feeling of intergenerational guilt), the belated seeing of Gwangju photographs—or that of other events—cannot simply be summed up as a matter of guilt induced by the shock of evidentiary representation, but, as Seo also hints at, the unruliness of temporal discombobulation and its potentiality. Ironic as it may sound, the images' anachronistic advent adds to the event's affective power, retrospectively speaking, and to its haunting memories conjured at later events. Through this belated affect, the photographs of Gwangju refuse to fix the uprising merely as an event photographed.

An Indelible Image: June 1987

The absence of widely disseminated photographic images of socially provocative issues from the 1960s through the 1980s, including military and police brutality against civilians, is crucial to understanding the affects—be it guilt, anger, or shock—such images generated for the public when they were finally on view, closing that temporal gap and causing the historical times to overlap, converse, and reverse. In June 1987, however, a photograph of another martyred student activist appeared, dramatically influencing and coming to represent the June Democracy Movement of 1987.

Chun Doo-hwan, the successor of Park Chung Hee and the figure responsible for the massacre in Gwangju in 1980, continued to enforce censorship on all types of publications. For reporters and journalists, self-censorship was standard practice during the years of military government.[68] As a result, many ended up leaving the field.[69] At the same time, the public was becoming increasingly critical of the newspapers and journalists for their apparent incompetence. Eventually, however, the "brick" facade created by official censorship began to crack. The new turning point for the democratization movement, and photo publication, came with the deaths of two university students. In January 1987, a Seoul National University student, Pak Chongch'ŏl, was killed while being tortured in the notorious *taekongbunsil*, "interrogation room," at the National Police Agency's Namyeong-dong Anti-Communist

Investigation Office.[70] Pak drowned during water torture, although police claimed that he died of a heart attack induced by shock when an interrogator banged on a desk with his fist.[71]

Following the report of Pak's death, students, professors, and many others gathered for a massive memorial at Seoul National University, which in turn led to a series of rallies at major locations in Seoul. Encouraged by this solidarity, journalists declared a new "freedom of the press" statement.[72] From then on, more photojournalists began to breach official restrictions on press materials.[73] Although most print media still would not publish protest photographs, reporters and photographers attended student protests, which frequently became violent exchanges of teargas grenades and Molotov cocktails with the police.

Finally, on June 10, 1987, *Joongang Ilbo* reproduced a new protest photograph in their *sahoemyŏn*, the Society Section. This photographic event brought back the specter of Kim Chuyŏl's murder in Masan twenty-seven years earlier—and likewise came to usher in dramatic changes to the government and Korean society as a whole. The photojournalist Chŏng T'aewon (Tony Chung), then Reuters' director of photography for the Korea office, took a photograph of an attack on a student protester, Yi Hanyŏl.[74] The image shows two young college students in front of a rally at Yonsei University on the afternoon of June 9, 1987 (figure 3.9). A masked student, Yi Chongch'ang, holds Yi Hanyŏl, who is collapsing after being hit by a teargas canister in the side of his head. The canister had penetrated Yi's skull. He fell into a monthlong coma and died on July 5.

Chŏng's photograph put newspaper editors to the test.[75] The image, showing blood dripping from Yi's head and nose, was supposedly too graphic to be published. More importantly, it was understood that the photograph would generate intense public reaction against the military regime and engender more sympathy for the student protesters. Critical decisions had to be made by the editorial team, knowing that publishing the photograph put both the job and life of Yi Ch'angsŏng, the director of photography at *Joongang Ilbo*, in danger.[76]

As expected, the revelation of Yi Hanyŏl's injuries shocked the public, igniting a series of massive protests throughout the month of June. The human casualty in the photograph also visualized the metaphorical wounding of the collective body. In doing so, it united students, religious leaders, public intellectuals, and ordinary citizens for *minjuhwa*, the democratization of South Korea.[77] Thousands of middle-class, white-collar workers—known as "tie-

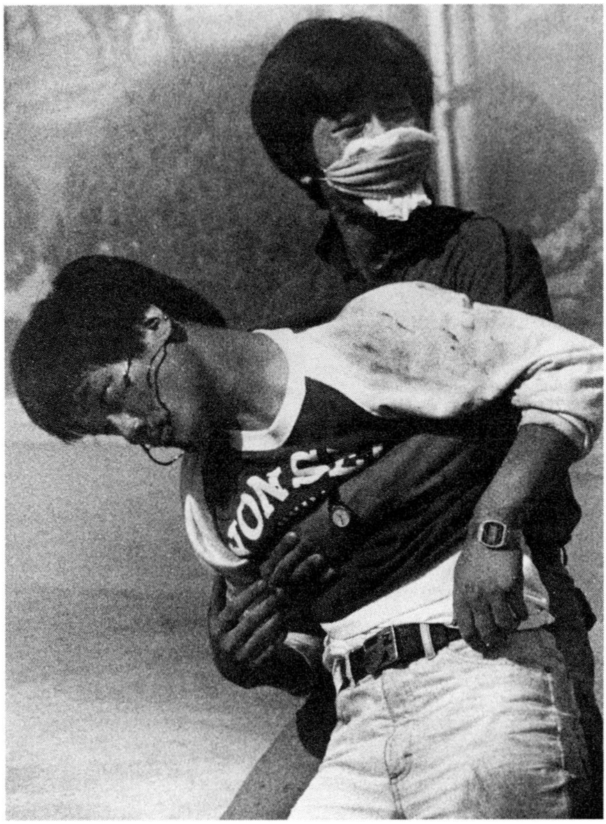

FIGURE 3.9 Chŏng T'aewon (Tony Chung), *Yi Hanyŏl Hit by a Teargas Canister*, Yonsei University, June 9, 1987. Courtesy of Chŏng T'aewon and Noonbit.

troopers" ("*nekt'aiputae*")—joined demonstrations that lasted nineteen days (figure 3.10). Criticism from the international community of the government's violent suppression of student and labor movements—crucially, coming during preparations for the 1988 Summer Olympic Games hosted in Seoul—put further pressure on the military regime.[78] Ultimately, on June 29, 1987, known as 6.29 Sŏnŏn, Roh Tae-woo, the head of the ruling Democratic Justice Party and a former army general, announced that the presidential election to be held the next year would be a direct election guaranteeing individual electoral rights. Furthermore, Roh promised to release Kim Dae-jung, a democracy activist (and future president, 1998–2003) who was serving a life sentence. The photograph of Yi Hanyŏl collapsing thus quickly became a representation of individual and collective sacrifice for democracy, summoning up a new phase of the tumultuous civic struggle against militarism.[79] It is now

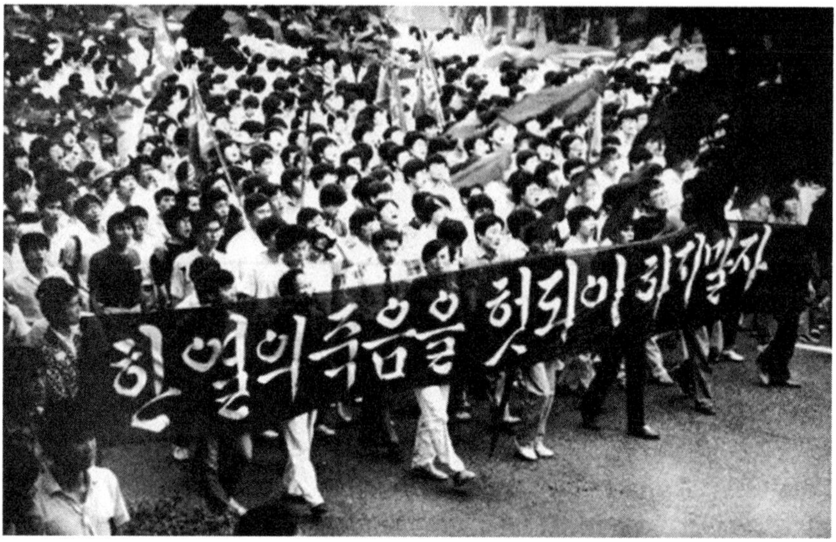

FIGURE 3.10 Photographer once known, “Hanyŏriŭi chukŭmŭl hŏttwei hachimalja (Let’s not make Hanyŏl’s death useless),” Seoul, June 1987.

one of the most iconic pieces of photojournalism in the last quarter of the twentieth century in South Korea.[80]

The photograph has since been appropriated in paintings, banners, and commemorative items. Following its publication, the photograph was reproduced on large banners student activists hung on the facades of campus buildings (figure 3.11). Minjung artist Ch’oe Pyŏngsu’s stylized painting on a large banner in the style of the Minjung woodcut medium was based on the photograph, as was Ch’oe’s painting of Yi’s ID portrait, also used during his funeral.[81] Ch’oe’s images were reproduced on handkerchiefs and scarves used by student activists and distributed to the public.[82] Chŏng T’aewon’s photograph and Ch’oe’s banner and portrait are now used depending on the nature of events and what the users wish to emphasize, including at the annual appearance on the Yonsei University campus in June—acknowledgment of the decades of student democracy movements that culminated in June 1987 and commemoration of Yi’s death (plate 12). Chŏng’s photograph of Yi renews and updates the memory of 1987 like objects used in commemorative events or one’s own keepsakes do. The attempt to preserve the memory of 1987, therefore, has largely depended on the multiple ways in which the photograph is

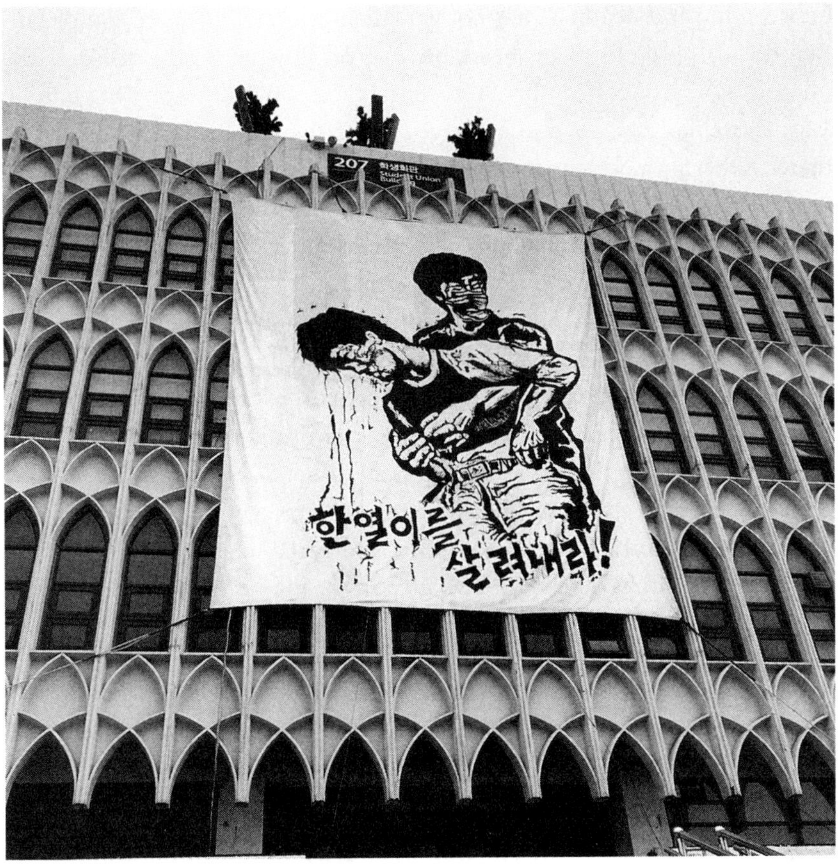

FIGURE 3.11 Ch'oe Pyŏngsu, *Hanyŏrirŭl Sallyŏnaera* (1987), acrylic on canvas. A commemorative event at Yonsei University, 1989.

used in the material reproduction of the event. Here, the event of photography encompasses the (intermedial) materiality of reproduction in the making of memory, just as it encompasses the haptic experience of the photograph of Kim's mutilated body cast on the Masan plaque. As such, and to repeat, the temporal and sensorial experiences of photography become inseparable.

Yet there is another crucial aspect of temporality we must return to: the deferral of Yi's death in Chŏng's photograph and what it does as the event of photography. The visual shock comes from the violence itself; the result of that violence—Yi's death—can only be forthcoming in the image. Through the photograph, Yi Hanyŏl is caught forever in the limbo of unconsciousness between life and death: Yi has not yet fallen or closed his eyes completely. Blood is dripping from his head, but not yet flowing on the ground. The photograph, as Geoffrey Batchen characterizes photography in general, "suspend[s] its subjects, and ourselves, somewhere between life and death, thereby offering a permanent deferral of the otherwise fatal onset of passing time."[83] This deferral, especially as used to sustain the memory of June 1987, becomes a powerful ritual of the collective memory of the event. The repetition and return created by the ongoing ritual of seeing Yi in the limbo of life and death "function as indices of trauma"—a trauma that also repeats the event of Gwangju in May 1980 and that of Masan in April 1960.[84]

Yet while this violence may summon the past events, the photograph of Yi differs strikingly, and obviously, as the event captured is metaphorically and literally stuck in the dureé of Yi's comatic state. Likewise, Yi's falling body is conspicuously held by Yi Chongch'ang, a comrade in this deadly fight for democracy, a "brother" who is calling out and beckoning to the world for Yi's life. The devastating state of the two men in the photograph crosses the line between life and death, history and imagination, and individual tragedies and collective trauma.

The political ontology of photography is dependent on the potentiality of the event of photography, including the crossing between these individual tragedies and collective trauma, which brings back the memories of other student deaths—both despite and through their historical and aesthetic differences. The singularity of the photographed event is subsumed by its possibilities. As Azoulay argues, this ontology requires "civil imagination," free from the binary of politics versus aesthetics—neither of which, in any case, solely generates the power of Yi's photograph. This power comes from the people themselves identifying what the fallen student's death meant. It is a power that can be activated when people reimagine their own subjectivity as a revolutionary one, and when they reimagine their futurity.

However, as Kwŏn points out, throughout Korean history, the people's desire for the closure of a violent revolution outweighs their sense of responsibility for the dead: "the fear of social destabilization, thus the fear of the living Other," is greater than the responsibility to bring justice to those responsible for inciting violence.[85] This may partially explain the disappointing outcome of the 1987 presidential election. The incredible event of June 10 was eclipsed by the outcome of the promised presidential election, where the majority vote went to the ex-military colleague of Chun, Roh Tae-woo, the last military-linked (but not junta) president in twentieth-century South

Korea.[86] The fear of becoming a new subject by "killing" the prerevolutionary Self led to the collapse of the collective, and therefore a return to the (semi) military state. The photograph of Yi's falling body to the Korean people was thus a multitemporal event of violence, the returning trauma of the cataclysmic events of the twentieth century—and this is not the violence experienced in the killing of young civilians, but the violence that followed when they try to reimagine themselves as a revolutionary subject.[87]

Yi Hanyŏl's photograph, therefore, should itself be considered an event. Azoulay writes that a photograph is an event. I add that the photograph is an ongoing eventualization to emphasize the contingency of photographic meaning making. By that, I mean the multitemporal return of the image, and its changing significance and meaning within the context of a new event, may transform what the *photographed* event once had meant; the depicted event comes to mean something different and reactualize differently at later times. Hence, the event of Yi's photograph depicts not only the dying student, but the eventual collective refusal to appose the civic responsibility for Yi's death to the reactive desire for protecting the community of the living. To witness the event, therefore, is to confess the politics of death that followed his death.

4

The Photo Public in the *Kwangjang*

Almost thirty years after the June Democracy Movement, nationwide weekly candlelight protests over a series of government corruption scandals involving President Park Geun-hye swept across South Korea. The movement ultimately led to the congressional vote to impeach Park, upheld by the Constitutional Court in March 2017. The transformational impact of the 1960 and 1987 events reverberated throughout the new series of protests. At the same time, many critical aspects of the movement, including photo practices, had shifted dramatically over the intervening decades. From the photographic perspective, the most notable change is the transition from the singularity of the photographed event (e.g., of Kim Chuyŏl's floating corpse or Yi Hanyŏl's fall) to the plurality of photographic performance: photographs of social movements are no longer taken, published, and viewed individually, but performed—made, shared, and reacted to—together, discursively.

Through this performance, the participating bodies come to make a polity, pixelated on screens.

Continuing the discussion on the event of photography and the potentiality of new political subjectivity, chapter 4 focuses on the changes in the photo practices of social movements, namely the ascent of a plural, performative photography during the 2008 candlelight protests, through which the crowd becomes what I call a "photo public." In exploring this plural performativity, I examine what photography can do beyond its expected function of reportage in the 2000s—"the age of deep mediatization"—and how it converges with and diverges from the photo practices of 1960 and 1987 in collective memory.[1]

The power of photography in these events derives not from its iconic signification, but from its affective capacity to transform individuals into a photo public—what I see as a collective of nonbinding goals and motivations that becomes photography—through making, editing, meming, posting, reposting, deleting, and so on. In these events, the plural performance of photography becomes a process through which political subjectivization occurs.[2] The photography of twenty-first-century social movements is thus also about its transformation via the "technologies of representation and media of contestation," from the iconicity of images to the plural performativity of the photographic act.[3] The desire to visualize a public, therefore, is entangled in the desire to be part of a networked society.

Indeed, I invoke the plural performativity of photography in social movements not only to examine the South Korean struggle against neoliberal capitalism and the experiences of those at the margins of life, but to understand the medium's affective engagement in social movements in a rapidly changing yet still-militarized society vis-à-vis the everyday experience of that struggle.[4]

Performing Photography Together and Separately: A Photo Public

That something which could be considered the national Korean experience of photography exists does not, of course, mean that the people of the nation have a uniform experience of the medium. This is especially true for photography of social movements in the twenty-first century.[5] Photography is, after all, a medium of multiplicity—in reproduction, circulation, and viewership. A key point of this multiplicity is the recent extension of such photographs' viewership through the reproduction and circulation of images by participants. The relationship between this plurality and photographic representations is in turn central to understanding the role of photography in social movements, as photography has become a collective performance by the people.[6]

My thinking about the plural performativity of photography is heavily informed by the observations of Judith Butler and Rosalind C. Morris regarding the concept of "the people" in their struggles against states and militarism.[7] Butler addresses the collectivity of "we the people," particularly in relation to the performative power of assembly. Acknowledging the impossibility of ever knowing "the people" as "we" and their political representation, Butler claims "that any designation of 'the people' works through delimiting a boundary that sets up terms of inclusion and exclusion"; an effort to establish "the people" often leads to presumptions about those included and excluded within a population.[8] An assembly does not represent a unity, and looking closer at the assembly will reveal its internal divisions and disagreements.[9]

Rosalind C. Morris examines the transformation of a public, *öffentlichkeit*, in today's protest movements: "'The people' extends in time and place, encompasses those who have vanished, those who have yet to come—as well as those who, quite simply, stayed home. But this excess is not limited to those national-political formations that organize themselves under the rubric of 'the people.' The social is always larger than what can ever be present. This excess is not merely to be measured in quantitative terms, however; it is also a function of the communicative dimension itself."[10] Photography is part of this communicative dimension that mediates the representation of the social. Since the 2000s, the photography of social movements has extended well beyond the visual representation of a given movement as it activates what Morris calls "the technomediatic environment" in which the social is performed in plurality.[11]

However, plural performativity is not simply many individuals acting upon a shared goal. Butler and Athena Athanasiou explore the performativity of the people and seek possibilities in ethical relations between them: "The 'I' is already social, and must begin its reflection and action from the presumption of a constitutive sociality."[12] In their critique of (neo)liberal democracy as disembodying collective power and disengaging the public in the name of the free market, Butler and Athanasiou propose the "performativity *of* plurality and performativity *in* plurality"—the performance of public dissent by the multitude as a way to find the "space for objecting to neoliberal regimes of economization of life."[13] Specifically, collective gatherings, such as rallies, protests, and candlelight vigils, "enable and enact a performativity of embodied agency," and share the reality of vulnerability facing state power.[14] Plural performativity, therefore, is about the affective becoming of an embodied agency, which enacts collective dissent against that state power.

Because photography exceeds the visibility of the public in protest movements, the act of photography, rather than the photographed event, is at the center of my discussion. The plural performativity of photography involves the act of making the crowd see themselves as a speaking self—speaking against the state, speaking to others, and speaking to themselves—while the dissemination and circulation of their utterance captures its immediacy.[15] This is the becoming of photo public.

Diversity in social production is key to the makeup of photo publics—and that diversification broadly characterizes twenty-first-century social movements in South Korea. A photo public is an ambivalent (and often inconsistent) network of social desires eroding the boundaries between the inside and outside of the public;[16] per Homi Bhabha, the radicalism of difference does not come from some extraordinary individuality but from the "liminal enunciative position" of difference, "located somewhere between affective pressures exerted on the inside and forces summoned by political contingencies on the outside."[17] The people gathered in the *kwangjang*—the Korean word for public square, which came to carry the symbolic meaning of "public forum" in the 2000s—did not collectively declare a (political, sovereign, or national) unity, but shared an "open relationship that the singularities set in motion."[18] As such, the power of the people did not come from the mobilization of masses under a unity, but "the ability to act in common without unification," combined with their own capacity to work through political contingencies on the outside and internal affective pressures on the inside.[19]

This public in South Korea, however, is "more polarized, individualized, and shrinking in scale [*sochunghwa*] than ever," according to Ch'ŏn Chŏnghwan.[20] Despite the vulnerability of a small or sub-scale public [*sochung*]" whose "life [is] defined by consumption [*sopi*] and taste [*ch'wihyang*]," Ch'ŏn notes that public dissent is a traditional and valuable resource in Korean democracy, tracing its genealogy from the anticolonial movement of 3.1 Undong in 1919 to the 2016–17 events.[21] The dissenting body, however, is no longer described by Ch'ŏn as *minjung* (as in 1987) but *tachung*, the multitude, with an emphasis on inclusivity, diversity, and freedom from institutionalized mobilization.[22]

Since the turn of the millennium, plural performativity has transformed photography from a medium that establishes and maintains the iconicity of a photographed event to a series of engagements in plural making, sharing, modifying, and reproducing—what Karen Strassler calls an "image-event."[23] Iconic photographs of twentieth-century social movements were viewed at the same time by hundreds of thousands of people who had access to major newspapers. Furthermore, for the most part they were only viewed via mass publication and public installations. With the advent of plural performativity in photography, images can be reproduced and circulated at will by the individual viewer. Essential to this transmission is the act of making the image social, through posting, hashtagging, retweeting, liking, and so on—user modifications to distribution that increase the traffic of the image even as they diversify the meanings and intents attached to those images and to their distribution. Photo making in the *kwangjang* is not only a popular media practice of solidarity, but the performance of political becoming: the act of imagining (and imaging) a new political subjectivity, *now*. Such photography is not an evidentiary index of some collective agenda. Rather, it offers processes of affective, spatial, sensorial, temporal, technological, and performative mediation.[24]

The Emergence of *Irinmidiŏ* and the Photo Public of 2008 Candlelight Vigils

In June 2002, ordinary Koreans massed in larger numbers and over a longer period than had been seen since the June Democracy Movement of 1987. But rather than protesting, crowds blasted music and cheered on the Korean soccer team during the Korea-Japan World Cup games. Places where protesters like Pak Chongch'ŏl and Yi Hanyŏl once threw stones and Molotov cocktails in the face of tanks and teargas grenades were brimming with cheering crowds wearing red, the Red Devils being the name of supporters for the national team. The mobilization has been read in different ways: some Korean scholars, such as Han Sangjin, view this collective fervor as a sign of improved civil consciousness, resulting from the nation's economic, cultural, and athletic achievement.[25] Others, however, identify the phenomenon with totalitarian conditioning, a kind of collective hysteria removed from reality.[26] Regardless of the reading, the message to South Koreans was clear: citizens were able and willing to come together for a common cause, whether in defiance or celebration.

This ability was soon actualized for a far more somber purpose. On June 13, 2002, two fourteen-year-old girls were struck and run over by a Second Infantry Division armored carrier vehicle on a civilian road in Yangju, north of Seoul. Although anti-American and antimilitarism sentiments were aroused, for the most part, the deaths of Sim Misŏn and Sin Hyosun were overshadowed by the World Cup (May 31–June 30). However, when the drivers of the military vehicle were found not guilty of manslaughter, a candlelight vigil was held on November 26. This ignited a series of vigils in major cities across the country, continued through the end of 2002, at which thousands of people gathered.[27] Most of these events remained nonviolent, with many participants being high school students. Following the precedent of earlier memorializations, Hyosun and Misŏn's school ID pictures served as their funerary portraits and were carried as placards.

Shifts in public mobilization again became apparent in 2008 through events organized by high school students which erupted into nationwide protests against government policies. From May to August, gathering spots across the nation were filled with candlelight vigils in the form of festive events (*munhwache*) with invited speakers and performers, attended by people from all walks of life. The specific target was a new agreement on importing American beef from cattle over thirty months old—reported as carrying a higher risk of bovine spongiform encephalopathy (BSE), or "mad cow disease."[28] More broadly (although the exaggeration of the fear of contracting BSE has been much critiqued since), the uproar over BSE became a proxy for the neoliberal policies of newly elected President Lee Myung-bak and his administration.[29] Expanding rapidly, the protest events were characterized by new political sensibilities building on humor and parody, such as creative placards with memes and slogans against combat police.[30] This was especially noticeable following the airing on April 29 and May 13 of Munhwa Broadcasting Company's investigative program, *PD Such'ŏp*, on the lifting of the ban and safety concerns. The protests were further fueled by the prime minister and president's announcement on strengthened safety measurements, which were considered by the public to be temporary and ill-planned, and therefore indicative of the government's apparent posture as performing a merely managerial role within transnational capitalism, especially concerning Korea-US free trade.[31] Between the months of May and August, activists held candlelight vigils over 100 times in Seoul and 2,359 times countrywide.[32] On June 10, the day commemorating the June Democracy Movement, over eighty thousand people (by police estimate) gathered in Seoul for a candlelight vigil.[33]

The immediate difference in photography between the gatherings of 2002 and 2008 was that protesters now held digital cameras and phone cameras in their hands along with their candles. Participants and spectators, equipped with digital cameras in cellular phones, camcorders, and even laptop computers, acted as creators and publishers, simultaneously protesting and broadcasting news of their protests in both words and images (plate 13). Countless photographs of the rallies accompanied articles and online posts, some journalistic reportage, and extensive individual commentary. The so-called *irinmidiŏ* (one-person media; this term was in use prior to the advent of popular social media such as Twitter, Instagram, and YouTube) and protesters' live posts of still and moving images offered people inside and outside South Korea vicarious access to the events as they unfolded.[34] Newspapers had published photographs of the candlelight vigils since the announcement of the US-Korea agreement on beef imports.[35] However, print media and TV were no longer the main mode through which the public engaged with the vast majority of these photographs.

The technological developments that paved the way for the *irinmidiŏ* phenomenon also greatly changed how such events were organized, and who organized them.[36] The first of these candlelight vigils was initiated by a group of fifty-one high school students from seven youth organizations in Ch'ŏnggye Kwangjang (Ch'ŏnggye Square) on April 18, 2008, the day the Lee government announced that the United States and Korea had sealed an agreement on the import of US beef.[37] Although the civil movements of the 1950s and 1960s were also led by junior high and high school students, in 2008, the key organizers of this group were high school girls. Women overall—not coincidentally, citizens normally excluded from the male- and adult-centered discourses of civil society[38]—made up the majority of participants.[39] Many of the events were planned and promoted on the now defunct Korean internet message board Agora, provided by one of the major internet portals, Daum.[40] Furthermore, the events' successful execution relied in part on virtual communication. According to Kim Chongyŏp, the vigils remained uniformly peaceful events—despite the Lee administration's attempts to disperse the gatherings by instigating violent reactions—thanks to the preplanning and discussion enabled by the internet forums.[41]

The events and online mobilization in turn signaled a subversion of mainstream politics; Jiyeon Kang explains that while making it difficult to define "the difference between frivolous play and political criticism on the Internet," the three types of online community, "alternative [news] media, parody sites, and discussion forums," were responsible for the unprecedented scale of on- and offline communication and mobilization.[42] Adding to Kang's salient point, these communities provided the platforms through which photographs and recordings were shared and circulated before Twitter, Instagram, or YouTube.

The key issues brought to the *kwangjang* were more than incidentally related to the inequality and injustice that adolescents and women experienced every day.[43] For instance, the high school students protested against school policies such as mandatory attendance of *yŏnggyosi* (zero-hour class), a self-study session before the regular school hours which was thought to make school environments even more competitive.[44] The young protesters also felt that the Lee administration was too fixated on the 1970s-style land development projects such as the Grand Canal Project and should have been instead focused on addressing the precarity of their job securities and labor conditions. As such, the main reason for the months of candlelight vigils was not simply objections over the import of US beef, but over the ways that the administration handled it, foreshowing a US-Korea free trade agreement negotiation among many other issues. The lack of public discourse or disclosure reflected the general lack of communication from the government on administrative, political, and social issues considered critical by the public, such as education, food, and the environment.

The gathering of the protesters across the country both enabled and was enabled by the formation of a photo public, those participant-performers in the *kwangjang* who not only produced and circulated photographs but also become the subjects and inspirations of others' (photo) activities. This collective consisted of individuals from diverse backgrounds, especially young women who had never participated in political rallies prior to the event. Unlike the student protests in 1987, there was no unity in terms of political, social, and economic identification. The collective—those who activated the photo public (whether deliberately or inadvertently)—is aptly described in Sylvère Lotringer's account of the multitude as "immaterial workers": "mobile and detached, adaptable, curious, opportunistic and cynical, also toward institutions; they are inventive and share knowledge through communication and language; they are mostly de-politicized, also disobedient."[45] Indeed, according to Kang, the women who filled the *kwangjang* with creative slogans and placards speaking back directly to authority, with their sharp critiques on education and inequality, lost their interest when the protests began to focus on "institutional goals" familiar to the 1987-generation protesters.[46]

Performativity, Plurality, Relationality

In the *kwangjang*, plural performativity becomes the premise—and the right—of a photo public. When confronting suppression of the right to fight for and act toward personal well-being, and of the subsequent expression of discontent and dissent, a public is enacted by "a performativity of embodied agency, in which we own our bodies and struggle for the right to claim our bodies as 'ours' (as we ask, for example, that the state keep off our bodies)."[47] In addition, as Athanasiou contends, the claims of a public do not apply merely to a group of individual bodies, but to "the relationality of these bodies."[48]

This constantly forming, shifting, drifting, and re-forming relationality was indeed the potentiality of the 2008 *kwangjang* event. While the *kwangjang* crowds were frequently referred to by the opposition as "conspirators," "commies," and "pro-North," the emergence of this public in empathetic alliance (albeit not without internal tensions) strikingly defied the Korean identitarian trope of communist versus anti-communist ideology. The photo public of 2008 was not beholden to a hypostatized foundation of unity; they self-organized against what they saw as "life-threatening violence of profit extraction" and shared an "affective economy of motivation, endurance, changeability and vitalization."[49] As such, they shared a sense of belonging, not a binding power.[50]

The act of photography, which encompasses related postphotography activities such as online posting and sharing, was especially important to this collective performativity. While enacting a public together in the square, protesters constantly made photographs of the site and of themselves, holding their cameras and camera phones above their heads to photograph the gathering (plate 14). The (extended) act of photography in the *kwangjang* was a performance that activated the relationality of the gathered. In 2008, performance sites included South Korean social media platforms such as Cyworld and Ap'ŭrik'at'ibi,[51] launched in 1999 and 2005, respectively, not to mention the widely practiced, familiar and fashionable conventions of *selka* (selfies, short for self-camera).[52] The phenomenological and affective shift from June 1987–style photojournalism was immediately evident in the images and footage being seen, shared, and commented on through such social media.

In the *kwangjang*, photographic activities brought plural performativity into the on- and offline network in real time. The citizens gathered at the vigils activated themselves, as the subject of revolutionary potentials, through performativity; in this, the photography was no longer refracted as a language, signifier, or representation of a political subjectivity. The plurality of the photo making itself offered an aesthetic means of resistance.[53] With the movement being experienced in mediated forms, photography was no longer a supplementary medium of communication, but was inseparable from the formation of solidarity.[54] Once the photograph was taken, it lived its life online, without needing to travel the narrative path of, say, newspaper publication and reproduction on protest banners. It was all nearly immediately online—as was the photography which had earlier traveled those long paths to iconicity.

The photographs of the *irinmidiŏ* had a self-sustaining and self-fulfilling life cycle. As Kang posits, online activities including sharing and circulating of photographs and footage "captivated" viewers, leading many to join the vigils physically. They then returned to online communities to share their experiences and thoughts.[55] In their perpetual circulation back and forth between the *kwangjang* and various online communities, the photographs of the 2008 candlelight vigils were thus both the catalyst for and a result of the new relationality between political subjects—sometimes leading to collective actions, other times only remaining online, but never remaining in the binary of action versus nonaction.

Irinmidiŏ, "YOU," and the Illusion of a Networked Community

As one of many following the 2008 movement closely, I encountered the vigils on the internet, becoming a long-distance, virtual participant.[56] For those with a desire to participate, despite not being physically present in the location, the experience of these events through others' experiences created a sense of collectivity (and belonging), albeit virtual. For the first few days, at least for someone like myself, encountering hundreds of digital images online, these images felt affectively ephemeral. Keeping track of where I saw the images seemed futile, since similar (or the same) images appeared in many spaces, whether on message boards of major portal sites, personal blogs, or other social networking sites.

However, this remote experience took a different turn when the event on the ground turned into bloody clashes between the police force and protesters.

Cameras were now used to record the acts of brutality and as a preventive measure against police repression, despite their quick co-optation by the police to record and identify the faces of protesters.[57] Carol Martin, discussing the Lebanese artist Rabih Mroué's 2012 performance on the aesthetics of Syrian protests, notes that "the target of security forces is no longer people with guns with the intent to kill, but people with mobile phones with the intent to record. The target of people with mobile phones is people with guns, and their intent is to stop the killing by recording it. The instant uploading of digital recordings on the internet has become lethal to both its users and its subjects."[58] As what was occurring on the ground shifted, the online activities accordingly reacted by sharing and reposting the violence on the ground.

In response to the growing number of assemblies, participants, and locations, heavily armored police units began to appear at the vigils, blocking and encircling the crowd. By late May, the police force was shooting water with high-pressure hoses directly at protesters to break assembly (figure 4.1).[59] The evening of June 10, the police blocked the Sechongno, the major road leading to Kyŏngbokkung (Kyŏngbok Palace), with massive shipping container boxes, resulting in close, and often injurious, encounters between the protesters and the police force.[60] Photographs of these clashes include one showing an injured man facing a combat police unit called in for riot control (plate 15). As he holds his hand up in the air, blood runs down the side of the man's forehead and his hand. Similar images and events were widely photographed and recorded by protesters and quickly posted on their blogs, Agora, and other photo- and video-sharing platforms.

Because these images were typically participant-sourced, the candlelight vigils of 2008 saw a transformation of the ways in which such violence was communicated at large. This was one of the earliest points at which photography and social media together became a critical medium for the affective politics of plural performativity; when a violent confrontation between the police force and protesters occurred, one would hear about and watch what was happening live on Ap'ŭrik'at'ibi or other online venues, as posted by individual protesters, well before TV news programs or newspapers reported on them. Indeed, the rise of *irinmidiŏ* indicates the limits of mass media's one-way communication. During these months in 2008, the significant changes in digital technology and the immediate adaptation of users to those changes was crucial to the spread—and validity—of *irinmidiŏ*.[61]

The phenomenon of *irinmidiŏ* is also about the transformation of relationality among the individuals that make publics and of the performances

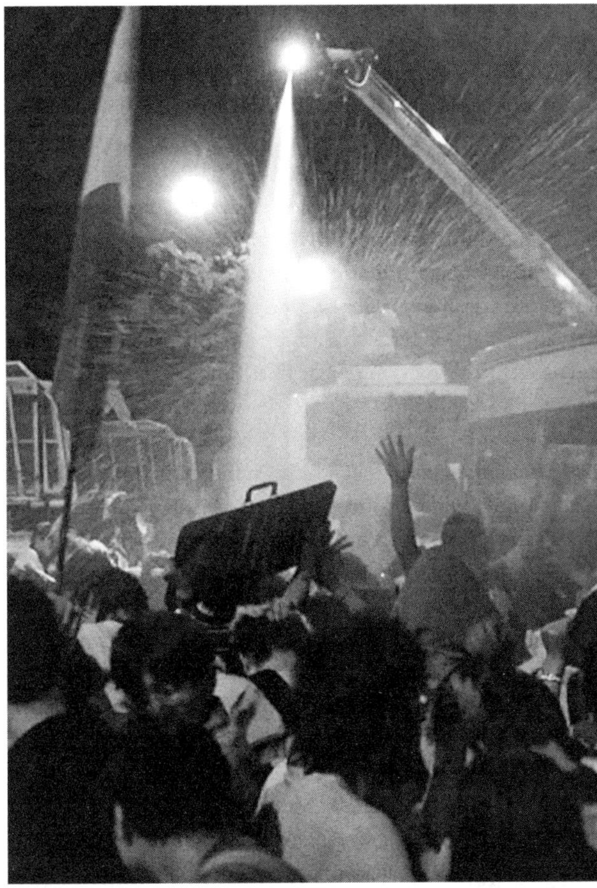

FIGURE 4.1 Police water carrier shooting water at protesters, Seoul, June 1, 2008. Courtesy of P'urŭn kŭrim.

through which a photo public is enacted. Simply put, the rise of *irinmidiŏ* brought forth a new kind of activation of (seeing and being seen as) a political subject. Rather than constituting a political subjectivity in reaction to a photograph of violence, the event of photography in 2008 showed that the performativity of photography taking place as *irinmidiŏ* activated political subjectivities. *Irin*, an I—a singularity, if you will—is "from the start implicated in the lives of the other that the 'I' is already social, and must begin its reflection and action from the presumption of a constitutive sociality."[62] That first-person "I" in *irinmidiŏ* is thus inevitably implied in the photo public of the 2008 event. The significance of 2008 assemblies lay in this performance of individuals in activating the relationality of the gathered, in this case through making images of themselves from a positionality differing from those defined by the institutional politics of the Cold War ideology, as in 1960, 1987, or even 2002.

But, as Morris contends, "increased visibility... does not connote potential power (of the kind that could grant recognition)";[63] moreover, in a so-called networked society, connection ("the fantasy of a digital hook-up") can replace communication and satisfy, for the moment, the desire for being seen as a speaking self.[64] As such, Wendy Hui Kyong Chun asks if such mediated processes merely create an illusion of unity so that the multiplicity becomes a functioning public,[65] and, I would add, if such mediation is even "necessary for the construction of a political subject, a fiction which is nonetheless essential to the real operation of constituent power."[66] The "fiction" in the formation of a political subject is the equation of "I" as "we," or the assumption that "I" embodies "we" in social movements.

Since then, Chun has in the past decades experienced the repeated returning of the fantasy of a networked society while that fantasy is controlled by, and in turn reproduces, what she calls "discriminatory data"; her persistent warning against the allure of data democracy becomes ever more crucial in examining the relationship between photography and the social movements of the twenty-first century.[67] Chun's warning against the logic of Big Data in defining and grouping "I," "you" (which Chun writes in all-uppercase "YOU"), and "we" in the guise of connectivity and democratic relationality therefore becomes a warning against simply celebrating the transformation of the relationship between photography, social movements, and "we."[68]

How is the illusion of "we" maintained in networks? Chun argues that networks move "away from subjects and narratives toward actors and captured actions that they knit into a monstrously connected chimera. They imagine connections that transform the basis of the collective imaginary from 'we' to YOU: from community to an ever-still-resolvable grouping that erodes and sustains the distance between self and other."[69] Certainly this follows, given that photography, so often hailed as the medium of democracy, has also proven that its seeming democratic qualities—reproducibility, accessibility, and instant shareability—can just as easily be co-opted for surveillance, distortion, invasion of privacy, and so on. Neither networks nor photography are inherently democratic or capable of handing out freedom. Rather, they continuously update to renew its capacity to co-opt, transform, and expand.[70]

Photography via *irinmidiŏ* shifted the experience of photography documenting social movements. So many photographs and reports posted and shared online depicted the same events and perspective due to sheer sample size. At the same time, in large part due to the vast number of images available, no one photograph has been singled out as an iconic image of the 2008 vigils. Instead, certain aesthetic types of images have created a kind of mass symbolism. Photographs of huge crowds of people holding candles at night, of young students holding picket signs, and bird's-eye-view shots of vigils—all share a collective association with the movement (plate 16).[71] In particular, because no death or severe casualty was captured on camera during the 2008 vigils, there is an absence of images carrying the shock value present in photographs such as those of Kim Chuyŏl and Yi Hanyŏl.

Rather than forming around the nexus of an existing photograph, the photo public wanted to see themselves being heard—performing photography not to just see, but to become the public outcry itself. The photo public enacted themselves as new political subjects, their visibility widely acknowledged and affirmed . . . by themselves. The events of 2008 and their chronicling thus signaled that the days of iconic photographs produced primarily by heroic photojournalists have passed. The new images and image makers create very different experiences.[72]

The posting and reposting of images depicting virtually the same scenes during the vigils—repeated actions of photography—created a visual and virtual common ground for the "we" and for the transition from the "I" to the "we" (and to "YOU"). The repetition of the act of photography is closely related to the understanding of the relations between individuals in a public. Chun cautiously reasons, referring to Deleuze, that habits—repetitions—make difference "conceivable as generic relations." Although Chun's critique is directed at the glossy allure of Big Data and networked society, her discussion also applies to the affective workings of repeated actions of photography—this time, online activities that were seemingly enabled by networks. The networks of *irin* and their repeated postings of protests and vigils made "it possible to imagine and elucidate connection, as well as link humans and machines together as beings that repeat."[73] Of course, the act of photography (photo making, filtering, posting, reposting, and so on) is repetition that helps people imagine connection (just think of Instagram). Hence, despite the lack of unity in a public, the act of photography makes it possible to imagine connectivity, through which the affect of being together, whether physically proximate or not, is substantiated.

Slacktivism 2008 and Reactions

The move from photographs reproduced in newspapers and journals to personal digital photographs posted online and viewed on computer screens or cell phones also means changes in the physicality of photography. In the case of the 2008 candlelight vigils, the photograph was no longer a printed object, but manifested as pixels on a liquid crystal display. This physical change in turn transformed the traffic of images. The online circulation of protest images by citizen journalists demonstrates that, currently, "the goal of any one image may not be to sum something up, but to trigger others in response."[74] Viewed today, the photograph by Chŏng T'aewon of Yi Hanyŏl falling sums up the struggle for democracy in South Korea in the 1980s. At the same time, like the photographs of the 2008 candlelight vigils, those of Yi triggered, or "ignited" (as Kang puts it) mobilization in response. What was significantly different for the 2008 event was how the photographs of the vigils influenced viewers not just to participate in the vigils, but also to take more pictures and post them online—and subsequently, to repost them online, whether in lieu of one's own in-person participation in the vigils or not.

The possibility of performing "affective information"—by disseminating digital photography and footage online as political subjects, photo publics, and performative collectives—distinguished the 2008 event of photography. For the photo public to maintain its potentiality, however, requires defiance against the instant lure of networked society. To connect with each other online as the social movement is being organized, and "to read 'voice' in systems designed to deny voice," Chun proposes that

> we need to "*listen*" for actions that are embedded in infrastructures and settings and learn to speak through these actions. The desire to capture and to draw connections, maps, and models can open a future that defies what is captured, but only if we dwell in the disconnect between map and action, model and future—only if we occupy the collective chimera we are offered and become characters, not marionettes.[75]

This call to "listen" for actions is not merely a metaphor, especially in the context of photography. The affective vibrancy of photographic repetition, whether in social media or physical archives, must be attended to in order to understand the relationality created by the photographic act in the becoming of a public.

Does the photo public then also include the networked communities of slacktivism? Is slacktivism a side effect of photography gone digital on social media? Or does slacktivism, in fact, engage with a wider public, those who otherwise would have no interest or means to participate? Chun asks if any forms of humanitarianism are not slacktivism in the first place, if any networks are not banal. As Jacques Rancière puts it, a spectator does not simply occupy a passive position which fails to materialize as action. Rather, the emancipation of the fixed position of a spectator and actor occurs when their positionalities are confirmed or transformed by the act of viewing.[76]

Likewise, Kang's ethnographic studies conducted in 2012 on the generation of high school participants of the 2008 events, surveying their engagement or lack thereof with politics and past events, suggest that "low-risk protest or feel-good activism (so-called slacktivism) is *not* an antithesis of meaningful protest."[77] For the young participants of 2008 events, those who grew up "embodying the logic of the Internet in the real world," the fluidity between on- and offline is not a matter of institutional politics but depends on "the circulation of captivating objects, the affective networks and temporary alliances surrounding those objects, and the irreverent subversion of authority without fear of persecution."[78] Hence, obtaining news about the candlelight vigils online and engaging in them virtually ultimately led to particular actions online and offline.[79] In this way, individuals who once feared the violence of becoming a new political subject were emancipated, something impossible during and in the immediate aftermath of the military regime.

Of course, this was possible only because of the events of 1960 and 1987, and the continued collective struggles against the militarized structure manifesting in various aspects of life. Crucially, dictating what knowledge was to be accessible, to whom, and when, was impossible in the early stages of the broadband society. According to Zeynep Gürsel, "amateur and professional image brokers [use] the same networks to view and circulate images."[80] As such, the 2008 events revealed a democratization of photography in the civic sphere; the government was not (yet) cracking down on individuals taking photographs or circulating them, and protesters had far more accessible means for making, keeping, and sharing photographs and footage. Furthermore, the users of these online services acted in anticipation of censorship, for instance by taking screenshots of posts before they could be deleted by website administrators.

In several ways, in fact, even as the kind of censorship that existed during the military regime was rendered obsolete in this environment, the 2008 event intensified the degree and modes of censorship online.[81] Members of the Grand National Party accused internet users of posting false information about the beef imports and the dangers of mad cow disease. This soon led to formal accusations and trials of users. For instance, Pak Taesŏng, whose online handle was Minerva, was arrested and tried in 2008 for falsely accusing the government of pressing financial institutions to control foreign currencies, influencing a drop in overseas investment in South Korea. He was later acquitted of the charge, but his handle disappeared from online communities and social media soon after.

Soon enough, Congress, led by the Grand National Party, proposed a "New Media Law," which was enacted partly to facilitate censorship on the internet. Discussions held on portal sites such as Daum or on individual blogs, linked together with various functions that made the postings more accessible for users, gradually petered out even as social media proliferated. Agora was later folded under other forums, becoming less visible and popular, and eventually shutting down in 2018.[82] For all that various online social media services enabled—access, exchange, dissemination, manipulation, and detection of information at an unprecedented level—the backlash against "citizen journalism" rapidly curtailed these ways of using online forums for civic purposes. Although images no longer needed to be hidden in an earthenware pot and buried underground, image makers and disseminators were quickly exposed to the same principles of censorship and silencing that had earlier held sway.

Eventually, the uproar against imported US beef subsided. While South Koreans still prefer homegrown beef, imported US beef is readily available in markets and restaurants.[83] Rather, the change ushered in by the (photographic) events of 2008 was of a larger scale: a transformation of the ways in which people experienced social movements and their aftermath. Tens of thousands of people took to the streets of cities across the nation for more than three months consecutively in 2008—and even more people experienced the movement or participated in it online. The movement was less violent and more participatory, more fast-paced, and quicker to adapt to new circumstances. In part because of this, none of the thousands of digital photographs of the 2008 vigils that circulated and were posted on the internet communities ultimately became widely known as individual photographs.

Yet the enormous potentiality, and problems, of one-person media was now firmly part of the public engagement.

Because the Revolution Is Still Ongoing

Observing images of the Egyptian past circulating online, Lucie Ryzova posits that these images offer "an infinite range of resignification. In the case of the revolution, the meanings are unfixed because of the absence of closure, *because the revolution is still ongoing*."[84] Likewise, in looking back, one of the most striking aspects of the 2008 protests is the collective performativity of visualizing the people's political subjectivity, which has continued to evolve. The winter months of 2016–17 saw yet another collective enactment and experience of dissent, again turning the populace into agents of historical conjuring—that of the people against the state, as in 1960, 1987, and 2008. Every weekend, tens of thousands of people again congregated in public squares across the country, standing for hours in freezing temperatures to chant and sing together in protest against the Park Geun-hye administration. Primarily in response to a series of corruption cases involving her family friends, close allies, and *chaebols* including Samsung, animosity against the leadership had also been heightened by the cause and failed emergency management of the Sewol Ferry disaster that killed 304 passengers (mostly high school students).

The wintry months of public gatherings in the square were extensively photographed and broadcast on private channels, often featuring the practice of *injŭngshat* (photo shot confirming being there and then), widespread since the mid-2000s.[85] In protest movements, *injŭngshat* cannot simply be defined as evidentiary signification in the manner of indexicality. Rather, it manifests the desire to take part in the traffic of photography in the network, to become a photo public. This desire is also part of the *kinyŏmsajin* (commemorative photographs) vernacular discussed in chapters 2 and 6, and therefore cannot be dismissed—as Chun warns against, and under the same principles behind derision of slacktivism—as falling for the illusion of a networked society. At the same time, photographs that made it to mass media were aerial, long-exposure shots of the collectives holding candles, looking like fiery, swirly masses from above (plate 17). Various cable and online channels livestreamed the protests, effectively co-opting—at a distance—the way protesters conveyed the photographic event of 2008.

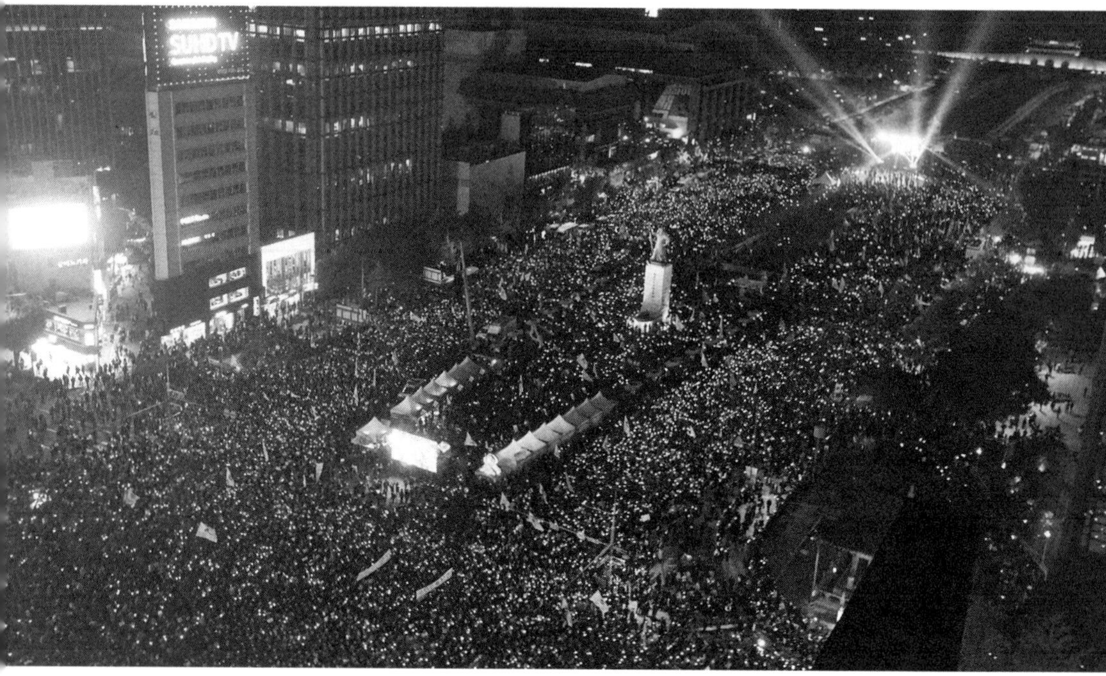

FIGURE 4.2 Candlelight vigil, Seoul Kwangjang, December 3, 2016, © KBS News.

Perhaps in consequence, despite their recency, it is harder to find well-known individual images of the 2016–17 candlelight vigils than those of 2008 (to say nothing of the iconic photographs of 1960 and 1987). Photographs and footage of the continued protests inundated social and mass media, but the event is now remembered with aerial photographs of the *kwangjang*, beautifully lit with tens of thousands of candles and cell phone flashes, forming a river of lights (figure 4.2). Once again, images showing the photo public as massive swirls of fiery dots at night became the emblematic image of the 2016–17 movement. Whereas the urge to see the individual *injŭngshat* by the public may have continued, news outlets clearly expressed "a need to visualize the sheer mass of individuals at the rally" with spectacular images of the masses.[86]

While individual photographs of protests or movements in the twenty-first century will not compete with the iconicity of the 1960 and 1987 photographs, the act of photography as a collective performance did lead to a bloodless revolution. However, the internet and social media cannot be depended on to salvage the event of photography in today's social movements. The photograph, before anything else, is made by the bodies on the streets—which are, as Butler describes, precarious.[87] The bodies in collective resistance activate the people and the power of plural performativity. At this moment, the performance of photography becomes "a defense of our collective precarity and persistence in the making of equality and the many-voiced and unvoiced ways of refusing to become disposable."[88] It was so in South Korea in 1960, 1987, 2008, and 2016–17, and it has been so in squares across the world, time and again, for the precarious lives standing against militarism and state violence. The performance of photography is thus critical in this becoming of a public, recognizing and remembering the rise (then and now) of political subjectivities. As such, the act of photography is always a performance of multitemporality, embodying the social movements of the past and the memory of the photo public.[89]

At the same time, news outlets' emblematic image of the vigils also indicate that reciprocity is no longer possible between the image maker (in this case, the drone) and the subjects of the photographs (the people). The subjects of aerial photographs, even via viewers, cannot return the gaze of the photographer—the lens of a drone camera. Likewise, the reciprocity between journalists and the public, though rarely symmetrical in the first place, has been broken. The information warfare proliferating during the campaigning months leading to the March 2022 presidential election characterizes today's problems with information dissemination and fact checking.[90] Just as the distance and detachment between the drone "photographer" and a photo public disallows visual reciprocity and no longer makes visible the bodies on the ground, disinformation, fake news, and orchestrated character assassinations rolled out toward the March 2022 election once again reveal the kind of complex, concerted, and combative work required to fight against the violence of networked society.

PART III

SENSING BORDERLANDS

5

The DMZ, Camptowns, and the Theater of Repetition

Decade-marking anniversaries of the outbreak of the Korean War provide an opportunity for reaffirming the sense of ethno-nationality, as well as making and sustaining the collective memory of the war. The 2020 seventieth anniversary, of course, could not possibly follow the normal routine. A global pandemic meant no lead-up to the June anniversary, no official 6.25 anniversary ceremonies with large gatherings of state officials, politicians, and veterans. Organized by the 70th Anniversary of the Korean War Commemoration Committee (the 6.25Chŏnjaeng 70Chunyŏn Saŏpch'ujinwiwŏnhoe), co-chaired by the prime minister of South Korea, the ceremony was held on June 25, 2020, but only after the scorching summer sun had completely set, to provide a more comfortable environment for those veterans now in their eighties and nineties wearing KF94 masks. It was still somewhat odd to witness the South Korean state virtually commemorate foreign contributions to the war by donating face masks to the countries from whence UN soldiers came.

The press coverage for the sixtieth anniversary seemed to consist almost entirely of "never-before-seen" images of atrocity-stricken landscapes below the 38th parallel, with an emphasis on (orphan) children. By contrast, the seventieth anniversary media publicity used war imagery sparsely, and was largely limited to footage and stills, perhaps due to the difficulties in retrieving photographs from archives during the pandemic.[1] The key memorial event—an act of national gratitude—was presented on YouTube.[2] Starting with montages of select veterans' recent black-and-white photo-portraits, the video goes on to show mixed footage of air bombings, with an insert of a crying Korean child with her mouth wide open (figure 5.1). The blurry black-and-white war footage abruptly shifts to a bird's-eye view of contemporary Seoul and rapidly successive images of the high-tech industry that South Korea has been known for in recent years. After more recent images of UN veterans commemorating the war, the pandemic context is addressed with images of people wearing PPE and captions proclaiming that Korea is now paying back its debt to its friends.[3] The video includes a few grim stills of (seemingly) a mother and her baby wearing masks and patients and medical workers in PPE; footage of mask shipments, delivered by a fighter plane; group *kinyŏmsajin* (commemorative photographs) featuring military personnel, flags, and "#Thanks to UN Veterans" on a banner, as well as *kinyŏmsajin* of the recipients. Many people appearing in this part of the video are people of color—unlike the veterans themselves (with two exceptions, including an Ethiopian veteran stating that he has never regretted fighting in Korea even though he lost his limbs during the war).

The video emphasizes Koreans' continuing gratitude to the veterans and their selfless sacrifice and, more importantly, their ability to help others in the current situation as a leading nation, first with its industry, and later with its advancements in medical and pandemic control capacity (at the time). But did anything really change about the ways in which imagery was used to commemorate and memorialize the war? With the war victims symbolized by the images of a crying Korean child (past) and later a foreign baby and mother (present) in the video, the narrative of debt and gift unfolds once again through the images of children, just as a decade before. In a model repetition of what Mimi Thi Nguyen calls "the gift of freedom," the victim, now grown up and super advanced, shows *their* gratitude by protecting the newly vulnerable descendants of the former saviors.[4] Strangely, however, the "victim" of the global pandemic deliberately excludes elderly white veterans of the Korean War. Instead, the victims of the pandemic "war" are represented

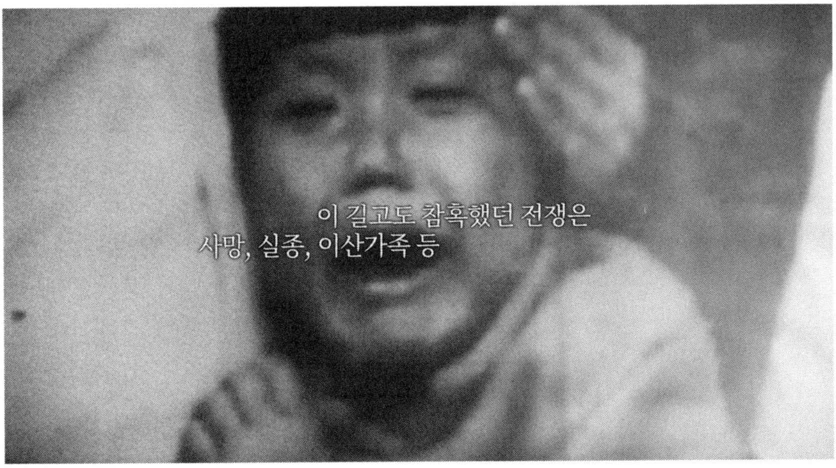

FIGURE 5.1 Still from *Urika Tangsinŭl Kiŏkhanŭn Pangbŏp (6.25chŏnjaeng Yuench'amjŏnyongsa'eke Masŭk'ŭrŭl Chiwŏnhada)*, Kukkapohunch'ŏ, YouTube video, May 28, 2020.

by a mother and child, and a patient of color lying on a hospital bed. Taking advantage of the national health and safety orders that effectively controlled the infection rate during the lead-up to the seventieth anniversary, the South Korean state thus attempts to seize this moment of global attention to present itself as the victim turned savior, even as it maintains racial dynamics traditionally associated with sympathy for less "advanced" countries.

As much as the global context of the seventieth anniversary was unexpected, the repetition of the victim-savior binary, whether reversed or not, has continued to capitalize and rely on war imagery. It is easy and logical enough to imagine that the framework employing photography to reproduce the ethno-nationalist, masculinist, and imperialist rhetoric of transnational militarism will likewise reappear for the eightieth anniversary. A notable addition to the repeated representation of war is the representation of peace, symbolized by the North-South borderlands, in particular the DMZ, as the signifier of a conflict zone turned ecological sanctuary—the symbol of peace in, and with, nature.[5] The 160-mile long, 2.5-mile-wide border between North and South Korea, the DMZ, is a buffer zone between the two states and is one of the most heavily guarded borders in the world, with an estimate of one million land mines buried in the DMZ and up to two million troops stationed across the border from each other.[6] Bouts of violent exchanges between the sides continue.

But repetition can take on unexpected paths, as Gilles Deleuze sees: "Difference inhabits repetition"—hence "repetition *in* difference"—disrupting the state-sanctioned rhetoric of peace in borderlands with the North that is repeated in commemorative sites and events.[7] Rather than reprise my critique of photography's usurpation in national commemorative events of the war, I explore in this chapter the unexpected paths of repetition via photographic representation. Indebted to studies on photography's affect and multisensorial experiences, not just as the subject of inquiry but as the onto-epistemological critique of knowledge production, the chapter examines the ways in which selected art and photography projects undo the national rhetoric of futurity prescribed in relentless adherence to, while seemingly oscillating between, ideology (이데올로기) and neoliberal desire. The chapter further attends to how such projects in the process create novel paths for repetition to take—or, for that matter, refuse to take, stalling the neoliberal imagination of cosmopolitan redevelopment. Hence, I pay attention to the ways that repetition also manifests in the reverberation of the sonic and somatic fields of sensing. Focusing on repetition as a rupture to the spatial ideology of the national partition and military expansion of the everyday, the chapter examines repetition in the ongoing *Real DMZ Project* and reverberations in and of landscape photographs depicting expropriated lands, and lives, for military purposes. While temporality is a central aspect of repetition and reverberation, I expand my discussion to bring in multisensorial and spatial encounters with photography and art, especially in yielding the mediated experiences of the borderlands while being near the DMZ.

Repetition, the Real, and the *Real DMZ Project*

The repetition of commemoration, as discussed in previous chapters, is key to imagining, making, and updating collective memory. Repetition, however, inherently presents difference, as no one event, regardless of how many times it has been repeated or how much it resembles previous occasions, is the same event as others. At times, the reenaction in repetition can itself take an unexpected path, veering from its intended affirmation.

The *Real DMZ Project* (*RDP*) is a case in point: the *RDP* has presented a rather unexpected outcome by repeating itself. As its title indicates, the

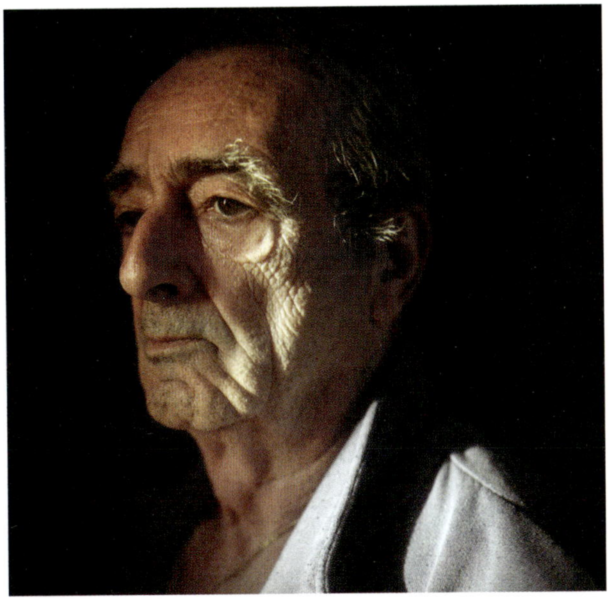

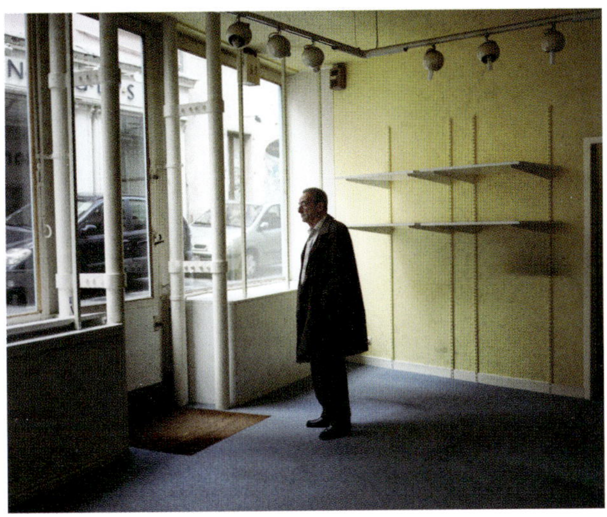

PLATE 1 (*top*) Agnès Dherbeys, from *Retired*, 2013–15, c-print. Courtesy of the artist.

PLATE 2 (*bottom*) Agnès Dherbeys, from *Retired*, 2013–15, c-print. Courtesy of the artist.

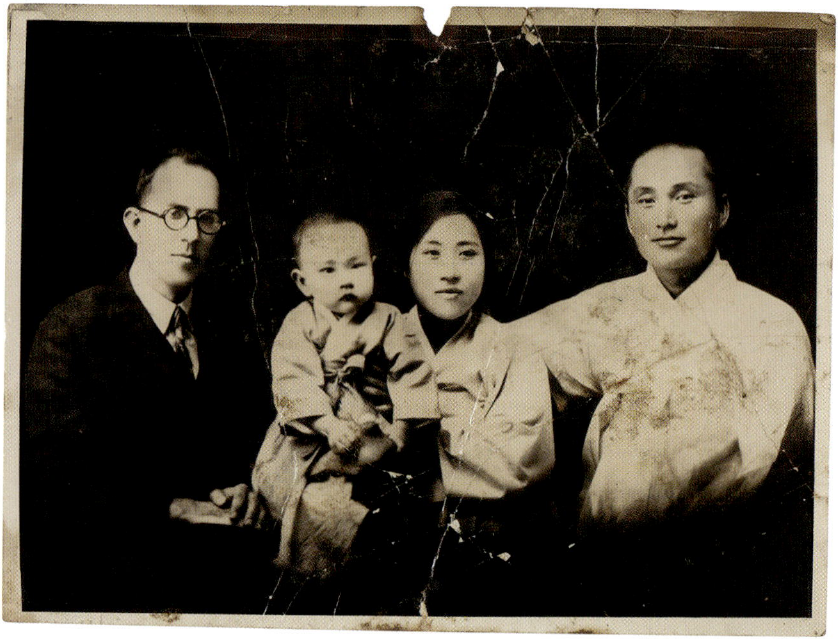

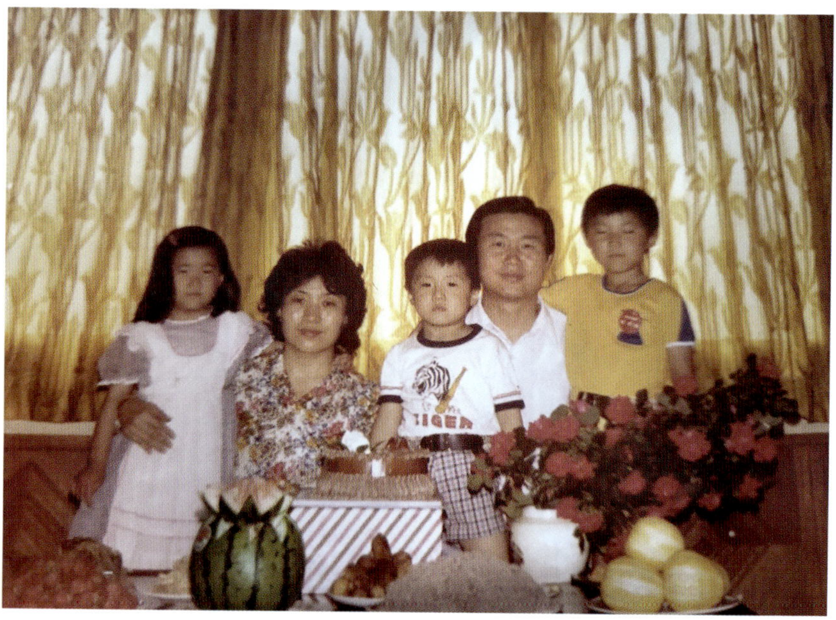

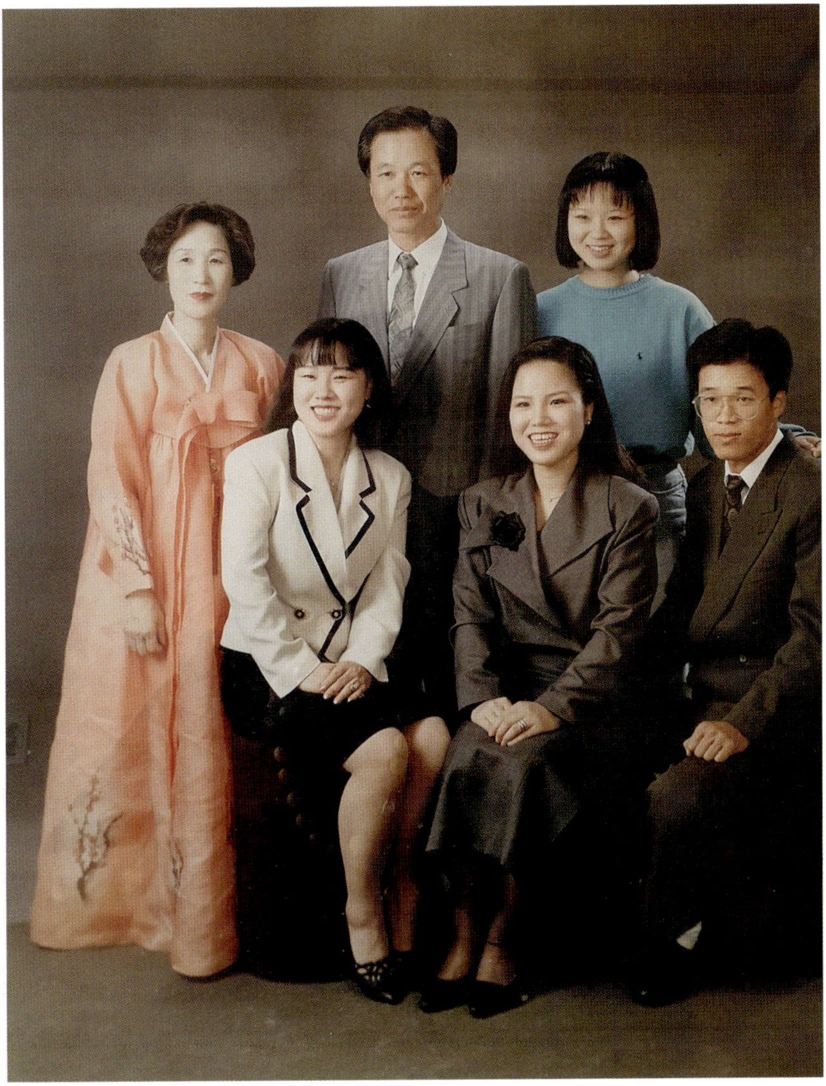

PLATE 3 (*opposite top*) Photographer once known, Yi Kwangsu's family portrait with an American friend, 1929, gelatin silver print, 13.2 × 17.3 cm. Courtesy of Museum Hanmi.

PLATE 4 (*opposite bottom*) Family portrait taken at home on a birthday, 1983, c-print. Courtesy of Cheon Chin Soon.

PLATE 5 (*above*) Studio family portrait, 1992, c-print. Courtesy of Kyungsook Yoon.

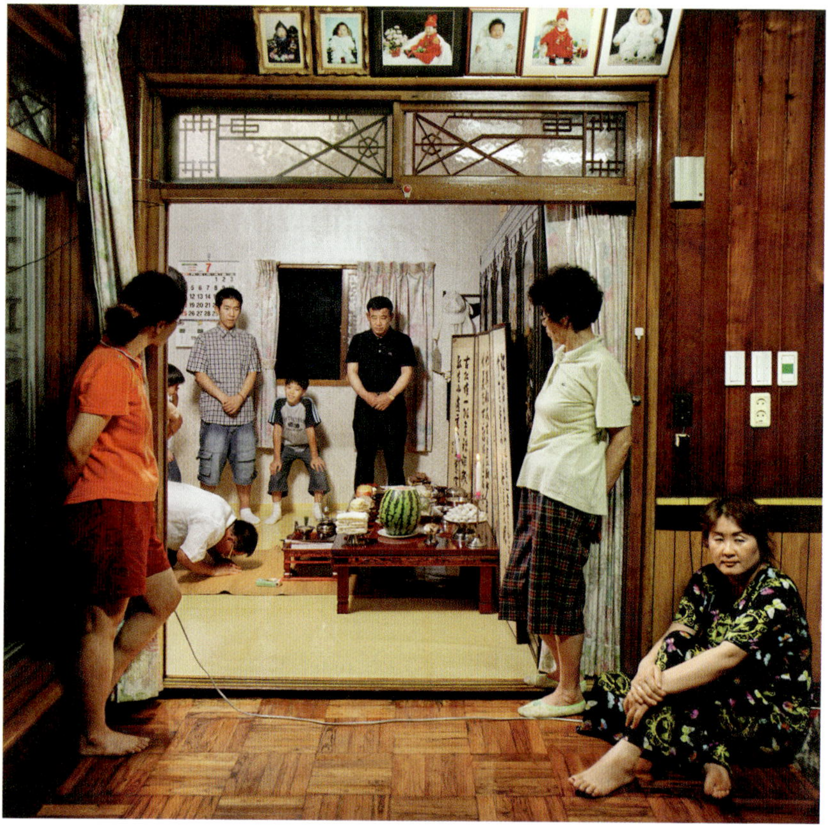

PLATE 6 Sunmin Lee, *Sunja Lee's House #1—Ancestral Rites*, from *Woman's House*, 2004, c-print. Courtesy of the artist.

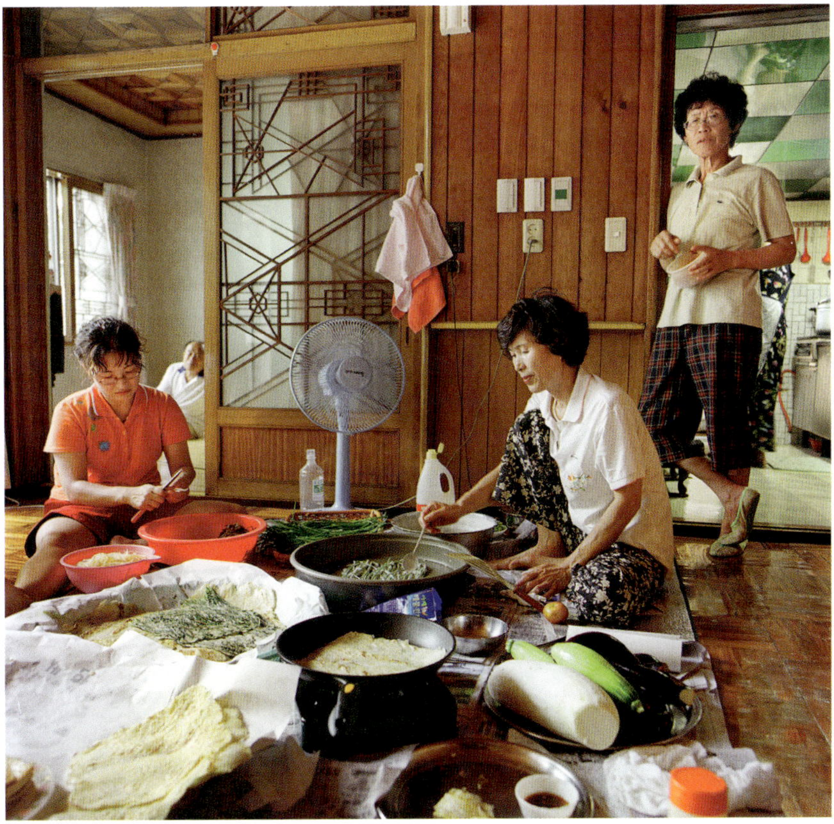

PLATE 7 Sunmin Lee, *Sunja Lee's House #2—Ancestral Rites*, from *Woman's House*, 2004, c-print. Courtesy of the artist.

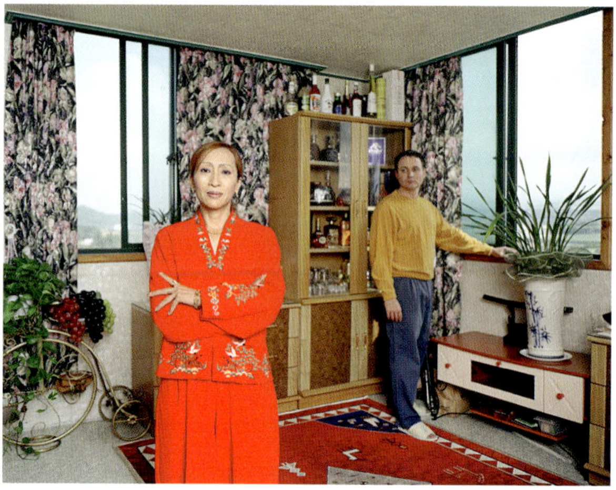

PLATE 8 Oksun Kim, *Candie and Ray*, from *Happy Together*, 2002, digital c-print, 96 × 114 cm. Courtesy of the artist.

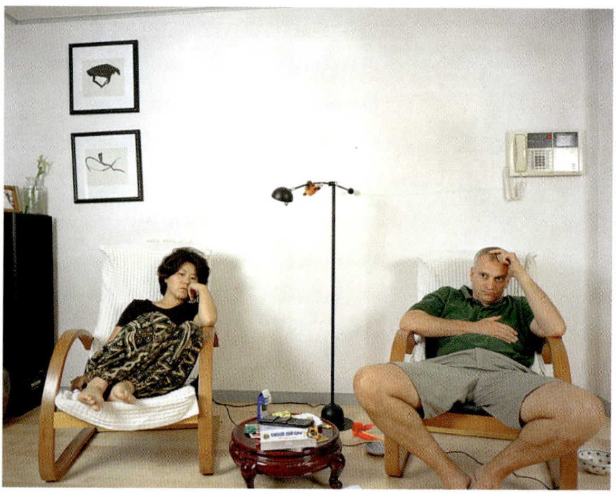

PLATE 9 Oksun Kim, *Oksun and Ralf*, from *Happy Together*, 2002, digital c-print, 96 × 114 cm. Courtesy of the artist.

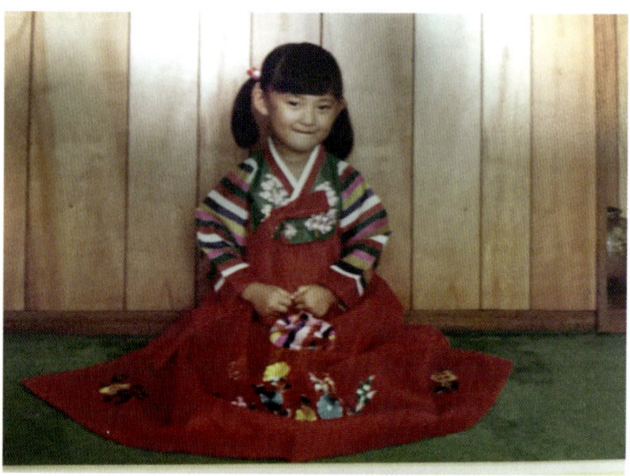

PLATE 10 Pak Lisa wearing *hanbok* at home in Sakai at age four, 1978, c-print. Courtesy of Pak Lisa.

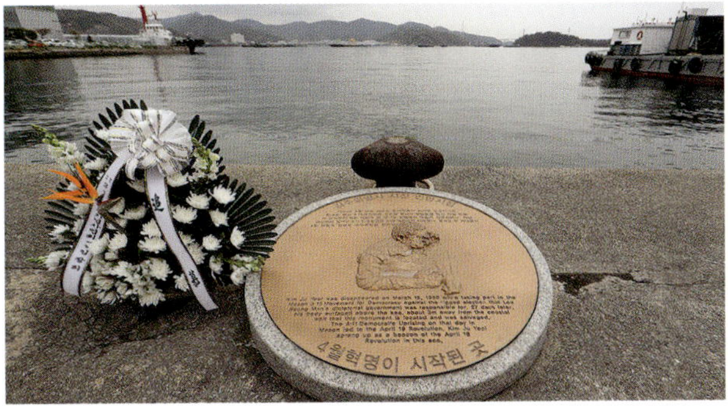

PLATE 11 Memorial plaque for the location where Kim Chuyŏl's body was found floating on April 11, 1960, 2019. Courtesy of Yonhap News.

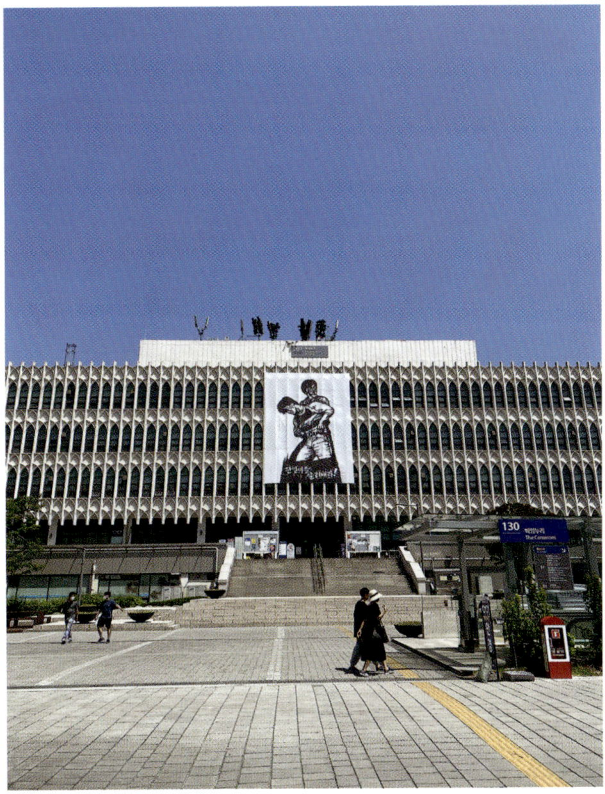

PLATE 12 Student Union Building, Yonsei University, June 2022. Photograph by the author.

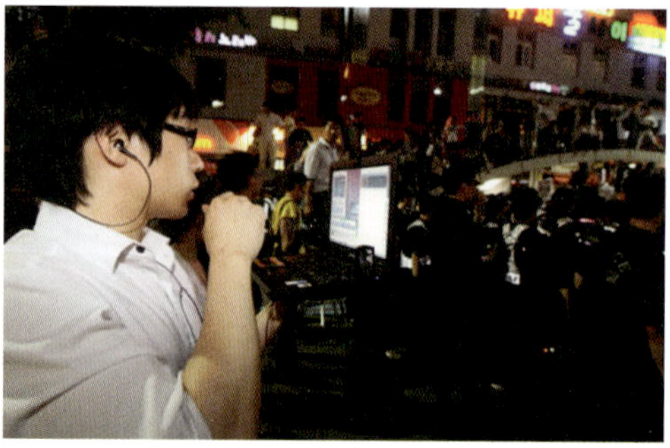

PLATE 13 An Hit'ae, a man broadcasting a candlelight vigil, Seoul, 2008. Courtesy of An Hit'ae.

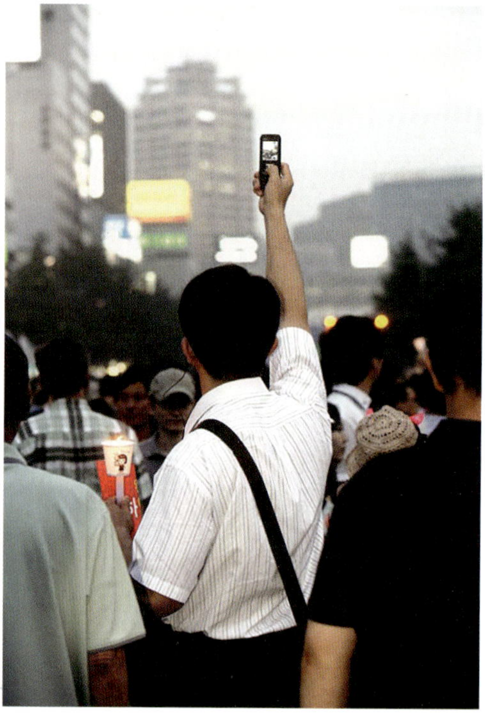

PLATE 14 A man taking a photograph with his cellular phone at the 2008 candlelight vigil, Seoul, June 2008, © dkb news.

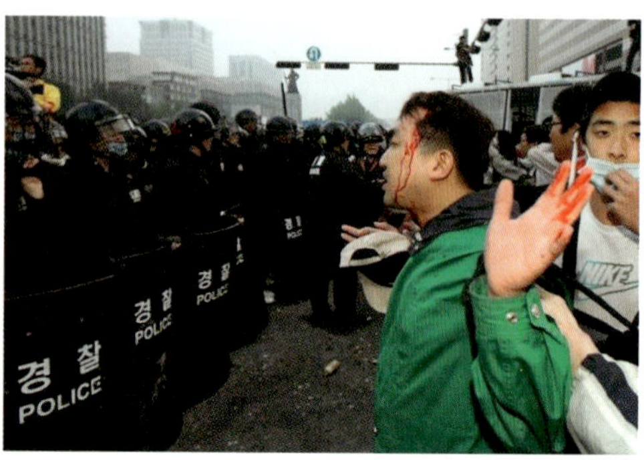

PLATE 15 Confrontation between candlelight vigil protesters and police force, Seoul, June 7, 2008, © Yeonhap News.

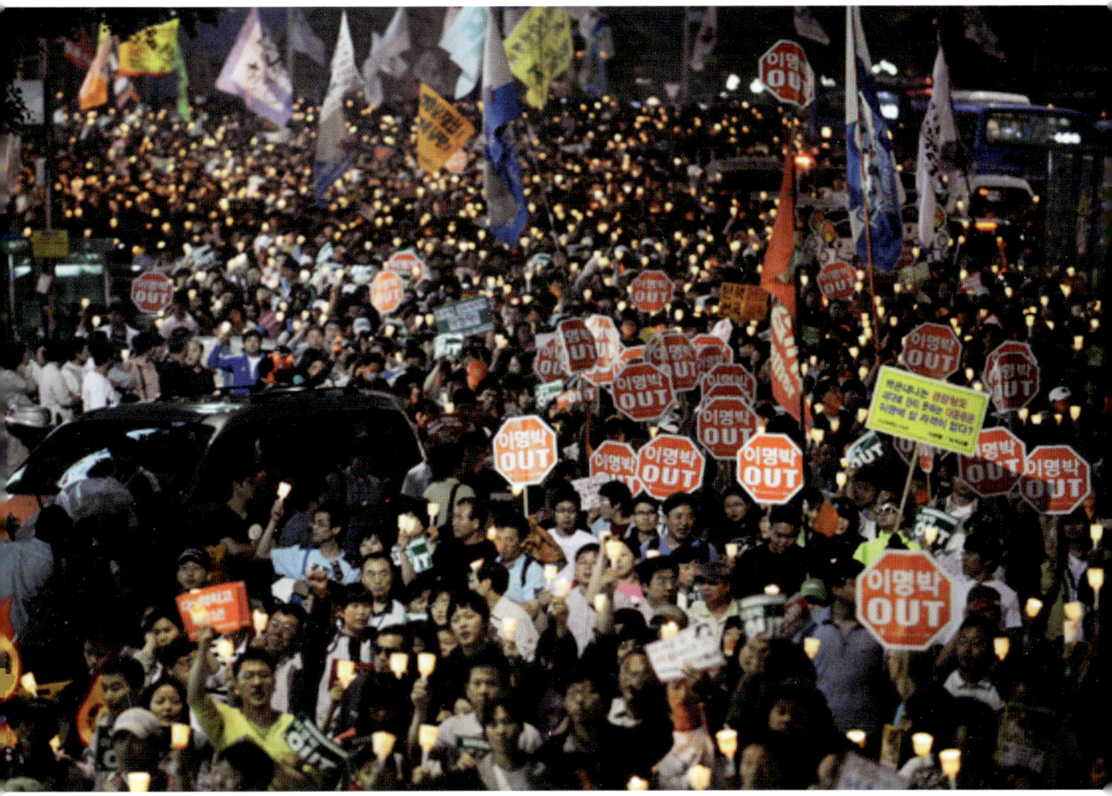

PLATE 16 Candlelight march, Seoul, June 7, 2008, © Newsis. A large crowd fills a major road, marching toward the viewer of the photograph. Most of the people are in short sleeves and hold electronic candles raised high in one hand. Others, on the right side of the photograph, hold pickets that resemble a red octagonal traffic sign, reading "Lee Myung-bak Out (이명박 Out)." There are various colorful flags raised in the middle and background above the crowd. The candlelight becomes more prominent as bright dots suffusing the background.

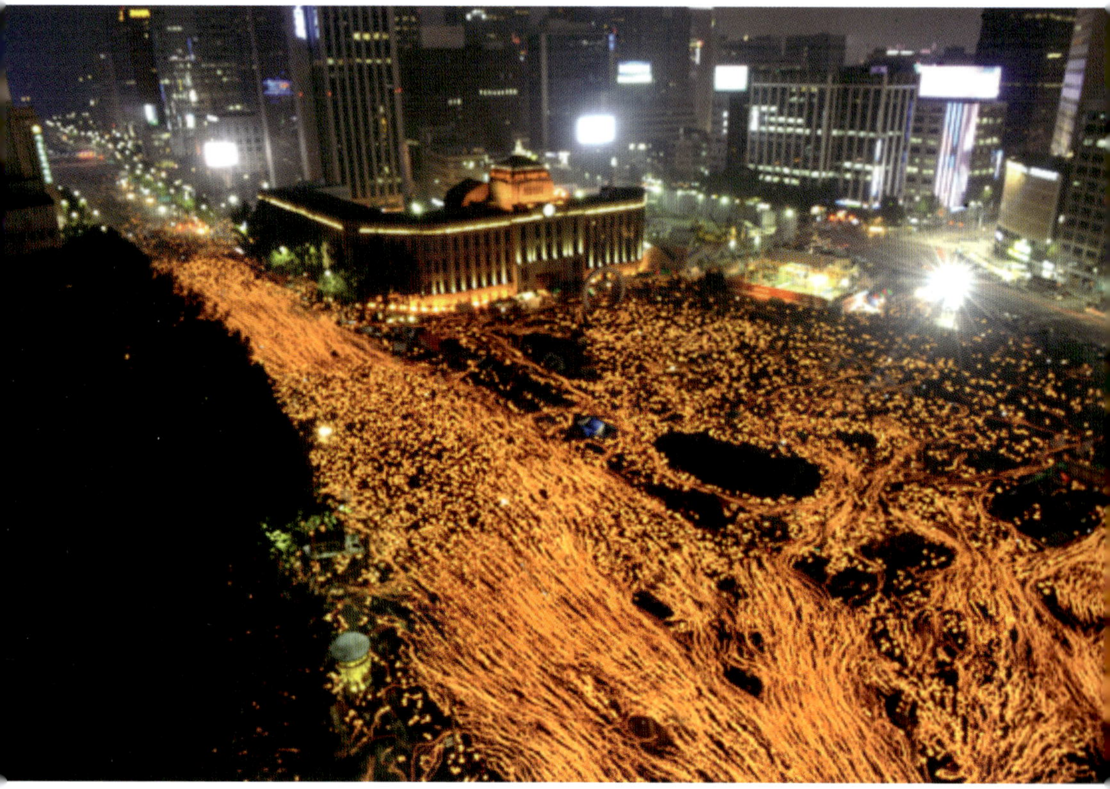

PLATE 17 Candlelight vigil and march in the city hall square, Seoul, June 7, 2008, © Newsis. The bird's-eye-view photograph, taken at night, gives a view toward the Seoul Kwangjang and the (now) old city hall building. The Seoul Kwangjang, at the right of the photograph, is filled with tiny lights—protesters holding candles—as is Sejongdaero to the left. The lights in Sejongdaero form elongated lines of lights, the result of taking the photograph with extended exposure—hence capturing the motion of the candlelight. The effect is fiery and dynamic against the dark background.

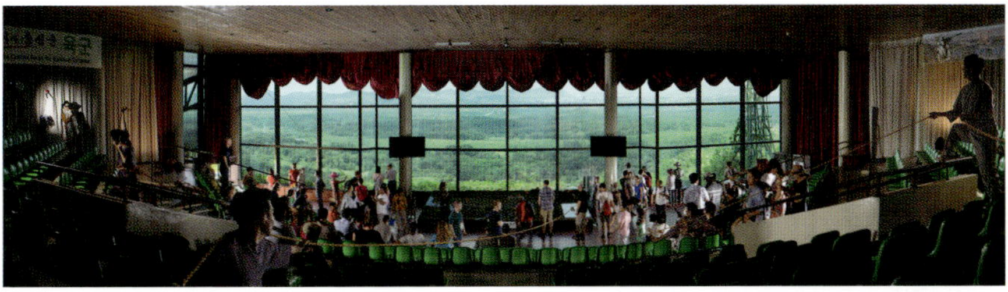

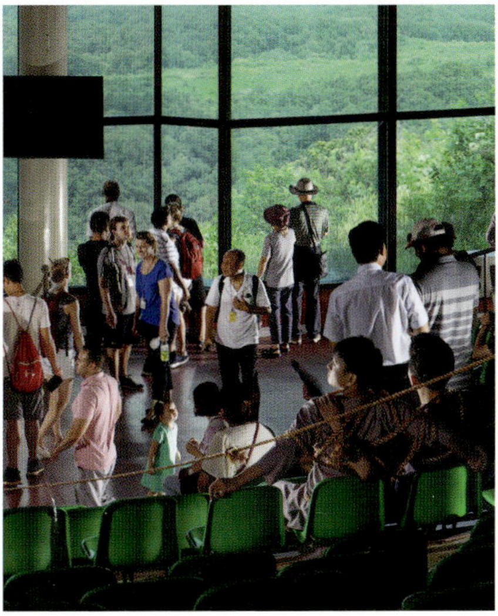

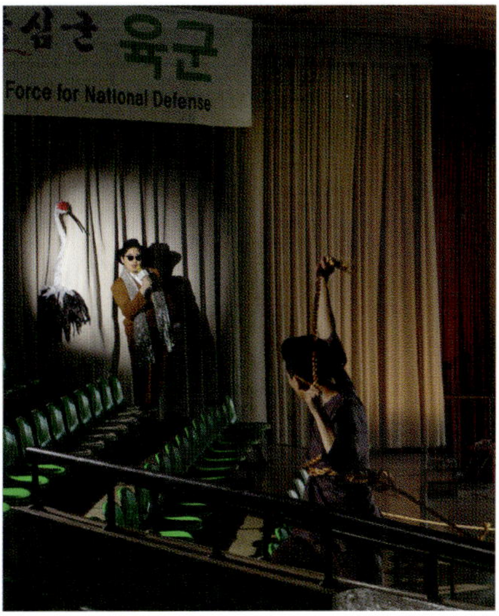

PLATE 18 (*top*) Yeondoo Jung, *DMZ Theater–Dora Theater*, 2019, solvent print and LED lightbox, 757 × 222 cm. Courtesy of the artist.

PLATE 19 (*bottom left*) Yeondoo Jung, part 2 from *DMZ Theater–Dora Theater*, 2019, c-print. Courtesy of the artist.

PLATE 20 (*bottom right*) Yeondoo Jung, part 1 from *DMZ Theater–Dora Theater*, 2019, c-print. Courtesy of the artist.

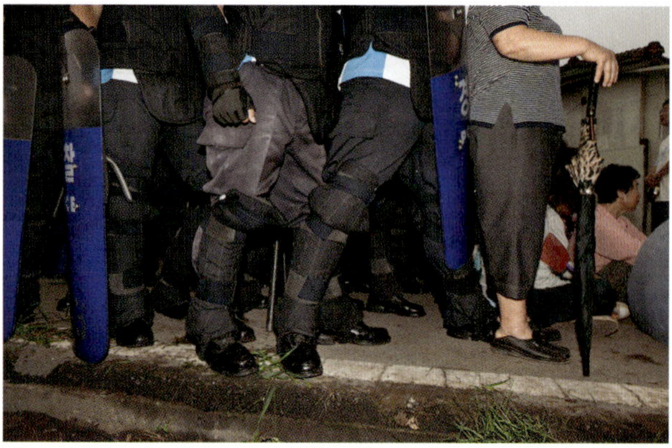

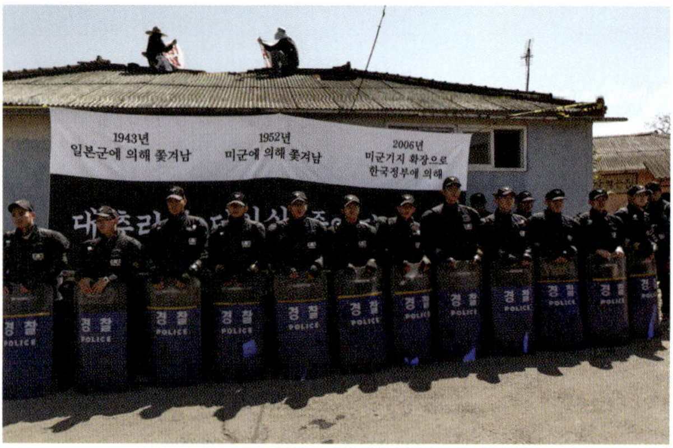

PLATE 21 (*top*) Suntag Noh, from *Noh Suntag: State of Emergency*, #BFH1001, Daechu-ri, Pyeongtaek, 2005, archival inkjet pigment print. Courtesy of the artist. A civilian woman wearing a black-and-white striped short-sleeve shirt and gray pants stands in profile and facing to the right of the photograph, holding the handle of an umbrella that she plants vertically on the ground parallel to her body. Immediately behind her are police officers in black full-armor uniform holding police shields against her back. The photograph crops out the woman's head and police officers above their chests. Next to the woman are elderly residents of Daechu-ri sitting on the ground.

PLATE 22 (*bottom*) Suntag Noh, from *Noh Suntag: State of Emergency*, #BGJ1301, Daechu-ri, Pyeongtaek, 2006, archival inkjet pigment print. Courtesy of the artist.

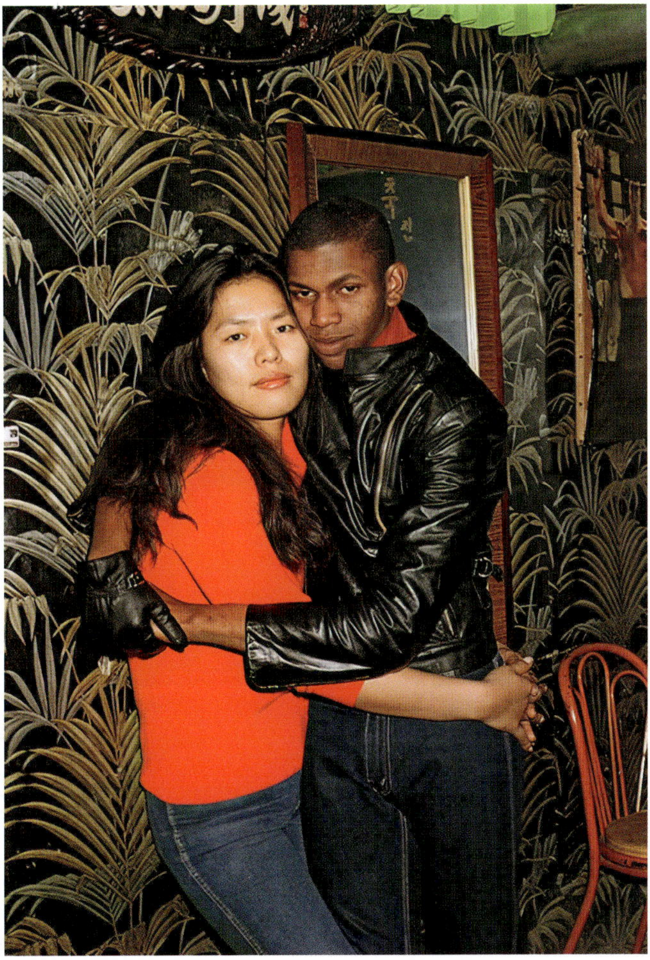

PLATE 23 Yong Suk Kang, from *Tong-duch'ŏn Kinyŏmsajin*, 1984, c-print. Courtesy of the artist.

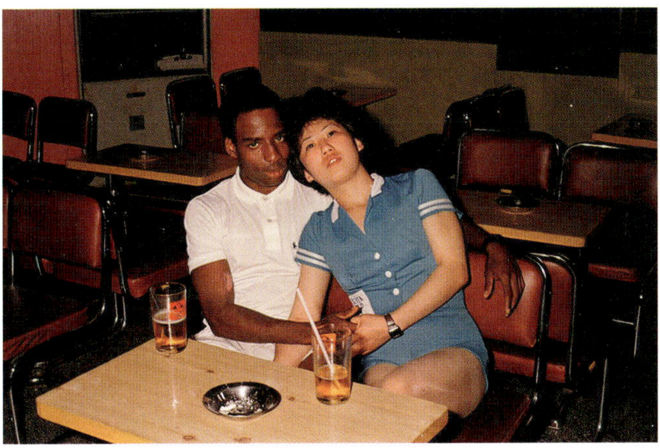

PLATE 24 Yong Suk Kang, from *Tong-duch'ŏn Kinyŏmsajin*, 1984, c-print. Courtesy of the artist.

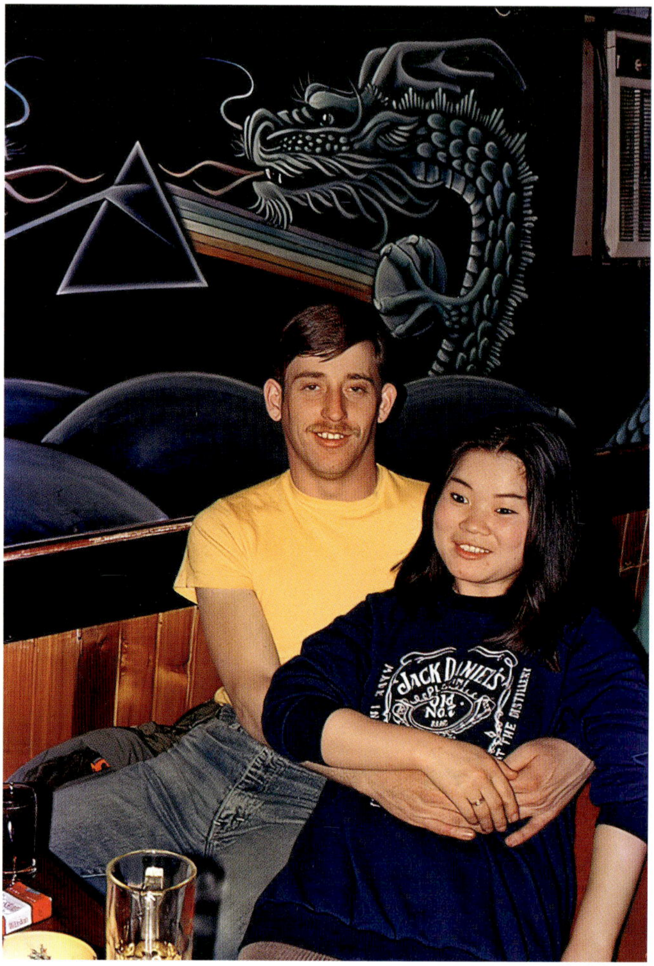
JACK DANIEL'S

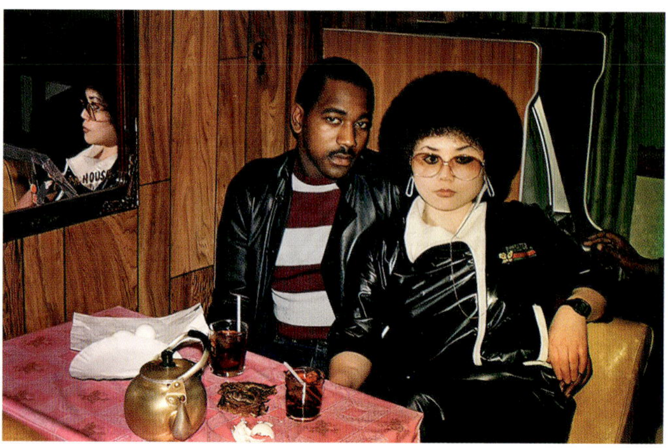

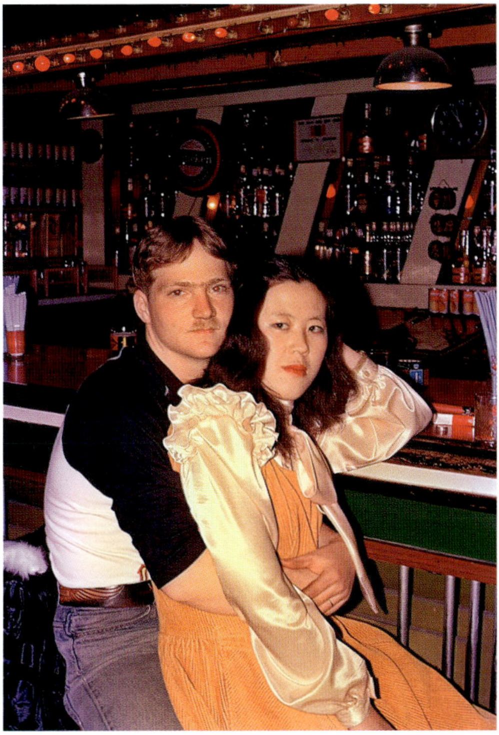

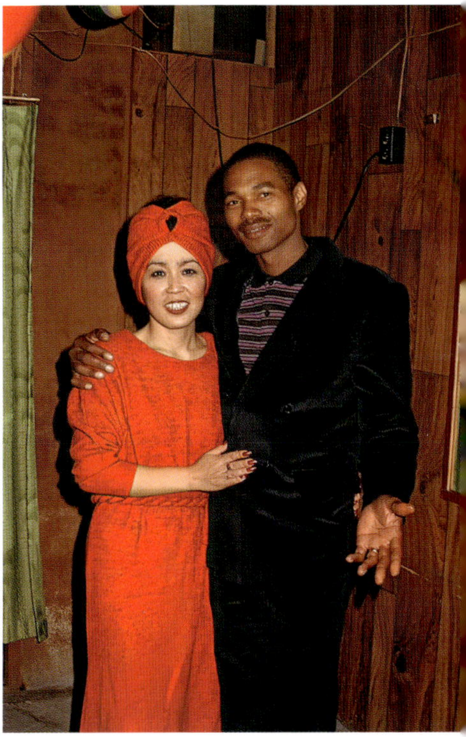

PLATES 25–28 Yong Suk Kang, from *Tongduch'ŏn Kinyŏmsajin*, 1984, c-print. Courtesy of the artist.

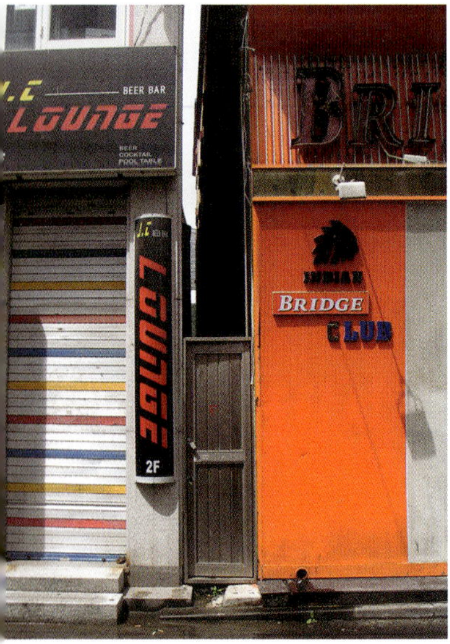

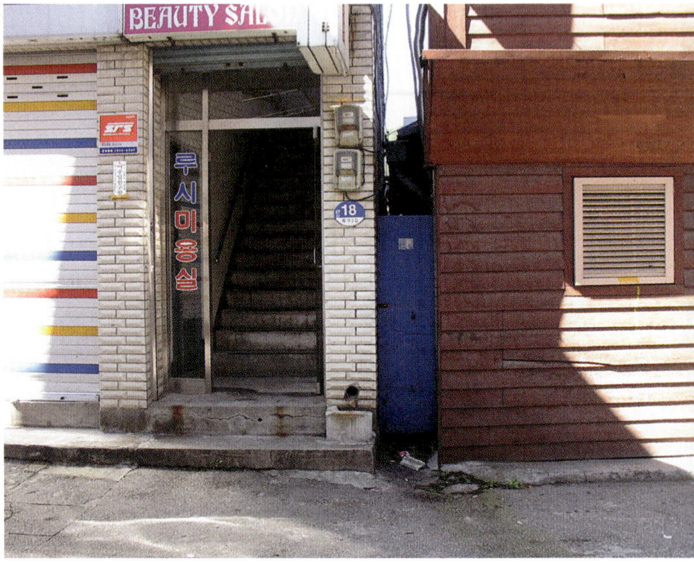

PLATE 29 (*left*) siren eun young jung, document image for *Narrow Sorrow* photo series, 2006–2009, digital image. Courtesy of the artist. In the center of the photograph, a very small and short aluminum door appears to be squeezed between two buildings. On the right is an orange-colored facade with signage for the Bridge Club bar in orange, white, and blue. Above the signage is a stylized black silhouette of an Indigenous chief wearing a headdress; below it reads "INDIAN." The tiny space between the buildings is especially notable in reference to the entrance to the left of the door, which leads into a building and stairs to a bar, with signage reading "J.C LOUNGE 2F" in yellow, red, black, and white. A metal shutter with alternating stripes of silver, red, blue, yellow, and red is drawn at the entrance.

PLATE 30 (*right*) siren eun young jung, document image for *Narrow Sorrow* photo series, 2006–2009, digital image. Courtesy of the artist.

South Korean project centers on the geopolitical and cultural conditions of the DMZ and the adjacent military and civilian areas to the south. In addition, the *RDP* has brought attention to the ways in which the DMZ has also become a symbol of ecological sanctuary and peace[8]—values oddly juxtaposed with the continued tensions between the two Koreas, and, to use Jinah Kim's phrase, the afterlives of the Pacific wars.[9] DMZ tourism, especially focusing on the ecology of the site, has expanded in the past decade, although tourists can only visit designated landmarks and tourist sites close to the Civilian Control Line. Quite often, when people refer to the DMZ—as in DMZ tourism, research in the DMZ, and photographs of the DMZ (including the *Real DMZ Project*)—they likely mean locations near the DMZ, or the Joint Security Area, which is indeed a special area within the DMZ, not the unpeopled forests or land-mine-laden areas inside the demarcation lines on either side.[10]

The state-led revenue-generating projects near the DMZ include ecotourism and art and architectural projects. According to Suk-Young Kim, the DMZ area has become a popular tourist destination precisely because of "the fact that the zone itself cannot be accessed for mass tourism."[11] Other recent developments include shopping malls and amusement rides as part of tourist attractions, which, as Kim states, "link the sites of national trauma more directly to the conventional tourist sites where consumption—whether labeled pleasurable or profane—is not only encouraged but also a foundational goal."[12] The DMZ has thus become a much anticipated theater of peace, where national trauma blends with consumptive desires.[13]

The *RDP* is a key artistic exploration of the DMZ and its adjacent civilian areas. Initiated in 2011, the project began with a group of South Korean scholars, art administrators, and curators visiting the Civilian Control Zone of Cheorwon County just below the 38th parallel. Originally consisting of an exhibition and organized "National Security Tours" and later expanding to incorporate workshops, conferences, and residency programs, the project sought to initiate dialogues between artists, scholars, curators, and students, thereby promoting a network for international collaborations on artistic and ecological projects based in the Cheorwon area. The *RDP* committee invited artists and critics from abroad to participate in talks, workshops, and exhibitions, and to explore landmarks near the South Korean side of the demilitarized zone such as the DMZ Peace Culture Park and Cheorwon Peace Observatory, as well as adjacent towns. These collaborations have continued annually as site-specific installations, artists' talks, workshops, and an exhibition with a catalog that records the year's activities.

The initial years of the *RDP* focused on the organization of group tours to the DMZ and security sites. These tours had three main purposes: to educate outsiders on what the DMZ is "really" like, to promote visits to local exhibitions and site installations, and to introduce the artistic collaborators to the local communities and locations for their site-specific projects. As the years went by, however, it became clear that the *RDP*'s exhibitions and catalogs were also becoming about finding ways to archive its work in "real" time.

The *RDP* has been archiving each year's activities, including art installations, exhibitions, conferences, workshops, and publications making them available online as well.[14] From March to May and from June to July in 2019, a retrospective exhibition giving an overview of the past eight years of the *RDP*, titled *DMZ*, opened at the Culture Station Seoul 284 museum with the English tagline "*DMZ* seeks to explore the art's ongoing value aiming to consider what the DMZ really is and what it is going to be in the future." In many ways, this retrospective exhibition's archival displays were aimed at rejuvenating the project, and, with the repeated articulations of what the project is about and what it does, reminding the audience of its ongoing nature, vis-à-vis the various geopolitical turns taken in the Asia-Pacific since 2016—particularly the rapidly changing tone of communication between the North and South, and between North Korea and the United States.

Considered alongside the repetition of commemorative events, including the Korean War anniversaries, the project's repetitions of itself are a curious phenomenon.[15] Observing its annual iterations, the project's encouragement of public and private interest in (and efforts emphasizing the ecological and aesthetic values of) the DMZ apparently becomes less about positioning the "real" demilitarized zone as a capital-generating site and place of peacemaking. Rather, it is becoming a site for its own struggle with the temporality of national (art) history. The ongoing *Real DMZ Project* is both an attempt to remember the DMZ and a critique of the current methods of doing so.

By contextualizing the *Real DMZ Project* as a live archive in the making—building and dismantling memories as it collects—we can rethink the "real" in this practice of remembering South Korea's militarized history, partly through the Lacanian concept of the "Real" applied to repetitions in visual art and partly alongside the "unreal" norms of transnational militarism as the condition of colonial and neocolonial legacies. The temporalities of repetitions expose the violence of modernization—in this case, in the writing of (art) history itself—as a national project.

In the 2013 exhibition catalogue of the *RDP*, Sunjung Kim, the founding artistic director of the *RDP* and former director of Art Sonje Center, states:

> The Civilian Control Line lies within an area that is ten kilometers south of the military demarcation line, defining a space that the public is prohibited from entering. The discrete psychological and physical separations between the inside and the outside of the line have created distances and hierarchies that are for the most part *invisible*. In addition to these borderlines, the separate roles taken by each part of society—the military, the government, and the civilians—have further entrenched ideological divides in amongst the citizens of South Korea, where different attitudes and emotions continue to play out in regards to Korea's separation.[16]

This introduction to the 2013 events was largely a repetition of the 2012 promotional material, and it was reiterated pretty much every year thereafter. The introduction made it clear that the project aims to expose the real DMZ by making what is invisible visible, remembering what has been forgotten, and ultimately, replacing the unreal DMZ—what the organizers believe is the commonly known DMZ—with the *real* DMZ through their art projects redefining it. Kim continues: "In adapting themselves to the circumstances of this ongoing and unresolved war, Koreans seem to have been trying to forget this border. Perhaps this is because they have been educated to forget the cease-fire, or the confrontations that have been connected to the military demarcation line, or because they have buried and repressed such memories away in the unconscious, in spite of the fact that renewed conflicts continually rise to the surface under pressure from various political agendas."[17]

According to Kim, the real border has been made invisible by the Korean unconscious swept up in the politics of memory. As if to counter this invisibility and forgetting, the *RDP* continuously repeats facts about the DMZ and their mission in their publicity materials for each new slate of annual events. In this way, while the project aims to expose the "real" history of the DMZ, a drive that David Eng describes as "the repetition compulsion of history—the continual political rehearsal of history as the way-it-really was"—the *RDP*'s practice of remembering through obsessive repetition begins to complicate, if not challenge, their own positivist desire for the revelation of the real.[18]

Examining Andy Warhol's compulsive repetitions of photographs depicting macabre scenes in his *Death in America* series, Hal Foster finds that trauma is central to the subsequent realist turn—what Foster calls the superrealist—in post-pop art in the United States.[19] The Lacanian notions of the unconscious and repetition compulsion are central to his argument that the real cannot be represented, but only be repeated. Repetition is not reproduction, Foster states, "in the sense of representation (of a referent) or simulation (of a pure image, a detached signifier). Rather, repetition serves to *screen* the real understood as traumatic."[20] Here, Foster's "screening" references Freud's concept of screen memories—that memories about childhood can be distorted to protect oneself from the traumatic experience—while also punning on Warhol's medium of choice, silk-screen printing, that repeatedly "screens" the photographic images of *Death in America* onto the surface of the canvas. For Foster, therefore, the Warholian image's excessive illusionism appears "anxious to cover up a *trou*matic real" (*trou* meaning a hole or gap in French) that is the missed encounter with the real, while it "cannot help but indicate this real as well"—a paradox he sees in superrealist art.[21]

If repetition cannot represent the "really real real," but only anxiously attempt to cover up the traumatic real, then what the *RDP* has done over the years in its repetitions cannot reveal the "real" DMZ.[22] All the viewer sees is the *screen*, the traumatic real in both the Freudian and Warholian senses. The DMZ in the *Real DMZ Project* is a missed encounter. Because the repeated representations of the DMZ cannot represent the real, the repetitions instead become a refusal of the functioning as a positivist production of knowledge.

Foster's analysis of the turn to the traumatic in visual culture offers one way to examine the anxiously self-historicizing *Real DMZ Project*. Nevertheless, the live archiving and ongoing repetitions of the *RDP* do more than reveal the trauma discourse in art.[23] In the introduction to the *RDP*'s 2019 exhibitions, the organizers write that they want to remember the present by conjuring the future—in this case, a future toward peace, and possibly reunification: "While the future of Korea is still mired in uncertainty, we are united in our wish for peace and a new life along the border and beyond it as well. We hope *DMZ* [the exhibition] will provide a meaningful time and space for visitors to reconsider the division and reflect on the Korean border's past, present, and future."[24] Put differently, the "real" in the *Real DMZ Project* is no longer just about the *revelation* of the real in a modernist sense, but the *enactable* possibility of the multitemporal—in remembering the DMZ in the present and imagining the futurity of a new life in peaceful unity. Here, the past of the DMZ remembered is projectional, even as *RDP*'s repetitions seem to slow down; what it slows down is not its futurity but "the linear, progressive time of modernity to reveal its gestures, its *tempi*."[25] As such, the anxious repetitions of the *RDP*'s information about the DMZ, the project's history, and its mission disrupt the temporal linearity expected in the writing of (art) history: that time is a universally experienced phenomenon.

To repeat (tongue in cheek) Bliss Cua Lim, "Modern time [is] projected in every direction to include even what exists outside of prior to its minting as a concept, entertaining an 'ideal of objectivity,' a belief that its conception of history is the 'overarching language,' the universal narrative to which all specific instances can be subsumed."[26] The history of the DMZ as something that can be revealed and made truthful—an "ideal of objectivity," as stated in the mission of the *RDP*—follows this insistence on the homogenizing temporality of modern time. Such temporal linearity has always grounded ethno-nationalist-masculinist approaches to history in South Korea. These approaches treat the present as indebted to the past, particularly in the civilian political struggles against the military regime, while the present also constantly needs to undo the wrongs of the past and do better (repeating the developmentalist ideology) by, for example, revealing the real. Temporality in the *RDP*'s repetitions of the traumatic real, however, complicates such linearity.[27] The *RDP*'s repetitions discombobulate the timeline of the truthful revelation. The traumatic real returns as bouts that disrupt the developmentalist, ethno-nationalist-masculinist, and neoliberal historicization of the DMZ, as the neoliberal timeline has set its path toward future developments in the name of reconciliation, reparation, and ecological preservation.

Of course, for many, this repetition can be a frustration—a symptom of the frustratingly stalemated peace talks between the Koreas and the United States.[28] If the *RDP*'s repetition represents this continued Cold War standoff, do multimillion-dollar state-funded architectural projects and peace festivals represent, let alone encourage, peace in the region? Suppose they did—whose peace will it be? And who maintains this peace, as it is defined by neoliberalism vis-à-vis ethno-nationalism, in the rhetorical absence, yet physical proximity of, North Korea and its imminent threat to national security in the rhetoric of peace?

The *RDP* is a project unlike others because it tries to remember a present (the state of the division, the borders, and the life under the division) which cannot be represented by reproducing the past. After all, the DMZ is unapproachable by civilians, including the *RDP* organizers and most participating artists, thus remaining—quite literally—a missed encounter; it cannot and will not represent the real of the DMZ. Rather, the project undoes "the borders" of the timeline, the ideology of the developmentalist future-driven present. The undoing of such timeline indeed enables the annual project's repetition in difference and the multispatiality of the artistic iteration-enunciation. Such repetition in difference, and the deterritorialization of the post and neocolonial history, could be seen in *RDP*'s recent repetition in the collaboration with the NIROX Sculpture Park in Krugersdorp, South Africa, where *RDP*'s 2021 outdoor exhibition *Margins of Error* was shown.[29] In his analysis of postcolonial Caribbean literature, Homi Bhabha posits that repetition's focus shifts from "the nominalism of linguistic imperialism to the emergence of another history of the sign. It is another destiny of culture as a site—one based not simply on subversion and transgression, but on the prefiguration of a kind of solidarity between ethnicities that meet the tryst of colonial history."[30] The DMZ, embodied in the sculptural installations, has now travelled all the way to another continent, metaphorically and physically representing *RDP*'s existence outside of the DMZ. This internationality is not a subversive attempt to report on the prolonged war and militarism, but the RDP's "DMZ diplomacy" backed by public sponsorships of the Korean Foundation for International Cultural Exchange and the ROK embassy in South Africa, resulting in, perhaps inadvertently again, a forging of a relationship in the postcoloniality of incommensurable spatiotemporality—the place of decolonial utterance—in South Africa.[31]

"Life on the Border"

Similar approaches to the "real" of the DMZ, as a site to be revealed, can be found in the South Korean exhibition at the 2014 Venice Architecture Biennale, titled *Crow's Eye View: The Korean Peninsula*. The 38th parallel that divides North and South Korea has been understood to function under three typologies of borders: land (the DMZ), river (the Han River Estuary), and open waters (of the West Sea). But in her article for the exhibition catalog, "Korean Borders: Real to Imagined," Yehre Suh argues that "real" physical borders are malleable and fluid.[32] As the title indicates, Suh's essay is an attempt to expose the real Korean border as "an active site of interpretation and negotiation." She concludes that "this unique yet unavoidable anomaly in the middle of the disputed territories reveals imaginative possibilities of the 'real' border. The collaborative discussions of governance and maintenance of ecological environments that no longer pertain to definitive, predetermined boundaries, invoke alternative methods of co-habitation and collaborative management."[33] The invocation of future cohabitation and collaboration in the DMZ is alluring; but what could such alternative methods be? What would cohabitation and collaborative management mean for the residents living in and around the borders, real and imagined?[34]

In 2019, the *Real DMZ Project* exhibition partly tried to answer the questions by picturing life near the DMZ. "Section C" of the *RDP* exhibition was devoted to photographs of "Life in the DMZ and Border Areas: Soldiers, Residents." Photographs in the first half of the section depicted conscripts, many from the Army Photographic Archive (figure 5.2), and works by frequent *RDP* participants Suntag Noh and Heinkuhn Oh. Chongwoo Park's photographs and video work, which he obtained permission to film from the South Korean side in 2015, shows the North Korean guard posts inside the DMZ.

The second part of "Life in the DMZ," "Village Residents and Life on the Border," presented images from the photographic archives of the municipalities of Yangji-ri and Daeseong-dong, the so-called *minbuk* villages, as well as from residents' personal collections.[35] Even as the exhibition dichotomizes the life near the DMZ into that of the conscripts and civilians, it also tries to emphasize their codependency, in contradiction to how the media has portrayed the residents as either victims of the military complex or opportunists leaching off of conscripts.[36] But most critically, their cohabitation and collaborative management are imagined and imaged by viewers outside of the villages, while the viewers themselves are absent in this picture of cohabitation. What, then, does cohabitation mean?

To consider this question, it must be remembered that the return of the traumatic real does not discriminate against the sites of transnational militarism. While cultural events such as film festivals, musical concerts, and art projects have promoted public interest in the DMZ, camptowns throughout the country have long been neglected and forgotten in the collective consciousness, as examined in the following chapter. The camptowns west of Cheorwon, especially, have been affected by the massive relocation of former US military bases to Pyeongtaek. Prior to the *Real DMZ Project*, art projects such as the *Tongduch'ŏn P'ŭrochekt'ŭ* (*Dongducheon Project*) focused on the camptown hosting and serving United States Forces Korea (USFK) base camps as a critical site of the transnational militarism in a period of dramatic decline. Thus, it is critical to consider the works here in relation to photographs of camptowns and former camptowns.[37] While representations of camptowns near the DMZ have been used to signify national tragedy in the past, the DMZ, increasingly, has represented the global interests in ecological

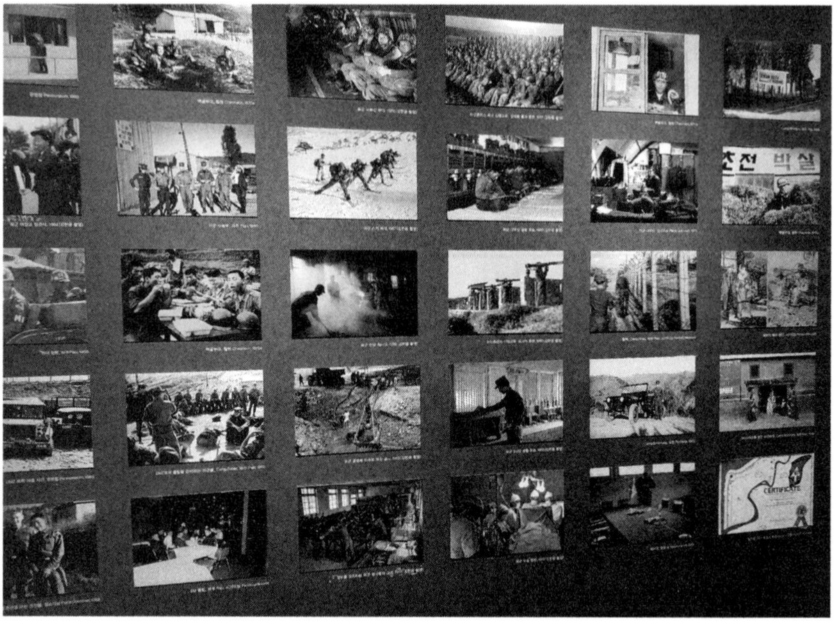

FIGURE 5.2 Installation view, Section C, *DMZ*, Culture Station Seoul 284, June 2019.

preservation and peace. At the same time, even as the DMZ undergoes rehabilitation and resignification, the stereotypical media portrayals of camptowns continue to alienate them from the rest of the country, especially in the age of successive "K-culture" booms.

The life of cohabitation and unity may be reimagined beyond the sites of the National Security Tour in Cheorwon, art spaces in Seoul, and international venues where individual works and recent *RDP* exhibitions have been organized, as perhaps *RDP* being the most successful project of its kind in continuation. In hopes of locating the DMZ together with other sites of transnational militarism (i.e., camptowns) in this future of cohabitation, I ask: If civilian-military and interspecies cohabitation is the ideal future of the DMZ, where are camptowns in this future? Does this cohabitation include or exclude civilians and the service members of both the Republic of Korea Armed Forces and USFK? Where are the places of affect—especially of kinship or other intimate, sometimes violent, relationships between civilians and service members? The questions linger in repetition.

The Compulsion to Repeat: *The DMZ Theater*

The concept of repetition was recently on the mind of the curatorial team at the Seoul Museum of Art (SeMA). The museum organized an exhibition, *Kangbak²* (*Compulsion to Repeat* or *Compulsion²*). The exhibition "explores how compulsion operates within the complexity of the capitalist system and emancipatory potentials . . . [and] highlights the repetitive trait of compulsion while pointing to the very repetitiveness as a potential of overcoming it. A way out of compulsion lies not on the outside—violation of the norm or inauguration of alternatives—but on the inside. The drive to repeat oneself within the habitual compulsion, or the 'compulsion of compulsion' is the strategy of artistic appropriation that runs through the exhibition."[38] Thematizing the compulsion to repeat as strategies of "artistic appropriation," nine artists were selected for the exhibition, including Yeondoo Jung (b. 1969), who is known for his photographs exploring the imaginative performativity of everyday. His DMZ *Theater–Dora Theater* (2019) was shown (plate 18).

Jung visited sites near the DMZ between 2017 and 2019. In collaboration with the producer Surya, he created works at peace observatories in thirteen locations near the border. The DMZ *Theater–Dora Theater* depicts the interior of the Dora Observatory located at the peak of the Dora Mountain in Paju, close to P'anmunjŏm. The scenery, like the genre of history painting, unfolds from the cascading plastic-cast seats in the foreground, where a couple of men are playing tug-of-war, to the middle ground of bright green seats, down to the ground level where foreign visitors appear, and finally to the unending, varying shades of greens beyond the grills of the glass panels in the observatory.

Some of the people in the theater, who look like members of a theatrical troupe, appear oddly rigid and obviously conscious of the photo shoot, others seemingly oblivious (plates 19 and 20). In fact, the work is a composite of panoramic multiexposure shots that include the same figures multiple times. Near the wall in SeMA on which this panoramic image hangs, albums of photographs document how the piece was made, in the style of a film journal (figure 5.3). The 752 × 222 cm solvent print lies on an LED lightbox, accentuating the theater-like scenery of the photograph (figure 5.4).

For those who have visited any South Korean peace observatories, the space appears familiar; except for the mismatched movements of the subjects, the interior view of the Dora Observatory is a lot like that of the Cheorwon

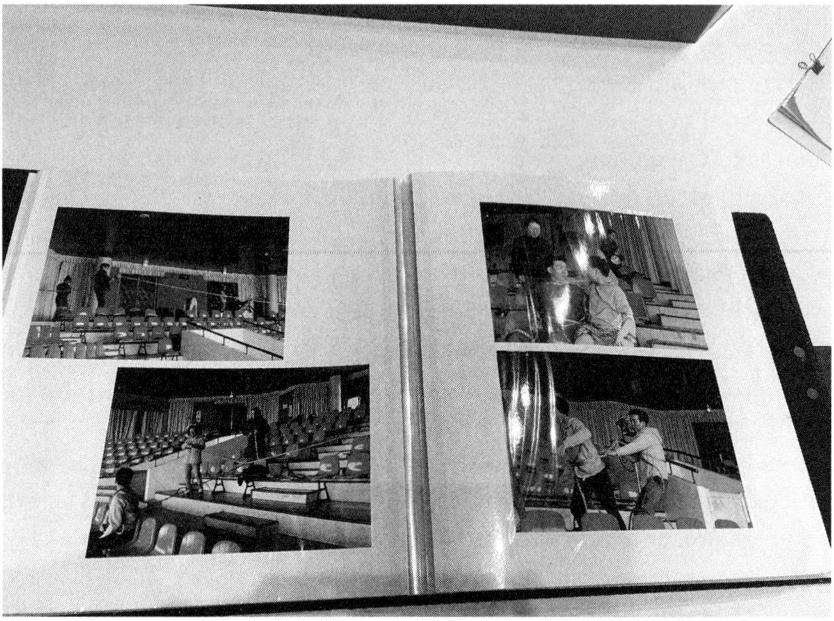

FIGURE 5.3 Yeondoo Jung, installation view of *DMZ Theater–Dora Theater* photo albums, 2019. Seoul Museum of Art, January 2020. Photograph by author.

Peace Observatory, which I have visited. Jung is known for his photographic works blurring the line between fiction and truth, with a focus on performative aspects of the everyday and identity making.[39] But rather than overlapping, or creating a hazy space between, fiction and truth, the *DMZ Theater* series is a work of performance that problematizes the site's historically militarized conditions and the ways in which the site has always required the visitor to perform their ideological position when facing the DMZ—and North Korea. The Dora Observatory is a theater that obligates the visitor to associate or identify the DMZ with an ethno-nationalist ideation of peace, seeing ethno-nationalism as the only viable power-yielding paradigm of the nation to survive, sustain, and thrive in the fraught geopolitical situation of and between Northeast Asia and the United States.[40]

In peace observatories, a prerecorded audio guide plays as tour groups enter the space, summarizing the national tragedy—the war—and postwar conflicts in the DMZ and insisting that this rich green ecological sanctuary dotted by heavily armed guard posts (many supposedly taken down after the September 2018 North-South summit meeting) is a representation of peace

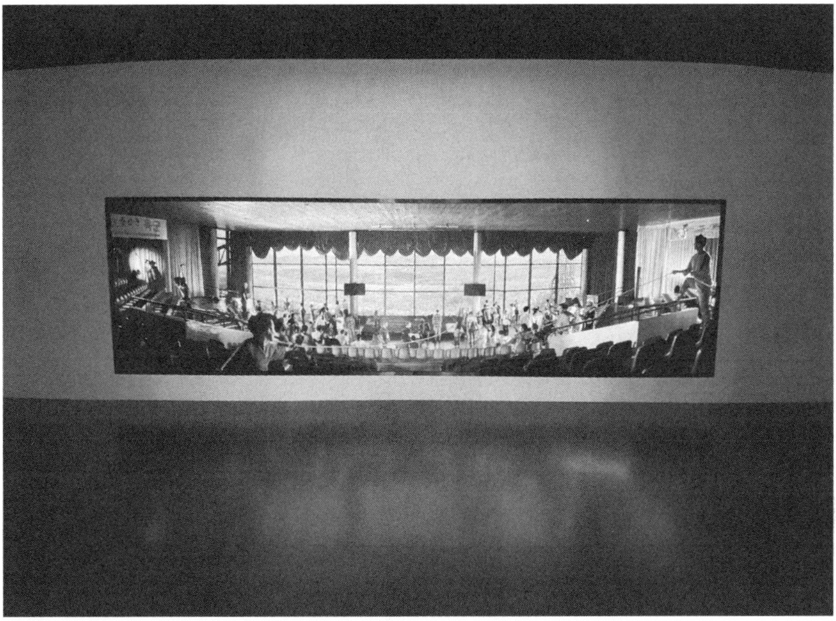

FIGURE 5.4 Yeondoo Jung, installation view of *DMZ Theater–Dora Theater*, 2019. Solvent print and LED lightbox, 757 × 222 cm. Seoul Museum of Art, January 2020. Photograph by author.

to come.[41] The multiple observatories located along the DMZ are steeped in the didactics of ideology, one which, according to the SeMA curatorial team, South Koreans find normalcy within—"the structure of the collective unconsciousness at work."[42] With its fantastical reconstructions of the DMZ observatories, the *DMZ Theater* series messes up the timeline didactically preserved and ideologically performed in these spaces.

The compulsive repetition of this "Theater of Peace" along the DMZ is a "Theater of Repetition." The SeMA states that "Repetition is the only move that could open up a gap within the compulsion of the era, and a critical element of art as a compulsive act." However, they also admit that it is not the repetition but the pause in it that provides a moment for reflection and artistic exploration: "When repetition that produces difference puts a stop to meaning, the repetition's potential [for] rupturing meaning is found. If art has the potential to interrupt the obsession with meaning, an artwork that appropriates the mechanism of compulsion in terms of content and form could act as a compulsion that is disruptive to its own. The moment of pause is the very ground for skepticism that allows a reflection on life as well as a time to image the outside from the inside without restraint."[43] If what they mean by this pause is a rupture to the everyday repetition they see as compulsion-driven acts, it is worth noting that "pause" is not the title and main subject of the exhibition—"compulsion" is.

Perhaps pause itself is part of the compulsion if we apply SeMA's concept of repetitions and pause to geopolitical events. Were the unusually optimistic peace talks between North and South Korea and between the United States and North Korea in 2018 a pause of the Korean conflict and its corresponding legacy of Cold War frictions in the Asia-Pacific? If so, what about the usual disappointments that followed the talks, which quickly turned cold and intensified public distrust? Living these familiar repetitions and occasional ruptures (pauses), the anticipation of sudden turnover and desensitization to the need for "real" ruptures become part of the realpolitik of repetition. Where, then, do the repetitive ruptures take us?[44]

While repetition may feel increasingly futile, it may also have been one of the things that keeps the DMZ from turning even further into a fetishized theater of peace, one directed by an amalgam of capital, ethno-nationalism, and state ideology, while delaying rapid, neoliberal development propped up by the allure of green consumerism. The indeterminacy of change through repetitions is not particularly welcome by those that seek empirical evidence of advancement. The local residents have also been waiting for years while their patience is wearing thin. But it may be necessary for reimagining the cohabitation of many, and different, lives in Korea and the Asia-Pacific. The process of this reimagining includes our affective responses to the indeterminacy of change and, as Bhabha saliently puts it, to "transform the temporal medium through which we interpret the world and act upon it."[45]

As such, Jung's *Dora Theater* brings temporal disjuncture to the historization of the DMZ, displacing the visitor or viewer from the compulsorily ideological theater of peace, into an indeterminacy through which they encounter their own "fear, ambivalence, terror, shame, disorientation, or dispossession . . . with an imminent sense of sensory and bodily attentiveness to the task of change."[46] The temporalities of change, therefore, cannot be sensed without personal involvement in this indeterminacy of change. The measure of temporality in the theater of peace in contingent and indeterminate circumstances demands one's affective unlearning of the DMZ as inscribed in the road map of ethno-national advancement and projection. "Affect is the acute measure of the *time* change takes—in particular, the temporalities of transition or transience."[47] The (re)sensing of the DMZ in *Dora Theater*, for example, initiates this affective measure of the time change takes, and does so differently than the imminent futility of repetitions that the teleology of advancement brings—such as real estate redevelopment of former camptowns into gentrified, consumer-inviting theme parks. The multitemporal scenes in *Dora Theater* dramatize the strangeness of the DMZ's temporality, unable to move forward in the future of peace. Jung's collaborative performances based on local histories and myths and the subsequent composite photographs turn the theater of state-led performances into a place of reconnection with its local histories and people. In these collaborations, the theater of repetition may finally be imbued with reparative potentials.

Expropriation, Repetition, and the Photographic Reverberation

Sensing the photography of everyday militarism involves the possibility of the kind of historical ruptures discussed above and realized in the works discussed in this section, exploring the affect of reverberation (and thus repetition) in the experience of photographs by Yong Suk Kang (b. 1958) and Suntag Noh (b. 1971). The landscape of militarism is the key visual and conceptual methodology shared by Kang and Noh. Although they take dissimilar approaches to exploring that landscape, their photographs are fundamentally about the conflicts between the army bases and towns and the position and acts of the state in these conflicts. Their work on expropriated landscapes of military bases reverberates with the impact of haptic and sonic experiences of living with and in transnational militarism; the images of the landscapes and residents of camptowns (or soon-to-be camptowns) call for multisensorial scrutiny of the violence of expropriation and military drills.

Kang's oeuvre is chiefly representations of the lingering consequences of the Korean War, from the casualties of military drills to the visualization of the state's ideology in military memorials, in addition to his camptown portraits discussed in the following chapter. Kang received increased attention from critics and audiences in the late 1990s with a series of photographs depicting Maehyang-ri, a fishing town in Hwaseong, Gyeonggi Province. A compilation of these photographs was published in 1999 as part of the *Portfolio* series, curated by the Korean photography book publisher Noonbit. *Maehyangni P'unggyŏng* (*Maehyang-ri Landscape*) reveals the damage done by US

Air Force activities to the small town, whose residents' livelihoods depend almost entirely on earnings from the tidal marshland. The United States Air Force (USAF) conducted aerial bombing target practice drills in the area most nights from 1952 until 2005, the result of the 1952 Korea-US Mutual Defense Treaty in which off-sea areas were designated as a USAF firing range. Under the treaty's state of exception, the K'uni Range was created by the state expropriation of the lands and fishing areas of Maehyang-ri residents. The roaring of the bombs, and the misfires, affected the town for many years, resulting in numerous cases of psychological and physiological damage manifesting as miscarriages, chronic ailments, and suicides.[48] For many years Maehyang-ri residents pleaded for termination of the drills, but the government maintained their necessity for national defense and peace.

The images in *Maehyangni P'unggyŏng* show this barren marshland during ebb tide in the aftermath of target practice. One photograph in the series depicts bombshells stuck in the middle of the tidal marsh (figure 5.5). The black-and-white photograph, whose tonal intensity is minimized, subtly delineates the marsh, the seawater on the horizon, the buildings in the town of Maehyang-ri, and the sky. This otherwise serene landscape is disrupted by bombshells in the center of the image. The largest appears extremely corroded, as if it has been stuck in the marsh for a very long time. Next to it are smaller piled-up shells that could have been gathered by the residents of Maehyang-ri. Another photograph shows a large shell half-buried in a mound of soil overlooking the marsh, with Maehyang-ri residents at work visible in the upper right corner (figure 5.6). A mound cratered by the shell's impact indicates the degree of its destructive force, while the presence of a crumpled shell in the mounds below the crater reveals that this spot has been used as a target multiple times. Other photographs show residents gathering or inspecting shells left by new drills. Even as the delicate tonality of the photographs conveys the tranquility of the natural landscape, that very serenity emphasizes the incongruity of the bombshells and metal scraps.

The publication of the photograph series caused public uproar, leading to a collective campaign against the use of the K'uni Range. In 1999, the investigative television program *Sisa Maekŏchin 2580* broadcast a story on the plight of the Maehyang-ri residents, revealing the uncooperative attitude of the USAF and the Korean government's complicity and incompetence in dealing with the problem. Less than a year after the publication of *Maehyangni P'unggyŏng*, student activists and citizens began to hold protests and meetings in the town alongside the Maehyang-ri Residents' Committee. As

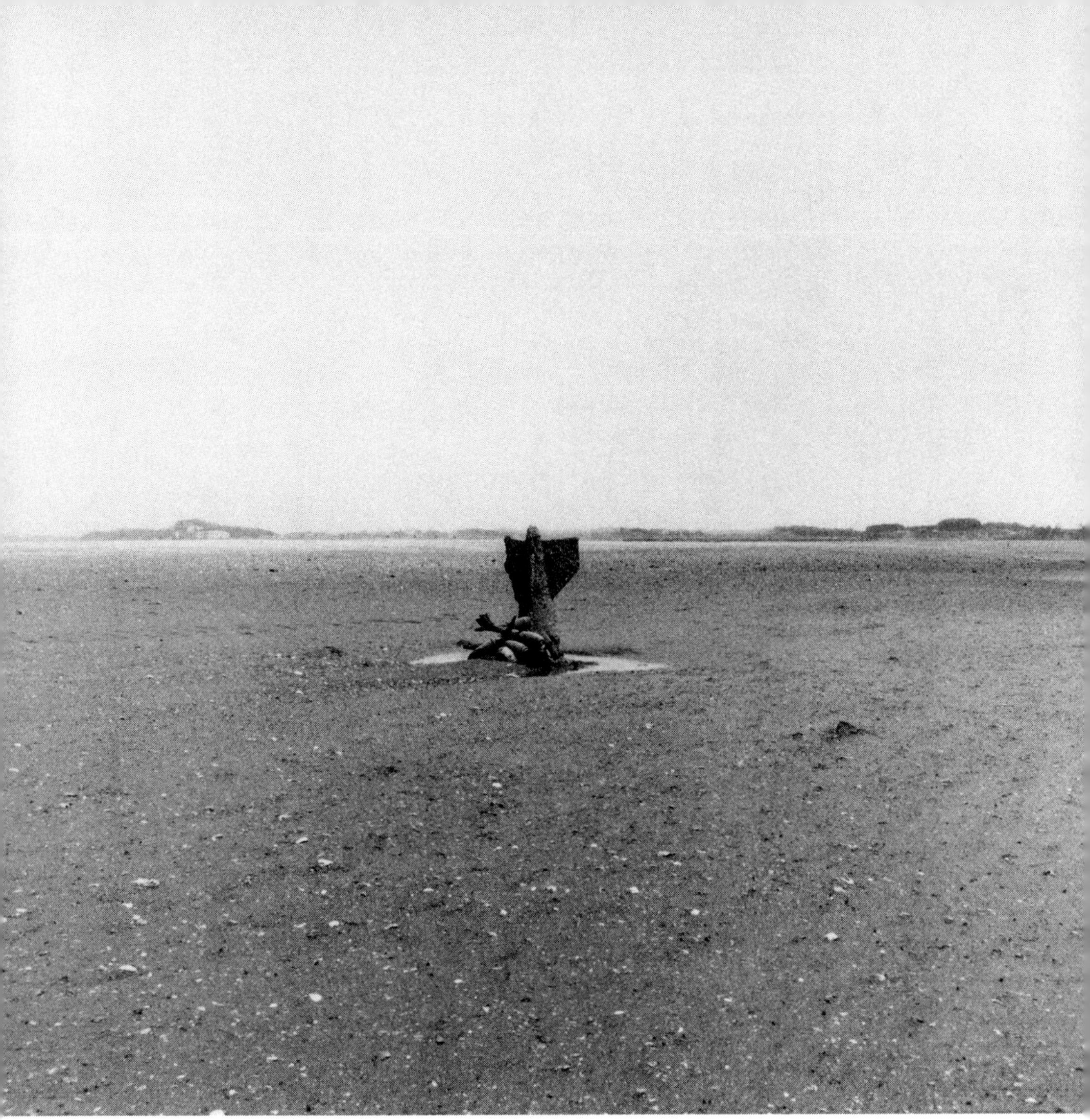

FIGURE 5.5 Yong Suk Kang, from *Maehyangni P'unggyŏng*, Maehyang-ri, 1999, gelatin silver print. Courtesy of the artist.

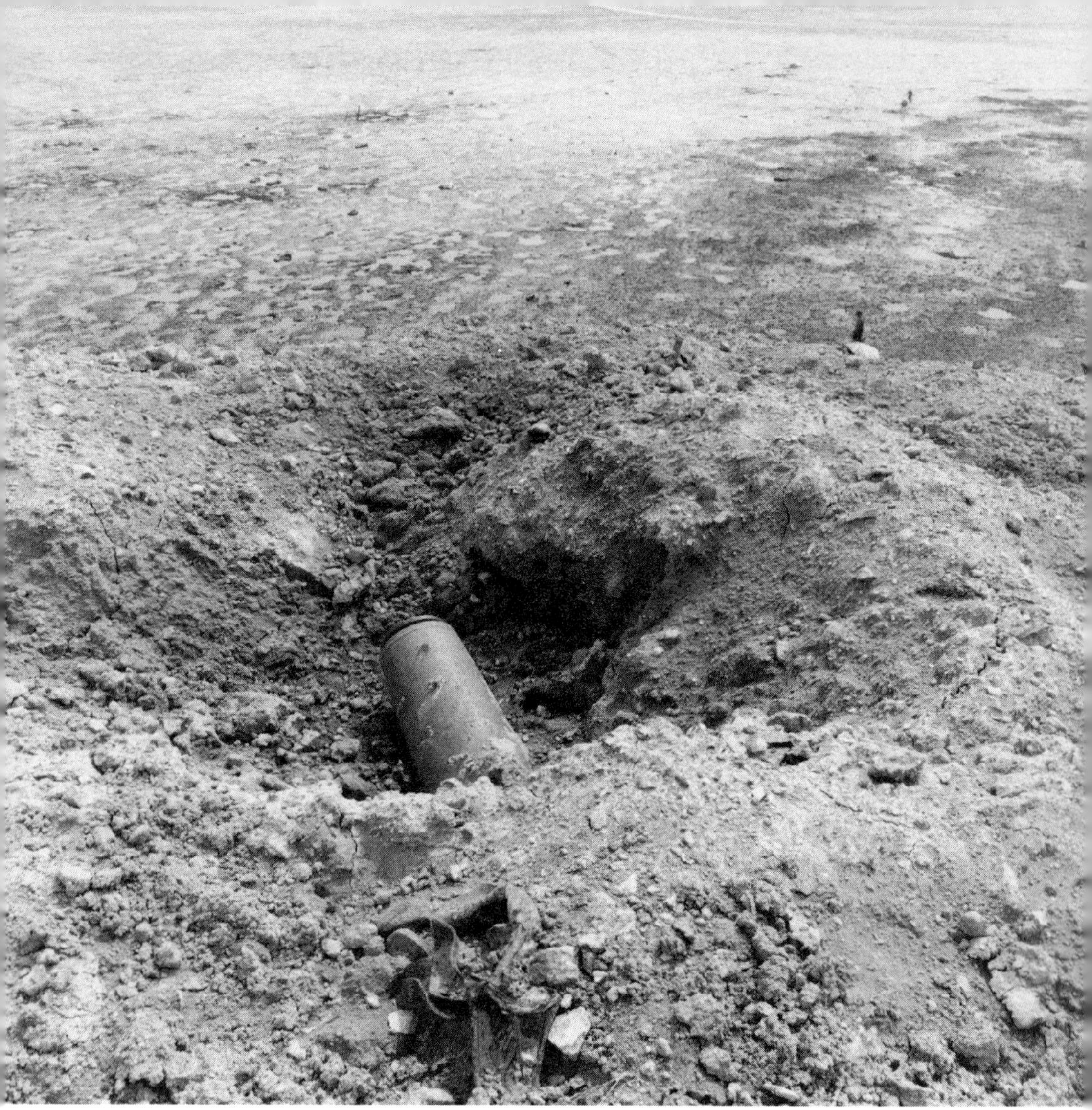

FIGURE 5.6 Yong Suk Kang, from *Maehyangni P'unggyŏng*, Maehyang-ri, 1999, gelatin silver print. Courtesy of the artist.

a result, in 2004, the USAF in South Korea announced plans to terminate aerial drills at the K'uni Range, and by August 2005, Maehyang-ri was finally relieved of aerial bombings and the land was reappropriated by the Ministry of National Defense. However, it took another nine years for the land to be officially accessible to the residents. The city of Hwaseong began laying out plans for a public park in 2015 and began working with the Office of Forestry after acquiring part of the reappropriated land with funds from both the central and city governments.[49] But of course, years of abuse remain embedded in Maehyang-ri's soil and people: bits and pieces of USAF refuse are still buried in the marshland (unsurprisingly), while many residents have had difficulty shaking off the echoes of daily drills, not to mention coping with economic loss.

Kang states that he tried to accentuate the landscape as a means to represent Maehyang-ri, "articulating how the topography of Maehyang-ri and the air that surrounds the landscape transforms through the gray tones of the photographs."[50] The emptiness felt after the dissipation of an aerial bombing drill becomes ironically corporeal through the muted gray tones of the photographs, leaving the sensation of an unsettling aftertaste and its eventual reverberation. Kang's subtle landscape photographs thus capture and echo the scathing sounds of the aerial bombing and the thundering silence they leave in their wake. The quieter the landscape appears in subtle gray tonal ranges, the louder the mnemonics of military drills echoes. Kang, as he states, intended to convey the underrecognized politico-historical significance of this small village, employing subtle gray tones rather than color to provide a "cool" approach to the subject.[51]

Whereas Kang focused on accentuating the flatness of the landscape through his careful treatment of tonality to prevent the photographs from becoming evidentiary documents, which tended to frame his earlier work in camptowns against his wish, the reverberation of *Maehyangni P'unggyŏng*—not merely the visual indexes—intensifies the work's documentary efficacy as evidence of violence.[52] According to Elspeth Brown and Thy Phu, "the central claims of documentary photography and photojournalism toward the irrevocable reality of their work also hinge upon the haptic qualities of feeling."[53] As such, *Maehyangni P'unggyŏng* is also about the silence (of fighter jet drills) in photography, not only the thundering noise that had tortured the residents for decades before Kang's photographs were on view. When Kang's landscape photographs absorb the screeching thunder into a resounding silence which in turn bursts open upon the black-and-white landscape—thus transforming the sonic into the haptic via the visual—the body feels the photographs without delineating the boundaries of the senses. The viewer's experience depends on their affective engagement with the landscape as sound and touch, beyond its visibility.

The historicization that makes the work an effective document might limit the multisensorial possibilities of photography. Nonetheless, sensing the landscape of militarism and imperialism, and not just "witnessing" it, encourages different ways of engaging with and challenging the everyday militarism normalized in the Cold War Asia-Pacific.

Today, although the aerial drills have been terminated in Maehyang-ri, other towns and their residents are still suffering, including Pocheon, where the Rodriguez Live Fire Complex and several other firing ranges are located.[54] Soon after the aerial drills stopped in Maehyang-ri, the farming village of Daechu-ri in the city of Pyeongtaek was expropriated by the state to make room for the expansion of US military base Camp Humphreys, the USFK headquarters since the closure of the Eighth Army and the Yongsan Garrison, under the Korea-US Mutual Defense Treaty. The houses and farmland of 1,372 residents were seized.[55] The town's residents repeatedly petitioned both United States and Korean officials for redress, which uniformly was refused. By 2006, tension was escalating between residents, mostly farmers (notably, without participation from residents who worked at or operated businesses in the town), and the Korean police forces.

Suntag Noh went to Daechu-ri to photograph the confrontations. The photographs taken in Daechu-ri constitute a major segment of his multiseries project *State of Emergency*, chronicling the struggle of the Daechu-ri residents from 2005 to 2006. Doing away with the victimology prevalent in representations of the relation between the United States and South Korea, Noh's project brings to light the complicit role of the South Korean state within the shifting geopolitics of the Asia-Pacific in service of the US military hold on the region, as increasingly expansive and neoliberal transformation of the released land takes shape.

When, for the sake of the USFK's realignment of forces in South Korea and the Asia-Pacific, the Korean state dispossesses its citizens of the right to their property, Daechu-ri residents come to exist in the juridical phenomenon of the state of exception. As Giorgio Agamben explains, the state of exception is created by the merging of the military authority's wartime powers over civil life and the subsequent suspension of constitutional norms of civil liberty.[56] More broadly, in Noh's words, it signifies "the national state of emergency:

the arbitrary abrogation of civilian law governing property on the basis of the disavowed nation state South Korea."[57]

Noh's Daechu-ri images center the Korean government in the landscape without mimetically representing it, exposing the ways in which it has mediated between the US military bases and Korean civilians. One of the few color photographs in the mostly black-and-white series depicts a confrontation between a mass of young policemen and Daechu-ri residents (plate 21).[58] A presumably middle-aged woman turns her back to the soldiers, firmly planting herself on the spot, resting her hand on an umbrella. The colors are crisp and clear, accentuating the contrast between the black-clad police and the woman's casual and humble attire. While the vulnerability of the Daechu-ri residents is evident in the juxtaposition of her everyday clothes against the full armor of the police, the woman's adamant stance is equally apparent. The seemingly immovable positioning of herself alludes to her staunch will to sustain her land—her life—in the face of coercion by her own government.[59]

The series includes many such photographs of physical confrontations between the police force and residents, such as one showing police threatening to bulldoze the resident protesters. Noh also depicts both the passive and active (and mysterious) presence of the "*yongyŏk kkangp'ae*"—"contract mob"—employed by the contractor of the camp's expansion (and ignored or tolerated by the police) to threaten and attack residents (figure 5.7). The police and these contractors began forcefully evacuating residents over the course of a couple of years, starting March 15, 2006.[60] One of the last photographs in the series includes an image of the police force in front of a small building in Daechu-ri, where two residents are folding banners on the roof (plate 22). A banner hung on the building reads: "1943, Expelled by the Japanese; 1952, Expelled by U.S. Army; 2006, By the Korean Government for the Expansion of the U.S. Army Base Camp." The banner succinctly, and damningly, historicizes the fate of Daechu-ri's residents: perpetually displaced, this time for the relocation of most USFK forces, the USFK headquarters, and United Nations Command to Pyeongtaek.[61]

Noh's photographs indict the "state of emergency" that has led to the life-and-death struggle of townspeople to protect their homes and lands. From its start, the series is clear about what the images are intended for: not just to document the sympathetic situations of the camptown subjects, but to visualize the Korean government in this process of dislocating and uprooting camptown residents. Indeed, part I of *State of Emergency* ends with a

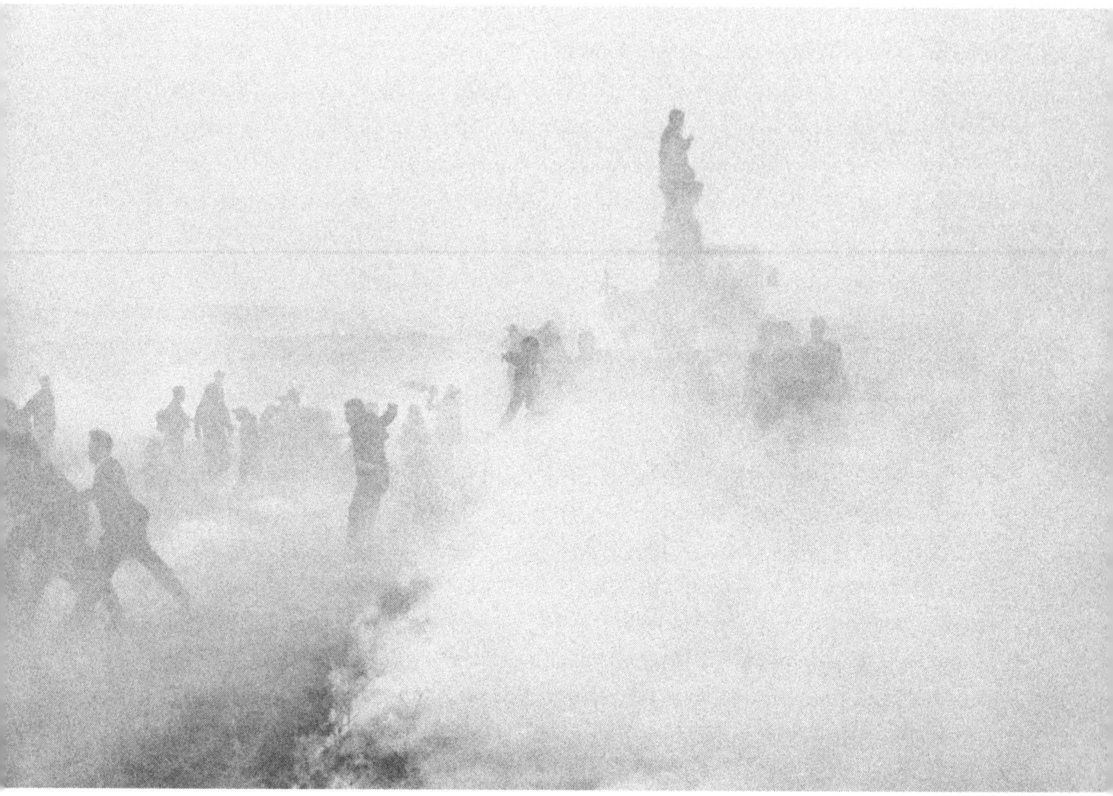

FIGURE 5.7 Suntag Noh, from *Noh Suntag: State of Emergency*, Daechu-ri, Pyeongtaek, 2006, pigment print. Courtesy of the artist.

photograph depicting the dome of the Korean National Assembly as visually echoing the helmet of a riot-control policeman sitting on top of a police bus (figure 5.8).[62] As the state of emergency becomes, for Korean citizens, the nation's condition of normalcy, the militarized nation itself has been in a perpetual state of exception since the war.

Public attention to the struggles of Daechu-ri residents has been eclipsed by the glossy, green urban development plans for Pyeongtaek. The stake of reenvisioning the camp as a new cosmopolitan urban center is, however, as high as always: the stigma of the *kijich'on* (literally "camptowns," and often referring to their red-light districts) north of Seoul haunts the local government and residents.[63] Moreover, issues of environmental pollution and damage still need to be addressed by the US Air Force and the Korean gov-

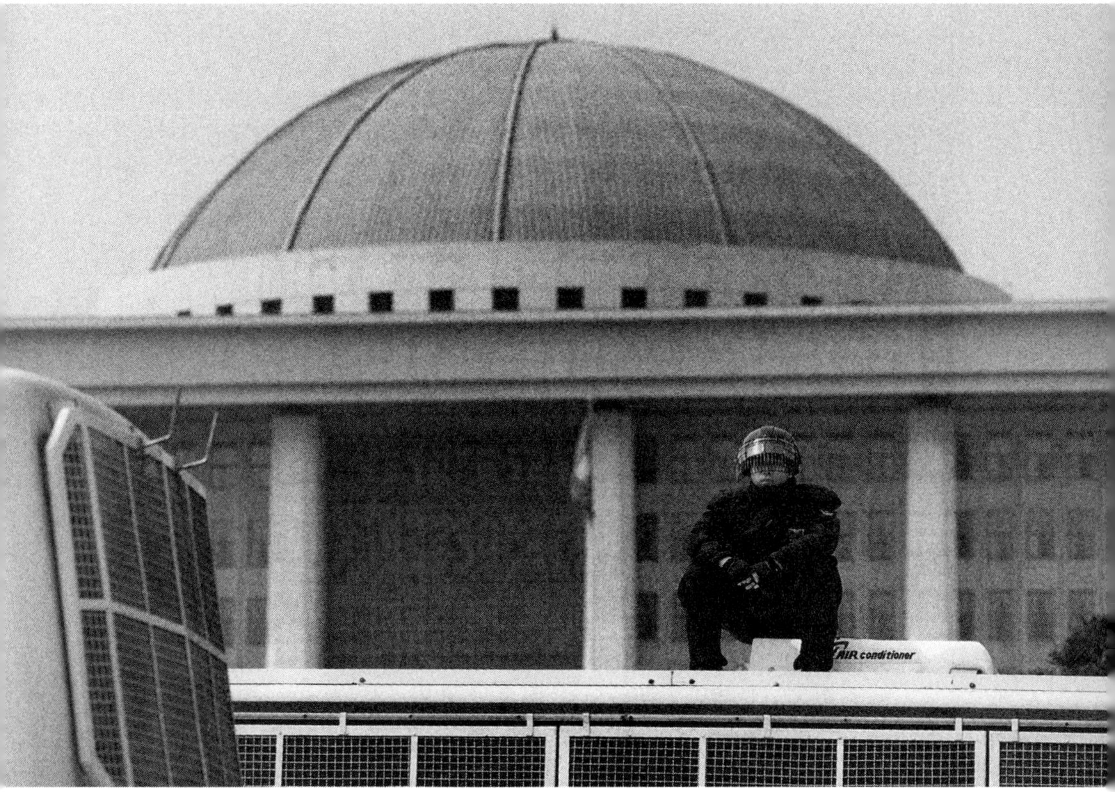

FIGURE 5.8 Suntag Noh, *Smells Like the Division of the Korean Peninsula*, National Assembly, Yeouido, Seoul 2003, pigment print. From Noh, *Noh Suntag: State of Emergency*. Courtesy of the artist.

ernment. Meanwhile, reparations for harm in Maehyang-ri, as with many other camptowns, have been conceived in two overlapping paradigms: real estate development and green space making as a symbol of peace and reconciliation. As for the former K'uni Range site, various efforts for closure and reparation had been made by Maehyang-ri residents, such as organizing peace festivals. After over a decade of anticipation, the city of Hwaseong, the municipality overseeing the site, completed the Maehyang-ri Peace Ecology Park (P'yŏnghwasaengt'aekongwŏn, MPEP) in 2021 (figure 5.9). In this guise, the site once again appeared in a TV program, this time in a popular entertainment game show (*Running Man*) on a network TV channel, Seoul Broadcasting System (SBS).

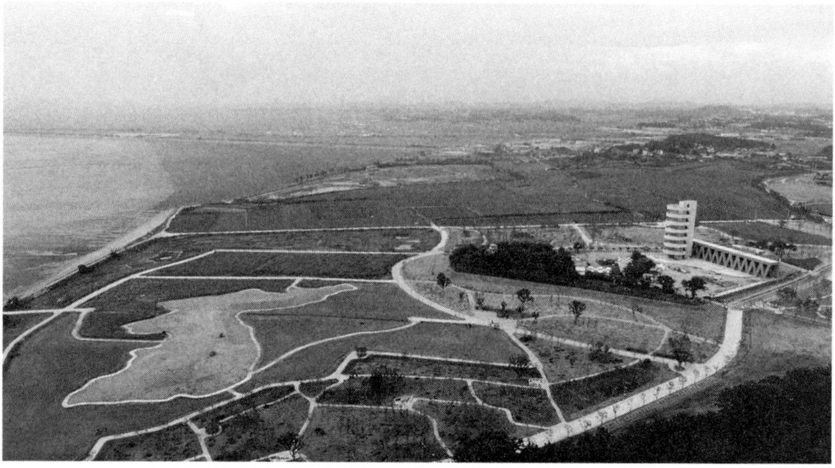

FIGURE 5.9 Maehyang-ri Peace Ecology Park (Maehyangni P'yŏnghwasaengt'aekongwŏn), July 2021, Chungangsinmun.

The MPEP certainly appears to be a long way from the landscapes of K'uni Range depicted in Kang's photographs. Its representation of the Korean peninsula as a miniature covered with young green grass, the demarcation of the 38th parallel now absent, symbolizes the reclamation of military and militarized land and the peace of a unified Korea. Like other peace parks, the MPEP's starkly literal visualization of national, securitized peace presents itself as proof of successful demilitarization and restoration of public space. Yet according to Bridget Martin, this is merely a new form of land enclosure, another example of the Defense Land Brokerage Scheme: the USFK installations first relocate; the city then sells the land to developers. In the case of public parks, the construction is made possible through the municipal (and the central government's) budget slated for the purpose.[64] The development of the area, which uses public money, is the main attraction and incentive for residents. But, to put it bluntly, the taxpayers of Hwaseong, not the USFK, are paying to reclaim the land, and that land will be used by private developers and contractors to make their fortunes.

Underneath the green grass of the model peninsula is the fact that the construction of these peace parks (let alone the residential and business developments) is in fact an essential part of the Defense Land Brokerage Scheme, allowing the central and local governments to work together with private developers in order to pay $9.72 billion (USD) back to the USFK to compensate for the base closures and relocation to Pyeongtaek.[65] The construction of peace parks and the real estate development projects as means to fund the expansion of bases elsewhere is the kind of temporal advancement that the Korean state visualizes in glossy advertisements of new property developments and urbanization. Likewise, the MPEP has become an example of the representation of peace and reclamation in the temporality of neoliberal developments, imagined as national advancement.[66]

Indeed, to ameliorate the angst of Daechu-ri residents and attract new residents and businesses to Pyeongtaek, the local government and developers, according to Martin, "are fervently promoting the idea that the arrival of the [white] Americans will give the city an international, cosmopolitan atmosphere."[67] The ongoing base (en)closures and the impact of expropriation and dispossession are closely tied to the technology of neoliberal land transformation—the work that local and central government, real estate developers, construction companies, local real estate agents, and investors have been executing as the USFK moves on with their long-term and short-term strategic planning in the Asia-Pacific. The map for the old military installations, purportedly reclaimed for the public, is subsidiary to the new military appropriations.

The futurity visualized in this map is the future of capital and its management of and by the military-industrial complex. Indeed, this rebranding strategy of turning militarization into desirable urban redevelopment projects has become much savvier than that of the Park regime, when local and national advancement was proclaimed by the same processes behind the establishment of "special entertainment districts."[68] The trope of national advancement articulates the relentless desire for developments "by offering the promise of sequence as the royal road to *con*sequence."[69] In this temporality of national advancement, the compulsion to repeat and reverberate is a roadblock. Rather than point to the time of national advancement in securitized peace, the compulsion of repetition in representing the DMZ, USFK bases, and camptowns refuses the chronology and procession of developments. Frustrating though the repetition may feel, these continued reverberations crawling our skin are the signifiers of the images' temporal demand, the demand that we make time to see what is really being transformed in the DMZ and base areas, in the theater of securitized peace.

6

Listening to Camptown Photographs

The history of Korean camptowns—cities and towns that host military bases, especially the United States Forces Korea (USFK) installations proliferating since the 1950s—provides a compact précis of the geopolitics of the Asia-Pacific and its continued grip of the country. Commonly known as camptowns in the Anglophone academic context, the sites of these US military bases correspond closely to Japanese military settlements during the colonial period. For example, Paekmajang (now Sangok-dong) in Bupyeong became a Japanese Army base in 1939 and was taken over by the US military after Japanese evacuation in 1945. Yet as the US bases in Paekmajang and elsewhere relocated in the 1970s, the town's economy was devastated. The rise and fall of such camptowns thus traces the modern history of the nation from the colonial experience, through the Korean War and military regimes, to the country's accelerated economic growth in the 1970s and 1980s.

While the six major USFK areas still operative in 2021, hosting approximately 23,500 service members, present a dramatic reduction from earlier eras, for former camptowns the effects of their past use remain economically and socially profound.[1] The decades-long government exploitation of camptown policy and development, as well as nationwide stigmatization, have especially impacted former camptowns in terms of the real estate market and private investment. More recently, camptowns have been directly hit by the relocation of most of USFK installations to Pyeongtaek, south of Seoul in Gyeonggi Province. At the same time, this relocation involved further government violence in the removal of local residents and farms by mandates, conciliation, and force.

As discussed in the previous chapter, artists working in and around camptowns and the DMZ have photographed the landscape and questioned the legacy of the Korean War and the presence of US military bases. However, photographic works about camptowns only began to draw public interest and critical attention in the 1990s and 2000s. The rarity of images depicting camptowns available to viewers until the very end of the twentieth century echoes the scarcity of public discourse about them up to that point. This was the desired effect of military suppression of the topic. By controlling what was reported about army bases and camptowns, and thus what the public knew of them, the military state silenced camptown residents. Social stigmatization added to a disinterest in camptowns, and particularly, camptown women, also referred to as *mikun wianbu* ("comfort women" to the US military).

The consanguine relationship between USFK base camps and camptowns is deeply rooted in gendered labor and exploitation of women that leads back to the Japanese occupation. Camptowns and camptown women have been further marginalized and stereotyped through media portrayal. While praised at the time for raising awareness, movies such as *Silver Stallion* (*Ŭnmanŭn ochianŭnda*, dir. Chang Kilsu, 1991) represent camptowns as bleak, near-abandoned, and dilapidated, populated by women who turn to prostitution in their desperation.[2] Similarly, the rare photographs taken in camptowns prior to the 1990s, which became available to general viewers only after the end of the military regime, mostly depict the camptown's entertainment districts, sex workers, and GIs. Only a small community of scholars and activists had examined the complexities of the relationship between the US military presence in South Korea and camptown sex work.

This is particularly striking in contrast with the discourse and public awareness of "comfort women" during Japanese colonial rule, which human rights activists and victims of Japan's sexual slavery brought to light in the 1990s.[3] Kim Haksun first spoke about her experience in 1991 in South Korea, followed by Kim Poktong, who testified at the United Nations Commission on Human Rights in 1993. Since then, colonial-military sex slavery has been of both academic and public interest. Nonetheless, there has been a concerted effort to dissociate camptown sex workers from the understanding of sex slavery.[4] While it is certainly necessary to delineate the historical and political differences between the two, the refusal until recently to address institutionalized sex work in camptowns starkly demonstrates how even social activists tend to consider camptown sex workers as "morally loose" beneficiaries of the business of camptown prostitution.[5] As Katharine Moon states, compiling a history of camptown prostitution is exceptionally difficult because it "is a history that most Koreans do not want to see immortalized in books and taught in schools."[6]

The postindependence United States Army Military Government's adoption of the colonial practice of "comfort stations" in camptowns (1945–48) and the post–Korean War extension of camptowns serving the USFK—even when the Republic of Korea (ROK) government officially banned state-operated prostitution in 1948—are entangled in the remapping of American imperial power in the Asia-Pacific region and the ROK's intensive positioning of itself as the United States' loyalist ally. This mapping and positioning cannot be explained without the systemic abuse and exploitation of camptowns and camptown women backed by the South Korean state. Indeed, camptowns and their residents, although officially under the Korean Constitution and laws, perpetually exist in a limbo between the USFK and ROK, both in legal terms and in the collective memory of that limbo. At the same time, the USFK bases and United States Army Garrisons have occupied parts of Korean territory under laws that exist neither completely within nor outside of the ROK and the United States: the occupied land is considered the territory of the United States, as the federal and military laws apply within the base.[7] Nonetheless, camptowns officially do not belong to USFK territory, and are under South Korean sovereignty and laws.

Existing neither under the South Korean law nor under the Status of the Forces Agreement (SOFA) when it comes to their rights, camptowns and camptown residents, in particular those working in the service industry, inhabited a seemingly perpetual state of exception, at least until the massive closing down and relocation of bases to Pyeongtaek.[8] For American service members, camptowns become the space of incompatible (and asymmetrical) rights; because camptowns exist(ed) for service members, camptown workers' rights under the South Korean law were only guaranteed selectively. In particular, by approaching camptown sex workers as potential carriers of venereal disease that may harm USFK operations, the South Korean state effected extrajudicial control over camptown women's bodies. Hence, even within the state of exception of camptowns, the conditions of the exception differed dramatically for US service members and Korean camptown residents.

While Giorgio Agamben's "state of exception" may not detail the legality of camptown rights and restrictions in the USFK military context, it is at least an apt descriptor for the state of camptowns in the collective memory formed largely by cultural production—exception legitimized by the unfinished war, which, in turn, requires that very exception.[9] Photographing camptowns not as a space of exceptionality but as a space of the everyday life—which Jin-kyung Lee calls service economies—can therefore become an act of conscientiously and conspicuously presenting what is physically invisible in the images: the relational complexities of service labor and its imperial history, not to mention the actors in these relations (the Korean government, business operators, and USFK as the forces institutionalizing service labor) behind the faces captured in camptown photographs.[10] With this context, the chapter examines the representation of camptowns in varying genres of photographic images, from reportage to snapshots to art, illuminating the ways in which they exist within the territory of the Republic of Korea as a sovereign state, and how they may continue to signify or interrupt the visualization of this state.

The use of camptown images, namely those of camptown sex workers and GIs, has consistently sensationalized outside society's approach to camptowns, both reinforcing and manipulating the pressing issues in and of camptowns that perpetuate the gendered nature of militarism in South Korea, even as the state, local governments, and real estate corporations seek to revamp the image of camptowns as "gentrified, cosmopolitan cities with craft beer and tacos."[11] This chapter examines the ways in which camptown images have typically helped viewers outside of camptowns suspend their anxiety about situating themselves within the place by imagining the place as outside their ethics of sovereignty, laden with foreign desire and currency.

Many camptown images have contributed, deliberately or otherwise, to the sexually and politically dichotomized representations of South Korea and the United States, allegorizing the women's occupied bodies as the nation's postwar condition and the GIs as the new occupier. This gendered allegorization is addressed through rare examples of documentary photographs, taken in the 1960s by Kuwabara Shisei and René Burri, that exceptionalize the camptowns from Korean sovereign territory.

Photographic works on camptowns diverging from this perspective appeared in the 1980s (other than personal examples), as demonstrated in the Korean photographer Yong Suk Kang's images of camptowns through snapshot portraits. Envisioning camptowns and service labor through the vernacular aesthetics of snapshots, a photographic genre familiar to most people, Kang creates his own archives of camptown intimacy, as they mostly were personal commissions by GIs.

The public imagination does not easily envision putting an end to the state of exception in which camptowns reside. This chapter is grounded in the possibility that interrogating photographic representations of camptowns may go some ways to address this difficulty. To this end, the chapter concludes with an exploration of siren eun young jung's work in the city of Dongducheon, which does away with the representation of bodies and faces in favor of spaces and voices. jung's multimedia work asks uneasy questions to viewers who find comfort and pleasures in seeing imagery as partaking in the semiotics of visual representation: How do the images/*imiji* visualize the state of exception that camptowns have endured?[12] How do representations of camptowns relate to maintaining (or ending) the state of exception, which has trapped camptown women in the gridlock of a service labor deemed necessary for national and regional security and condemned at the same time?[13] What does our—the viewing selves'—encounter with camptown photographs mean and do? For a start, how do (and how can) viewers, the people outside of camptowns, predicate themselves in the photograph?[14] In exploring these questions, camptown photographs illuminate how camptowns become the site/sight of transnational militarism in the state of exception, and the exploration provides ways in which the viewer can interrogate and resist the ethno-nationalist symbolization of camptowns and camptown women as a binary of promiscuous traitors and victims of the American empire.

Camptown Photographs and the Military State

While photographs of camptowns had long been unavailable or of no interest to the wider public, one such photograph caused a sensation in the fall of 1992—a forensic photograph of a murdered Korean woman. On October 28,

Yun Kŭm'i, a sex worker in Dongducheon, a camptown 30 kilometers (19 miles) north of Seoul, was murdered by Kenneth Markle, a white US Army private. Markle brutalized and desecrated Yun's body by shoving a Coke bottle into her vagina and the trunk of an umbrella into her rectum, placing matches in her mouth, and spreading detergent powder all over her body. How the forensic photograph of Yun's body, "found in a pool of blood in the small room that she rented in [a camptown]," was initially made public is unclear.[15] The photograph of the murder scene quickly spread through channels including weekly journals and student papers. The degree of brutality in the murder was obvious in the photograph of Yun's mutilated body.

While the murder induced extreme anger, it also brought forth the mixed feelings of sympathy and shame so frequently associated with camptown sex work. Many activists, especially university students, believed that this photograph revealed the intrinsic injustice of camptown life. Of course, many Koreans were shocked by the graphic, sexualized descriptions of Yun's mutilated body even without seeing the photograph. But while funerary portraits are usually displayed for the purpose of commemoration and activism in memorials, the use of Yun's forensic photograph as propaganda for memorial meetings and protests was, and is, extraordinary.[16] Although the photograph was widely reproduced under the logic that it needed to be seen by as many people as possible to alert the public as to what was happening in camptowns, women activists have problematized the explicit portrayal of extraordinary violence against a woman as misogynistic sensationalism, capitalizing both on the shock of the physical damage and on the sexualized content.[17]

This ambivalent reaction toward camptown victims of sexual violence is closely related to the contradictory reception of the history of camptown sex industry and the military regime's cultivation of it. The history of the US military presence in South Korea began with the fall of the Japanese colonial empire. By August 1945, seventy-two thousand US soldiers were stationed on the peninsula, initiating a military occupation lasting until the 1948 declaration of the Republic of Korea. Within the base camps, the US Army Military Government developed an unofficial system of regulated prostitution as a means for both the entertainment and control of male soldiers, as well as to limit the spread of venereal disease.[18] The succeeding Syngman Rhee government continued to regulate sex work in camptowns, even as it publicly condemned and criminalized it. The system served Allied forces and Korean soldiers by adopting the Japanese institution of "comfort stations," allowing the government to claim that it would "protect respectable women and reward soldiers for their sacrifice."[19] This systemic prostitution of Korean women after 1945 was therefore a remnant of colonial practice, reconfigured by the US forces and maintained by the Korean government in the name of the military's—and thus the nation's—good.[20]

The armistice agreement of the Korean War, the signing of the Mutual Defense Treaty of 1953, established permanent US military bases in South Korea. During the 1950s, camptowns developed rapidly to fulfill the needs of US soldiers. Camptowns are referred to in South Korea as *kijich'on*, "a village of a military camp." Over the years, the term has come to specify the "red-light district" of the camptowns, especially as part of terms such as *kijich'on yŏsŏng*—literally "camptown women," which refers to camptown sex workers. Regulated prostitution comprised a significant portion of the camptown economy, even as it was criminalized in formal law.[21] Park Chung Hee created 104 "special districts" and rules overhauling the system of regulated prostitution, bringing in an unprecedented amount of foreign currency in the 1960s.[22] Indeed, the Park regime "viewed camptown prostitution not only as necessary for American soldiers to continue protecting South Korea, but also as beneficial for economic development."[23] However, camptown prostitution saw a steady and continuous decline after the end of the Park regime, and fell sharply in the 1990s and 2000s even as it became increasingly transnational in its employment of sex workers from the Philippines and Russia, among other countries.[24]

Between the 1950s and 1980s, the South Korean state publicly detached itself from camptowns and state-managed prostitution. Camptown issues, including violent crimes committed by service members against camptown residents, were portrayed as personal, local, and particular, limited to the problems of morally tainted (Americanized) camptown activity—thus allowing the public uproar against the United States and USFK to bypass the South Korean state.[25] But in reality, the now-(seemingly)displaced issues of camptowns were deeply related to "the nation-wide development of sex industry, asymmetrical developments, and the ideology of patriarchy."[26] Against this backdrop, just as Yun's forensic photograph brought new attention to camptown violence in the 1990s, the case came to dominate the public imagination of camptowns.

The lack of photographic interest in and exposure of camptowns until the 1990s was, as with many things in Korea, primarily due to the military domination of Korean politics and culture since 1945, throughout the nation-building decades and the subsequent military regimes. It is also deeply related to the purposeful eclipsing of Korea's history of militarism by the nation's rising economy. Hence, a lens turned toward camptowns exposes the many domestic, diplomatic, military, social, and gender issues brought into being by the state and military regime. Camptowns became the sites of an embarrassing past-present for the hyperdevelopmentalist society.

The Park regime's declaration of a state of emergency in December 1971, and the rolling out of the presidential Emergency Decree No. 1 of the Yushin Constitution in October the following year, made it even more difficult for Korean photographers to take photographs freely and show their work to the public without being censored.[27] The military regime also condemned and suppressed public criticism of the US forces in Korea. As discussed in previous chapters, the alliance was considered crucial to guarding against the threat posed by North Korea, and criticizing US-related issues in South Korea was considered a threat to the security of the state.[28] As a result, publication of camptown images, especially those depicting entertainment establishments, brothels, and sex workers, was eschewed to avoid raising public interest in the workings of the system.

In this near absence of photographic representations of camptowns, the photograph of Yun's mutilated body came to represent camptown sex workers with both positive and problematic results. The brutality of Yun's murder finally alerted South Koreans about the sexual violence prevalent in camptowns, while escalating anti-American sentiments among Koreans.[29] However, as a symbol of camptown sex workers as a whole, the photograph presented them as universal victims even as it warned them, and the wider public, of what happens to immoral women. The subsequent media sensationalism swiftly switched the public's focus from the representation of chastised camptown sex workers to the representation of a helpless victim of American imperialism. Inevitably, by emphasizing the heinousness of the murder, more attention was paid to the camptown women who were dead, ignoring and silencing the living women;[30] in this, "the violence, discrimination, and injustice the women experience every day became invisible."[31]

This invisibility was of course necessary for the Korean government, for while the photograph of Yun's body pointed to violence of the USFK, the violence to other, living bodies was largely committed by the state. For example, registered sex workers were forced to undergo sexually transmitted infection (STI) testing twice a week until 1978, and once a week thereafter.[32] Pak Chŏngmi, referring to the testimonies of former camptown sex workers, explains that if they refused, they were (extrajudicially) arrested, detained in jail, and tested, for violating Yunnakpangjipŏp (Law against Prostitution)—the local ordinance on "Preventive Measures to Contagious Diseases" did not contain judicial sentencing powers.[33] Ironically, the law prohibiting prostitution was exploited by the state to enforce control over sex workers' bodies, maintaining systemic prostitution. The enforced treatment was extremely harsh; many women suffered side effects and overdoses of penicillin, extending even to some deaths during treatment.[34] The majority of the camptown facilities (*punyŏpohochidoso*) for mandatory STI testing of camptown sex workers, where they were also detained and treated, were closed only in the mid-1990s—coinciding with the rise of entertainment visa issuances to women from Russia and the Philippines.

According to Hyun Sook Kim, Korean nationalist activists have further silenced camptown residents by denying them a strong voice in the movement condemning the illegal activities of the USFK and the South Korean government.[35] In this way, activists, inadvertently or not, treat the sex workers as symbols rather than people, and the camptowns themselves as mere tokens of US oppression, thereby allowing the South Korean state (and people) to avoid being implicated. Appropriating the voices of camptown sex workers, these nationalist activists erase "any historical specificity of women's locations in particular social and cultural power relations."[36] Disenfranchised and chastised for their "shameful" activities, the camptown women are made into scapegoats for blame and subsequent purification, since, according to Chungmoo Choi, "the discourse of anti-colonial nationalism demands moral purity."[37]

Even as the military regime institutionalized prostitution in US military base camptowns across South Korea—and enjoyed the institution as a lucrative source of foreign currency—camptown sex workers were reviled for not upholding the dignity of the nation. As such, these women were caught in the power dynamics between the new occupier (the US military) and the once-again-occupied Korean state and Korean men, who chose to ally themselves with this new occupier and remasculinize themselves through the (sexual) labor of even more heavily marginalized Koreans, presumably including gay men and trans women. In this environment of hypermasculine competition between the US military and Korean men, the intense abhorrence toward women stems from the meeting between the ideology of patriarchy and the damaged masculinity of the post-colonial nation.[38]

Photographs of camptown sex workers and GIs, especially those in the style of documentary or reportage, thus acted as rare but essential visual proofs of the transactions between Korean women and GIs. Such representations of camptown women effect a regulatory power in defining what "normal women" should be and how the "proper women's" subjectivity is formed against the "improper women." The signification of the "*yanggongju*" ("Western princess," a slur for camptown sex workers who serve Western men) induces internalized shame and self-degradation among camptown sex workers, enforcing a given frame of subjectivity upon them which maintains the regulatory power and reproduction of the *yanggongju* rhetoric.[39]

Notably, this process of shaming, purifying, and resurrecting the body, a Christian analogy, is associated with the rise of Protestantism since the Korean War—among both the military government and the activist opposition.[40] This analogy is also associated with the military regime contriving the transformation of a damaged nation into a healthy one capable of competing in the global market. In her discussion of "curative violence," Eunjung Kim states that the desire to cure disability and heal others' wounds is, however, deeply associated with violence—especially since, in South Korea, "the overwhelming association between debilities and colonial domination, racism, exploitation, war and violence makes it easy to simply devour disabled bodies to feed the unchanged desire for health and normality, which is often entangled with the idea of sovereignty."[41] During the military regime, economic sovereignty, along with the ideology of anti-communism, was considered crucial for national sovereignty. Ironically, however, the recovery of the nation depended on foreign currency, including that which came from camptown businesses. In this swirl of exploitation, "female bodies were subsumed symbolically into the national body politic."[42] Hence, the symbolic and patriarchal "cleansing" and thus curing of the sexually "violated" bodies of sex workers was used against the sex workers, both exploiting their wounds and forcing them to heal through this curative violence.

Korea's military government, in collaboration with the USFK, was the principal force establishing this public consensus on camptowns and camptown prostitution. For the sake of the alliance, sex workers were privately and systemically provided but publicly portrayed as immoral aberrations. Even as some legal recognition and restitution has recently been accomplished by camptown sex workers,[43] they have been further disenfranchised due to their complicated place in the geopolitics of the Cold War represented in the US–South Korea relationship.[44] A crucial signifier to this relationship is evident in the terms of the SOFA regarding crimes committed against camptown residents by service members, protecting offenders from arrest and trial under Korean law.

For instance, on July 16, 1971, a white American serviceman murdered a camptown sex worker near the city of Daejeon, which hosted Camp Ames. As with almost all other cases of crimes committed by GIs, the USFK was reluctant to turn the accused man over to the South Korean legal system.[45] A similar case was the murder of Kim Yŏnsun, a camptown woman, in 1999. Kim Hyŏnsŏn chronicles the immediate aftermath of the murder, describing the ways in which the Korean police violated proper procedures of investigation in order to protect a prime suspect, a GI, who lived with Kim Yŏnsun. According to Kim Hyŏnsŏn, Korean police officers were acting inferior to the USFK investigators and even attempted to violate orders given by Korean prosecutors.[46] The police forces' voluntary submission to USFK, a form of imperialist self-subjugation, is worth reemphasizing here: Why were they insistent on abusing the basic rights of ROK citizens, these camptown women who were victims of homicide? And how were they able to get away with it? Bringing these questions to the focus of this book—the politics of image making, viewing, and consuming—the following section examines early examples of camptown photographs and what is at stake with representing camptowns and camptown women with them.

Representing the State of Exception: Kuwabara and Burri

During the early days of the junta, the few photographs of camptowns reproduced in and outside of South Korea were taken by a handful of foreign photographers. Among them was the Japanese photographer Kuwabara Shisei, whose documentary work in the years following Park's military coup received substantial attention in South Korea.[47] Kuwabara (b. 1936) came to South Korea in 1964, photographing Seoul and protests against the reestablishment of Korea-Japan diplomatic relations.[48] He then made two to three annual trips throughout the 1960s and 1970s. His photographs show the lives of Koreans struggling to recuperate from the war while also dealing with the rise of an authoritarian military regime.

On his return visits, Kuwabara moved from explicitly political events to photographing the bustling camptown of Dongducheon, mostly capturing interactions between sex workers and GIs.[49] As photographers had limited access to political and military matters, the subject of camptowns—namely GIs and Korean women—was a sideways look at the geopolitics of US militarism in the Koreas. Indeed, it was the exceptional state of camptowns—a front of the Korean War that was simultaneously a state of normalcy—that attracted foreign photographers to them in the first place. Access to the military bases would be limited, if not nonexistent at the time; camptowns, and their encounters between civilians and GIs, provided an oblique approach to the censored and taboo topics created by Korea-US military relations.

One of Kuwabara's Dongducheon photographs shows GIs in uniform walking on the street with Korean women—escorts (figure 6.1). The couple on the right hold hands, glancing toward their right as they walk. The GI on the left looks at the front of a parked car, smiling or talking. In front of him is a Korean woman touching up her hairdo. A third couple stands behind these four people, their legs and heels visible behind the couples in the foreground. Another photograph depicts a group of GIs and two women by the entrance of an establishment, presumably a brothel (figure 6.2). The GIs seem to be talking with someone inside the humble building, their backs to the camera. A well-dressed woman turns her head toward the camera; Kuwabara frames her with a metal structure resembling the horizontal bar used for exercise. To her right is another Korean woman, looking much more lethargic.

Both photographs, taken outside and from a distance, allow for a reconstruction of the situation. Having seen the GIs and escorts walking on the street, Kuwabara chose them as his subjects, yet maintained a good distance to avoid disturbing the couples, walking backward while waiting for the right moment for exposure. Kuwabara's representation of the GIs and escorts in his photographs in turn creates a distance between the subjects and viewers. As is typical of a photojournalistic work, it is not an image captured through direct communication with or consent from the subjects.

This working style is present throughout Kuwabara's Dongducheon images. In another scene, two GIs and two women walk side by side on the street (figure 6.3). While the soldiers appear undisturbed by Kuwabara's presence, the women, wearing sunglasses, are trying to cover their faces: the woman on the right is about to cover her face with her hands, and the one on the left holds up an object blocking her face and waves her hand to the right, as if to tell Kuwabara to move to the side. The women's gestures show that they do not want to be documented. In this photograph, Kuwabara has also caught a couple embracing in the distance, behind the bush on the right; the couple is clearly unaware of being photographed. Kuwabara's images of the interactions

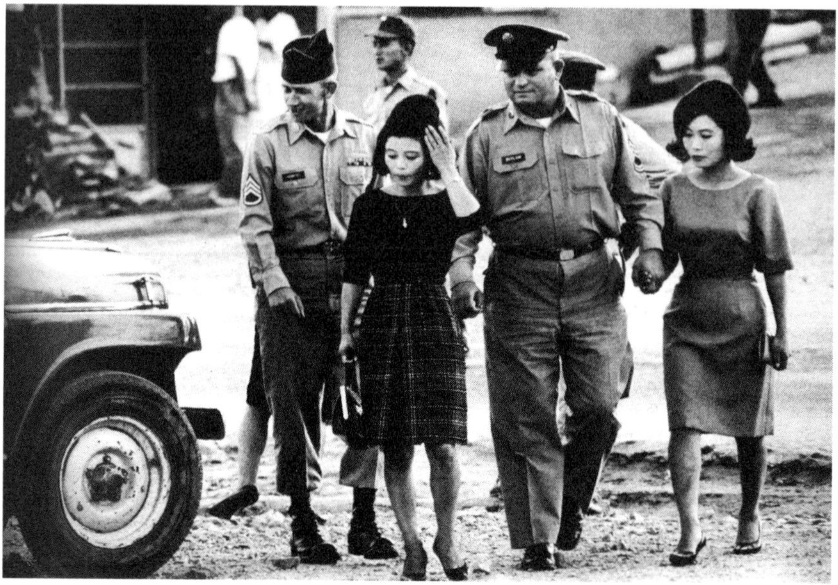

FIGURE 6.1 Kuwabara Shisei, *Tongduchŏn*, 1965, gelatin silver print. Courtesy of Noonbit.

between American soldiers and their escorts in Dongducheon, reveal what goes on in camptowns in the 1960s and thus entail the intrusiveness of the photo making that (while applying to all street photographs) here also reflects the power dynamics at play in the production and consumption of service labor in camptowns—and in the camptowns' very existence, as an intrusion of one nation's prerogatives on another's.

The same phenomenon comes into play in works from the Swiss photographer and filmmaker René Burri (1933–2014). As a Magnum photographer, he traveled extensively throughout Europe, the Middle East, Latin America, and Japan from 1956 to 1959. In 1961, the year of Park's coup, Burri went to South Korea and photographed the recent political transitions. Burri's main subjects were the interactions between soldiers and civilians, whether Korean soldiers arresting a young man smoking the American cigarettes banned by the junta, or US soldiers courting Korean sex workers in "special districts."

Burri managed to photograph interior scenes in a brothel in the special district of Daeseong-dong. These are striking images for their rarity, due in part to the lack of access to camptown bars and brothels for Korean nationals.

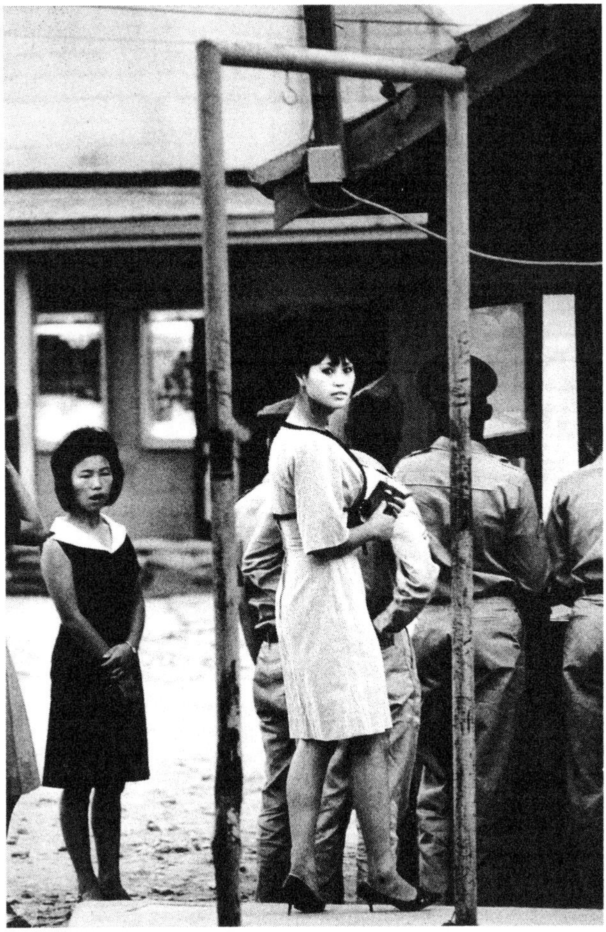

FIGURE 6.2
Kuwabara Shisei, *Tongduch'ŏn*, 1965, gelatin silver print. Courtesy of Noonbit.

Burri, a white European, could gain access to the bar more easily to take his photographs showing sex workers and GIs engaged in much more intimate actions than those in Kuwabara's photographs. One example is an image in which a woman wearing a pearl necklace and a dress is whispering in a GI's ear (figure 6.4).[50] The photograph is highly composed, with a clearly focused couple in the foreground and another couple in the blurry background. The viewer does not see the face of the GI, whose back is turned, but views that of the woman, with half-closed eyes and dark lipstick. In the out-of-focus background, another couple is kissing, sitting on a couch. Because the focus is on the couple in the foreground, it is difficult to detect further details of the couple in the background, although the GI appears to be white. The woman

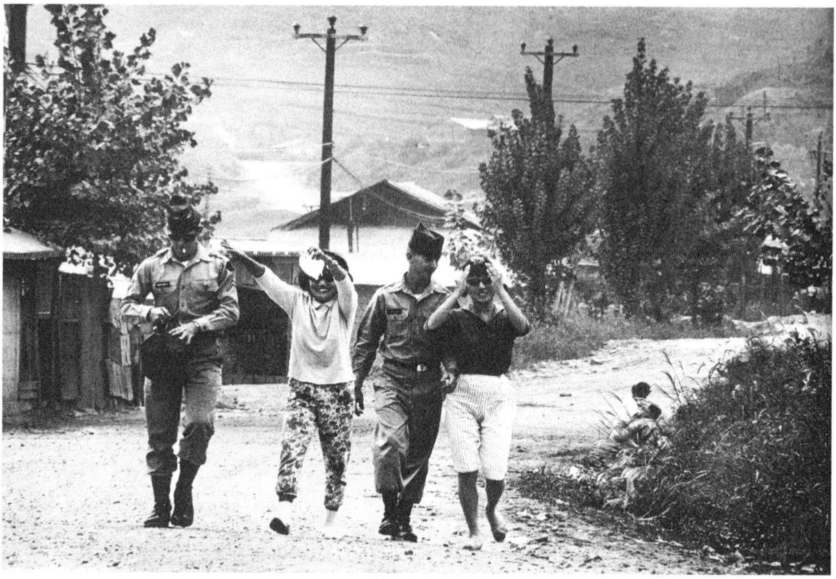

FIGURE 6.3 Kuwabara Shisei, *Tongduch'ŏn*, 1965, gelatin silver print. Courtesy of Noonbit.

in the foreground projects intense pleasure. The intensity of her facial expression makes the scene appear dramatized—appropriately perhaps, as, indeed, she is performing her service.

Another photograph by Burri shows a sex worker standing by the door of a brothel or bar with two GIs about to enter (figure 6.5). The woman facing Burri holds a fan close to her face to cover it while the viewer sees the GIs from behind. The pose reappears in a photograph of a woman who looks as if she is giving a lap dance to a GI (figure 6.6). She holds a fan close to her face while turning back to see what is going on behind her. Her eyes barely peek above the fan. The GI, whose face is blocked by the woman's body, holds the woman by her waist. Judging from the outfit and the painting of goldfish on the fan, the women in these two photographs, and possibly also the GI, are the same. If so, this photograph likely represents the beginning of this "episode," with Burri following the couple from the bar entrance inside.

Even as it is clear that the woman hiding her face behind the fan did not want to reveal her identity, there is a deliberate focus on the sex workers' faces. The woman's covering of her face shows that she is aware of the threat photography poses for her should she be publicly identified as a *yang-*

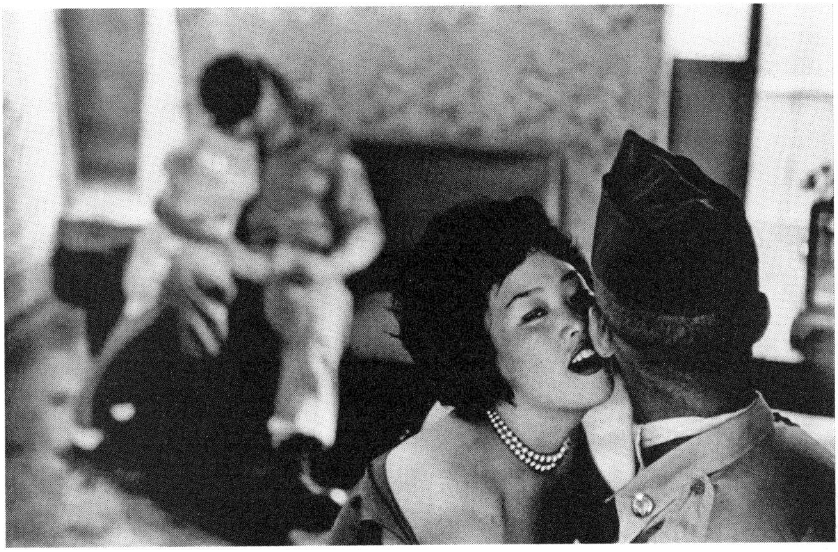

FIGURE 6.4 René Burri, *Tae Song Dong, South Korea*, 1961, gelatin silver print, © Magnum Photos.

gongju who serves American service members. This is also in stark contrast to the generally unseen faces of the GIs—only one of the six photographs by Burri that I have seen shows the face of a GI, and that is blurry as he is turning his head.

By following the GIs and sex workers from the street into their working establishments, Burri creates a narrative, constructing the story he wishes to tell the viewer. He chronicles their interactions from meeting to service, portraying the women as mysterious, seductive, provocative, and yet shy. The effect of such narration has the viewer reading the erotic story from the GI's, or at least the man's, point of view, while Burri's deliberate shielding of the GIs' faces in the photographs allows the (male, Western) viewer to immerse himself in the story. This also puts Burri himself in the position of power over his female subjects. Burri's photographs are, therefore, products of both occupier and male desire, as much about fulfilling his own imagination and the fantasy of *kijich'on* women as capturing its real manifestation.[51]

Crucially, both Kuwabara and Burri violated the women's will not to be photographed and thus possibly subsequently identified. As such, the photographers' and viewers' desire to look—through the male gaze—at the postwar conditions of the divided nation, via the dichotomized and sexualized figures

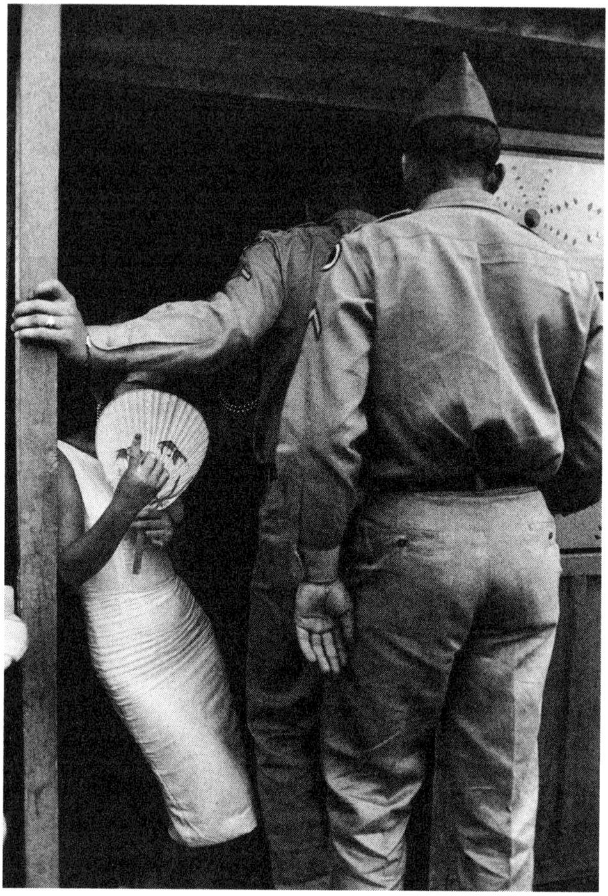

FIGURE 6.5 René Burri, *Tae Song Dong, South Korea*, 1961, gelatin silver print, © Magnum Photos.

of American service members and Korean women, has overruled the violence (and violation) of that gaze upon the women.

Nonetheless, being among the very few photographs of camptowns made at the time, such images have taken on possibly disproportionate significance. They are valuable records, reproduced in publications, and even reenacted for movie posters. For example, a poster for the Korean film *Silver Stallion* had the actors reenact Kuwabara's photograph of a GI holding a Korean woman's waist from behind in front of a club entrance in Paju (figure 6.7). The same photograph was also reproduced on the front cover of a scholarly publication examining the US military empire across the world.[52] In the movie poster, the awkward distance between the photographer and subjects invites the viewer to activate a voyeuristic gaze; in the book, the captioned

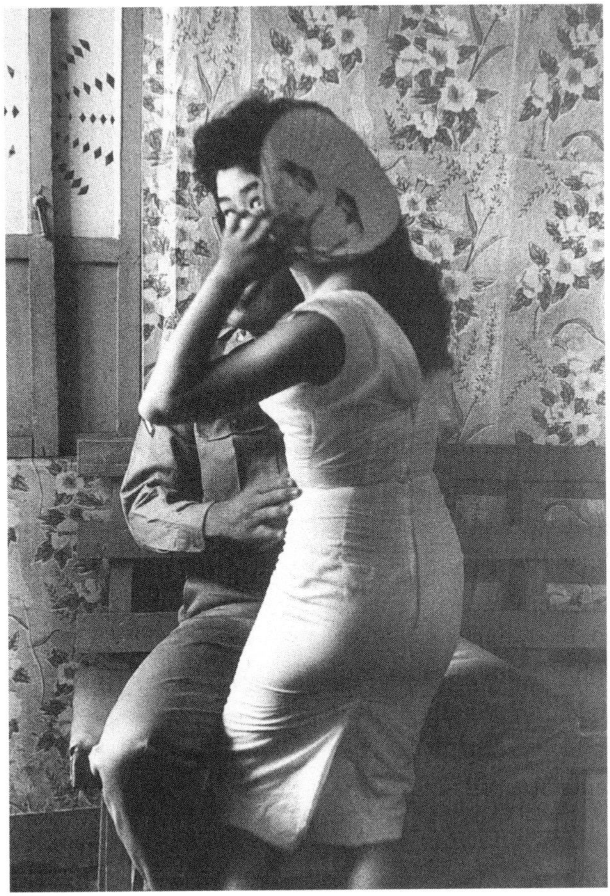

FIGURE 6.6 René Burri, *Tae Song Dong, South Korea*, 1961, gelatin silver print, © Magnum Photos.

reproduction, "A couple outside a GI club in Paju, Gyeonggi Province," becomes the signifier of the geopolitical relationship between South Korea and the United States that the book examines. Notably, neither of the reproductions introduce Kuwabara Shisei or why he was in Paju in 1964. Consequently, the photograph seems to have been offered to illustrate and supplement the film and book, bypassing critical examination of the imagery itself as a mediated production.[53]

Beyond the symbolic, binary identification of the subjects in Burri and Kuwabara's photographs, their images of camptowns also provide the viewer signs of the state of exception. Perhaps more importantly, they reveal that this reduction to signs helps maintain the collective memory of the state of exception, which in turn continues to legitimize its conditions and consequences—that

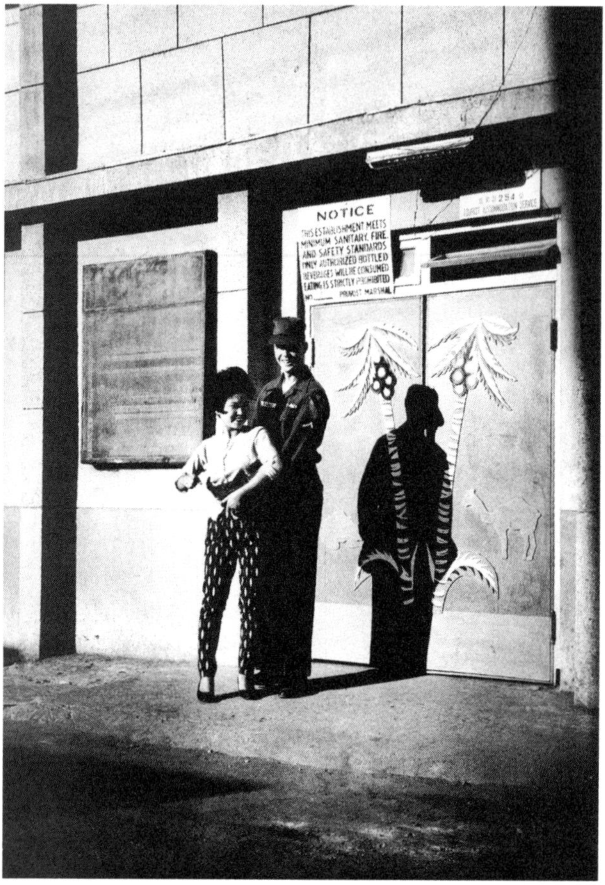

FIGURE 6.7 Kuwabara Shisei, *P'aju*, 1964, gelatin silver print. Courtesy of Noonbit.

the USFK is necessary for the national security of South Korea, and thus camptowns and sex workers must exist under this state of exception.

Such camptown photographs are then perceived as the essential, truthful representation of the Korea-US geopolitics, forestalling other narratives. This leads to the consistent assignment of identity to the women in these photographs: the camptown sex worker, a victim of both the US military and the Korean government. As a result, the representational relation formed between the media (i.e., film and book) and Kuwabara's photographs both buries the camptown sex workers' agency and makes it difficult for the photograph itself to be an object of critical inquiry. The protagonists of the text and photographs are not allowed to form their own subjectivities even in the text. The sex workers in Dongducheon have to be represented by a photojournalist from Japan, or spoken for by activists and academics. Similarly, without any information on the making of the photographs, the city of Dongducheon (and Paju) and the US military bases then located in and around the city—Camps Casey, Nimble, Hovey, Castle, and Mobile—come to represent the unspecified site of camptown-related topics, of the state of exception, itself a representation of the Cold War orders of power.[54]

The gendered metaphor of US military presence as masculine GI and South Korea as feminine and subservient Korean women is ultimately a product of this order, and its hierarchy, as practiced by the rank and file. Chungmoo Choi recounts how US soldiers in passing military trucks used to call out for "saekssi (young women)" in the years following the Korean War.[55] She argues that the call was not just "a public declaration of the soldier's intention to violate Korean women," but "an indiscreet threat of metaphorical rape of the nation," "a display of masculine domination over the women and men of Korea, constructing all Korean people as the sexualized feminine Other."[56] This is also critically related to the racial politics and cultural imaginary within the United States and its territories, where, as David Eng has argued, the settler colonial state uses racial emasculation—what he calls "racial castration"—through which "the impact of gender and sexuality in the racial formation of Asian American men" contribute to containing, subjugating, and exploiting Asian Americans as well as other racialized minority groups in the settler colonial state.[57]

Moreover, the racial emasculation of indentured Asian laborers in the nineteenth century, such as the British introduction of the Chinese and Indian laborers in West Indies, has been part of the liberal empire's tactics to reimagine the global order and economy at the time of emancipation. This reimagining is enacted by charging what they called "free laborers" to take "an intermediary position" between former slaves, native workers, and the colonialists and by having them "enter voluntarily into contract[,] a dominant mode for the initiation of the 'unfree' into consensual social relations between 'free' human persons."[58] According to Lisa Lowe, Asians have been expected to perform a position of triangulation (always in relation to Black and white in the American context)[59] for the liberal empire to legitimize the use of violence to suppress possible revolts of former slaves and native workers (which unexpectedly was met with these "free laborers'" resistance) in the West Indies, for example—a labor coup which still resonates painfully in the United States and its history of anti-Asian racism vis-à-vis anti-Black racism. In other words, the USFK's emasculation of the Korean public is part and parcel of the making of the US empire; the empire relies on regulating racial and gender dynamics in those places under its power for consolidating and strengthening its role as a liberal state promoting the global free market. This is conflated with the notion of freedom in anti-communist states and inseparable from transnational militarism. Thus, in the gendered utterance of "saekssi," the metaphorical assignment of the Korean nation vis-à-vis the US occupation is clear.

Alongside the machination of the military occupation for building, expanding, and strengthening the US empire, I wish to bring acute attention to what the Korean military state did with its memories of violent militarization of the nation by Japan and the United States. As discussed throughout the book, everyday South Korean life during the military-developmentalist regime was overcome with less conspicuous but more habitual culture of militarism (as the naturalized order of things) in order to shed its past of the "feminized" former colony and "to recuperate its virility and join the ranks of the imperialistic order."[60] The visual culture of camptowns, reproduced to provide the evidentiary signs of US imperialism, therefore requires analyses that move beyond reinforcing the binary identification of foreign oppressor versus native victims, as such binary identification ignores the South Korean state and people as the agents of history. Thus, once again, the US is treated as the singular subject of all-consuming imperial power—and this may in fact still be the case. But imperial paths require constant and careful negotiations with its collaborators as well, maintaining their collaboration through various political, material, and psychological means.

To return to the use of camptown images—and keeping in mind the interconnectedness of US imperial and the Korean racial and gender politics—Choi's assessment of the gendered state of South Korea as a postcolonial nation becomes corporeal in the images of sex workers and GIs when they are reproduced to illustrate discourses on camptowns. This holds true even if that discourse is intended to revise and rectify the history of camptown prostitution in South Korea. Despite the good intentions behind much of the current use of these photographs, their expected indexical power not only contributes to the silencing of sex workers, but paints them as passive victims. Should they claim their own subjectivity, they would be quick to be identified by the public as morally and sexually loose, having aligned with imperial power by providing sexual services. With their identities defined by the combination of text and image,[61] the subjects of the photographs more broadly come to represent the perpetually gendered metaphorization of the East-West relationship.[62]

Conspicuously, then, in this early camptown imagery—and the Cold War Orientalist allegorization more broadly—the figure missing thus far is the Korean man. Despite this absence, the women in the pictures were dealing with both American servicemen and Korean men, albeit in different capacities—the Korean men might be their fathers, husbands, brothers, sons, employers, and the local officials and administrators of public health divisions that regularly tested registered sex workers for venereal disease.[63] For example, Bruce Cumings has described how, when he arrived in South Korea for the first time as a Peace Corps teacher in 1967, Korean men approached him in hotels, restaurants, bars, and streets and constantly offered sexual services involving Korean women.[64] Hence, questioning the absent subject of South Korean men—who could symbolize the South Korean state in the same vein of allegorization—is in fact a purposeful complicating of the context.[65]

Hiding in this absence, the military government maintained its alliance with the United States by propagating the metaphorical representation of transnational militarism in which the masculine figure of the USFK (and, at other times, South Korean mandatory conscription) is the protector of the feminized South Korean. This creates a sense of emergency—and thus exception—and solidifies popular support.[66] And when the public questions the history of oppression and violence in camptowns and transnational militarism, the state, whether symbolically or corporeally, is nowhere to be found in camptown representations.

The allegorization of the nation as a victimized woman, then, is a narrative that further exploits its subject—women—without providing the context in which the victimization occurs. Having exploited Korean women in positions without socioeconomic or public health safety nets, the Korean kyriarchy then exploit their suffering, subsequently commemorating it in cultural production. The state thus creates continuous material for exploitation. Its attempt to virilize the emasculated past of Korea requires this formulaic narrative, whether ending with complete silencing, or, as in literature and films, patriarchal purification and redemption in order to accept the fallen women back in the family-*minjok*-nation.[67]

Tongduch'ŏn Kinyŏmsajin (Dongducheon Commemorative Photographs)

Censorship during the regime was a life-and-death matter for photographers, especially under the Emergency Decrees.[68] With the rise of the Minjung Movement in the arts in the 1970s and 1980s, artists intent on producing works about ordinary working-class people and their lives under military oppression—subjects the regime deemed ideologically corrupt—had to develop conceptually and stylistically different approaches to photo making. In this vein, photographers who do not necessarily identify themselves as artists experimented with documentary modes they found specific to the Korean situation at the time. This is the case with *Tongduch'ŏn Kinyŏmsajin (Dongducheon Commemorative Photographs)*, a series of snapshot portraits by the Korean photographer Yong Suk Kang, which begin to complicate the omnipresent metaphors in the discourse on camptown service labor.[69] *Tongduch'ŏn Kinyŏmsajin*, photographed in 1984, consistently deploys a snapshot aesthetics. Used among families and loved ones by the 1960s, the snapshot aesthetics had by then become banal. Most significantly, the sitters, Korean women and GIs, are directly involved in the photo-making process: commissioning, posing for, paying for, and owning the snapshots. As a result, Kang's snap portraits are much more intimate and personal than those of his predecessors.

Since the 1980s, Kang has taken photographs that depict the lingering impact of the Korean War, especially the effects of militarism in the lives of the Korean people. As a third-year university student majoring in photography at Joongang University in Seoul in 1982, Kang first ventured into Bosan-ri, today the old town within Dongducheon, after returning from his mandatory military service with a sense of duty to record the marginalized lives in the city.[70] Once a bourgeoning camptown, by the 1980s and 1990s, Dongducheon faced a crumbling economy and political negligence, a decline brought on by its history of hosting foreign army bases since the colonial period. Almost 40 percent of Dongducheon city's territory was then occupied by military bases, most of which have since been relocated to Pyeongtaek. Dongducheon has long been a synonym for "military camptown" among Koreans, as represented by the imagery produced by Kuwabara and Burri and reinforced by other media portrayals of camptowns.[71]

Kang graduated with his degree in photography in February 1984 with a body of black-and-white photographs from Dongducheon, largely depicting the landscape and residents. He then decided to return to Dongducheon the same year, not just on weekends to shoot, but to live there for an extended period.[72] There, he met an elder Korean photographer who took photographs inside clubs; in the 1980s, commercial photographers were present inside camptown clubs and bars to take *kinyŏmsajin* (commemorative photographs) for clients who wanted them.[73] As the photographer grew ill, Kang took over as a club photographer for about a year.

Most of Kang's "commemorative" portraits of US servicemen and Korean barmaids were later exhibited and published as *Tongduch'ŏn Kinyŏmsajin*, comprising scenes from "a small-town club, the door of which had a warning sign of 'No Korean Citizens Allowed.'"[74] Couples sit or stand close to each other with their arms locked (plate 23) or holding hands (plate 24). Some sitters appear as if they do not care about posing for Kang, forgoing typical poses and manners such as smiling or looking directly at the camera lens. One after another, they appear to be taken in the same bar, or similar bars in the neighborhood. The very multiplicity of the color portraits invites the viewer to observe the humble interior and art of the bar as well as the differences and similarities between the sitters. Like other snapshots, the subjects' faces, hair, makeup, clothes, and poses become the highlights of the vernacular, resonating with viewers' own experiences of making photographic souvenirs.

Having done some documentary work for his photography degree,[75] the challenge Kang faced now was, as Tirdad Zolghadr puts it, "not to summon selfless good will or progressive content but to find intelligent forms of voyeurism," with the potential to expose camptown service labor while marking the laborer as vulnerable.[76] In its outlook, *Tongduch'ŏn Kinyŏmsajin* turned the act of taking photographs into a service for the sitters, depicting the sex workers and GIs as they wished to present themselves for their own recollections, not for Kang or the prospective viewers. Certainly, as a series of snapshots, while the photographs exist in the context of camptown sex industry, Kang's images of the GIs and barmaids are distinct from the images of eroticized camptown sex workers in Burri's photographs, possibly stemming from the sitters' familiarity with Kang as a staple bar photographer added to their intimacies with their GI partners. Granted, this does not mean that the women sat for photographs through their own desire, as it may be that they are servicing the GIs when agreeing to take photographs.[77]

Kang's seemingly casual, snap portraits were met with shock when they were shown in exhibitions and publications in the 1990s; images of US servicemen and sex workers had rarely been exposed to the public, and certainly not in the form of an artwork where audiences viewed private moments inside the bars that Korean nationals were barred from entering.[78] However, this shock value, I argue, was due less to the prurient subject matter or entry into forbidden spaces than to the images' affect of intimacy. All the photographs in Kang's series exhibit the couples' closeness—crucially, including their seeming comfort with the presence of the photographer. Kang stepped into the private moments of his subjects, but with their consent, and often for their own desires (at least on the part of the service members). Rather than affectively distant reportage in black and white, the viewer encounters the camptown subjects as if having accidently opened someone's family album. In being invited (more or less) to view someone's memories, and with the affective familiarity from the mode of photography, the images moved from representing camptowns to providing the viewer encounters with the camptown subjects.

The settings of the photographs are casual and personalized. It appears there was minimum intervention by the photographer in the portraits, and the subjects had control over how they would be depicted.[79] In most photographs, Kang includes objects surrounding the sitters such as bar tables and chairs, wall mirrors, clocks, and paintings (plate 25). The glasses and other objects on the tables show the simplicity of the kind of entertainment that goes on in a camptown bar. Variation among subjects is on display, reflecting the practice of sex workers in camptowns adopting different styles of fashion depending on their client groups. For instance, a woman with a Black American partner wears an afro and makeup with a pair of sunglasses (plate 26), while a woman with a white soldier sitting in front of the bar wears a yellow shirt underneath a golden corduroy dress (plate 27). A woman with a stern expression does not wear makeup, while other women wear colorful eye shadow and faux eyelashes as well as flashy accessories. Another photograph shows a couple standing by a corner of the bar; the Black GI wears a dark suit that contrasts with the brightness of the barmaid's red dress and headdress (plate 28).

Rather than posing for idealized and aestheticized shots, the GIs and barmaids make gestures and expressions which, in their variation, do not necessarily allow viewers to make assumptions about the mood or relationship between them. For example, in the bulk of the fifteen photographs most frequently reproduced in publications regarding *Tongduchŏn Kinyŏmsajin*,[80] the GIs—twelve Black and three white soldiers—are smiling, albeit sometimes awkwardly.[81] The Korean women, on the other hand, show a range of expressions and gestures: where one barmaid smiles, another might appear sad, and yet another, stern. Sometimes the women convey subordination and reluctance, other times confidence and self-containment. The different expressions of the women in the photographs of *Tongduchŏn Kinyŏmsajin* make it difficult for the viewer to generalize the women and their feelings about the moment, as well as their relationships with the GIs. In all these nuances, the casualness of snapshots appeals to the viewer with their vernacular familiarity. This intimacy and familiarity in turn warps the comfortable distance that the viewer has kept between themselves and the camptown. Invited into this intimacy, the viewer has no choice but to confer their affective knowing of camptowns.

Black Portraiture in Camptowns

With Kang's portraits of intimacy in the camptown, another critical confrontation occurs to viewers of *Tongduchŏn Kinyŏmsajin* in and outside of Korea: their own racial biases grounded in anti-Blackness. Racial discrimination against Black Americans has existed in USFK bases and camptowns since their establishments, and camptown residents generally adopted their white clients' anti-Blackness. In 1971, Camp Humphreys' Black service members protested discrimination, including the blatantly worse services and treatment they received compared to their white peers. This led to violent clashes between Black service members and Koreans in Anjeong-ri.[82] According to Seungsook Moon, camptown clubs were racially segregated, reflecting the unofficial (and technically illegal) segregation within the US military in South Korea and elsewhere. Camptown entertainment areas were divided into white versus Black areas, and escorts were divided into "those who served white GIs and those who served black GIs."[83] This in turn led to more extreme discrimination against camptown women who served or lived with Black men. Kang has also stated that, as a stranger to the camptown, he was only able to work in the Black area of Dongducheon as those businesses tended to be more flexible about who can and cannot work in their establishments.[84]

The discomfort potentially entailed by this boundary-crossing extends to the images' effect of challenging viewers'—especially Korean viewers'—anti-Blackness as well. People outside of camptowns have treated this history of camptown anti-Blackness as either cultural misunderstanding (that "Koreans don't actually discriminate against Blacks, they are just fascinated or ignorant"), something that happens extranationally, or taboo. Needless to say, however, this history of racism vis-à-vis transnational militarism is indeed a national phenomenon, just as the systemic exploitation of camptown women is.[85] Reading the women in *Tongduchŏn Kinyŏmsajin* as victims, and the GIs—including Black GIs systemically discriminated against in the United States and South Korea—as corrupting and powerful American imperialists is a convenience propping up the masculinist, and anti-Black, allegory of the nation, even as the Korean state and men are conveniently absent.[86]

In their Bosan-ri snapshots, the Black GIs and their partners make the camptown bar a space of their perhaps fleeting intimacy. Unlike studio portraits with elaborately painted backdrops, the humble interior of the bar accentuates their relationship of service labor bluntly.[87] In these instances and spaces of temporary intimacy, some six thousand miles and an ocean away from the GIs' home, they insist on, as Leigh Raiford puts it, emplacing Black life in an anti-Black world—this time, as the diasporic bodies navigate one of the most rigid structures of life, the military service.[88] The Black (and Korean) portraiture by Kang (and others) from the camptown is not a representation of the unmoored spatiotemporality uniformly replicated by the US military and its hosting cities. Rather, it could be explored as a performance of a home or world making, a temporary home or world for their own service labor—to the US military. The images of Black GIs have been usurped as the symbol of American imperialism and violence in the South Korean context of anti-neocolonialism, but their significance as images of the Black diaspora and as sights of emplacing Black life is salient.

That is not, however, to say that the Black GIs and Korean women all had nurturing relationships or that their children were coparented when they did or did not marry each other. As Young Min Moon notes, the barmaids' relationships were not always those of sex workers and GIs; nor did the women always desire romantic relationships or marriage with them. Rather, the variance among those relationships needs to be recognized.[89] Doing so could be part of the unlearning Raiford asks for. And now, looking at their images, we have to ask ourselves: What do we have to unlearn in order to reimagine Black lives, here in the place of Korean camptowns, with their "temporary" Korean partners and those who became their lifelong partners with children?

Camptown portrait making, a world making toward "a different modality of existence," should also be considered alongside what Tavia Nyong'o refers to as the cinematic capturing of "a certain fundamental criminality that accompanies being-sent" in reading Blackness.[90] The doubly diasporic undertaking of Black GIs "being-sent" to the military base in South Korea is made un-visible in the fiction of the ethno-national capture through which Koreans see race as "a marker that strengthened ethnic identity, which in turn was instrumental in defining the nation."[91] The failure to "see" the un-visiblity of Black emplacement and world making in the reading of camptown photographs is thus critical, conflating the criminality of American imperialism with "a certain fundamental criminality that accompanies being-sent." The portraits of Black GIs become hypervisible even as Blackness and its diaspora remain un-visible.[92]

How, then, can we reclaim camptown portraits from falling into the ethno-nationalist rhetoric of national tragedy, which predicates on anti-Black racism and in turn, ironically, aligns with the racial politics of US imperialism? How do we undo gendered racialization and hypersensitized visibility that numbs the varying sensorial experiences offered by these portraits? How can we—as implicated in the history of transnational militarism—make memories of Dongducheon differently? Here, we may return to the humble objects of snapshots and studio portraits as an antireportage archive, one that encourages the viewer to read the images against the grain. The very title of Kang's series, *Dongducheon Commemorative Photographs*, suggests remembering the camptown not as evidence of transnational militarism and American imperialism, but as the site/sight of residents, who provide transnational service and temporary labor as they experience everyday affect and struggle against and within the geography of transpacific kinship. This in fact extends beyond the genre of the photographs as *kinyŏmsajin* to articulate the "archive drive": the desire for archiving in the human condition of, as Derrida puts it, "the radical finitude, [the] possibility of a forgetfulness which does not limit itself to repression."[93] Camptown "entertainment" was a known secret to most Korean nationals, even as the state would not open camptowns for public scrutiny lest the ways in which they systematized sex work be revealed. In a situation close to the collective amnesia regarding camptowns, Kang's drive to portray the sitters' varying gestures and expressions and where their interactions (service labor) happen is an attempt to work against the near impossibility of knowing the place—the radical finitude.

As such, Kang's portraits are not about the past of camptowns, as recorded to inform or document. Rather, it is about the future of camptowns, "the question of a response, of a promise and of a responsibility for tomorrow" for Dongducheon, the people who made it, and all the other places like it.[94] In line with Tina Campt's temporality of Black feminist futurity, "the future real conditional, or *that which will have had to happen*," the commemorative photographs now ask the viewer what the camptowns, the women and GIs, will have had to become, knowing what has already happened since 1984—the military regime ending, many base camps closing or relocating—even as the gendered racialization of US imperialism continues.[95] The futurity that the images ask from us needs to be radically reimagined and re-tensed (to the future real conditional)—this time, against the spectatorship of ethno-nationalism, attending to the multisensoriality of camptown portraiture and transpacific kinship.

For that reimagining—and reimaging—we must be able to sense the portraits of Black GIs and Korean women and their children beyond their visibility as a trans-temporal and trans-spatial experience thus far dominated by accessible and inaccessible archives, circulation as artworks in exhibitions, and use as academic evidence in publications. A possible example for this undertaking is a project by the artist siren eun young jung, *Narrow Sorrow* (2006–2009). Combining photography, performance, video, oral history, and research, it is a project about Dongducheon, requiring the audience to activate different modes of sensing the camptown and camptown lives.[96] The following, and the last section of the book, invites all to try to un-see camptown photographs, and instead to listen to them, with jung's work.[97]

Narrow Sorrow: To Listen to Dongducheon

In the summer of 2008, an exhibition centering on the city of Dongducheon was coorganized by and shown at New York's New Museum of Contemporary Art (May–July) and Insa Art Space (July–August), curated by Kim Heejin. The exhibition, *Dongducheon: A Walk to Remember, a Walk to Envision*, was the first major US museum exhibition to focus solely on artworks about South Korean camptowns. New Museum was at the time enthusiastically engaging with artists and art institutions across the world through programs such as "Museum as Hub," of which this exhibition was a part. Alongside related educational and public programs, the exhibited artworks, by siren eun young jung, Ko Sŭnguk, No Chae'un, and Kim Sangdon, made a strong case for the importance of engaging US viewers with camptowns' future real conditional (of what it will have had to become), as opposed to their past or present; the artworks also highlighted where the United States and its militarism (and the viewer) is situated in the map of the camptown the exhibition created.

Among the artworks included in the exhibition was a multimedia project by siren eun young jung (b. 1974). *Narrow Sorrow* (2006–2009), for which jung lived in Dongducheon over extended periods of time, combines photography, performance, video, oral history, and research, in a site-specific installation that attempts to "awake[n] the memories of [*kijich'on*] women, who wandered through the dark nights like apparitions or vanished over time."[98] The work explores the camptown's narrowest—literally, and symbolically—spaces: where camptown sex workers and their families, including their children with GIs, live (plate 29). jung's videos, photographs, and text depict the extraordinarily short and narrow doors between buildings leading to the humble living spaces (plate 30). As jung notes, it is difficult to imagine that people can pass through such narrow doors and alleyways. Yet these are also the homes of real women, homes in which their laughter, tears, joy, and despair are shared and contained.

The state needed these women to serve the USFK, but pushed and squeezed them into what usually would be considered nonspace (what zoning ordinance could possibly apply to such spaces?). This is the space allowed for the camptown women and their children under the state of exception; they were on the frontlines of the Cold War in the name of national security but elbowed past the national boundaries into the state of exception due to the very exploitation of their bodies they were conscripted for.[99] And with the decline of the camptown, many of these women have been further marginalized by the mainstream of the city and society. jung therefore questions not just how one remembers the camptown, but what happens to the memories of camptown women.

While publications for and exhibitions of *Narrow Sorrow* highlight the photographs, posters, and poems of the installation, the videos and recordings of the voices of camptown women require the audience to listen to the sounds of the camptown: "The voices in Korean, English, and Tagalog engage in casual conversations with their neighbors, solicit their customers, pray at Sunday worships, hum, sing, and, most importantly, mourn."[100] These are frequently the voices of immigrant workers and their children, reverberating with the changing demographics of camptown sex workers and, in Kim Yŏngok's words, "the globalization of prostitution."[101] They are, in fact, the sounds that the state (and the "pre-state") has tried to mute since independence.

At the same time, jung resists the fantasy of transcendental authorship, by exposing where and how she—an artist-researcher-collaborator from outside the camptown—is situated in the work. This work is, by necessity, a reflection on jung herself. In *Narrow Sorrow*, jung therefore implicates herself in the memories of Dongducheon—a phenomenon avoided (and, potentially, not even considered) by the male photographers discussed earlier in the chapter and by male critics of their works.[102] The reasons for jung's effort to grapple with her position are nuanced, but the result of the artmaking is a long performative process, encompassing her own extended presence in the camptown as something more than a spectator.[103] To put it bluntly, Kuwabara, Burri, and Kang were not as much at risk of being objectified, sexually or not, by service members in the camptown while making their work. This was, however, part of the condition of being a woman, even if not a sex worker, living in the camptown. The male artists and photographers had a priori access to the distance, literal and affective, from sexualized service labor in a way a woman could not.

jung states that "the work given to the participating artists was not to spectacularly re-present the history and its landscape, or expose 'Dongducheon' as a national trauma; but to produce a different artistic strategy that 'refuses' collective recovery that cancels out all injuries via victimization and nationalism."[104] Photography has been employed over and over as representation of camptowns through the bodies of sex workers and service members. jung's "strategy" instead resists the endless, and rote, repetition of this imagery toward a narrative of victimization and ethno-nationalization for the sake of national redemption and remasculinization. Indeed, in *Narrow Sorrow*, Dongducheon is never represented by faces of camptown women or GIs, but by the spaces and sounds (that jung cannot make out) of the camptown as a totality. As Kim Yŏngok posits, the absence of the camptown subjects' faces pushes the viewer to "feel" their identities instead; rather than, say, peeping in on the photographer's attempts to expose an escort, the experience creates an ethical relationship between the viewer and subject.[105]

By recording the spaces and sounds of Dongducheon, jung emphasizes that she is not creating but adding another voice to the work long in progress by the camptown women. She palimpsestically writes on top of these women's work: their labor, their lives, and the work of their history. At the same time, the palimpsest jung creates holds relevance to the multitemporal aspect of the event of photography—a continuum without temporal directions, which leaves the work unfinished. Unlearning (the nationalist-masculinist representation of camptowns) is an exhaustive process, and that through which jung creates *Narrow Sorrow*. The layers upon layers of spaces and sounds jung collects and curates demand that the viewer, too, unlearn the representations of camptowns. They are the sounds of protest against allowing camptown imagery to become merely the mimesis of the state of exception.[106] They are the sounds that require us to listen to photographs.

NOTES

Introduction. The Time of Korean Photography

1 Benjamin, "Theses on the Philosophy of History," 261–62.

2 For example, Justin Carville questions the boundary of Irish photography when photographs resist national identification in the historico-political complexity of Northern Ireland and the postcolonial memories of the place. Carville, *Photography and Ireland.*

3 The translation I find most accurate is "Front leaning rest position!"

4 Chatterjee makes an important claim that informs the epistemological challenge in producing a national history of photography (emphasis added): "History, it would seem, has decreed that we in the postcolonial world shall only be perpetual consumers of modernity. Europe and the Americas, the only true subjects of history, have thought out on our behalf not only the script of colonial enlightenment and exploitation, but also that of our anti-colonial resistance and postcolonial misery. Even our imaginations must remain forever colonized. . . . *The most powerful as well as the most creative results of the nationalist imagination in Asia and Africa are posited not on an identity but rather on a difference with the 'modular' forms of the nation society propagated by the modern West.* How can we ignore this without reducing the experience of anti-colonial nationalism to a caricature of itself?" Chatterjee, "Whose Imagined Community?," 214–25.

5 Although nationalism is not necessarily a driving force for the historicization of a national photography, it readily becomes a defense mechanism against applying modern genres of photography shaped in Europe and the United States (an example will be discussed later in the chapter). Chakarabarty, on the other hand, finds that nationalism presents a meaningful question regarding vision and imagination, challenging the easy identification of realism or facts with the political. Chakrabarty, *Provincializing Europe*, 149–50.

6 It is common to refer to specific photographic works of countries according to nationality—for example, British photography, Japanese photography, and so on. However, treating photographs as capable of representing the national approach to the medium as a whole—if such a thing exists—is a fallacy. For studies on the discourse of the nation and photographic archives, see Caraffa and Serena, *Photo Archives and the Idea of Nation*.

7 Geoffrey Batchen has critiqued how "photography's other history is to be fashioned from accounts of the medium's representations of non-Western peoples." Batchen, "How the Other Half Photographs: Looking Globally." Jasbir Puar also discusses how difference continues to be "difference from," not "difference within." This "'difference from' produces difference as a contradiction rather than . . . recognizing it as a perpetual and continuous process of splitting." Puar, "'I Would Rather Be a Cyborg than a Goddess,'" 53.

8 Historians and critics of photography have debunked the myth of photography as an invention. Yet the scholarship of the medium's history still demands the establishment of an identificatory, ethnographic index for a non-Western history of photography, an index that is compatible, understandable, and parallel to the epistemology of photography as inherently European.

9 Chow, "Theory, Area Studies, Cultural Studies," 114. Emphasis added.

10 Pinney, "Locating Photography"; Cadava and Nouzeilles, *Itinerant Languages of Photography*.

11 Jennifer Nash draws from the voices of feminists of color, which "have been deeply critical of diversity logics, arguing that it is a practice of 'benign variation' that 'bypass power as well as history to suggest a harmonious empty pluralism.' [. . .] Taken together, these scholars reveal the host of ways that diversity operates in apolitical and often anti-political ways to selectively usher a few bodies into exclusive institutions." Nash, *Black Feminism Reimagined*, 24.

12 Lowe, *Intimacies of Four Continents*, 7. Similarly, Jasbir Puar discusses the "cherished categories of the intersectional mantra—originally starting with race, class, gender, now including sexuality, nation. Religion, age, and disability—are the products of modernist colonial agendas and regimes of epistemic violence, operative through a Western/Euro-American epistemological formation through which the notion of discrete identity has emerged." See Puar, "'I Would Rather Be a Cyborg than a Goddess,'" 55.

13 It has been difficult to do so when the liberal university uses non-white, non-Western identities as signs of an inclusive and diverse place of knowledge making and sharing.

14 Puar, "'I Would Rather Be a Cyborg than a Goddess,'" 55. Also see Nash's thoughtful analysis of reclaiming intersectionality through the affect of defensiveness in black feminism today. Nash, *Black Feminism Reimagined.*

15 This task of satisfying identitarian logics is familiar to anyone whose studies involve non-Western, nonwhite, or nonnormative subjects, and this familiarity is part of the fatigue Puar discusses via Chow. In defiance against such identitarian logics, the Burmese photographer Min Ma Naing, for example, discusses how she is often confronted with the critique from international curators and editors seeking images of political turmoil and civilian oppression: "I don't find Burmese aesthetics in your work." Min Ma Naing, "Beyond Burmese Esthetics."

16 Chuh, "It's Not about Anything," 175.

17 Chuh, 174.

18 Chuh, 176.

19 Yoneyama, *Cold War Ruins*, 57.

20 Puar, "'I Would Rather Be a Cyborg than a Goddess,'" 50.

21 Muñoz, *Sense of Brown*, 78. In his discussion on Nao Bustamante's performance as Carmelita Tropicana, Muñoz relates the shifting personifications to queer assemblage itself, to always becoming. Resonating with Puar, becoming, for Muñoz, "eschews notions of fixed organic unity for anticipatory formations. . . . Becoming is a kind of deterritorialization of the body itself, where stable molar identities are interrupted and new molecular formations take place. Becoming is about the interstice, about the threshold, dislocation, and destabilization."

22 Gi-Wook Shin describes how Korea's ethno-nationalism, based on common ancestry and heritage, was not only shaped by modernity, but also determined "the forms and nature of modernity" the country took on. It is not uncommon to see conflations of nation and nationalism, nation and modernity, and nationalism and modernity in that context. Shin, *Ethnic Nationalism in Korea*, 13.

23 Benjamin, "Theses on the Philosophy of History."

24 Barthes, *Mythologies*, 137–50. Emphasis in original. Pinney, "Locating Photography," 30.

25 Barthes's antithesis of "bourgeois ex-nomination" is "revolutionary denomination," which "announces openly as revolution and thereby abolishes myth." Barthes, 147; Pinney, "Locating Photography," 40.

26 For instance, in *Itinerant Languages of Photography* (36), Eduardo Cadava emphasizes "itinerancy" as the essence of photographic images; it also helps to shift the focus from "the relation between photography and travel" to "the itinerancy

of the practices and discourses of photography themselves." Yet while Cadava and Gabriela Nouzeilles remark on "an explosion of 'world photography'" and how all of its archives and histories "deserve to be studied 'independently' and in relation to one another," they nonetheless immediately turn to the "nominated" difference of Latin America being at "the forefront of the development of new aesthetic paradigms in modern and contemporary photography," which was the focus of their 2013–14 exhibition and accompanying catalogue. The itinerancy of photographic practices and discourses does help us reach more nuanced scholarship of the violent and entwined histories of capital, industry, colonialism, technology, and knowledge production; but the nominated difference is still presented as the very episteme that "deserves" to receive scholarly attention and institutional funding. Cadava and Nouzeilles, *Itinerant Languages of Photography*, 18.

27 Barthes, "Great Family of Man," 100–102.

28 Barthes's work has inspired contemporary reflections on photography's essence, including its relationship with death. For example, see Batchen, *Photography Degree Zero*; "Life and Death," 108–29.

29 Barthes, *Camera Lucida*, 97. Pinney considers Barthes's conjuring of the three tenses an ontological exploration of photography, which is potentially a more meaningful question than focusing on cultural differences as the medium's ontological beginnings. Pinney, "Troubled by Photography."

30 Barthes's powerful and deeply admired reflection on the "death in the future" of photography, as he writes on Lewis Payne's portrait, is commensurate with death in Christianity: "There is always a defeat of Time in them: *that* is dead and *that* is going to die . . . they are dead (today), they are then *already* dead (yesterday)" (*Camera Lucida*, 96). The impending yet suspended death, which has happened at the time of viewing, showcases the multiple tenses of photography. It is, however, the possibility of conflating these deaths, including those of Payne, Jesus, and Barthes at different times and locations, that the default of ex-nomination allows. In other words, it is not the different times that a photograph engages with per se that a project of "national" photography finds its onto-epistemological limits, but the ex-nominated location from which different times are conjured, iterated, and compared. And conversely (and subsequently), to conjure, iterate, and compare different times in hopes of being ex-nominated. Subjects are legitimized and valorized as academic when they are mapped onto the temporality of modernity vis-à-vis European thoughts.

31 Gordon, *Ghostly Matters*.

32 Barthes, "Great Family of Man," 102. By contrast, Ariella Aïsha Azoulay's more recent approach to the *Family of Man* exhibition sheds light on its lasting humanitarian impact as a "visual universal declaration of human rights," countering Barthes's critique. Azoulay, "'Family of Man.'"

33 Moten, *In the Break*, 203.

34 Moten, 204–5.

35 Moten, 205.

36 Moten, 196.

37 Moten, 208.

38 Barthes, *Camera Lucida*, 34, cited in Smith, *At the Edge of Sight*, 28, 30.

39 Smith, *At the Edge of Sight*, 35.

40 Smith, 38.

41 Eng, "Feeling of Photography, the Feeling of Kinship," 346n10. Also, Elizabeth Abel examines Barthes's essentialization of the language of photography, juxtaposing it against Benjamin's approaches. Abel, *Signs of the Times*, 62–67, especially "Signs of Race in the Language of Photography."

42 For example, to self-reflect on and reassess their interventionist guerilla performance at the opening of Matthew Barney's solo exhibition at the San Francisco Museum of Modern Art, Tina Takemoto pays attention to the ways that Barney and Barthes both deploy Japan in their work as "an inspiring 'situation for writing' that need not bear any resemblance to any actual location." Referring to him as the master of semiotics, Takemoto notes that Barthes is "willfully indifferent to the historical, cultural, or political realities of Japan in order to fulfill 'the possibility of difference, of a mutation, of a revolution in the propriety of symbolic systems'"; Japan is approached "as an empire of foreign, traditional, and antiquated signs that can be manipulated to create entirely new symbolic systems for the West." See Takemoto, "Drawing Complaint," 87–88.

43 Hirsch, *Family Frames*.

44 This logic operates efficiently in linear time as we are asked to look back (usually through the image of the Other) and to look forward (in anticipation of the diversified Self). See Smith and Sliwinski, *Photography and the Optical Unconscious*, 15.

45 Smith and Sliwinski, *Photography and the Optical Unconscious*.

46 Benjamin, "On the Concept of History," 389–400.

47 Benjamin, "Little History of Photography," 510, quoted in Smith and Sliwinski, *Photography and the Optical Unconscious*, 11–12.

48 Benjamin, "On the Concept of History," 391, quoted in Smith and Sliwinski, *Photography and the Optical Unconscious*, 12.

49 Chakrabarty, *Provincializing Europe*, 107.

50 Chakrabarty, 100.

51 "Minor" methods and affect have been explored by authors such as Hentyle Yapp and Cathy Park Hong. Yapp, *Minor China*; Hong, *Minor Feelings*.

52 Gordon, *Ghostly Matters*.

53 Gordon, 27.

54 Chakrabarty, *Provincializing Europe*, 108.

55 Chakrabarty, 109.

56 Kracauer and Kristeller, *History*, 155.

57 Bhabha, "'Race,' Time and the Revision of Modernity," 203. Emphasis in original.

58 Bhabha, 201.

59 Bhabha, 202.

60 Bhabha, 194. Bhabha refers to Fanon, "The Fact of Blackness," 109–40.

61 Bhabha, "'Race,' Time and the Revision of Modernity," 202.

62 Bhabha, 202. Emphasis in original. He goes on to claim, "Hidden in the disavowing narrative of historical retroversion and its archaism, is a notion of the time-lag that displaces Foucault's spatial analytic of modernity and Anderson's homogenous temporality of the modern nation." See 209.

63 Lim, *Translating Time*, 18.

64 Lim, 50–51.

65 Lim's "immiscible temporality" is therefore comparable to the temporality of photography. See Lim, 32.

66 Azoulay, *Civil Imagination*, 25. Azoulay critiques the concept of "a certain instance framed by a photographer" as overemphasizing the particular time represented and doing so by erroneously conceptualizing the time of photography as if it is given by the photographer. Azoulay writes that "a photograph is never the testimony of the photographer alone, and the event of photography, unlike the photographed event, continues to exist despite all other considerations.... The event of photography is never over. It can only be suspended, caught in the anticipation of the next encounter that will allow for its actualization," 25.

67 Tsai Ming-liang explores the dehomogenization of global time (and being) in his 2001 film, *What Time Is It There?* Though the event of photography undoes a universal time, the concept of the camera as a clock continues to enable a particular kind of temporality in national photography by acting as a framing device for putting different spaces in a unified time via the special distance of history's enunciation.

68 Yoneyama, *Cold War Ruins*, 49. Emphasis added.

69 Thy Phu has similarly discussed the temporal and spatial disjuncture and misalignment that happens during the reenactment of the Vietnam War in the forests of Virginia in An-My Lê's *Small Wars*. Phu, "Reenactment and Remembrance."

70 Chakrabarty, *Provincializing Europe*, 113.

71 Chow, "Theory, Area Studies, Cultural Studies," 111.

72 Indeed, it would not be hyperbole to say Ch'oe shaped the foundation of the history of Korean photography and launched it as an academic field as the director of RIHP. He died in 2016 at age seventy-five. In 2018, the institute was given a new name, Research Institute for the Visual Language of Korea (RIVL), directed by Ju Suk Park at Myongji University. In honor of Ch'oe and his work, RIVL founded the Ch'oe Injin Center for Photo Research in the same year. Lee, *Han'guksajinŭi Chip'yŏng*.

73 Park, "Han'guksajinŭi Doip Kwajŏng Sŏlmyŏnggwa Chŏng Haech'ang Sajinŭi Haesŏge Nat'anan Munjechŏm Koch'al," 103–4.

74 Park, 116.

75 Park, 117.

76 However, I note that RIHP's—now Research Institute for the Visual Language—epistemic shifts and diversification are apparent. For instance, in the introduction to his publication *Han'guksajinsa* (*The History of Korean Photography*), Park takes a more investigative position to examine how the "Western" medium and discourses have clashed and evolved in the unique context of Korea. Park, *Han'guksajinsa*.

77 In examining the rise of national narratives in modern China, Prasenjit Duara aptly points out that history has been treated more as "a transparent medium of understanding than as a discourse enabling historical players (including historians) to deploy its resources to occlude, repress, appropriate and, sometimes, negotiate with other modes of depicting the past and thus, the present and future." National narratives in modern China, in turn, "transformed the perception not only of the past but also of the present meaning of the nation and the world." Duara, *Rescuing History from the Nation*, 5.

78 Kim, *Interrogation Rooms of the Korean War*, 3.

79 Shin, *Ethnic Nationalism in* Korea, 7.

80 Shamsul A. B.'s discussion on "methodological nationalism," referred to by Yoneyama, is applicable here. Yoneyama, *Cold War Ruins*, 243n30.

81 Curiously, the group is more concerned about Western imperialism than the Japanese colonial era, during which photo groups and salon competitions were popularized.

82 Sakai, "Translation and Image," 85.

83 Sakai, 86.

84 Sakai, 86.

85 Liu, "Eventfulness of Translation," 18.

86 Lim, *Translating Time*, 250. Emphasis in original.

87 Lim, 250. Lim refers to Johannes Fabian and Dipesh Chakrabarty.

88 Marker, *Coreénnes*; *Puknyŏksaramdŭl (Coreénnes)*.

89 See, respectively, Jongwoo Park, *Inside DMZ-Guard Posts*, 2009–2017, chromogenic color print; Suntag Noh, *Red House I, II & III*, 2001–2005, color photography. Noh's newly edited series was shown at Seoul Metropolitan Museum of Art's exhibition, "North Korea Project (Pukhan Project)," which was held for the seventieth anniversary of independence in July 21–September 29, 2015.

90 One is Boyoung Chang's work on the representation of North Korea in Europe and North America juxtaposed against South Korean artists' work, exploring the ramification of Western representation of the North Korean leaders and authoritarian state. Chang, "Imagining the Other Korea."

Chapter 1. War and the Image of an Orphan Nation

An earlier version of this chapter was published as "Orphan Nation: Representations of Korean War Orphans in Contemporary Visual Culture," in *The Eye on War: Constructing the Memory of War in Visual Culture since 1914*, edited by Ann Murray, 226–36 (New York: Routledge, 2018). The photo series by Agnès Dherbeys was introduced previously in "Undoing the Cold War Temporality: Transnational Adoption in Agnès Dherbeys's *Omone* and *Retired*," in *Visual Representations of the Cold War and Postcolonial Struggles: Art in East and Southeast Asia*, edited by Midori Yamamura and Yu-Chieh Li, 212–31 (New York: Routledge, 2021).

1 Yoneyama, *Cold War Ruins*.

2 Yoneyama, 49. Emphasis in original.

3 The UN forces combined soldiers from sixteen countries, listed here in order of the number of soldiers sent to Korea: the United States (302,483), the United Kingdom (14,198), Canada (6,146), Turkey (5,455), Australia (2,282), the Philippines (1,496), New Zealand (1,389), Thailand (1,294), Ethiopia (1,271), Greece (1,263), France (1,119), Colombia (1,068), Belgium (944), South Africa (826), the Netherlands (819), and Luxembourg (100).

4 The Korean War was crucial to the process of the United States becoming the world's most militarized nation and expanding its political influence across the world. Around the time of the Korean War, the US signed treaties with forty-two allies, which enabled it to establish over 2,700 US military bases outside the United States. This political change is referred to as "Globalization of Containment Policy." Yi Wanbŏm, "Han'guk chŏnjaengŭi chŏngch'ichŏk yŏnghyang," 8.

5 The United States' two-per-family international adoption limit was annulled in 1955 so that Harry and Bertha Holt could adopt eight Korean war orphans. Mass Western adoption of Korean children followed.

6 The juxtaposition was a critical curatorial decision at the exhibition of Agnès Dherbeys's photo series *Omone* and *Retired* at the Museum of Photography, Seoul, in the winter of 2016–17. The exhibition, titled *아녜스 데르비 Agnès Dherbeys #K76_3613*, was part of the museum's yearlong program, which introduced selected French photographers in collaboration with various French institutions in celebration of "2015–2016 Korea France Year."

7 Thy Phu examines the different meanings of "orphan images," including "orphaned images," those that have lost their places and owners, and of those implications in the Vietnamese diaspora, especially in different generations. Phu, "Diasporic Vietnamese Family Photographs."

8 Hübinette, *Comforting an Orphaned Nation*, 38–39.

9 The captions of the photographs use the term "adoption" to describe the relationship between orphans and GIs. These photographs have been reproduced in Pak, *Chiulsuŏmnŭn Imigi 3* (*The Indelible Image 3*). English title in original.

10 War commemorations work toward consolidating different war and postwar experiences and memories. The conjuring of such varying experiences and memories at the same time (via commemorative events) yields the feeling of unity and the feeling of homogeneous temporality.

11 See, for example, Brown and Phu, *Feeling Photography*; Olin, *Touching Photographs*; Campt, *Listening to Images*.

12 Campt, *Listening to Images*, 72.

13 English title in original.

14 Wisch-Ray, "Dallas Doings."

15 One of the ten photographs included in *Abandoned Children* is a now-iconic photograph of a girl with a baby—wrapped in a quilt and strapped to the girl's back, a common way of carrying children in Korea—from the NARA Korean War photography collection. The title *Abandoned Children* tacitly leads the viewer to identify the girl and her sibling as orphans. The caption of the photograph reads: "With her brother on her back a war weary Korean girl tiredly trudges by a stalled M-26 tank, at Haengju, Korea, 06/09/1951." This photograph was also selected as the poster for the exhibition.

16 Kim, "Dallas 'Han'gukchŏnjaengt'ŭkpyŏlsajinchŏn' Haninbalkil Soedo." The now-defunct Dallas-based Korean American news outlet continued to report on local Korean War memorial events using similar children's photographs. See, for example, Kim, "'Beibi Soljyŏwa 'Pudaechigye'e Tamkin Yugio Han'gukjŏnchaengŭi 'Ch'amsang.'"

17 Kim, "Dallas 'Han'gukchŏnjaengt'ŭkpyŏlsajinchŏn' Haninbalkil Soedo."

18 A common postwar collective consciousness, *postmemory* is a term coined by Marianne Hirsch in her assessment of shared memory among Holocaust victims' children. Hirsch, *Family Frames*.

19 Phu's analysis is centered on the rhetoric of reunion, forgiveness, and the symbolic "rapprochement between East and West" in the aftermath of the Pacific and Vietnam Wars. Her point about a "sense of embodied vulnerability," shared by those "who signify traumatic encounters between the United States and Asia," is relevant to the Korean American community viewing the Dallas exhibition. Phu, *Picturing Model Citizens*, 87.

20 Similarly, South Korea's first four-star general, Paik Sun Yup, expresses his gratitude to the United States in his foreword for a photo book by John Rich published in 2010: "We the people of the Republic of Korea humbly express our recognition and respect to those troops and their families. This nation owes them a great debt. Now the Republic of Korea must repay that debt to them." This debtor-creditor approach to remembering the forgotten war—not very different from that observed in Dallas—is immediately presented visually with the book's cover spread, which shows a South Korean orphan boy posing on a crashed North Korean fighter plane. This narrative continues with photographs of South Korean and US officials, United Nations service members, and South Korean civilians. See Rich, *Korean War in Color*, vi, cited in Lee, review of *Korean War in Color*. In the same vein, Korean Americans acknowledged their "debt" to Korean War veterans of Texas and bowed to them at a Korean War anniversary event. Kim, "Han'gukchŏnjaeng Yuksipchunyŏn Kinyŏmhaengsa 'Ch'amjŏnyongsatŭlkke Chinsimŭro Kokaesugyŏ Kamsatŭrimnita.'"

21 Rai, *Rule of Sympathy*.

22 Rai, xi.

23 Chaudhary, *Afterimage of Empire*, 172.

24 Chaudhary, 173.

25 Rai, *Rule of Sympathy*, xiii, xix.

26 Kwŏn, "Mosŏngsinhwaŭikiwon, Kŭ P'asijŭmjŏk Hyŏngsigekwanhayŏ"; "Yŏsŏngsunansa Iyagi"; "Yŏsŏng·sunansa Iyagiŭi Yŏksajŏk Ch'ŭngwi."

27 Kwŏn, "Mosŏngsinhwaŭikiwon, Kŭ P'asijŭmjŏk Hyŏngsigekwanhayŏ," 53.

28 They are considered the periods of national humiliation and emasculation.

29 Scholars such as Sheila Miyoshi Jager, Sang Mi Park, and Tobias Hübinette also discuss the gendered representation of the Korean nation and family; however, they overlook the ways in which the representation of familial transformation requires a priori gendering of individual members as "natural." Jager, "Women, Resistance and the Divided Nation"; Park, "Paradox of Postcolonial Korean Nationalism"; Hübinette, *Comforting an Orphaned Nation*; Hübinette, "Orphaned Nation"; Hübinette, "Korea(n) Divided."

30 Kwŏn, "Yŏsŏng·sunansa Iyagiŭi Yŏksajŏk Ch'ŭngwi," 154.

31 Kwŏn, "Munyeyŏnghwawa Kongyugiŏk (Commemoration) Mandŭlgi," 131.

32 Hübinette, *Comforting an Orphaned Nation*; "Orphaned Nation."

33 Kwŏn, "Yŏsŏngsunansa Iyagi," 110.

34 Chaudhary, *Afterimage of Empire*, 179.

35 Kim, "Dallas 'Han'gukchŏnjaengt'ŭkpyŏlsajinchŏn' Haninbalkil Soedo."

36 Kim, "Dallas 'Han'gukchŏnjaengt'ŭkpyŏlsajinchŏn' Haninbalkil Soedo."

37 South Korean publications of Korean War photographs by American veterans and war correspondents include Veterans of Foreign Wars, *Kŭtŭripon Han'gukchŏnjaeng 2*; and To Pak, *Chiulsuŏmnŭn Imigi 3*.

38 Lim, "Victimhood Nationalism in Contested Memories."

39 Lim, 138–39.

40 Lim, 139.

41 Kwŏn, "Munyeyŏnghwawa Kongyugiŏk (Commemoration) Mandŭlgi," 131.

42 Lim, "Victimhood Nationalism in Contested Memories," 140.

43 Carter Eckert writes that "South Korean army culture and practice continue to be ingrained in government, business, education, and virtually every other sphere of social activity, as well as in many facets of everyday Korean life." Eckert, *Park Chung Hee and Modern Korea*, 2.

44 Kim, *Adopted Territory*, 50.

45 Sarri, Baik, and Bombyk, "Goal Displacement and Dependency," 92.

46 According to Sarri, Baik, and Bambyk, the vast majority of US adopters of non-US children are white, and their most highly desired adoptees are from northeast Asia. Although it is beyond the scope of this article, the racial issues surrounding international adoption are immense. For studies on the issues of race in international adoption, see Choy, "Race at the Center"; Kim, Suyemoto, and Turner, "Sense of Belonging."

47 Sarri, Baik, and Bombyk, "Goal Displacement and Dependency," 93–94.

48 An increasing number of studies on diverse adoption-related issues, from adoption policies to portrayals of adoptees in pop culture, have been produced by scholars across the world since the 2000s. Several of those scholars have analyzed the imagery of Korean orphans and adoptees in visual culture. For instance, as mentioned, Eleana Kim examines the use of orphan photographs in adoption advertisements in the formative years of Korean international adoption in her book *Adopted Territory*; Hübinette (2005, 2006) assesses portrayals of Korean adoptees in popular culture media; Arissa Oh (2005, 2012) examines the rhetoric of "Christian Americanism" in constructing the figure of the Korean orphan; Chrystal Mun-hye Baik (2015) assesses adoptee artists' contemporary artworks in the context of US-Korea militarized debt; Hosu Kim (2016) examines Korean birth mothers through what she refers to as "virtual mothering"; Kim Park Nelson (2016) provides ethnographic studies of the transnational adoption of Korean children in North America through

racial and cultural dynamics, through which the adoptees become "invisible Asians"; SooJin Pate's work (2014) on military film footage is discussed later in this chapter.

49 Chaudhary, *Afterimage of Empire*, 179.

50 Kim, *Adopted Territory.*

51 Phu, *Picturing Model Citizens*, 86.

52 Such as the Nogeun-ri massacre of 1950.

53 Pate, *From Orphan to Adoptee*, 56. Nonetheless, Pate does not examine photographs of camptown sex workers or, notably, of Korean servicemen with or without GIs for her arguments on such allegorical representations.

54 Pate, *From Orphan to Adoptee.*

55 Although Pate makes the analogy of the boys as American GIs and girls as *kijich'on* (camptown) women, I argue, to follow this analogy, that the boys were also sexualized via their representations as vulnerable beings in need of homosocial care, as seen in the Mosey and Pak photograph.

56 This concept of pan-Koreanness is especially pertinent in the case of the Dallas exhibition.

57 An exception which remains frequently referenced is the photographer Joo Myung Duk's 1966 exhibition, *The Mixed Names*, at Chunganggongbokwan (Central Information Services) in Seoul, depicting mixed-race orphans in the (then) Harry Holt Memorial Orphanage. According to Joo, while he had no difficulties showing this body of work in 1966, it was suppressed by the state in the following decade. Myung Duk Joo, "Q&A."

58 See Sarri, Baik, and Bombyk, "Goal Displacement and Dependency"; Choy, "Race at the Center." On birth mothers, see Kim, *Birth Mothers and Transnational Adoption Practice in South Korea.*

59 For instance, in the 1991 film *Susanne Brink's Arirang*, directed by Chang Kilsu. Hübinette, "Nationalism, Subalternity, and the Adopted Koreans," 118.

60 Hübinette, 121.

61 Kim, *Adopted Territory*, 137–38.

62 Kim, *Adopted Territory*, 137.

63 Kim, *Adopted Territory*, 137.

64 Hübinette, *Comforting an Orphaned Nation.*

65 For this series, the individual photographs come with brief captions hinting at what is going on: for example, a caption for a photo depicting Mr. Dherbeys' dining table reads, "Ever since I can remember, my father has been hammered by insomnia. Every night around 4 A.M., he sets up the table for breakfast for the morning after." Reprinted with permission of the artist.

66 Dherbeys first noticed during the shooting that her father's face was "very cinematic, like an actor." Dherbeys, FaceTime interview with the author, January 11, 2020.

67 Comparatively, the steep rise in transnational adoptions from China is an alarming indicator of where transnational adoption stands in neoliberal temporality. Over 150,000 children, mostly girls, were adopted internationally since the introduction of the one-child policy in 1979, the annual number peaking in 2005. It has since been decreasing. See Monica Dowling, "Globalisation and International Adoption from China," 305–20.

68 Nelson, *Invisible Asians*, 152–53.

Chapter 2. The Place of Women in Family Photography

An earlier version of this chapter was published as "Envisioning Modernity, Practicing Desire: Baby and Family Photographic Portraiture in Korea," *History of Photography* 37, no. 3 (August 2013): 312–25.

1 Throughout the chapter I use the terms *photo-portraits* and *photo-portraiture* rather than *portrait photographs* or *portrait photography* to place an emphasis on the photographic genre of portraiture.

2 According to Jung-ha Kim, the rise of photo-portraits in Korea in the early twentieth century is closely related to the distribution and hanging of *ŏchin*—the portrait of Kochong, the emperor of the Taehanchekuk (Korean Empire, 1897–1910)—as a sign of resistance against Japanese colonial rule. Kim adds that the practice of hanging of *ŏchin* and portraits of one's ancestors at the top of the wall resembled the custom of hanging a photo-portrait of the Japanese emperor in the Korean homes of Japanese colonials. Kim, "Kŭndaesingminchuŭie Taeŭnghan Saenghwalmunhwa Cho'sangsajin," 154, 158.

3 Hye-ri Oh traces the etymology, genealogy, and practice of *sajin*, the Korean word for photography, which initially meant portrait painting, in relation to premodern and modern discourses of visuality in Korea. See Oh, "Translating 'Photography.'"

4 For a brief comparison between portrait paintings and photo-portraits, see Lee, "Envisioning Modernity, Practicing Desire," 313–15.

5 *Chungin* literally means the middle people—those holding lower managerial/administrative positions within a municipality.

6 Ch'oe, *Han'guksajinsa*, 171–72.

7 An embossed seal in an art nouveau-style typeface on the lower right corner of the mount board indicates the name of the photographer, "M. Kikura Seoul Corea."

8 Given that all of them appear to be in a similar age group, their relationships and the occasion of photo-taking are not obvious.

9 Hirsch, *Family Photographs*, 32–33.

10 Israel, *Enlightenment Contested.*

11 Pak, *Kajogŭl Kŭrita*, 28.

12 Hirsch, *Family Photographs*, 32–33.

13 Choi, "Kajoksajin,"143.

14 Another photographic work that explores women's life, labor, and psyche in Korean society is the photography series *Mich'innyŏn p'urojekt'ŭ* (*Mad Women Project*, 1999) by Young Sook Park.

15 Campt, *Listening to Images*. Campt has taught me to pay attention to the ways that the images, collections, and archives exist and make meanings differently than the ways photo archives have functioned and been studied under the disciplinary practices of Eurocentric institutions.

16 Yi was an independence activist until about 1921. In 1922, he became a writer for *Dong-a Ilbo* (*Dong-a Daily*), writing articles about the need to modernize before protesting against colonial power. He announced his procolonialist collaboration in 1938 and continued to write both fiction and newspaper and journal articles. In 1950, Yi was abducted by the North Korean military, dying mysteriously the same year. Although the exact circumstances of his death are unknown, it is assumed to be related to his abduction.

17 Ponggŭn was born in 1927 and died in 1934.

18 For a study of changes in the treatment of infants and children in the West, from indifference to nurturing, see "Mother and Infants" and "The Rise of the Nuclear Family" in Shorter, *Making of the Modern Family.*

19 Among pro-*kaehwa* (prowesternization/promodernization) intellectuals, Yi Kwangsu was considered especially "anti-past" or "anti-tradition." He has been criticized for insisting on "moral transformation" while ignoring "political transformation," thereby limiting the movement to "elitist discourse." See Kwŏn, *Kajok Iyaginŭn Ŏttŏke Mandŭrochinŭn'ga*, which examines the *kaehwa* movement initiated by intellectuals during the colonial rule from a psychoanalytical perspective. *Kaehwa* literally means "to bloom" but it is also used to refer to "civilization" and "modernization" specifically during the colonial period. In other words, westernization/Japanization equaled modernization, which also means colonization—and self-degradation as subjects to become "civilized" through colonization. For a historical analysis of the *kaecho* (reform/reconstruction) thought on Yi, see Choi, "Yi Kwangsu and the Post–World War I Reconstruction Debate."

20 In the May 1922 issue of the journal *Kaepyŏk* (개벽), Yi wrote an article titled "Minjok Kaejoron (The Theory of National Reformation)," which argued for

ethical reformation of the Korean race based on Confucian virtues. Having previously called for the abolition of the Confucian doctrine long embedded in the Korean life, he was criticized for his new insistence on its importance.

21 Tan'guktaehakkyo pusŏl tongyanghak yŏn'guso, *Ilsangsaenghwalgwa Kŭndaekyŏrhonjedo Chapchip'yŏn*, vii.

22 Paek, *Sŭwit'ŭ Homŭi Kiwŏn*, 15–16; Kim, "Ilcheha Ŏrinikiŭi Hyŏngsŏnggwa Kajokpyŏnhwae Kwanhan Yŏn'gu," 104–6.

23 Paek, cited in Pak, *Kajogŭl Kŭrita*, 76.

24 Paek, *Sŭwit'ŭ Homŭi Kiwŏn*, 21–24.

25 Paek, 24.

26 Choi, "Yi Kwangsu and the Post–World War I Reconstruction Debate," 39.

27 Na, *Ilchesitae, Uri Kajogŭn*. Throughout this book, Na describes the influence of Japanese education on her parents and other elite members of the group they associated with. While they felt despair and anger during the colonial period, they also wished to transform their "backward" country into a modernized state.

28 Kim, "Kŭndaesingminchuŭie Taeŭnghan Saenghwalmunhwa Ch'osangsajin," 154.

29 The stamp shows a Japanese name in a Romanized transliteration, "Y. Sato." This was possibly the name of the photographer.

30 Western-style attire as opposed to *hanbok*, traditional Korean clothes. Today *yangbok* generally means men's suits.

31 Although the hundredth day and the first birthday are also celebrated in other parts of East Asia, such as China, these photographic practices specifically developed into an idiosyncratic cultural practice particular to South Korea. In China, one month after birth, called *moon-yut*, is much more commonly celebrated than the hundredth day; similar to Korean practice, the biggest celebration during childhood is the first birthday, as with many other cultures.

32 On the practice of baby photo-portraits in South Korea, see Hong, "Study of the Specialization of Baby Photos"; Chŏng, "Beibisajine Kwanhan Yŏn'gu," 18–31; Ko, "Sinsaengasajin p'yohyŏne Kwanhan Yŏn'gu."

33 For an examination of the gender-differentiated practice of baby photo-portraiture in Korea, see Lee, "Envisioning Modernity, Practicing Desire."

34 For Park's military career in the Japanese Imperial Army and its relations to the militarization of ROK during his time, see Eckert, *Park Chung Hee and Modern Korea*.

35 Serk-Bae Suh discusses Yi's status as a "failed-father" figure of modern Korean literature, being both a wound and the inflictor of that wound through which modern Korean literature was born, regardless of the conflicting receptions of his life and work as independence activist turned colonial collaborator. The issue of self-sacrifice in Yi's defense of colonial collaboration is examined in

his autobiography, *Naŭi kopaek*. Notably, Suh explores the patrilineal rhetoric of nation as family in Yi's claim for his collaboration as self-sacrifice, and his "sons," the young Korean men whom he encouraged to enlist in the Japanese Imperial Army during the Asia-Pacific War, the most "valuable thing" he is sacrificing for the Korean nation, hence, insisting himself as the ultimate victim of his colonial collaboration. Suh, "A False Martyr's Wager."

36 Kwŏn, *Ŭmnangwa Hyŏngmyŏng*, 35.

37 Kwŏn, 35.

38 Kim, *Curative Violence*, 64–65.

39 Kukkakirogwŏn, "In'gu Chŏngch'aek: Chuyo Isyu Mannaki"; "Idarŭi Kirok: 2010nyŏn 02wol: 'Mojapogŏnpŏp' Chejŏng."

40 The name of the act deliberately puts the state's will to intervene over the rights of the mother, and only the mother.

41 Kim, *Curative Violence*, 50. Kim argues that eugenics was an "intellectual" and paranoid fallout of new interest in "modern marriages" based on love: "Eugenic ideas and methods to 'fix' and 'improve' the 'essence' of race were introduced to colonial Chosŏn through Japanese adoption of British eugenics and by Korean elites who studied in Europe, Japan, and the United States during the colonial era." Kim, 44.

42 Sin, "Sanŏphwaihu Il-Kajok Munjeŭi Tamnonjŏk Chihyŏnggwa Pyŏnhwa," 91. See also Kim, *Curative Violence*, 64–65.

43 I recall making numerous posters in watercolor and acrylic for school competitions while attending elementary school in the 1980s. The themes of the competitions varied, including *pan'gong* (anti-communism), *chŏnki* and *multcha chŏryak* (energy saving and product consumption control), *hwacheyepang* (fire prevention), and more. Best posters were awarded with award certificates and sometimes opportunities for municipal or citywide competitions.

44 For different approaches to family planning from the 1960s to the 1990s, see Lee, "Envisioning Modernity, Practicing Desire."

45 Sin, "Sanŏphwaihu Il-Kajok Munjeŭi Tamnonjŏk Chihyŏnggwa Pyŏnhwa," 91.

46 The development of marshy land south of the Han River is often referred to as "the Miracle on Han River." This is today's Kangnam, literally meaning the south of the river.

47 Pak, Kang, and Yi, *1960nyŏndae Sahoebyŏnhwa Yŏn'gu*, 55–98. The prices of most of these single-family apartment units south of the Han River (Kangnam) have increased dramatically over the past three decades, as it has become one of the most expensive areas of South Korea. The units have become too small for high-income families in the area, and most of the apartment buildings have undergone or are slated for *chaekaepal* (reconstruction)—transformation into high-end, high-rise apartments.

48 Kim, "Kajoksajine Kwanhan Han Yŏn'gu," 27.

49 Kim, 28.

50 Kim, 29. "이 시기에 집중된 대형 가족사진은 중년기 여성들의 혼란된 감정을 정리해주는 역할을 한다는 측면에서 하나의 통과의례로 볼 수 있다."

51 Oh, *Kkumŭl Tchiknŭn Sŭtyudio*, 184–85.

52 While phone cameras transformed the ways family photographs are made and viewed, the desire to portray a family according to the prescribed patriarchal structure is still expressed by male, presumably heterosexual, Korean writers on photography. Chang Chŏngmin, for example, laments that digital family portraits have betrayed the essence of family photo-portraiture: to remember family values. For Chang, the cheapening of photo making from film to digital has devalued what it means to make family photo-portraits and keep them in one's memories. But what are those family values, and how do photo-portraits mediate one's memories in passing on such values? Whose values are remembered and whose memories are forgotten? Do the "new" digital portraits portray "new" values? Unlike Chang, Choi has argued that vernacular family photo-portraits, then and now, represent the desire for the "irrefutable collective consciousness" of the family. See Chang, "Kiŏgŭi Maech'eesŏ Manggagŭi Maech'ero," 333–34; Choi, "Kajoksajin," 146.

53 Kwŏn, *Muhani Chŏngch'ijŏgin Oeroum*, 150. Kwŏn examines the popularity of Sin Kyŏngsuk's 2008 novel, *Ŏmmarŭl Putakhe* (*Please Look After Mom*), and its positive reception from literary critics, including some antifeminists.

54 Kwŏn, 153.

55 Pak, *Kajogŭl Kŭrita*, 249.

56 Kwŏn, *Muhani Chŏngch'ijŏgin Oeroum*, 267–68.

57 *Hochuche* was an adaptation of the Japanese civil code in 1923. The code was repealed in Japan in 1948, but retained in South Korea under different titles until December 31, 2007.

58 The recent popularity of *minjokchuŭi* among Korean intellectuals as a shield against neoliberalism and global capitalism is discussed in chapter 5. That the promoters of *minjokchuŭi* are mostly men, whether from conservative or progressive communities in academia, is undeniably related to the masculinist-nationalist basis of such learned circles.

59 The artist Hye Sun Shin, for example, has photographed the portraits of *tamunhwa* families in rural areas. Shin, "Family Photo."

60 Hye-Kyung Lee, "International Marriage and the State in South Korea," 11.

61 For discussions on the "multicultural turn" of Korean identity, see Iain Watson, "Multiculturalism in South Korea"; Jun, "'We Have to Transform Ourselves First'"; Ahn, "Transforming Korea into a Multicultural Society"; Cawley, "Back to the Future."

62 Pak, *Kajogŭl Kŭrita*, 261–62. Even *kukchekyŏrhon* has become a less popular term with the rise of multiculturality, while the use of the term *tamunhwa kajŏng*—multicultural family—has grown.

63 Bonglim Choi argues that probing what is at stake in the Korean family requires examining art photography, such as Lee's and Kim's, as vernacular family photo-portraits only reveal "cliché formality, old social functions, and sitters' desire for an ideal family." Choi, "Kajoksajin," 156.

64 Although Rhee himself was married to Francesca Donner, a woman born in Vienna, Austria.

65 Chae, "Non-Western Colonial Rule and Its Aftermath," 175–76; Pak, *Kajogŭl Kŭrita*, 263.

66 In her artist's statement, Kim points out that international marriages are over 13 percent of all South Korean marriages, as of 2007. Kim and Kim, "Haep'it'ugedŏ-Sajin'ga Kim Oksŏn." In 2019, the rate was 11 percent, with a 4.2 percent increase from the previous year. While the overall number of marriages in South Korea declined dramatically over the last two decades, the ratio of international marriages remained rather consistent, seeing only slight fluctuations; so while the visibility of long-term non-Korean residents in South Korea has increased through media representation and *tamunhwa* campaigns, the number has not risen significantly in recent years. See Ch'oe, "2019 Honin Yihon t'onggye"; Yŏsŏngkachokpu Tamunhwakachokkwa, "Kukchekyŏron Hyŏnhwang."

67 Kim and Kim, "Haep'it'ugedŏ-Sajin'ga Kim Oksŏn."

68 For an assessment of such readings of family studio portraits in Kim Yongt'ae's photocollage, *DMZ*, and a new way of understanding his appropriation of studio portraits, see Lee, "1984: A Camptown Story."

69 The number of traditional neighborhood photo studios has decreased dramatically since the popularization of digital and cell phone cameras. In contrast, there has been a steep rise of sticker photo booth studios as their popularity soared again, notably around 2020. Sticker photo booths were previously popular in the 1990s.

70 Ran Studio is famous for making family photo-portraits of Korean socialites and famous politicians and proudly displaying them in their show windows.

71 The widely known gay director Kim Cho Kwangsu and his spouse's public wedding ceremony in 2013 attracted both popular support and anti-same-sex-marriage rallies.

72 Smith, "'Baby's Picture Is Always Treasured.'" This is also related to the lack of publicly displayed family photo-portraits including family members with disabilities.

73 Smith, 361, 363.

74 Roughly translated as the Pro-North Korean Residents' League in Japan.

75 The Zainichi are people of the Korean diaspora in Japan; they may be naturalized Japanese citizens, maintain their South Korean or North Korean citizenship, or be stateless, mainly due to nonalignment. According to Kim Pŏmsu, the varying terms referring to Korean Japanese are closely related to identitarian and political positionality of the referring self. Examining the changing ways in which South Korean media identified and marginalized (*chupyŏnhwa*) them, Kim, for example, uses "*chaeilhan'gukin*" for those with South Korean (ROK) citizenship and "*chaeilchosŏnin*" for those with North Korean (DPRK) citizenship when in need of discerning their citizenship. Kim, "Hyŏryukesŏ Kyŏnggyeinŭro," 167–68. See note 1 of the Kim article.

76 *Burakumin* refers to ethnic Japanese outcasts in the traditional social order of Japan, who live in special districts, *buraku*.

77 Mirinae, *Pot'ongi Anin Naldŭl.*

78 Ŏm, "Kajoksajin Kŭrigo Mainŏriti Yŏsŏng Chŭngŏnŭi Sŏsa, Ch'abyŏlgwa p'yŏnkyŏne Chŏhanghako Sot'onggwa Yŏndaerŭl Mosaekhanda."

79 Mirinae, *Pot'ongi Anin Naldŭl*, 81–89.

80 Mirinae, 88.

81 The original title is *Goku futsū no zainichikankokujin* (ごく普通の在日韓国人).

82 Kim, "Hyŏryukesŏ Kyŏnggyeinŭro," 188.

83 Bhabha, "'Beginning of Their Real Enunciation,'" 17.

84 Bhabha, 17.

85 I have encountered newspaper articles and blog posts that reproduce the portrait with Yi's American friend cropped out. In an article pleading for the building of a museum/center dedicated to Yi, only the left hand of the American friend is visible. Sim, "[Sim Kyusŏn taekijaŭi 人(in)] muchŏng 100nyŏn." In a blog post, the author uses a further manipulated image, without the American friend, that put Yi, Hŏ, and their son closer to each other. Sin'i, "D-Story 123."

86 I thank Samuel Perry for sharing his manuscript for his forthcoming book, *A Century of Queer Korean Fiction*, from Modern Language Association in 2023.

87 Perry, *Century of Queer Korean Fiction.*

88 *Kŭ ŭi chasŏchŏn (1936), Chunwŏn* chŏnjip, cited in Perry.

89 Hwang et al., "Yŏryu Myŏngsa Tongsŏng Yŏn'ae Hatŭn Iyagi," 120–23, cited in Perry, *Century of Queer Korean Fiction.*

90 Perry, *Century of Queer Korean Fiction.*

91 Yoneyama, *Cold War Ruins*, 49.

92 Yoneyama, 49.

Chapter 3. Shooting Social Movements

1 Minjuhwaundongginyŏmsaŏphoe (Korea Democracy Foundation), *Han'gungminjuhwauntongsa 1*, 89–103.

2 Minjuhwaundongginyŏmsaŏphoe (Korea Democracy Foundation), 33–34.

3 Minjuhwaundongginyŏmsaŏphoe (Korea Democracy Foundation), 33–34. Former procolonialists continued to serve in high-ranking positions even as Rhee's anti-communist policies continued to harshly persecute left-leaning intellectuals and their families; in 1960, 70 percent of the highest-ranking officers had previously worked for Japanese police. As cited by Atul Kohli, "Rhee Interregnum," 66.

4 The Constitutional Law of South Korea has been amended nine times as of 2021. Four of these amendments were made during the Rhee presidency.

5 Minjuhwaundongginyŏmsaŏphoe (Korea Democracy Foundation), *Han'gungminjuhwauntongsa 1*, 113.

6 Minjuhwaundongginyŏmsaŏphoe (Korea Democracy Foundation), 104, 113.

7 With their history going back to the March 1 Movement of 1919, student marches in particular became "one of the most powerful forms of organized protest" against the military regime in the following decades. Kim, *Youth for Nation*, 15.

8 Minjuhwaundongginyŏmsaŏphoe (Korea Democracy Foundation), *Han'gungminjuhwauntongsa 1*, 115.

9 Minjuhwaundongginyŏmsaŏphoe (Korea Democracy Foundation), 114–15.

10 An, *Saeroun 4.19*, 129–30.

11 Chang, *Han'guksinmunsajinnon*, 58–59. It was reported that Kim's body was "stolen" from the morgue by the police for several days, hence making it impossible to hold a proper funeral. In commemoration of the fiftieth anniversary of Kim's death and the discovery of his body, Kim Chuyŏl Ch'umosauphoe, a foundation memorializing Kim Chuyŏl, organized a funerary procession for March 15, 2010. This started in Masan and ended in Namwon, Kim's hometown and burial place. An, "Kim Chuyŏl Yŏlsa Changrye Osipnyŏnmane Ch'irŭnda."

12 Strict policies on grooming and uniforms follow colonial practices since the early years of the twentieth century, heavily based on Japanese military practices at the time. Colonial-style school uniforms were standard until the 1980s.

13 Hŏ Chong died on March 22, 2008. His obituary in news media commemorated him as the photographer who brought forth the 4.19 Revolution. See Choi and Yi, *Han'guksajinmunhwayŏn'guso Charyochip*, vol. 2. See also Chang, *Han'guksinmunsajinnon*, 58–59.

14 Chŏng Pŏmt'ae became one of the leading figures of Saenghwaljuŭi realism.

15 The office was moved to the Ch'ŏngwadae (Blue House) in 1961.

16 For the background, testimonies, and aftereffects of the 4.19 Revolution, see 4.19 Hyŏngmyŏngginyŏmsaŏphoe, *4.19 Hyŏngmyŏngsa*; Kim, *4.19 Hyŏngmyŏng*.

17 The unpublished photographs of students lying dead or dying in the streets were later made public by the 4.19 Revolution Library. The protests that followed weeks after the revolution, and after President Rhee's impeachment, were more easily documented by press photographers and were allowed for publication in newspapers.

18 Kim, *4.19 Hyŏngmyŏng*, 90–91; Minjuhwaundongginyŏmsaŏphoe (Korea Democracy Foundation), *Han'gungminjuhwauntongsa 1*, 135–41.

19 As with the previous chapters, I use the term "ordinary citizens," "the public," "the general public," or "the wider public" to refer to the majority of the Korean people, who were not directly involved in the events discussed in the chapter. The terms exclude military personnel and government officials.

20 Kim, *4.19 Hyŏngmyŏng*, 92–93.

21 Minjuhwaundongginyŏmsaŏphoe (Korea Democracy Foundation), *Han'gungminjuhwauntongsa 1*, 130, 142. Song was known to have been favored by the US military headquarters in Korea, which added more pressure on Rhee. Also see Kim, *4.19 Hyŏngmyŏng*, 95.

22 Minjuhwaundongginyŏmsaŏphoe (Korea Democracy Foundation), *Han'gungminjuhwauntongsa 1*, 142.

23 The two-year period following the 4.19 Revolution was the only time that the administration employed the parliamentary system, which was headed by a prime minister rather than a president.

24 Yi, "'Ch'oerut'an Pakhin Kim Chuyŏl' Sekyee Allyŏttŏn Hŏ Chongssi Pyŏlse"; Min, "Kimjuyŏl Yŏlsa Pŏmgungminjang Masanhangsŏ Nunmul Sok Ŏmsu."

25 Azoulay, *Civil Imagination*, 23.

26 The so-called 6.3 (Yuksam) Movement against the normalization of diplomatic relations with Japan in 1964 was possibly the next major student-led protest. However, while photographs of the student marches by, for example, the Japanese photographer Kuwabara Shisei, were published in photo books several decades later in South Korea, these photographs did not have an iconic effect under the military regime due to limited access. Kuwabara, *Ch'walyŏnggŭmji*; *Kuwabara Shisei*; *Takyument'ŏri Sajin'ga*.

27 English in original. The introduction on the plaque is written in Korean and English.

28 Although discussing vastly different events and historical contexts, I am drawn to Shawn Michelle Smith's words describing memory and photography regarding the photographs of Emmett Till in an open casket: "Images of his mutilated corpse refuse to stay in the past; they come back, like the repressed, to disturb the present." Till, a fourteen-year-old Black child, was abducted, tortured, and

shot in the head by at least three white men (Roy Bryant, J. W. Milam, and another unidentified man) in Money, Mississippi, on August 24, 1955, and was thrown in the Tallahatchie River with a metal cotton gin fan fastened to his neck with barbed wire. Smith, *Photographic Returns*, 113.

29 Retrospectively speaking, the event of photography had been suspended during the junta, as Azoulay puts it, "caught in the anticipation of the next encounter that will allow for its actualization." Azoulay, *Civil Imagination*, 25.

30 Kwŏn, *Ŭmnangwa Hyŏngmyŏng*, 256–57. Despite their topical differences, Kwŏn's use of "a politics of death" is relevant to Achille Mbembe's work on "necropolitics." As Mbembe theorizes the colonial/postcolonial "ordeal of the world" via Frantz Fanon, Kwŏn also finds that the military's counterrevolutionary powers "affect and diminish their [Korean civilians in this case] capacities to consider themselves moral agents"; the militarization of life is a processual characteristic of colonization. Mbembe, *Necropolitics*, 5.

31 During the Park regime, the nation's previously agriculture-based economy transformed dramatically. Park, a draconian anti-communist, launched a series of Five-Year Economic Development Plans in January 1962, ironically modeled after those of Chairman Mao, which focused on the urbanization and industrialization of rural areas. A decade of development of an export-oriented economy resulted in the rise of the annual GDP growth rate from 4.94 percent in 1961 to 11.7 percent in 1968. The GDP of the Republic of Korea further rose from 2,764 million won in 1970 to 1,023,937 million won in 2008, which is a 370-fold increase. See NationMaster, "GDP Growth Annual % Statistics—Countries Compared."

Although Park's modernization efforts were successful, the rapid development was possible only because of the harsh working conditions and extremely low wages of the labor force, underscoring the lack of even the most basic labor laws and guidelines during the 1960s and '70s. The severe exploitation of both light and heavy industry workers, who were mostly migrants from rural areas, continued in the name of economic advancement. Dissenting voices were suppressed by the military regime, allowing business owners to resist unionization. Anyone critical of the military regime was regarded as procommunist and a threat to the economic advancement of the nation.

32 State repression is, however, argued to have helped various protest groups form alliances for future democracy movements, the result of a "dialectical interplay between authoritarian regimes and social movements." See Chang, "Unintended Consequences of Repression."

33 Chang states that this is the second period that photojournalists underwent hardships, the first being the period under Japanese colonial rule. Chang, *Han'guksinmunsajinnon*, 58.

34 This martial law was in effect from May 16, 1961, to December 6, 1962.

35 Military Revolution Tribunal Law No. 1 Article III (Kunsahyŏngmyŏng wiwŏnhoeryŏng che1ho, che3hang), "3. 언론, 출판, 보도 등은 사전검열을 받으라. 이에 대해서는 치안 확보 상 유해로운 기사, 논설, 만화, 사진 등으로 본 혁명과 관련하여 선동, 과장 등 비판하는 내용을 공개하여서는 안된다. 본 혁명에 관련된 일절 기사는 사전에 검열을 받으며 외국 통신의 전재도 이에 준한다."

36 Chang, *Han'guksinmunsajinnon*, 60.

37 Chang, 58.

38 As discussed earlier, Kuwabara Shisei photographed the protests in June 1964 and the photographs were reproduced in publications since the 1990s in South Korea. See Kuwabara, *Ch'walyŏnggŭmji*; *Kuwabara Shisei.*

39 Chang, *Han'guksinmunsajinnon*, 61.

40 Pak, *Han'guksajinsa*, 452–53.

41 Hye-ri Oh discusses why it is appropriate to translate Saenghwaljuŭi realism as Life-ism in Oh, "Photography, Technology, and Realism in 1950s Korea."

42 Im founded Han'guksajinjakkahyŏphoe (the Association of Korean Photographers) in 1952, which became the springboard for recognition of the movement. He also taught photography in the early days of visual arts and photography curricula at universities, notably teaching students of the Photo Club, Sungmihoe, at Sookmyung Women's University from 1974 to 1982. *Han'guksajinsa Kusulp'ŭrojekt'ŭ*, 107.

43 Pak, *Han'guksajinŭi Sŏn'gujatŭl*, 101.

44 Ch'oe and Park, *Century of Korean Photography*, 97. English in original.

45 Ch'oe and Park, 97. English in original.

46 "Straight photography" is a term supposing the objectiveness and truthfulness of the photographic work. Straight photographs are generally expected to depict scenes without manipulation of the subject or in the print process. Though a widely, and normatively used term, its expected signification of objectivity is undergirded by the positivist, hetero-masculinist framework, believed to represent the highest purity of the medium. For a discussion on "queer and straight" photography in the context of the photo history of the United States, see Ribbat, "Queer and Straight Photography."

47 See, for example, the monographs of Im Ŭngsik, Sŏng Tukyŏng, Yi Kyŏngmo, and Yi Hyŏngnok. Im, *Im Ŭngsik Sajinjip*; *Naega Kŏrŏon Han'guksadan*; Kwŏn, *Sajin'ga Im Ŭngsik k'ameraro Chinsirŭl Marhada*; Sŏng, *Tasitorawapon Sŏul Sŏng Tukyŏng Sajinjip*; Yi, *Kyŏktonggiŭi Hyŏnjang Yi Kyŏngmo Sajinjip*; Yi, *Yi Hyŏngnok Sajinjip*.

48 Pak, *Han'guksajinŭi Chasengnyŏk*, 16–17; Yi, *Han'guk Kŭndae Yesulsajin Akaibŭ*, 11–12. I have also encountered mixed use of *ssalongsajin*, *yesulsajin*, and *misulsajin* (art/aesthetic photography) by critics such as Cho Usŏk.

49 Pak P'yŏngjong argues that Im's work during the postwar period tends to mix the style of *ssalongsajin* and documentary photography. Im himself made photographs during the prewar period that are now considered *ssalongsajin*. Upon examining Im's photographs before and after the Korean War, there is a distinct focus on isolating the human subject in the photograph from the surroundings, indicating that Im's compositional approach to photography has not radically transformed with Saenghwaljuŭi realism. Pak, *Han'guksajinŭi Sŏn'gujatŭl*, 102–3.

50 Pak, 146. For example, Yi Hyŏngnok applied a technique called "pesŭt'ŭ tanhudŭ ppaeki" (베스트 단후드 빼기), popularized by the Japanese photographer Nakajima Kengichi in the early twentieth century. To produce a soft focus, Nakajima removed the lens hood from an Eastman Kodak Vest Pocket Camera, shooting with an open aperture. The technique was originally called "besu-tan hood hazushi" in Japanese. In 1935, Yi Hyŏngnok joined Kangnŭngsauhoe, a photography salon comprised of amateur photographers in the city of Kangnŭng. The salon was headed by Im, and the members of Kangnŭngsauhoe organized monthly critiques of their photographs that emulated Pictorialism and *pitkwahaejo* popular in Japan. At the end of the colonial period, however, Yi was drafted by the Japanese military to fight in the Pacific War, and a few years later, he became a war correspondent in the Korean War. His experience in the two wars led him to turn to realism from *ssalongsajin*, in search of a more "appropriate" aesthetic language to depict the aftermath of the war. As with Im, his postwar photographs focused on the struggle of Korean people after the war. Yi founded a photography group called Sinsŏnhoe in 1956, of which the members aspired to realism as "the path to be followed by contemporary photography." See Pak, 149. The members were also deeply influenced by the traveling exhibition *The Family of Man*, organized by Edward Steichen, the director of the Photography Department at the Museum of Modern Art. The exhibition was held in Seoul's Kyŏngbokkungmisulkwan (the Art Museum of Kyŏngbok Palace) in April 1956. Im was a key organizer of the exhibition in Seoul.

51 Cho, *Han'guksajin'garon*, Nunbit Sajinsŏnsŏ 15, 94, 97.

52 Cho, 94–95.

53 Ch'oe, *Najŭndero Imhan Sajin Naŭi Insaeng, Naŭi Sajin*, 22, 49–50.

54 Pak, *Han'guksajinŭi Chasengnyŏk*, 13–15.

55 Prominent adherents of Saenghwaljuŭi realism, including Chŏng Pŏmt'ae and Yi Myŏngdong, did not consider Ch'oe a member of the group, regarding his work as not academic enough and too saccharine. See their interview with Choi Bonglim and Yi Kyŏngmin at the Museum of Photography, Seoul (now Museum Hanmi). Choi and Yi, *Han'guksajinmunhwayŏn'guso Charyochip*, vol. 2.

56 Gee, *Photography of the Fifties*, 2.

57 Gee, 2.

58 The Martial Law Command announced that the number of civilian deaths was 144, a number disputed by various political groups and researchers. As of December 2018, families of 155 dead and 84 missing persons have received government recognition and compensation among other categories of civilian casualties. "5.18 Minjuhwaundong Kwannyŏn T'onggye (The May 18 Democratization Movement Statistics)."

59 Recent documentary films, namely *Kwangju Bidio: Sarachin 4(ne)sigan* (dir. Yi Chohun, 2020) and *Kimgun* (dir. Kang Sanghun, 2019) probe the truth of the Gwangju massacre through original photographs and footage, as well as interview footage and recent interviews with journalists. The latter film is especially interesting; its investigation centers on a photograph of an unknown protester and his identity.

60 Chang, *Han'guksinmunsajinnon*, 66.

61 Chang, 66. Most of the Gwangju photographs were only reproduced after the June Democracy Movement of 1987.

62 Sin, *Kwangjunŭn Marhanda*, 9–10.

63 Sin, 10. Sin's photographs were used at the hearings regarding the Gwangju Uprising as evidence of false testimony by military and government officials related to the massacre. Films such as *A Taxi Driver* (dir. Chang Hun, 2017), based on the true story of German journalist Jürgen Hinzpeter and Korean taxi driver Kim Sabok, who witnessed the Gwangju massacre, re-created scenes based on photographs, notably those taken by Sin.

64 Yi, "1980nyŏndae Kyŏmyŏlgwa Chetochŏk Minjuhwa," 160.

65 Seo, "Birth of an Ethical Subject," 262.

66 Seo, 262.

67 Seo posits that when it comes to the Gwangju Uprising, "there are few who can claim impunity by pleading ignorance." While this applies to all atrocious events, it is important to examine how "guilt" operates in postignorance reparative cultural productions. This is not within the book's scope, but I have to warn against "guilt" (to turn into "indebtedness") becoming a badge of honor in owning that piece of history, whether as an alibi for moving on or not, similarly to how "guilt" (and "indebtedness") is often substituted for filial piety when Korean children are asked about their parents, as a priori for returning parental—eternal and unconditional—love. Seo, 263.

68 In fact, the encouragement of self-censorship had already been included in the addendum to the Yushin-era press policy of 1972, "Podokŭmjisahang (Restrictions on news coverage)." Yi Pongbŏm points out the frightening description of systematizing self-censorship for "the perpetual movement of social purgation" in the policy. See Yi, "1980nyŏndae Kyŏmyŏlgwa Chetochŏk Minjuhwa," 164n15.

69 For instance, 134 journalists were forced out of their jobs after participating in a series of protests against censorship in 1975. See Chang, *Han'guksinmunsajinnon*, 62.

70 The building is set to reopen as the Democracy and Human Rights Memorial Hall in 2023. Room 509, the interrogation room, where Pak Chongch'ŏl died, was on view to visitors until the Memorial Hall project began.

71 Sin, "Kyŏngch'aresŏ Chosa Pattŏn Taehaksaeng 'Shokŭsa.'" The statement of the police commissioner at the time, Kang Minch'ang, "T'akhago chi'ni ŏkhago ssŭrŏchyŏ," ("Pak collapsed when the interrogator banged on the desk") has come to symbolize the military government's state of corruption and human rights abuse.

72 Chang, *Han'guksinmunsajinnon*, 70.

73 Chang, 70.

74 Kim, "Sŭlp'ŭmŭl Titko Sŏn Chakgaŭi Naengŏmhan Sisŏn." Chŏng had worked as the foreign news director of the United Press International (UPI) Korea since 1977. He retired as Reuters' director of photography, Korea, in 1994. In 2020, the Korea Democracy Foundation made 1,322 of Chŏng's photographs available on their digital archive, Open Archives: https://archives.kdemo.or.kr/main.

75 For a brief period, the state authorized selected publications of previously banned books; however, alarmed by their rapid circulation, the Chun regime enforced stricter control over publishers, editors, and staff writers in 1984. Editors and staff writers were often taken to interrogation rooms of the Agency for National Security Planning (former KCIA) and the National Police Agency and forced to halt the printing of materials in the press. The sabotaging of already printed materials was also common. Yi, "1980nyŏndae Kyŏmyŏlgwa Chetochŏk Minjuhwa," 172.

76 Chŏng, *Sŏulbal Sajinjonghap (Photographs from Seoul: Photographs by Tony Chung)*.

77 In 2017, the thirtieth anniversary of the June Movement, news media published a "never before seen" photograph of Yi Hanyŏl in the arms of Yi Chongch'ang from a greater distance. The "revelation" of the singular photograph resonated with the recent impeachment of the corrupt president after months of public protests.

78 James R. Lilley, the US ambassador to South Korea at the time, writes in his memoir that he met with Chun to pass on a letter from the then president, Ronald Reagan. Lilley stated that the Reagan administration was against the involvement of the military and the planned imposition of martial law. See Lilley, *China Hands*, 277–79.

79 The iconic images of the June Democracy Movement also include the funerary portraits of Pak and Yi, originally taken to be used as their ID photos.

80 Kim, "Sŭlp'ŭmŭl Titko Sŏn Chakkaŭi Naengŏmhan Sisŏn." A collection of Chŏng's photographs were bequeathed to the Korea Democracy Foundation, and among over 87,000 scanned images, 1,322 digitized photographs are available for view on the foundation's digital archive, Open Archives. Yun, "Minjuhwaundong Sajin DB Kuch'uk (Building Database of Korean Democratization Movements)," 252–53.

81 Cho'e's 1987 original banner painting is in the collection of the National Museum of Modern and Contemporary Art. The painting has also been reproduced as a bronze sculpture installed at the Yonsei University's Seoul campus.

82 Chang, *Han'guksinmunsajinnon*, 71.

83 Batchen, "Life and Death," 108.

84 Smith, *Photographic Returns*, 116.

85 Kwŏn, *Ŭmnangwa Hyŏngmyŏng*, 235.

86 The candidates from the opposition parties, Kim Young Sam and Kim Dae-jung, failed to agree on who would be the unifying candidate against Roh, thus splitting the opposition. As a result, the masses chose the candidate with the familiar military past and ties, although Roh had appealed to the public as a civilian.

87 Žižek, *Hyŏngmyŏngi Takaonda*, 111. Žižek's discussion of such violence is referred to in Kwŏn, *Ŭmnangwa Hyŏngmyŏng*, 234.

Chapter 4. The Photo Public in the *Kwangjang*

1 Cody, "Populist Publics," 52.

2 In social media, for example, photography's capacity to signify is taken for granted, and at the same time almost always ready to be disputed.

3 Cody, "Populist Publics," 60.

4 For example, the militaristic cultures of schools, universities, and workplaces (not to mention the impact of conscription) are closely related to some of the worst labor conditions and wage inequalities among OECD nations. In 2018, the OECD gender wage gap in South Korea was by far the largest, at 31.4 percent; Japan was second, at 24.5 percent. The OECD, "Earnings and Wages," 2020. *Kunbongmu kasanjŏm chedo* is a hiring policy giving extra points to job applicants who have completed their mandatory military service; service status also affects wage calculation (and negotiation) and promotion. The policy was ruled unconstitutional in 1999 in the case brought by five Ewha Womans University students and a male Yonsei University student with disabilities, but conservative parties have since promoted reintroduction of the policy. South Koreans also worked longer hours (1,933 per employee) in 2018 than all but two OECD

countries, Mexico and Costa Rica. The OECD, "Employment—Hours Worked," 2020.

5 Morris, "Theses on the New 'Öffentlichkeit,'" 99. Morris notes that contemporary protest movements do not assume "consensus as a goal," "in ways that specularize the capacity for communication while severing it from any structure of reciprocity." This leads to the transformation of öffentlichkeit and the concept of the political.

6 I am invoking here what Judith Butler and Athena Athanasiou call "plural performativity." Butler and Athanasiou, *Dispossession*.

7 Butler, *Notes Toward a Performative Theory of Assembly*; Morris, "Theses on the New 'Öffentlichkeit.'"

8 Butler, 164.

9 Butler, 166.

10 Morris, "Theses on the New 'Öffentlichkeit,'" 97.

11 Morris, 98.

12 Butler and Athanasiou, *Dispossession*, 107.

13 Butler and Athanasiou, 176. Emphasis in original.

14 Butler and Athanasiou, 178.

15 As Zeynep Gürsel argues, the production and circulation of a photograph in/of an event—a virtual witness—entails "the passionate uptake of the image by a public." Gürsel, "Visualizing Publics," S143.

16 Virno, *Grammar of the* Multitude, 26, 80. Virno, rethinking the multitude in contemporary forms of post-Fordist life, defines the characteristic of the multitude "*ambivalent*," like any other modes of being, with contradictions. Emphasis in original.

17 Bhabha, "'Beginning of Their Real Enunciation,'" 10.

18 Brown and Szeman, "What Is the Multitude?," 378.

19 Brown and Szeman, 379.

20 Ch'ŏn, "'1987nyŏnhyŏng Minjuchuŭiŭi' Chongŏn'gwa Ch'otpulhangjaeng Ihuŭi Han'guk Minjuchuŭi," 32.

21 Ch'ŏn Chŏnghwan, 32, 34.

22 Ch'ŏn Chŏnghwan, 34.

23 Strassler, *Demanding Images*.

24 For studies on the affect and sensoriality of photography, see Brown and Phu, *Feeling Photography*.

25 See Han et al., *(2002 Wŏldŭk'ŏp Ihuŭi) Munhwasimin'undongbalchŏnbangan Simp'osiŏm*; Dong-a Ilbo, "Wŏldŭk'ŏp Ihu Siminŭisik Kaesŏndwaetta."

26 Yi, "Pulgŭnangmawa Chuch'ehyŏngsŏng," 165, cited in Yoo, "Candlelight Girls' Playground," 63.

27 Jiyeon Kang states the "accident" transformed South Korea's online space with "a national furor that forced Koreans to reexamine the fifty-year relationship between the United States and South Korea." Kang, *Igniting the Internet*, 1.

28 The debates over the danger of BSE directly related to the US beef import became a partisan issue, in part through the curated use of the scientific information as presented by mass media; according to Bak and Kleinman, media accounts were also highly politicized by the partisan adherence of individual media companies. Bak and Kleinman, "Media Cultures." For instance, conservative newspapers and pro-American organizations accused the participants in candlelight vigils of instigating violence, some arguing that the assemblies had been organized by pro–North Korean activists who brainwashed the public into believing that consuming American beef (from cows over thirty months old) would expose them to BSE. See Yi and Pak, "'Hwachangp'um, Ttŏkpokkito Kwangupyŏng Wihŏm' Chŏndanji Ppuryŏ."

29 Kang points out that BSE-related concerns were expressed by the public as early as 2003, but the issue became particularly associated with President Lee's promises of economic growth based on neoliberal, developmentalist politics. Kang, *Igniting the Internet*, 114.

30 Kang, 126.

31 Kim, "Yŏsŏngchuŭi Kwanjŏmesŏ Pon Ch'otpulchiphoewa Yŏsŏngŭi Chŏngch'ichŏk Chuch'esŏng (Candlelight Rallies and Political Subjectivity of Women from the Feminist Perspective)," 27; Bak and Kleinman, "Media Cultures," 343.

32 Kim, "Study on the Photographs of Candle Demonstrations," 16. English title in original.

33 Yi, "Chŏngch'ich'amyŏ Yuhyŏngŭrossŏŭi Ch'otpuljiphoe," 20.

34 The rise of *irinmidiŏ* was, of course, possible due to the widely available high-speed internet connection. Between 2002 and 2012, South Korea had the highest "broadband penetration rate" in the world, at 98 percent in 2012. Kang, *Igniting the Internet*, 37.

35 Kim, "Study on the Photographs of Candle Demonstrations," 24. English title in original. The number of such published images varied considerably by source; for example, in May, the "progressive" newspaper *Hankyoreh* included thirty photographs of candlelight vigils, while the "conservative" *Chosun Ilbo* published thirteen photographs.

36 The phenomenon was liberating, and liberated from the ideological assumptions of the leftist, anti-Americanism undergirding the 1987 event. Kang, *Igniting the Internet*, 118.

37 Over 80 percent of the candlelight vigil participants in May 2008 were teenagers; among these, about 70 percent were female. Kang, 110.

38 Kim, "Ch'otpul Hangjaenggwa 87 (p'alch'i'il)Ch'eje," 42. In the *kwangjang*, then and there, the demarcations between these women's private space and the political (not the public) space were proven false. See Kim, "Yŏsŏngchuŭi Kwanjŏmesŏ Pon Ch'otpulchiphoewa Yŏsŏngŭi Chŏngch'ichŏk Chuch'esŏng (Candlelight Rallies and Political Subjectivity of Women from the Feminist Perspective)," 25.

39 The spike in participation among young women, from high school students to mothers with strollers, and the reasons for and ramifications of such changes, have been examined in articles including: Cho, "Pop'yŏnjuŭiwa Sangdaechuŭirŭl Nŏmŏ"; Hong, "Kamjŏnggujowa Ch'otpulhyŏkmyŏng"; Na and Kim, "Int'ŏnet Kwangjangesŏ t'aorŭnŭn Ch'otpul Iyagi Agorawa 82cook (p'arik'uk) Net'ijŭni Malhada"; Kim, "Ch'otpul Hangjaenggwa 87 (p'alch'i'il) Ch'eje,"; Kim, "[Chaengjŏmgwa Tonghyang] Dijit'ŏl t'ekŭnolojiŭi Palchŏn'gwa Saeroun Yŏsŏng Chŏngch'i Chuch'eŭi Kanŭngssŏng (Digital Technology and Young Women's Political Participation)"; Kim, "Yŏsŏngchuŭi Kwanjŏmesŏ Pon Ch'otpulchiphoewa Yŏsŏngŭi Chŏngch'ichŏk Chuch'esŏng (Candlelight Rallies and Political Subjectivity of Women from the Feminist Perspective)"; Kim, "Yŏsŏng, Kukka, Ch'otpul," 203; Ŭn, "Ch'otpulgwa Han'guksahoe Chungsanch'ŭngŭi Chahwasang," 225. All English titles in original.

40 A petition for the impeachment of President Lee was posted on Agora by a high school student with the username "Andante" on April 6, 2008. As many as 1.3 million users signed the petition over forty days. Yoo, "Candlelight Girls' Playground," 50–51; Kang, *Igniting the Internet*, 109–10. For first-person analyses by participants of activities led by Agora and 82cook (an online cooking community), see Na and Kim, "Int'ŏnet Kwangjangesŏ t'aorŭnŭn Ch'otpul Iyagi Agorawa 82cook (p'arik'uk) Net'ijŭni Marhada." Both Na and Kim praise the internet for enabling their coordinated investigative activities that unveiled corruption among a number of right-wing politicians, and promoting other offline activities such as boycotting companies that advertise in conservative newspapers, popularly referred to as "chojungdong": *Chosun Ilbo*, *Joongang Ilbo*, and *Dong-a Ilbo*.

41 Kim, "Ch'otpul Hangjaenggwa 87 (p'alch'i'il)Ch'eje," 46.

42 Kang, *Igniting the Internet*, 37–38.

43 Cho, "Pop'yŏnjuŭiwa Sangdaechuŭirŭl Nŏmŏ," 28.

44 Kim, "A Study on the Photographs of Candle Demonstrations (with a Focus on the Five Major Daily Newspapers)," 16. "o kyosi, uyŏlban, hakkyochayulhwarŭl pandaehanŭn ch'ŏngsonyŏnyŏndae."

45 Lotringer, "We, the Multitude," 17.

46 Kang, *Igniting the Internet*, 129.

47 Butler and Athanasiou, *Dispossession*, 178.

48 Butler and Athanasiou, 178.

49 Butler and Athanasiou, 178.

50 Kim, "Yŏsŏngchuŭi Kwanjŏmesŏ Pon Ch'otpulchiphoewa Yŏsŏngŭi Chŏngch'ichŏk Chuch'esŏng (Candlelight Rallies and Political Subjectivity of Women from the Feminist Perspective)," 16.

51 Ap'ŭrik'a (Afreeca) is short for "A Free Camera." An early equivalent of YouTube and Twitch, Afreeca TV was shut down for weeks by the Korea Communications Standards Commission during the summer of 2008 (Pangsongt'ongsinsimŭwiwŏnhoe).

52 Karen Strassler refers to photographs of masses gathered for political causes (such as for the 2014 presidential election in Indonesia) as "crowd-selfies." Strassler, *Demanding Images*, 233–37.

53 Mroué, "Pixelated Revolution," 22, introduction by Carol Martin.

54 The integral aspects of social media in social movements, whether as platform for spreading information, garnering solidarity, or just indicating support by "liking" a post, have been critiqued for encouraging armchair activism. As photographs of social movements disseminate and circulate in social media, the act of "participating" in the movements online—looking, clicking, liking, posting, hashtagging, following, reposting—has often been regarded as slacktivism. In any case, the phenomena are never uniform in the ways they manifest and in influencing subsequent events.

55 Kang examines the online and *kwangjang* civil movements through the concept of captivation, through which the audience immerses oneself in the event, and its impact leads to subsequent acts. The impact of captivation, she states, should be noted and differentiated when examining what many see as "failed" individual participation on the internet—such as occurred with the Occupy Wall Street movement—where "the particular collective dynamics . . . cannot be reduced to the sum of individuals." Kang, *Igniting the Internet*, 13.

56 Although Cyworld, a social networking site popularized in South Korea in the early 2000s, was once the most used social media in South Korea (with 25 percent of the population having a Cyworld minihomepage), it was not utilized for the purpose of candlelight vigils. Following the popularization of social network services such as Facebook and especially Twitter, the number of Cyword users dropped continuously. The company eventually discontinued their minihomepage service in September 2015. As of 2021, Cyworld was acquired by CyworldZ and revived their *minihompy* service for smartphones. Twitter, a potentially ideal mode for *irinmidiŏ*, was not launched in South Korea until 2011.

57 Undercover police forces carried student ID photos to crack down on student organizations in 1987. By 2008, facial recognition software was in the process of becoming the new normal.

58 Mroué, "Pixelated Revolution," 22.

59 Water-based weapons replaced the teargas grenades used in the 1980s in Korea. Conversely, in the United States, hoses and water cannons were used against civil rights protesters in the South in the 1950s and 1960s and fell out of favor given that association; however, with the intensified militarization of the police force due to the influx of materiel from the military-industrial complex, teargas and rubber bullets are now far more commonly used against protesters in the United States.

60 The Kyŏngbok Palace is the main royal palace complex that housed the royal family and court of Chosŏn.

61 The witnessing of events via mobile phone recordings has been the most affective result of *irinmidiŏ* today. Now, of course, this phenomenon is all too familiar, post–Arab Spring and later events such as public-sourced documentation of police violence against Black Americans. See also, for example, the performance work of Mroué, who has dealt directly with perhaps one of the most devastating examples of what recordings of protests mean. Mroué, "Pixelated Revolution," 35.

62 Butler and Athanasiou, *Dispossession*, 107. These are still meaningful questions to ask about civic movements that followed since 2008, especially against the government handling of the sinking of the *Sewol* ferry in 2014.

63 Morris, "Theses on the New 'Öffentlichkeit,'" 105–6.

64 Morris, 109.

65 Chun, *Updating to Remain the Same.*

66 Brown and Szeman, "What Is the Multitude?," 382.

67 Chun, *Discriminating Data.*

68 Chun, *Updating to Remain the Same*, 40.

69 Chun, 40.

70 The updating does not necessarily entail corruption or erasure. Lucie Ryzova posits that the "original" state and provenance of photography, the supposed stage before co-optation or transformation, does not matter for the everyday users of digital imagery online, even as it may be devastating for historians and researchers who see this as a silencing of their original contexts. Ryzova states that "for their contemporary users in Egypt, and for Egyptians across the world, such de-materialised digital photographs are, in fact, 'liberated.' As they are orphaned and de-signified, they are simultaneously re-signified with new meanings that were already there waiting. The more severed they are from their original contexts, the more 'free' they become to perform new kinds of cultural work. This is but one instance of local digital vernacularity in the post-photographic age." Ryzova, "Nostalgia for the Modern," 304.

71 Meanwhile, the sharing of photographs online exhibits the characteristics of the "revolutionary demands in the politics of art" imagined by Benjamin. Benjamin, "The Work of Art in the Age of Mechanical Reproduction," 218.

72 Around the time of and following the 2008 events, many graduate theses were written on the flow of digital photography and issues particular to the South Korean situation regarding digital photography, "digital culture," and candlelight vigils: see, for example, Kim, "A Study of the Transformation in Internet Cultural Contents through the Entrace [*sic*] of Digital Cameras"; Yang, "Characteristics of Digital Culture in Candle Rallies"; Park, "A Study on the Expression and Thinking Method of Digital Photo Image"; and Kim, "A Study of the Process of the Formation of the Online Public Opinion and Transformation to the Political Power." My research on the 2008 events is also indebted to their work. The titles of the theses and transliteration of their names have been provided by individual authors.

73 Chun, *Updating to Remain the Same*, 53.

74 Heiferman, "Has Facebook Killed the Photo?," 56.

75 Chun, *Updating to Remain the Same*, 62. Emphasis added.

76 Rancière, *Emancipated Spectator* 13.

77 Kang, *Igniting the Internet*, 130.

78 Kang, 130.

79 Kang, 134.

80 Gürsel, "Visualizing Publics," S143.

81 The Korea Communications Standards Commission censors materials published and posted online which may contain materials infringing, for example, the National Security Law and the restrictions of the Korea Food & Drug Administration.

82 Agora lost its significance in empowering civil movements around 2012–13. Daum removed a link to Agora from its main page and never again displayed headlines of its major discussion topics until it was removed.

83 Despite the changes brought forth by the 2008 candlelight vigils, they have been assessed and critiqued as lacking consolidated political structure (here Hobbes comes back), and being based on the neoliberal, middle-class interests of progressive activists and intellectuals. See, for example, Ŭn, "Ch'otpulgwa Han'guksahoe Chungsanch'ŭngŭi Chahwasang." Such criticism may have been rewritten in post-2016–17 events—the impeachment of President Park Geunhye and overturning of the ruling party—that have resulted in consolidating the political agenda. The author, Ŭn, herself became a member of the National Assembly in 2012 and was elected mayor of Seoungnam, Gyeonggido, in 2018.

84 Ryzova, "Nostalgia for the Modern," 317. Emphasis added.

85 Similarly, Strassler describes the crowds gathered for the Indonesian presidential candidate Joko Widodo's campaign in 2014 as "performatively model[ing] a collectivity made up of self-aware, self-governing citizens." Strassler argues that the candidates' "image management," including the depictions of mass gatherings of their respective supporters, was a critical component of their campaign strategies and the result of the election. Strassler, *Demanding Images*, 222.

86 Gürsel, "Visualizing Publics," S147.

87 Butler states that "those bodies are obdurate and persisting, instating on their continuing and collective 'thereness.'" Butler and Athanasiou, *Dispossession*, 187.

88 Butler and Athanasiou, 187.

89 Chun refers to recent studies on memory in neuroscience that "there is arguably no involuntary memory separate from perception. Every involuntary repetition trains perception, calling into question the notion of memory as an entity we recall." Chun, *Updating to Remain the Same*, 70.

90 Uroskie, "Far Above the Madding Crowds," 315.

Chapter 5. The DMZ, Camptowns, and the Theater of Repetition

1 "6·25chŏnjaeng 70chunyŏn Saŏpch'uchinwiwŏnhoe."

2 Kukkapohunch'ŏ, *Urika Tangsinŭl Kiŏkhanŭn Pangbŏp*.

3 The video's opening caption following the portraits is "Tangsineketo irŏn t'ŭkpyŏrhan ch'in'guka issŭmnika? (Do you have special friends like these [Korean War veterans]?)."

4 Nguyen, *Gift of Freedom*.

5 In examining the ways they are imagined and represented in artworks and photography, my use of the term "borderlands" includes both the physical and conceptual sense of the area. I am reminded by Eleana Kim of the various Korean terms used in South Korea to refer to the North-South border without literally using the term "border": *pimuchangjitae*; *kunsapun'gyesŏn*; *samp'alsŏn*; *hyuchŏnsŏn*; and *chŏpkyŏngjiyŏk*. Each has different purposes and nuances related to historical memories and politico-militaristic usages. Kim, *Making Peace with Nature*, 10.

6 Kim, 8; Bleiker, "Visual Autoethnography and International Security."

7 Deleuze, *Difference and Repetition*, 76; Kennedy, *Deleuze and Cinema*, 75, cited in Barea, "Cinematographic Refrain," 16. Emphasis in original.

8 For discussions on the DMZ peace tourism and ecology, see Koh, "Place-Ness of the DMZ"; Westing, "Towards Environmental Sustainability," 20–23; Brady, "Life in the DMZ"; Healy, "Korean Demilitarized Zone"; and Kim, *Making Peace with Nature*.

9 Kim, *Postcolonial Grief.*

10 For example, when Roland Bleiker discusses the potential of autoethnography using his photographs of the DMZ in a scholarly article, most of the examples he uses were taken in the JSA, P'anmunjŏm, and Pyongyang. Bleiker, "Visual Autoethnography and International Security."

11 Kim, *DMZ Crossing*, 138.

12 Kim, *DMZ Crossing*, 142.

13 Dong-Yeon Koh critiques the state's superficial approach to peace in promoting tourism. Koh, "The Place-Ness of the DMZ," 654–57.

14 "REAL DMZ PROJECT" website, http://www.realdmz.org/.

15 Kim, "REAL DMZ PROJECT and Dongsongsewol," 11. In this short essay in the 2015 catalogue, Nam-See Kim briefly explores the *RDP*'s initial concerns about the project becoming an event only about remembering the past.

16 Kim, *Real DMZ* (2013), 6. Emphasis added.

17 Kim, *Real DMZ* (2013), 6–7.

18 Eng, *Feeling of Kinship*, 188.

19 Foster, *Return of the Real.*

20 Foster, 132. Emphasis in original.

21 Foster, 138. Emphasis in original.

22 In her discussion of photographs of Emmett Till, Shawn Michelle Smith states the photographs themselves are like traumatic memories, as they return repeatedly "but refuse to give one access to the events they signal." Smith, "Afterimages of Emmett Till," 25.

23 Foster concludes that "trauma discourse magically resolves two contradictory imperatives in culture today: deconstructive analyses and identity politics," 168. I find his wholesale categorization of "trauma discourse," "deconstructive analyses," and "identity politics" reductive historicization and a fine example of homogenizing temporality in the discipline of art history.

24 Kim, *Real DMZ* (2019), 6.

25 Bhabha, "Freedom's Basis in the Indeterminate," 56.

26 Lim, *Translating Time*, 18.

27 The temporality I discuss here is indebted to Lee Edelman's critique of "futurism's redemptive temporality" in a roundtable discussion on queer temporalities. Dinshaw et al., "Theorizing Queer Temporalities," 195.

28 Comparatively, Ren Ellis Neyra offers an analysis of senses that resist and undo the US imperial regimes of senses in Latinx and Caribbean performances. Neyra's examination of US settler colonialism and imperial violence that "romanticized sadism and nationalism and violent self-legitimation as reason" and

of the Latinx "performative unincorporation" and refusal of assimilation are especially pertinent to repetition as refusal in the context of RDP and the multisensorial landscape photographs discussed later in the chapter. Neyra, *Cry of the Senses*, 57.

29 The exhibition was held from May 8 to August 29, 2021. In 2020, the RDP organized two-part exhibitions in Paris titled *Negotiating Borders*; "to mirror" the situation of North and South Korea, as they state, one took place at Centre Culturel Coreén and the other, at Foundation FIMINCO.

30 Bhabha, "Freedom's Basis in the Indeterminate," 51.

31 This new place of utterance demands a deeper dive into RDP's transnational and transregional meaning making, in this case, in a settler colonial state, which will continue in my next research project.

32 Suh, "Korean Borders," 183–88.

33 Suh, 188.

34 For an exploration of the ethics of interspecies cohabitation near the border, see Kim, "Invasive Others and Significant Others."

35 *Minbuk* villages were established for civilian (re)settlement north of the Civilian Control Line and south of the *Namhan han'gyesŏn* (southern border limit) after the Armistice was signed. In Cheorwon between 1959 and 1980, fourteen *minbuk* villages were established; nine were dissolved, leaving five villages in the area. For a study of the value of *minbuk* villages as "living heritage" in their historical and urban context, see Park, Yun, and Zoh, "Characteristics of Minbuk Village."

36 Yi, "'Kunin Hyutaep'on Sayongsigan Churyŏdalla' Kangwŏn Chumin Hosohan Iyu."

37 Chapter 6 examines photographic representations of camptowns in depth.

38 Seoul Museum of Art, *Kangbak²* (*Compulsion to Repeat*), unpaginated.

39 The Zainichi writer Sŏ Kyŏngsik offers his affective introduction to Jung's work through an interview with the artist. Sŏ, "Wan'gohan Madadŭl-Chŏngyŏndu."

40 In the early 2000s, witnessing the nationalist fervor of the 2002 World Cup games in South Korea, some believed "peace-nationalism" ("*p'yŏnghwaminjokchuŭi*") offered a way out of the intensifying ethno-nationalistic antagonism against South Korea's neighbors, emphasizing the need for attending to the particular situation in northeast Asia. For example, Park Myoung-Kyu argues for "controlled" nationalism when needed, in the context of global competitions and conflicts. Park, "Pundanch'eje, Segyehwa, Kŭriko p'yŏnghwaminjokchuŭi (Regime of National Division, Globalization, and Peace Nationalism)." English title in original. I also note that, even though it may be redundant to mention here, salient discussions on ethno-nationalism and cultural production, especially Korean literature and theater, continue in South Korea with critical

reexaminations of colonial modernity, necessarily extending to issues of gender, race, and neoliberal desires. See, for example, Yi et al., "Chwadam."

41 For example, the North and South Korean states agreed to demolish eleven guard posts in the DMZ; this was included in the 9.19 Kunsapunya nambuk habŭisŏ (9.19 Inter-Korean Military Affairs Agreement) as part of the 9.19 Kongdong sŏnŏn (9.19 Joint Declaration) of the third summit meeting of the two states on September 19, 2018.

42 Seoul Museum of Art, *Kangbak²* (*Compulsion to Repeat*).

43 Seoul Museum of Art, *Kangbak²* (*Compulsion to Repeat*).

44 A short note on "pause," after living through the global COVID-19 pandemic for more than two years. Although the pandemic paused many things, many others have definitely accelerated and intensified: the rate and degree of inequality in health and safety of the working class and impoverished people, essential workers, and all those exposed to purportedly pandemic-caused (so described, but profoundly common across contexts) attacks around the world. This global pause has exacerbated the worst of systemic racism, labor exploitation, and exclusion of those repeatedly abused by the neoliberal economy vis-à-vis settler colonialism and neocolonialism. It certainly is a rupture; but, contrary to popular idealizations of revolution and the mantra of disruption as capitalist progress, ruptures to repetitions always take as hostage society's least protected. We know how this story ends (if it ever ends!).

45 Bhabha, "'Beginning of Their Real Enunciation,'" 8.

46 Bhabha, 8.

47 Bhabha, 8. Emphasis in original.

48 Between the 1960s and 1990s, twenty-nine Maehyang-ri residents (among about two hundred families) attempted suicide; twenty-six died. The father of Chŏn Mankyu, the chair of the Maehyang-ri Residents' Committee, was one such victim; Chŏn states that his father's suicide was induced by the psychological damage done by years of bombings. Pak, "Ripaiŏtŏn—Maehyangni," 8.

49 Kim, "Maehyangnisakyŏkchang P'yeswae 10nyŏn . . . Sangch'ŏŭi ttangesŏ haengbogi ssakt'ŭnda."

50 Kang, *Maehyangni P'unggyŏng*, 98.

51 Kang, 98.

52 Kang, interview with the author, March 17, 2022.

53 Brown and Phu, *Feeling Photography*, 15.

54 Martin, "Field Notes from South Korea," 237. Martin explains the demands Pocheon residents have made—to meet with US commanders and to receive compensation from Washington and Seoul—which have not been heard.

55 Christ and Dressler, *Noh Suntag*, 70.

56 Agamben, *State of Exception*, 5. In the camptown context, what is particularly striking in Agamben's state of exception is, while it presupposes a return to an original state with consolidated power, it constitutes "the kenomatic state, an emptiness of law," and thus the need to consider the presupposition that "a legal mythologeme analogous to the idea of a state of nature" (6). The absence of an "original state" of the sovereign territory from 1910 to 1949 (the Provisional Government was based in Shanghai from 1919 to 1948) made a legal mythologeme—the fantasy of a sovereign modern state prior to the Korean War—possible.

57 Christ and Dressler, *Noh Suntag*, 70. English in original.

58 These policemen, who performed their mandatory military service in the police force, were called *ŭikyŏng* (short for *ŭimukyŏngch'al*).

59 Christ states that the contrast in the subjects exposes "the existential bareness of civilian life." Christ and Dressler, *Noh Suntag*, 70.

60 At the same time, it is important to remember that the residents were not a singular body representing the opposition to base expansion, especially considering their shifting opinions (support rose from 37.8 percent to 49.5 percent between 2003 and 2010)—those based primarily on the city government redevelopment plans and publicity. See Martin, "From Camp Town to International City," 969. The relocation of the residents, of course, had to happen. In May 2018, former residents rallied in front of the Blue House to take back the name of the village, Daechu-ri, and to secure release of the imprisoned then village chief (*ichang*), Kim Chit'ae, and other imprisoned residents. Former residents testified that they were threatened to sign the relocation agreement when Kim and others were arrested. See Chŏng and Kim, "Taech'uri Chumindŭrŭi 11nyŏn Oech'im 'Maŭrirŭmŭl Tolyŏ Chuseyo.'"

61 Although the move was largely completed in 2018, service members, contract workers, and their family members continue to relocate to the city. The complete vacation of the Yongsan bases, and the return of the lands, had been in negotiations to be completed by 2021; their current status is undoubtedly impacted by the COVID-19 pandemic.

62 Part II was published in 2017 in conjunction with Noh's solo exhibition at Art Sonje. Noh, *Pisang Kukka: Che 4ŭi Pyŏk (State of Emergency II)*.

63 Martin, "From Camp Town to International City," 970.

64 Martin, "Base En/Closures"; "From Camp Town to International City."

65 Martin, "Base En/Closures." In another case, Paju's Ŏmmap'umdongsan, a park created for transnational adoptees on the former market site of Camp Andrew, was a direct example of the Defense Land Brokerage Scheme, through which $141 million (USD) was channeled directly to Pyeongtaek.

66 Added to the complication of Maehyang-ri redevelopment, as of 2021, the city of Hwaseong has been pressured to provide land for the relocation of a Repub-

lic of Korea Air Force airfield from Suwon. As one of the candidate sites for the relocation, Hwaseong has publicized the ecological value of Maehyang-ri and its painful past, which has been an important aspect of the campaign against the relocation. Bae, "Hwasŏng Maehyangni ch'ajŭn Yuchesŏk."

67 Martin, "Field Notes from South Korea," 230.

68 Martin, "From Camp Town to International City." Martin's study examines how such process was made possible in the midst of head-on protests against the USFK expansion in Pyeongtaek through the rhetoric of international, high-tech, green developments deployed by local and central governments and participating parties such as planners and expert consultants. The promise of neoliberal redevelopment with the multibillion-dollar projects including the Samsung semiconductor plant in Godeok City and yet-to-be-realized Brain City, proposed as an international medical hub, invokes eminent domain and further expropriation of farmlands.

69 Dinshaw et al., "Theorizing Queer Temporalities," 181. Emphasis in original.

Chapter 6. Listening to Camptown Photographs

An earlier version of this chapter was published as "1984: A Camptown Story," *photographies* 10, no. 3 (August 2017): 245–64.

1 According to the USFK website these are Area I: US Army Garrison Red Cloud / Casey; Area II: US Army Garrison Yongsan; Area III: US Army Garrison Humphreys; Area IV: US Army Garrison Daegu; Area V: Osan Air Base; and Area VI: Kunsan Air Base. United States Forces Korea website, "Organization," accessed June 10, 2020, https://www.usfk.mil/About/USFK/Organization/#Installations.

2 Hyun Sook Kim's analysis of *Silver Stallion* argues that the movie allegorizes camptown sex workers as symbols of the nation, sustaining and supporting "the Confucian patriarchal notions of femininity." Kim, "Yanggongju as an Allegory of the Nation," 181–85.

3 Referring to the women in the camptown sex industry (including immigrant workers), I use several terms interchangeably, depending on the context: "camptown sex workers," "camptown women," "*kijich'on* women," and, as the plaintiffs of the 2014 class action suit refer to themselves, "*mikun wianbu*." At times, I also introduce derogatory terms and slurs that have been used for these women.

4 Moon, *Sex among Allies*, 9. This was a major concern for the 122 former sex workers who filed a class action suit against the South Korean government in June 2014. Many of these women stated that they were abducted and trafficked as sex workers. Hŏ, "Insinmaemaetanghandui maeilbam ulmyŏnsŏ mikunŭl patatta."

5 On the other hand, there also has been criticism of heightened interest in the cultural representation of camptown sex workers in the United States. For example, focusing on literary representations of "comfort women" and camptown sex workers (although the latter does not in fact receive much attention), Ko Jeongyun examines the rise of interest in the two subjects "as an American topic of literary and scholarly representation." Ko problematizes the "Americanization" of the subjects in contemporary American literature by Asian Americans "considered as interpreter[s], if not, in some cases, outright spokesperson[s] of Asian women," and argues that "persistent U.S. orientalism is related to the continuing rush in the representation of oppressed Asian women of the past and present." Ko, "Politics of Representation," 20–21. While Ko's critique aptly points to the continued victimization of the women by forestalling their agency in such representations (and through her own identitarian subjectivization of Asian Americans), she does not examine—perhaps because of her heavy focus on "comfort women"—the critical role of American (and Japanese) imperialism and militarism in South Korea, the Asia-Pacific, and especially *within* the United States, where Asian American women are implicated in the geopolitics of transnational militarism not just symbolically but more immediately as "military brides," embroiling their children, and their communities, within "long-distance" ethno-nationalism and masculinism. See, for example, Cho, *Haunting the Korean Diaspora*; Yuh, "Out of the Shadows."

6 Moon, "Stars and Stripes and Sex." As such, perhaps unsurprisingly, the rise of scholarship on camptown sex work is related to the rise of anti-sex-work activism.

7 However, although existing outside the sovereignty of the ROK, a few exceptions also apply—South Korean nationals are not required to obtain appropriate visas and passports to enter the bases.

8 Unlike the closure by 1954 of "comfort stations" for the Korean Army, those that served the UN troops continued in the form of clubs and dance halls for American troops, established and operated by civilians. Pak, "Han'guk Kijich'on Sŏngmaemaechŏngch'aegŭi Yoksasahoehak," 10. In this article, Pak examines the South Korean government's control over camptown sex workers' bodies through the analytical framework of biopolitics (Foucault) and the state of exception (Agamben).

9 Agamben, *State of Exception*.

10 Lee, *Service Economies*.

11 Martin, "Base En/Closures."

12 I deliberately invoke "images" in both English and Korean; in Korea, *imiji* (image) is closer to an impression or an outlook, which may differ from the actual subject, than to a visual representation. I notice a similar use of the term in Japan.

13 Along with these questions, I also find asking Lisa Yoneyama's piercing inquiries on the geohistories of the transpacific violence and the Cold War helpful: "The epistemic demarcation that perceives the pre- to postwar transition as a clear severance from the (Japanese) time of supposedly illiberal violence to a peaceful world of (American) life and liberty has rendered illegible both the transwar continuity and the transferability of violence between the new and the old military and imperial powers. In what way can we understand the violence of hot wars and Kwon's 'civil war or other forms of organized violence,' which are coextensive with injuries under the Cold War even as they are inflicted in the name of conviviality, aid, and friendship? What are the ways in which we can cast light even further on the failure of transitional justice by perceiving violence and injustice as constitutive parts of the Cold War empire's liberal and biopolitical governmentality?" Yoneyama, *Cold War Ruins*, 52.

14 Yi Nayŏng contends that studies of camptowns and "camptown sex workers have focused heavily on the experiences of camptown women as socio-structural issues by emphasizing the relationship between national policies and the state." Yi argues that this focus has completely missed an opportunity to position the self, or "we" (the researcher, reader, viewer, etc.), in the writing of the history of camptowns and decisively become the transcendental voice in this history, thereby silencing the subaltern subject—as Gayatri Chakravorty Spivak critiques, the *kijich'on* women "cannot speak." Yi wants to start by asking who "we" are in this writing of the history, not by whether the subaltern can speak or not. Yi, "Kijich'on Yŏsongŭi Kyŏnghŏmgwa Yunnichŏk Chaehyŏnŭi Pul/Kanŭngsŏng," 81–82. Although Yi has argued to give more nuanced analyses of sex work in South Korea than be caught up in the dichotomy between abolition versus legalization, she is known today as an outspoken anti-sex-work activist. While I cite the work of Korean feminist scholars such as Yi, I do so to examine the state's role in camptown sex work, and I do not align with their anti-sex-work activism.

15 Kim, "Yanggongju as an Allegory of the Nation," 189.

16 See chapter 3 on the use of student ID photos as funerary portraits of Yi Hanyŏl and Pak Chongch'ŏl.

17 Eun-A, "Ko Yunkŭmi hyŏnjangsajin achikto sayongdoena."

18 The rationale and processes through which the Japanese operation of *kongch'angje* (state-operated prostitution) transitioned to American and Korean oversight, even after the illegalization of *kongch'angje* in 1947. Yi, "Kijich'on Hyŏngsŏng Kwachŏnggwa Yŏsŏngdŭrŭi Chŏhang," 175–83.

19 Moon, "Regulating Desire, Managing the Empire," 41.

20 Referring to Itagaki Ryūta's research on the Peace Treaty of San Francisco, Yoneyama points out "the importance of considering the British colonial legacies as well as the history of Anglo-Japanese interimperial alliances in shaping the

postwar, postcolonial settlement in Asia." Itagaki, "Shokuminchi sekinin o teiritsu suru tame ni," 310, and "Datsureisen to shokuminchi shihai sekinin no tsuikyū," 260–84, cited in Yoneyama, *Cold War Ruins*, 29–30. For example, South Korea was excluded from the signing of the peace treaty due to Japan and the United Kingdom, "which raised concerns that redressing Koreans for Japanese colonialism might have ramifications for its own colonies and which hoped to prevent the issues of colonial restitution from entering the state of the peace treaty." According to Yoneyama, Itagaki's study of how "war reparations have in effect eclipsed colonial redress, paving the way for the United States and its allies to act with impunity in their joint continuation of de facto colonization and neocolonization of much of Asia and the Pacific region" in turn informs this chapter.

21 Pak Chŏngmi examines how the "illegality" of controlling the bodies of sex workers was sustained: rather than establishing *pŏmnyul* (law) to control venereal disease, the government established *pŏpkyumyŏngryŏng* (orders), *haengjŏnggyuch'ik* (administrative regulations), and *chipangjorye* (local ordinances) on "Preventive Measures to Contagious Diseases" that would not clash with the 1948 ban on state-regulated prostitution. Pak, "Han'guk Kijich'on Sŏngmaemaechŏngch'aegŭi Yoksasahoehak," 12.

22 According to Han Honggu, revenue in US dollars earned from entertainment establishments exclusively for USFK was $9.7 million, almost 10 percent of the total foreign currency income in South Korea. Han, "<20> Kijich'on Chŏnghwaundong." In the case of Dongducheon, merely twenty-six GIs-only clubs made $400,000 in 1967, while the national export in the early 1960s was about $40 million. Kim, "Chikuhwa Sitae Kaeibŭrosŏŭi Yesulsilch'ŏn'gwa Changsoŭi Munje," 83.

23 Moon, "Regulating Desire, Managing the Empire," 58. According to Yi Nayŏng, about twenty thousand sex workers were serving forty-five thousand US troops in 1970. As most of their family members depended on their income, the livelihood of at least eighty thousand people directly depended on the women's work at the time. Yi, "Kijich'on Hyŏngsŏng Kwachŏnggwa Yŏsŏngdŭrŭi Chŏhang," 185.

24 According to Pogŏnsahoet'onggyeyŏnbo, the number of "waitresses and dancers of foreign amusement restaurant[s]" decreased from 11,456 in 1985 to 4,240 in 1995. See note 9. Pak, "Han'guk Kijich'on Sŏngmaemaechŏngch'aegŭi Yoksasahoehak," 15.

25 Yi, "Kijich'on Hyŏngsŏng Kwachŏnggwa Yŏsŏngdŭrŭi Chŏhang," 171.

26 Yi, 171.

27 The Presidential Decree No. 1 "outlawed all activities or statements opposing the Yushin Constitution itself, as well as any press reports on those activities. Emergency Decree No. 2 allowed the authorities to take all violators of Decree

No. 1 into custody without arrest warrants and give them prison sentences of up to 15 years." See Breen, "Park Got Dictatorial Powers."

28 Moon, "Resurrecting Prostitutes and Overturning Treaties," 137.

29 Kim, "Yanggongju as an Allegory of the Nation," 189. Markle was sentenced to fifteen years in prison in 1994 and was taken to Ch'ŏnan'gyotoso (Ch'ŏnan Correctional Facility), a correctional facility for non-Korean nationals.

30 Yi, "Kijich'on Hyŏngsŏng Kwachŏnggwa Yŏsŏngdŭrŭi Chŏhang," 189–90. Yi argues Korean ethno-nationalists use camptown women selectively at their convenience: while camptown sex workers are excluded from the national narrative as "dirty *yanggalbo*" (another derogative slur for camptown sex workers), they "resurrect as the symbol of 'the poor daughter of minjok,' in order to expose the Empire's brutality and reaffirm their own *ethnonationalist masculinity*." Emphasis added.

31 Pak, "Han'guk Kijich'on Sŏngmaemaechŏngch'aegŭi Yoksasahoehak," 2.

32 Pak, 14.

33 Pak, 18–22.

34 Pak, 22.

35 Kim, "Yanggongju as an Allegory of the Nation," 191–92.

36 Kim argues: "Both nationalist and feminist activists need to elucidate the ways working-class women of Kijich'on struggle to define the personal meanings of Korean womanhood and their self-representation as subjects of the Korean nation." Kim, "Yanggongju as an Allegory of the Nation," 193.

37 Choi, "Nationalism and Construction of Gender in Korea," 24.

38 In this regard, Kim Yŏngok examines how *minjung misul* entrenched itself in ethno-nationalism and exploited the representation of women's bodies, especially their sexual organs, as in the case of Sin Hakch'ŏl's "epic" paintings. Kim, "Kiŏgŭi chŏngch'ihak: Kkŭtnachianŭn chŏnjaenggwa chendŏ."

39 Yi, "Kijich'on Hyŏngsŏng Kwachŏnggwa Yŏsŏngdŭrŭi Chŏhang," 96.

40 Protestant church groups have joined NGOs against violent crimes against sex workers in camptowns in South Korea. Moon, "South Korean Movements against Militarized Sexual Labor," 316.

41 Kim, *Curative Violence*, 19.

42 Eunjung Kim cites McClintock: "Women are subsumed symbolically into the national body politic as its boundary and metaphoric limit." Kim, *Curative Violence*, 20–21; see note 59. Hyun Sook Kim also writes, "female bodies were subsumed symbolically into the national body politic." See Kim, "Yanggongju as an Allegory of the Nation," 189.

43 Here, I am referring to the 2014 landmark class action suit by 122 former camptown sex workers against the South Korean government. See the final note of this chapter.

44 Over the past few decades, Korean sex workers in camptowns have been replaced by Southeast Asian women who have been trafficked into South Korea. For an assessment of the changes and problems of the camptown entertainment and service industry, see Cheng, *On the Move for Love*; Moon, "Camptown Prostitution and the Imperial SOFA"; Yea, "Everyday Spaces of Human Trafficking."

45 Organized by sex workers, protests broke out outside Camp Ames. As discussed later in this chapter, a further series of protests broke out in other camptowns, such as Anjeong-ri, where Camp Humphreys is located, in 1971. In response, the US-Korea joint force and the Korean government declared a "Camptown Clean-up Campaign" in the summer of the same year "as a direct response to the civil unrest and racial violence in Anjeong-ri." One result was periodical quarantines of sex workers due to sexually transmitted diseases. They also had to carry ID cards indicating their STI-positive status. See Moon, "Prostitute Bodies and Gendered States in US-Korea Relations," 161–63.

46 Kim Hyŏnsŏn is the founding director of Sae'umt'ŏ, a social-service organization based in Dongducheon for camptown sex workers, which assists them to become financially independent when they leave brothels. Kim, "P'okihamyŏn Kŭnyang Chukkettanŭn Kŏn'gayo?"

47 A retrospective of Kuwabara's documentary work during this period was held at the Museum of Photography, Seoul (now Museum Hanmi), in November 2008. An exhibition catalog includes photographs of *kijich'on* women. See Shisei, *Kuwabara Shisei*. Kuwabara gave a special artist talk at Noonbit Publishing's thirtieth anniversary celebration, held at Space 22, Seoul, November 7, 2018.

48 Despite widespread protests in 1964–65, the military government of Park Chung-hee signed the Treaty of Basic Relations between Japan and Republic of Korea on June 22, 1965, reestablishing diplomatic ties.

49 In his memoir, Kuwabara recalls being interrogated by officers of the Seoul Police Department in 1965. As he had previously had his film confiscated, he learned to hide his film before undercover agents could seize it. Kuwabara, *Tak'yument'ŏri Sajin'ga*, 118–21.

50 The photograph appears on the cover of Katharine H. S. Moon's *Sex among Allies*.

51 The semiotic reading of the subjects' bodies in Burri and Kuwabara's photographs as representative of the two nations is a practice of Cold War Orientalism, particularly of the East and Southeast Asian regions as a sexualized feminine Other, as discussed in chapter 1. The critique of Cold War Orientalism in the images of camptowns is belated; in South Korea, the continued political rhetoric of the consequential exceptionality of the Korean War, which has yet to end, functions powerfully in conflating militarism and patriotism, in this case, through visual and popular culture. See Klein, *Cold War Orientalism*.

52 Höhn and Moon, *Over There*.

53 By contrast, the testimonial book of Kim Chŏngja, a former camptown sex worker, only includes photographs depicting specific sites, buildings, streets, monuments, and camps. These photographs work powerfully with the incredible journey Kim takes with the activist Kim Hyŏnsŏn of Sae'umt'ŏ, to camptowns she worked and lived in across the country. Kim, *Mikun Wianbu Kijich'on Yŏsŏng Ch'oech'oŭi Chŭngŏnnok.*

54 Pak argues camptowns symbolize "the arrested sovereignty" of South Korea by the United States. Pak, "Han'guk Kijich'on Sŏngmaemaechŏngch'aegŭi Yoksa-sahoehak," 25.

55 Choi, "Nationalism and Construction of Gender in Korea," 15.

56 Choi, 15.

57 Eng, *Racial Castration*, 2.

58 Lowe, *Intimacies of Four Continents*, 27.

59 Lowe, "Asian American Studies 101."

60 Choi, "Nationalism and Construction of Gender in Korea," 18.

61 I am, of course, implicated in this subjectivization of camptown sex workers. My analysis of camptown photographs is an attempt to examine how such silencing occurs with the photographs and how they can also place viewers in the position to question their own subjectivity in this history.

62 Moon, "Prostitute Bodies and Gendered States in U.S.-Korea Relations," 142. While the binary is found commonly in critiques of US imperialism, scholars such as Hyun Sook Kim and Katharine H. S. Moon scrutinize the exploitation of sex workers and the dangers they are exposed to in their everyday life. Their contributions to the scholarship on militarism in South Korea have expanded beyond the allegory of the strong and weak states—represented by the perpetrator and victim, and usually through male GIs and female sex workers—by problematizing the limit of such configurations. Moon also tackles this issue by asserting that scholarship on the topic has largely excluded the Korean government and military from the picture. Moon, 167.

63 Enloe writes that camptown women "detail how their relationships with local male lovers and husbands created the conditions that make them vulnerable to the appeals of the labor-needy disco owners." Enloe, "It Takes Two," 24.

64 It is telling to learn about Cumings's firsthand experience of the 1960s, which he did not disclose until 1992. He states, "Although I have barely written about this aspect about Korean-American exchange before—partly because it is embarrassing to Korean pride, partly because I thought few were interested in a phenomenon simultaneously ubiquitous and unremarked upon, partly because of a male code that I will discuss shortly—it is the aspect that most struck me when I first lived in Korea, creating indelible impressions of a relationship that, because of the use made of Korean women, could not be what it was said to be:

a free compact between two independent nations dedicated to democracy and anticommunism." See Cumings, "Silent But Deadly," 169–70.

65 Moreover, businesses that provide prostitution for heterosexual men outside camptowns are easy enough to find throughout cities across South Korea. They vary in "business types" from "room salons," where young women are employed to assist their male customers, to "massage parlors," and even to "noraepang," commonly known as karaoke in North America. While these businesses are not brothels, the description as bars and massage parlors creates a tacit understanding that these places are likely to offer sexual services. Sex workers in general are more stigmatized than the proprietors or their "clients," who are mostly men, but, as discussed, camptown sex workers have been even more stigmatized due to their service to foreign men.

66 Choi, "Nationalism and Construction of Gender in Korea," 18.

67 I discuss Kwŏn Myŏnga's analysis of postwar Korean literature and *sunansa* in chapter 1.

68 Government censorship between the 1960s and early 1990s is discussed in relation to social and democratization movements in chapter 3.

69 English title in original.

70 As the Chun Doo-hwan military regime conducted surveillance of the activities of college students, going into a camptown to record the lives of its residents was a risky undertaking.

71 Joo Myung Duk has also taken photos of Dongducheon focusing on sex workers and GIs on the street. The themes of Korean movies about camptowns have been limited to camptown prostitution or the life of marginalized mixed-race children born of camptown sex workers and GIs, as depicted in Kim Kitŏk's *Address Unknown* (2001).

72 Kang and Chang, "Chaberŭi Mundapchangch'i 5 Hwa"; Yong Suk Kang, interview with the author, Iksan, South Korea, March 17, 2022.

73 Until the widespread use of cameras in the 1980s, *kinyŏmsajin* were usually taken by professional photographers at events such as graduations and sixtieth birthdays, as well as at famous landmarks like waterfalls and Buddhist temples. Those photographs were inscribed with the word "*kinyŏmsajin*" and dates in white acrylic on the bottom part of the photographs. See examples of family portraits in chapter 1 for similar inscriptions.

74 Kang, *Yong Suk Kang*, 89. While Korean nationals were not allowed to go inside clubs that sell tax-free alcohol, his status as club photographer let him in. Kang, interview with the author.

75 Kang states that in college his instructors focused mostly on documentary approaches, while he found the contingency between facticity and fiction in photography more interesting and meaningful. Kang, interview with the author.

76 Zolghadr, "Them and Us," 7.

77 It is tacitly understood that the sitters for the portraits did not know that their portraits were going to be part of an artwork by Kang.

78 Korean artist Ko Sŭnguk's video *Ch'imŭl purŭnŭn norae* (2008) also uses vernacular snapshot photographs of a camptown sex worker. In the video, however, Ko uses special effects to blur and darken the image so that the sitter's features become mostly unrecognizable. Of additional interest, although not discussed in this chapter, is a pivotal work by Kim Yongt'ae, *DMZ*, which consists of hundreds of studio portraits collected from camptown photo studios. I examine this work in my article "1984: A Camptown Story."

79 Pak, "Multilateral View on Reality of Division," 4; Kang, interview with the author.

80 Kang bought cheap Sakura-brand film cassettes, available in Dongducheon, and developed them at express photo vendors in Dongducheon so he could give them back to the GIs on the same day. He usually charged a dollar for each print. The fifteen select photographs are the ones that have been enhanced digitally for reproduction since most of the developed photographs have noises with "raw" qualities that were not appropriate for publications. Kang, interview with the author.

81 Five couples out of fifteen chose full-shot portraits, embracing while smiling at the camera.

82 Kim, "60–70nyŏndae Kijich'on Get'ohwaŭi Pyŏn'gokchŏm-t'ŭkchŏngchiyŏk," 165–68.

83 Moon, "Regulating Desire, Managing the Empire," 52.

84 Kang, interview with the author.

85 Frank B. Wilderson III posits, "Antiblack violence is not a form of racial hatred but the genome of Human renewal[,]" through which the social death of Black people enables the social life of Humans. Anti-Black racism in Korea, thus, is inseparable from both the US imperial racialization of non-US and US territories (i.e., camptowns and USFK base camps, respectively) taking place in other parts of the world, which is often overlooked as most studies of Korean ethno-nationalism zoom in on the postcolonial making and myth of monoracial nation-state. Quoting Lewis Gordon, Wilderson III states, "Whiteness is both full Presence and absolute perspectivity. 'To look at a black body is to look at a mere being-among-beings . . . [but] the white body, being human (Presence), doesn't live as a mere-being-among-beings. It lives with the potential to be a being that stands out from mere beings. Its being-in-itself ironically enables it to be a being-for-itself' (Gordon 1995, 100–101)." Wilderson III, "Afropessimism and the Ruse of Analogy," 43, 47.

86 The experience of race, in which the camptown sex worker's own race becomes conflated with her sex work, is critical. In an interview with the former camptown

sex worker by Yi Nayŏng, "Kim Myŏngsuk," in her seventies, refers to only one Black GI as "*uri mikun*" ("our American solider"), who loved and respected her deeply; this is the only endearing reference she uses for any of her former partners, including Korean and white men, and indeed, Kim recounts that it was Korean people who called her "*yanggalbo*" ("Western whore") and treated her as "subhuman." Such political positioning of race and gender also enables the order within the camptown, again interrelated with the gendered racial politics of the US empire elsewhere. In this context, anti-Blackness in Korea kept at bay the formation of Korean-Black solidarity against the white supremacism of the US military, its expansion, and the racial dynamics within bases and camptowns and supported the policing of service members. See Yi, "Kijich'on Yŏsongŭi Kyŏnghŏmgwa Yunnichŏk Chaehyŏnŭi Pul/Kanŭngsŏng," 108, 110.

87 Again, for an analysis of camptown studio portraits collected and used for Kim Yongt'ae's iconic work, *DMZ*, see Lee, "1984: A Camptown Story."

88 Raiford, "When Home Is a Photograph."

89 Young Min Moon, "Souvenir Photographs from the Military Camptown." Also see Moon, "Report from the Underside"; "Kim Yongt'aeŭi <DMZ>." Kang notes that many of the barmaids he met in Dongducheon were not interested in making money as sex workers or service providers to the GIs but eager to find ways to move to the United States with American dreams of their own. Kang, interview with the author.

90 Nyong'o, "Habeas Ficta," 288.

91 Shin, *Ethnic Nationalism in Korea*, 4.

92 As Avery Gordon points out in reading Ralph Ellison's *Invisible Man*, "Hypervisibility is a persistent alibi for the mechanisms that render one un-visible." Gordon, *Ghostly Matters*, 17.

93 Derrida, *Archive Fever*, 19.

94 Derrida, 36.

95 Campt, *Listening to Images*, 17. Emphasis in original.

96 siren eun young jung, *Narrow Sorrow*.

97 Once again, "listening" to camptown photographs has been inspired by Campt and other scholars who have argued for photography's multisensorial affects, along with siren eun young jung, who has been undoing the normative and sanctioned ways of seeing/knowing/making histories.

98 jung, *Narrow Sorrow*.

99 Camptown women's lives have been discussed widely through an approach Agamben theorizes as "bare life" (Agamben, 1998). Simply put, bare life refers to one's biological fact, given the priority for what constitutes life over all other aspects of life, but the concept also entails the legal, social, cultural, and political processes through which the potentialities of life (that are certainly emphasized

in other lives) are annulled. Rather than repeat the discussion, I have focused on what is at stake with photography representing the state of exception for camptowns and camptown women.

100 jung, *Narrow Sorrow.*

101 Kim, "Chikuhwa Sitae Kaeibŭrosŏŭi Yesulsilch'ŏn'gwa Changsoŭi Munje," 84.

102 Although the work of Kim Tongryŏng is not examined in this book, there is a theme of women and/or LGBTQ+ artists, such as Kim and siren eun young jung, making works grounded in their activism and long-term ethnographic research. Kim's "American Alley" (2008) consists of photographs and videos that Kim made while researching in Dongducheon. Kim's work is a long-term project that started at Turebang, a support organization for current and former camptown sex workers in Dongducheon. For a feminist analysis of her work, see Kim Yŏngok, "Chikuhwa Sitae Kaeibŭrosŏŭi Yesulsilch'ŏn'gwa Changsoŭi Munje."

103 Kim, 96.

104 jung, "Dongducheon p'ŭrojektŭrŭl Mach'imyŏ," cited in Kim, "Chikuhwa Sitae Kaeibŭrosŏŭi Yesulsilch'ŏn'gwa Changsoŭi Munje," 97.

105 Kim, 100.

106 On June 25, 2014, 122 former *mikun wianbu* filed a class action suit against the South Korean government for the "facts and casualties of the institutionalized system of *mikun wianbu*" and "tak[ing] responsibilit[y] for violating women's rights." They demanded "the state's apology and reparation to the victims of institutionalized camptown prostitution." On January 20, 2017, the Seoul High Court ruling partially "acknowledged that the state had justified and promoted the prostitution of U.S. military 'comfort women' via the operation and management of military camptowns, and the state unlawfully detained the women." Following the ruling, 117 plaintiffs appealed on March 16, 2017. On February 8, 2018, an appellate court ruling for the lawsuit regarding state compensation for U.S. military "comfort women" was announced. The plaintiffs demanded a statement from the United States government, but they have yet to hear from them. Kijich'onyŏsŏnginkwŏnyŏndae, "'Kijich'on Yŏsŏng' Kukka Sangdae Chiptan Sonbaesosong." On September 29, 2022, the Supreme Court upheld the 2017 and 2018 rulings, stating that "the second division of the Supreme Court (Presiding Justice Yi Tongwŏn) dismissed the appeals of both sides in a case in which plaintiffs, women from US military camps, claimed damages against the Republic of Korea for illegal acts, such as creation, management, operation, and justification and promotion of prostitution. The judgment of the lower court, which determined that the national liability for compensation did not expire because the statute of limitations had not been completed, was confirmed." Supreme Court of Korea, "Potocharyo/Ŏnnonjaryohaemyŏng."

BIBLIOGRAPHY

4.19 Hyŏngmyŏngginyŏmsaŏphoe. *4.19 Hyŏngmyŏngsa*. Seoul: 4.19 Hyŏngmyŏngginyŏmsaŏphoe, 2003.

6·25chŏnjaeng 70chunyŏn saŏpch'uchinwiwŏnhoe. "6·25chŏnjaeng 70chunyŏn Saŏpch'uchinwiwŏnhoe." 2020. http://koreanwar70.go.kr/?ckattempt=1.

Abel, Elizabeth. *Signs of the Times: The Visual Politics of Jim Crow*. Berkeley: University of California Press, 2010.

Agamben, Giorgio. *State of Exception*. Chicago: University of Chicago Press, 2005.

Ahn, Ji-Hyun. "Transforming Korea into a Multicultural Society: Reception of Multiculturalism Discourse and Its Discursive Disposition in Korea." *Asian Ethnicity* 13, no. 1 (February 2012): 97–109. https://doi.org/10.1080/14631369.2012.625703.

An, Tongil. *Saeroun 4.19*. Goyang: Wisŭdŏm, 2010.

An, Wonjun. "Kim Chuyŏl Yŏlsa Changrye Osipnyŏnmane Ch'irŭnda." *Segyeilbo*. March 11, 2010.

Azoulay, Ariella Aïsha. *The Civil Contract of Photography*. Translated by Rela Mazali and Ruvik Danieli. New York: Zone, 2008.

Azoulay, Ariella Aïsha. *Civil Imagination: A Political Ontology of Photography*. New York: Verso, 2012.

Azoulay, Ariella Aïsha. "'The Family of Man': A Visual Universal Declaration of Human Rights." In *The Human Snap Shot*, edited by Thomas Keenan and Tirdad Zolghadr, 19–48. Berlin: Sternberg, 2013.

Bae, Jaehong. "Hwasŏng Maehyangni ch'ajŭn Yuchesŏkkwa Rŏningmaen··· Usŭmimyŏnen 'ch'ŏmyehan kaltŭng.'" *Kyeongin Ilbo*, August 14, 2021. http://www.kyeongin.com/main/view.php?key=20210813010002749.

Bae, Myungji, ed. *DMZ Theater*. Seoul: National Museum of Modern and Contemporary Art, Korea, 2021.

Baik, Chrystal Mun-hye. "Unfaithful Returns: Reiterations of Dissent, U.S.-Korean Militarized Debt, and the Architecture of Violent Freedom." *Journal of Asian American Studies* 18, no. 1 (February 2015): 41–72.

Bak, Hee-Je, and Daniel Lee Kleinman. "Media Cultures and the Representation of Science in Korea and the United States: The BSE Case in 2008." *East Asian Science, Technology and Society: An International Journal* 11, no. 3 (September 2017): 331–52.

Barea, María Del Carmen Molina. "The Cinematographic Refrain: Memory and Repetition in the Films of Hong Sang-Soo and Apichatpong Weerasethakul." *Canadian Journal of Film Studies* 30, no. 2 (Fall 2021): 1–21.

Barthes, Roland. *Camera Lucida: Reflections on Photography*. Translated by Richard Howard. New York: Hill and Wang, 1980.

Barthes, Roland. "The Great Family of Man." In *Mythologies*, translated by Annette Lavers, 100–102. New York: Hill and Wang, 1972.

Barthes, Roland. *Mythologies*. Translated by Annette Lavers. New York: Hill and Wang, 1972.

Batchen, Geoffrey. "How the Other Half Photographs: Looking Globally." *New York Times*, July 12, 2003. https://www.nytimes.com/2003/07/12/books/book-review-how-the-other-half-photographs-looking-globally.html.

Batchen, Geoffrey. "Life and Death." In *Suspending Time: Life-Death-Photography*, 108–29. Mishima, Japan: Izu Photo Museum, 2010.

Batchen, Geoffrey, ed. *Photography Degree Zero: Reflections on Roland Barthes's Camera Lucida*. Cambridge, MA: MIT Press, 2009.

Benjamin, Walter. "Little History of Photography." In *Walter Benjamin Selected Writings*. Vol. 2, *1927–1934*, edited by Michael W. Jennings, Howard Eiland, and Gary Smith, 507–30. Cambridge, MA: Belknap Press of Harvard University Press, 1999.

Benjamin, Walter. "On the Concept of History." In *Walter Benjamin: Selected Writings*. Vol. 4, *1938–1940*, edited by Howard Eiland and Michael W. Jennings, 389–400. Cambridge, MA: Belknap Press of Harvard University Press, 2003.

Benjamin, Walter. "Theses on the Philosophy of History." In *Illuminations*, edited by Hannah Arendt, 253–64. New York: Schocken, 1968.

Benjamin, Walter. "The Work of Art in the Age of Its Technological Reproducibility." In *The Work of Art in the Age of Its Technological Reproducibility, and Other Writings on Media*, edited by Michael W. Jennings, Brigid Doherty, and Thomas Y. Levin, 19–55. Cambridge, MA: Belknap Press of Harvard University Press, 2008.

Bhabha, Homi K. "'The Beginning of Their Real Enunciation': Stuart Hall and the Work of Culture." *Critical Inquiry* 42, no. 1 (Autumn 2015): 1–30.

Bhabha, Homi K. "Freedom's Basis in the Indeterminate." In "The Identity in Question," special issue, *October* 61 (Summer 1992): 46–57.

Bhabha, Homi K. "'Race,' Time and the Revision of Modernity," in "Neocolonialism," edited by Robert Young, *Oxford Literary Review* 13, no. 1/2 (1991): 193–219.

Bleiker, Roland. "Visual Autoethnography and International Security: Insights from the Korean DMZ." *European Journal of International Security* 4, no. 3 (October 2019): 274–99.

Brady, Lisa. "Life in the DMZ: Turning a Diplomatic Failure into an Environmental Success." *Diplomatic History* 32, no. 4 (September 2008): 585–611.

Breen, Michael. "Park Got Dictatorial Powers with Yushin Constitution in 1971." *Korea Times*, October 31, 2010. http://www.koreatimes.co.kr/www/news/nation/2010/10/116_75537.html.

Brown, Elspeth, and Thy Phu, eds. *Feeling Photography*. Durham, NC: Duke University Press, 2014.

Brown, Nicholas, and Imre Szeman. "What Is the Multitude? Questions for Michael Hardt and Antonio Negri." *Cultural Studies* 19, no. 3 (May 2005): 372–87.

Butler, Judith. *Notes Toward a Performative Theory of Assembly*. Cambridge, MA: Harvard University Press, 2015.

Butler, Judith, and Athena Athanasiou. *Dispossession: The Performative in the Political*. Cambridge: Polity, 2013.

Cadava, Eduardo, and Gabriela Nouzeilles, eds. *The Itinerant Languages of Photography*. Princeton, NJ: Princeton University Art Museum and Yale University Press, 2013.

Campt, Tina M. *Image Matters: Archive, Photography, and the African Diaspora in Europe*. Durham, NC: Duke University Press, 2012.

Campt, Tina M. *Listening to Images: An Exercise in Counterintuition*. Durham, NC: Duke University Press, 2017.

Caraffa, Costanza, and Tiziana Serena, eds. *Photo Archives and the Idea of Nation*. Berlin: De Gruyter, 2015.

Carville, Justin. *Photography and Ireland*. London: Reaktion, 2011.

Cawley, Kevin. "Back to the Future: Recalibrating the Myth of Korea's Homogenous Ethnicity." *Asian Ethnicity* 17, no. 1 (January 2016): 150–60. https://doi.org/10.1080/14631369.2015.1051510.

Chae, Ou-Byung. "Non-Western Colonial Rule and Its Aftermath: Post-Colonial State Formation in South Korea." PhD diss., University of Michigan, 2006.

Chakrabarty, Dipesh. *Provincializing Europe: Postcolonial Thought and Historical Difference*. Princeton, NJ: Princeton University Press, 2000.

Chang, Boyoung. "Imagining the Other Korea: Photographs of North Korea." Panel hosted by Center for Creative Photography, Arizona, February 26, 2022.

Chang, Chŏngmin. "Kiŏgŭi Maech'esŏ Manggagŭi Maech'ero: Sajinŭi Mudŏme Much'in Kajoksajinŭi Sidae." *Hwanghae Review*, no. 3 (2018): 328–34.

Chang, Ch'ungjong. *Han'guksinmunsajinnon*. Seoul: Noonbit, 1998.

Chang, Paul Y. "Unintended Consequences of Repression: Alliance Formation in South Korea's Democracy Movement (1970–1979)." *Social Forces* 87, no. 2 (December 2008): 651–77. https://doi.org/10.1353/sof.0.0153.

Chatterjee, Partha. "Whose Imagined Community?" In *Mapping the Nation*, edited by Gopal Balakrishnan, 214–25. New York: Verso, 1996.

Chaudhary, Zahid R. *Afterimage of Empire: Photography in Nineteenth-Century India*. Minneapolis: University of Minnesota Press, 2012.

Cheng, Sealing. *On the Move for Love: Migrant Entertainers and the U.S. Military in South Korea*. Philadelphia: University of Pennsylvania Press, 2010.

Cho, Chuhyŏn (Joo-hyun). "Pop'yŏnjuŭiwa Sangdaechuŭirŭl Nŏmŏ: P'eminisŭt'ŭ Chŏngch'ihagŭi Silch'onchŏk Chŏnhwan (Beyond Universalism and Relativism: The Practical Turn of Feminist Politics)." *Sahoewairon (Society and Theory)*, no. 24 (May 2014): 7–42.

Cho, Grace M. *Haunting the Korean Diaspora: Shame, Secrecy, and the Forgotten War*. Minneapolis: University of Minnesota Press, 2008.

Cho, Usŏk. *Han'guksajin'garon*. Noonbit Sajinsŏnsŏ 15. Seoul: Noonbit, 1998.

Ch'oe, Chihyŏng. "2019 Honin Yihon t'onggye." T'onggyech'ŏng: Kukkat'onggyep'otŏl, March 19, 2020. http://kostat.go.kr/portal/korea/kor_nw/1/1/index.board?bmode=read&aSeq=381203.

Ch'oe, Injin. *Han'guksajinsa 1631–1945*. Seoul: Noonbit, 1999.

Ch'oe, Injin, and Ju Suk Park. *Han'guksajinŭi Hanseki* (*The Century of Korean Photography: Images from the Land of Morning Calm*). Seoul: RIHP, 2001.

Ch'oe, Minsik. *Najŭndero Imhan Sajin Naŭi Insaeng, Naŭi Sajin*. Seoul: Noonbit, 2009.

Choi, Bonglim. "Kajoksajin: Chŏnghyŏngsŏngesŏ Isankujoro (Family Photography: From the Formal to the Discrete)." *Misulsahakbo: Reviews on the Art History*, no. 45 (December 2015): 141–62.

Choi, Bonglim, and Kyŏngmin Yi, eds. *Han'guksajinmunhwayŏn'guso Charyochip*. Vol. 2, *Han'guksajinsa Kusulp'ŭrochekt'ŭ: 1945–60nyŏndae Sajin'gyeŭi Hwaltonggwa Tonghyang*. Seoul: Han'guksajinmunhwayŏn'guso, 2010.

Choi, Bonglim, Chiŭi Yu, and Sohŭi Kim, eds. *Han'guksajinmunhwayŏn'guso Charyojip* Vol. 6, *Han'guksajinsa Kusulp'ŭrojekt'ŭ: Sukmyŏngyŏjataehakkyo Sajinpu Sukmihoe 50(Osip)Nyŏnŭl Chinago*. Seoul: Han'guksajinmunhwayŏn'guso, 2013.

Choi, Chungmoo. "Nationalism and Construction of Gender in Korea." In *Dangerous Women: Gender and Korean Nationalism*, edited by Elaine H. Kim and Chungmoo Choi, 9–32. New York: Routledge, 1998.

Choi, Ellie. "Yi Kwangsu and the Post–World War I Reconstruction Debate." *Journal of Korean Studies* 20, no. 1 (Spring 2015): 33–75.

Ch'ŏn, Chŏnghwan. "'1987nyŏnhyŏng Minjuchuŭi'ŭi Chongŏn'gwa Ch'otpulhangjaeng Ihuŭi Han'guk Minjuchuŭi: Taechungminjuchuŭiŭi Munhwachŏngch'irŭl Chungsimŭro." *Munhwakwahak*, no. 94 (June 2018): 22–44.

Chŏng, Hwanbong, and Chŏnghyo Kim. "Taech'uri Chumindŭrŭi 11nyŏn Oech'im 'Maŭrirŭmŭl Tolyŏ Chuseyo.'" *Hankyoreh*, May 3, 2019. http://www.hani.co.kr/arti/society/society_general/843153.html.

Chŏng, T'aewon. *Sŏulbal Sajinjonghap: Jayuwa Minjuhwarŭl Hyanghan Taechangjŏng: Chŏngtaewon Sajinjip (Photographs from Seoul: Photographs by Tony Chung)*. Seoul: Noonbit, 2013.

Chŏng, Yujin. "Beibisajine Kwanhan Yŏn'gu: Beibisajin Sŭt'yudioŭi p'yohyŏn Stailŭl Chungsimŭro." MA thesis, Sangmyung University, 2005.

Chow, Rey. *The Rey Chow Reader*. Edited by Paul Bowman. New York: Columbia University Press, 2010.

Chow, Rey. "Theory, Area Studies, Cultural Studies: Issues of Pedagogy in Multiculturalism." In *Learning Places: The Afterlives of Area Studies*, edited by Masao Miyoshi,

Harry Harootunian, and Rey Chow, 103–18. Durham, NC: Duke University Press, 2002.

Choy, Catherine Ceniza. “Race at the Center: The History of American Cold War Asian Adoption.” *Journal of American-East Asian Relations* 16, no. 3 (Fall 2009): 163–82.

Chuh, Kandice. *The Difference Aesthetics Makes: On the Humanities After “Man.”* Durham, NC: Duke University Press, 2019.

Chuh, Kandice. “It’s Not about Anything.” In *Saturation: Race, Art, and the Circulation of Value*, edited by C. Riley Snorton and Hentyle Yapp, 171–82. Cambridge, MA: MIT Press, 2020.

Chuh, Kandice, and Karen Shimakawa, eds. *Orientations: Mapping Studies in the Asian Diaspora*. Durham, NC: Duke University Press, 2001.

Chun, Wendy Hui Kyong. *Discriminating Data: Correlation, Neighborhoods, and the New Politics of Recognition*. Cambridge, MA: MIT Press, 2021.

Chun, Wendy Hui Kyong. *Updating to Remain the Same: Habitual New Media*. Cambridge, MA: MIT Press, 2016.

Cody, Francis. “Populist Publics: Print Capitalism and Crowd Violence beyond Liberal Frameworks.” *Comparative Studies of South Asia, Africa and the Middle East* 35, no. 1 (2015): 50–65.

Cumings, Bruce. “Silent But Deadly: Sexual Subordination in the U.S.-Korean Relationship.” In *Let the Good Times Roll: Prostitution and the U.S. Military in Asia*, edited by Saundra Pollock Sturdevant and Brenda Stoltzfus, 169–75. New York: New Press, 1992.

Deleuze, Gilles. *Difference and Repetition*. Translated by Paul Patton. New York: Continuum, 2001.

Derrida, Jacques. *Archive Fever: A Freudian Impression*. Chicago: University of Chicago Press, 1996.

Dinshaw, Carolyn, Lee Edelman, Roderick A. Ferguson, Carla Freccero, Elizabeth Freeman, Judith Halberstam, Annamarie Jagose, Christopher Nealon, and Nguyen Tan Hoang. “Theorizing Queer Temporalities: A Roundtable Discussion.” *GLQ: A Journal of Lesbian and Gay Studies* 13, no. 2–3 (2007): 177–95.

Dong-a Ilbo. “Wŏldŭk’ŏp Ihu Siminŭisik Kaesŏndwaetta,” September 17, 2003. http://news.donga.com/3//20030917/7982950/1.

Dowling, Monica. “Globalisation and International Adoption from China.” In *Handbook on the Family and Marriage in China*, edited by Xiaowei Zhang and Lucy Xia Zhao, 305–20. Cheltenham, UK: Edward Elgar, 2017.

Duara, Prasenjit. *Rescuing History from the Nation: Questioning Narratives of Modern China*. Chicago: University of Chicago Press, 1995.

Eckert, Carter J. *Park Chung Hee and Modern Korea: The Roots of Militarism, 1866–1945*. Cambridge, MA: Harvard University Press, 2016.

Eng, David L. *The Feeling of Kinship: Queer Liberalism and the Racialization of Intimacy*. Durham, NC: Duke University Press, 2010.

Eng, David L. “The Feeling of Photography, the Feeling of Kinship.” In *Feeling Photography*, edited by Thy Phu and Elspeth Brown, 325–48. Durham, NC: Duke University Press, 2014.

Eng, David L. *Racial Castration: Managing Masculinity in Asian America*. Durham, NC: Duke University Press, 2001.

Enloe, Cynthia. "It Takes Two." In *Let the Good Times Roll: Prostitution and the U.S. Military in Asia*. New York: New Press, 1993.

Eun-A. "Ko Yunkŭmi hyŏnjangsajin achikto sayongdoena." *Yŏsŏngchuŭi Chŏnŏl Ilda*, August 1, 2005. http://www.ildaro.com/sub_read.html?uid=2510&section=sc1.

Fanon, Frantz. "The Fact of Blackness." In *Black Skin, White Masks*, translated by Charles Lam Markmann, 82–108. London: Pluto, 1986.

Foster, Hal. *The Return of the Real: The Avant-Garde at the End of the Century*. Cambridge, MA: MIT Press, 1996.

Gee, Helen. *Photography of the Fifties: An American Perspective*. Tucson: Center for Creative Photography, University of Arizona, 1980.

Gordon, Avery F. *Ghostly Matters: Haunting and the Sociological Imagination*. Minneapolis: University of Minnesota Press, 1997.

Gürsel, Zeynep Devrim. "Visualizing Publics: Digital Crowd Shots in the 2015 Unity Rally in Paris." Supplement, *Current Anthropology* 58, no. S15 (February 2017): S135–48.

Han, Honggu. "<20> Kijich'on Chŏnghwaundong." *Hankyoreh*, November 30, 2012. https://www.hani.co.kr/arti/society/society_general/563197.html.

Healy, Hall. "Korean Demilitarized Zone: Peace and Nature Park." *International Journal on World Peace* 24, no. 4 (December 2007): 61–83.

Heiferman, Marvin. "Has Facebook Killed the Photo?" *Art in America* 99, no. 4 (April 2011): 55–61.

Hirsch, Julia. *Family Photographs: Content, Meaning and Effect*. Oxford: Oxford University Press, 1981.

Hirsch, Marianne. *Family Frames: Photography, Narrative, and Postmemory*. Cambridge, MA: Harvard University Press, 1997.

Hŏ, Chaehyŏn. "Insinmaemaetanghandui Maeilbam Ulmyŏnsŏ Mikunŭl Patatta." *Hankyoreh*, July 4, 2014.

Höhn, Maria, and Seungsook Moon. *Over There: Living with the U.S. Military Empire from World War Two to the Present*. Durham, NC: Duke University Press, 2010.

Hong, Cathy Park. *Minor Feelings: An Asian American Reckoning*. New York: One World, 2020.

Hong, Misuk. "A Study of the Specialization of Baby Photos According to the Development of Portrait Photography." MA thesis. Seoul: Chung-Ang University, 2007.

Hong, Sŏngmin. "Kamjŏnggujowa Ch'otpulhyŏngmyŏng: 2008(Ich'ŏnp'al)Nyŏn'gwa 2016(Ich'ŏnsipnyuk)Nyŏn." *Siminsahoewa NGO* 15, no. 1 (2017): 79–110.

Hübinette, Tobias. *Comforting an Orphaned Nation: Representations of International Adoption and Adopted Koreans in Korean Popular Culture*. Seoul: Jimundang, 2006.

Hübinette, Tobias. "Korea(n) Divided: Third Space Existence in Kim Ki-Duk's *Wild Animals*." *Graduate Journal of Asia-Pacific Studies* 2, no. 2 (2004): 18–29.

Hübinette, Tobias. "Nationalism, Subalternity, and the Adopted Koreans." *Journal of Women's History* 19, no. 1 (Spring 2007): 117–22.

Hübinette, Tobias. "The Orphaned Nation: Korea Imagined as an Overseas Adopted Child in Clon's *Abandoned Child* and Park Kwang-Su's *Berlin Report*." *Inter-Asia Cultural Studies* 6, no. 2 (June 2005): 227–44.

Hwang, Sindŏk, Yŏngsuk Hŏ, and Tŏgyo Yi. "Yŏryu Myŏngsaŭi Tongsŏng Yŏn'aeki Iyagi," *Pyŏlgŏngon* 5, no. 10 (1930): 120–23.

Im, Ŭngsik. *Im Ŭngsik Sajinjip*. Seoul: Sajinyesulsa, 1995.

Im, Ŭngsik. *Naega Kŏrŏon Han'guksadan Im Ŭngsik Hoegorok*. Seoul: Noonbit, 1999.

Israel, Jonathan I. *Enlightenment Contested: Philosophy, Modernity, and the Emancipation of Man*. Oxford: Oxford University Press, 2006.

Itagaki, Ryūta. "Datsureisen to shokuminchi shihai sekinin no tsuikyū: Zoku/shokuminchi shihai sekinin o teiritsu suru tame ni." In *Rekishi to sekinin*, edited by Kim Puja and Nakano Toshio, 260–84. Tokyo: Seikyūsha, 2008.

Itagaki, Ryūta. "Shokuminchi sekinin o teiritsu suru tame ni." In *Keizoku suru shokuminchishugi: Jendā, minzoku, jinshu, kaikyū*, edited by Iwasaki Minoru, 294–315. Tokyo: Seikyūsha, 2005.

Jager, Sheila Miyoshi. "Women, Resistance and the Divided Nation: The Romantic Rhetoric of Korean Reunification." *Journal of Asian Studies* 55, no. 1 (February 1996): 3–21.

Joo, Myung Duk. "Q&A." Photography and Korea panel, hosted by Center for Creative Photography, Arizona, February 27, 2022.

Jun, Euyryung. "'We Have to Transform Ourselves First': The Ethics of Liberal Developmentalism and Multicultural Governance in South Korea." *Focaal* 2012, no. 64 (November 26, 2012): 99–112. https://doi.org/10.3167/fcl.2012.640109.

jung, siren eun young. *Narrow Sorrow*. siren eun young jung, 2008. http://www.sirenjung.com/index.php/dongducheon-project/narrow-sorrow/.

jung, siren eun young. "Tongduch'ŏn p'ŭrojektŭrŭl Mach'imyŏ." *Pol (Han'gukmunhwayesulwiwŏnhoe Insamisulgonggan)*, no. 9 (2008).

Kang, Jiyeon. *Igniting the Internet: Youth and Acitivism in Postauthoritarian South Korea*. Honolulu: University of Hawai'i Press, 2016.

Kang, Yong Suk. *Maehyangni P'unggyŏng*. Seoul: Noonbit, 1999.

Kang, Yong Suk, and Myŏnghun Chang. "Chaperŭi Mundapchangch'i 5 Hwa: Chŏnjaengŭi Sŏnjŏnkirok, Kŭkŏsi Kkŭtnanŭn Nal 1bu." *Kungnae ch'oech'o midiŏatŭ ch'aenŏl: Aelissŭon*, April 11, 2010. https://aliceon.tistory.com/1455.

Kennedy, Barbara M. *Deleuze and Cinema: The Aesthetics of Sensation*. Edinburgh: Edinburgh University Press, 2000.

Kijich'onyŏsŏnginkwŏnyŏndae. "'Kijich'on Yŏsŏng' Kukka Sangdae Chiptan Sonbaesosong." Chuhanmikunbŏpjoekŭnjŏrundongbonbu (National Campaign for Eradication of Crimes by US Troops in Korea). Accessed June 24, 2020. http://usacrime.or.kr/doku/doku.php?id=기지촌:기지촌여성인권연대.

Kim, Charles R. *Youth for Nation: Culture and Protest in Cold War South Korea*. Honolulu: University of Hawai'i Press, 2017.

Kim, Chŏngja. *Mikun Wianbu Kijich'on Yŏsŏng Ch'oech'oŭi Chŭngŏnnok: Mikun Wianbu Kijich'onŭi Sumgyŏchin Chinsil*. Edited by Hyŏnsŏn Kim. Paju, South Korea: Hanul, 2013.

Kim, Chŏngnam. *4.19 Hyŏngmyŏng*. Seoul: Minjuhwaundongginŏmsaŏphoe (Korea Democracy Foundation), 2004.

Kim, Chongyŏp. "Ch'otpul Hangjaenggwa 87 (p'alch'i'il)Ch'eje." *Ch'angjakkwa pip'yŏng (Creation and Criticism)* 36, no. 3 (September 2008): 36–59.

Kim, Elaine H., and Chungmoo Choi, eds. *Dangerous Women: Gender and Korean Nationalism*. New York: Routledge, 1998.

Kim, Eleana J. *Adopted Territory: Transnational Korean Adoptees and the Politics of Belonging*. Durham, NC: Duke University Press, 2010.

Kim, Eleana J. "Invasive Others and Significant Others: Strange Kinship and Interspecies Ethics near the Korean Demilitarized Zone." *Social Research* 84, no. 1 (Spring 2017): 203–20.

Kim, Eleana J. *Making Peace with Nature: Ecological Encounters along the Korean DMZ*. Durham, NC: Duke University Press, 2022.

Kim, Eunjung. *Curative Violence: Rehabilitating Disability, Gender, and Sexuality in Modern Korea*. Durham, NC: Duke University Press, 2017.

Kim, Grace S., Karen L. Suyemoto, and Castellano B. Turner. "Sense of Belonging, Sense of Exclusion, and Racial and Ethnic Identities in Korean Transracial Adoptees." *Cultural Diversities and Ethnic Minority Psychology* 16, no. 2 (2010): 179–90.

Kim, Hosu. *Birth Mothers and Transnational Adoption Practice in South Korea: Virtual Mothering*. New York: Palgrave Macmillan, 2016.

Kim, Hyekyŏng. "Ilcheha Ŏrinikiŭi Hyŏngsŏnggwa Kajokpyŏnhwae Kwanhan Yŏn'gu." PhD diss., Ewha Womans University, 1997.

Kim, Hyŏnsŏn. "P'okihamyŏn Kŭnyang Chukkettanŭn Kŏn'gayo? Kijich'on Yŏsŏngdŭrŭi Iyagi." *Yŏsŏnggwa p'yŏnghwa*, no. 1 (September 2000): 68–76.

Kim, Hyun Sook. "Yanggongju as an Allegory of the Nation: The Representation of Working-Class Women in Popular and Radical Texts." In *Dangerous Women: Gender and Korean Nationalism*, 175–201. New York: Routledge, 1998.

Kim, In'yu. "Maehyangnisakyŏkchang P'yeswae 10nyŏn . . . Sangch'ŏŭi ttangesŏ haengbogi ssakt'ŭnda." *Yonhap News*, August 19, 2015. https://www.yna.co.kr/view/AKR20150819137400061.

Kim, Jang Hee. "A Study of the Transformation in Internet Cultural Contents through the Entrace [*sic*] of Digital Cameras: Based on the Personal Homepage Media Providers Cyworld and Blogs." MA thesis, Sogang University, 2005.

Kim, Jieun. "'Beibi Soljyŏwa 'Pudaechigye'e Tamkin Yugio Han'gukchŏnjaengŭi 'Ch'amsang.'" *News Korea*. June 21, 2019, sec. Town News.

Kim, Jinah. *Postcolonial Grief: The Afterlives of the Pacific Wars in the Americas*. Durham, NC: Duke University Press, 2019.

Kim, Jung-ha. "Kŭndaesingminchuŭie Taeŭnghan Saenghwalmunhwa Ch'osangsajin." *Silch'ŏnminsokhakyŏn'gu (The Study of Practice Folkloristics)*, no. 32 (August 2018): 145–71.

Kim, Kungsŏn. "Dallas 'Han'gukchŏnjaengt'ŭkpyŏlsajinchŏn' Haninbalkil Soedo." *News Korea*, June 25, 2012.

Kim, Kungsŏn. "Han'gukchŏnjaeng Yuksipchunyŏn Kinyŏmhaengsa 'Ch'amjŏnyongsatŭlkke Chinsimŭro Kokaesugyŏ Kamsatŭrimnita.'" *News Korea*, July 19, 2014, sec. Town News.

Kim, Miae. "Kajoksajine Kwanhan Han Yŏn'gu: Sahoejŏk·chohyŏngjŏk Kwanjŏmesŏ Pon 1990nyŏndae Sŭtyudio Kajoksajin." MA thesis, Hongik University, 1998.

Kim, Monica. *The Interrogation Rooms of the Korean War: The Untold History*. Princeton, NJ: Princeton University Press, 2019.

Kim, Nam-See. "The REAL DMZ PROJECT and Dongsongsewol ('Lived Time of Dongsong')." In *The Real DMZ Project 2015*, 10–15. Seoul: SAMUSO, 2015.

Kim, Oksun, and Sŭnggon Kim. "Haep'it'ugedŏ-Sajin'ga Kim Oksŏn." iPHOS Webzine, August 27, 2004. http://webzine.iphos.co.kr/webzine/features/features_step03.asp?lrg_no=0&menu=15&ins_no=701.

Kim, Pŏmsu. "Hyŏryugesŏ Kyŏnggyeinŭro: 1980nyŏndaewa 1990nyŏndae Chaeildongp'oŭi p'yosanggwa Han'guk Minjokchuŭi (From a Blood Relative to a Marginal Man: Ethnic Koreans in Japan and the Change of Korean Nationalism in the 1980s and 1900s)." *Chŏngch'isasangyŏn'gu* 24, no. 2 (November 2018): 167–98.

Kim, Sooah. "[Chaengjŏmgwa Tonghyang] Dijit'ŏl t'ek'ŭnolojiŭi Palchŏn'gwa Saeroun Yŏsŏng Chŏngch'i Chuch'eŭi Kanŭngssŏng (Digital Technology and Young Women's Political Participation)." *P'eminijŭm Yŏn'gu (Issues in Feminism)* 12, no. 1 (April 2012): 193–217.

Kim, Su-jeong. "A Study on the Photographs of Candle Demonstrations (with a Focus on the Five Major Daily Newspapers)." MA thesis, Sangmyung University, 2009.

Kim, Suk-Young. *DMZ Crossing: Performing Emotional Citizenship Along the Korean Border*. New York: Columbia University Press, 2014.

Kim, Sunjung, ed. *The Real DMZ*. Seoul: SAMUSO, 2013.

Kim, Sunjung, ed. *The Real DMZ*. Seoul: SAMUSO, 2019.

Kim, Tae Jin. "A Study of the Process of the Formation of the Online Public Opinion and Transformation to the Political Power: A Case Study of 'Minerva' on the Online Public Sphere." MA thesis, Pusan National University, 2009.

Kim, Wŏn. "60–70nyŏndae Kijich'on Ket'ohwaŭi Pyŏn'gokchŏm-t'ŭkchŏngchiyŏk, Hanmich'insŏnhyŏbŭihoe, Kŭrigo Kijich'on Chŏnghwaundong." *Yŏksapip'yŏng*, no. 112 (August 2015): 153–85.

Kim, Yŏngok. "Chikuhwa Sitae Kaeibŭrosŏŭi Yesulsilch'ŏn'gwa Changsoŭi Munje: Tongduch'ŏn Chagŏbŭl Chungsimŭro." *Yŏsŏnghagnonjip* 27, no. 1 (2010): 73–109.

Kim, Yŏngok. "Kiŏgŭi Chŏngch'ihak: Kkŭtnachianŭn Chŏnjaenggwa Chendŏ." *Hyŏndaemisulsayŏnku*, no. 28 (December 2010): 311–34.

Kim, Yŏngok. "Yŏsŏng, Kukka, Ch'otpul." In *Kŭtaenŭn Wae Ch'otpurŭl Kkŭsyŏtnayo*, edited by Tongjin Sŏ, Yunhyŏng Han, Sŭnguk Paek, T'aekkwang Yi, Yŏngju Yu, Sanggil Yi, Yongt'aek Chŏng, et al., 201–14. Seoul: Sanch'aekja, 2009.

Kim, Yŏngok. "Yŏsŏngchuŭi Kwanjŏmesŏ Pon Ch'otpulchiphoewa Yŏsŏngŭi Chŏngch'ichŏk Chuch'esŏng (Candlelight Rallies and Political Subjectivity of Women from the Feminist Perspective)." *Asiayŏsŏngyŏn'gu (Journal of Asian Women)* 48, no. 2 (November 2009): 7–34.

Kim, Yŏngsik. "Sŭlp'ŭmŭl Titko Sŏn Chakkaŭi Naengŏmhan Sisŏn." *Wŏlgansajin (Monthly Photography)*, June 2007. Accessed June 30, 2020. http://www.monthlyphoto.com/webzine/st-jr_pt_view.asp?m_seq=15&s_seq=34&page=.

Klein, Christina. *Cold War Orientalism: Asia in the Middlebrow Imagination, 1945–1961.* Berkeley: University of California Press, 2003.

Ko, Jeongyun. "Politics of Representation: Americanization of Korean Comfort Women and Camptown Sex Worker Discourses." *Yŏngŏyŏngmunhak Yŏn'gu* 56, no. 1 (March 2014): 19–46.

Ko, Pyŏnggyu. "Sinsaengasajin p'yohyŏne Kwanhan Yŏn'gu: Aelbŏmchejak." MA thesis, Sangmyŏng University, 2005.

Koh, Dong-Yeon. "The Place-Ness of the DMZ: The Rise of DMZ Tourism and the Real DMZ Project." *Position: Asia Critique* 27, no. 4 (November 2019): 653–85.

Kohli, Atul. "The Rhee Interregnum: Saving South Korea for Cohesive Capitalism." In *State- Directed Development: Political Power and Industrialization in the Global Periphery*, 62–83. Cambridge: Cambridge University Press, 2004.

Korean Democracy Foundation. "Open Archives (오픈아카이브)." Accessed April 18, 2022. https://archives.kdemo.or.kr/main.

Kracauer, Siegfried. *The Past's Threshold: Essays on Photography.* Zurich: Diaphanes, 2014.

Kracauer, Siegfried, and Paul O. Kristeller. *History: The Last Things before the Last.* Princeton, NJ: Markus Wiener, 1995.

Kukkakirogwŏn. "Idarŭi Kirok: 2010nyŏn 02wol: 'Mojapogŏnpŏp' Chejŏng." Accessed July 11, 2017. http://theme.archives.go.kr/next/monthly/viewMain.do?year=2010&month=02.

Kukkakirogwŏn. "In'gu Chŏngch'aek: Chuyo Isyu Mannaki: Kajokkyehoek Saŏp." Accessed July 11, 2017. http://theme.archives.go.kr/next/populationPolicy/issue02.do.

Kukkapohunch'ŏ. *Urika Tangsinŭl Kiŏkhanŭn Pangbŏp (6.25chŏnjaeng Yuench'amjŏnyongsa'eke Masŭk'ŭrŭl Chiwŏnhada).* YouTube video, May 29, 2020. https://www.youtube.com/watch?v=xtivT2fNMT4.

Kuwabara, Shisei. *Ch'walyŏnggŭmji: Han'guk- Kyŏkttongŭi Sapanseki.* Seoul: Noonbit, 1990.

Kuwabara, Shisei. *Kuwabara Shisei: Naekaparapon Kyŏkttongŭi Han'guk.* Seoul: Noonbit, 2008.

Kuwabara, Shisei. *Tak'yument'ŏri Sajin'ga-Minamata·Han'guk·Bet'ŭnam Ch'wijaeki.* Translated by Sŭnggon Kim. Seoul: Noonbit, 2012.

Kwŏn, Myŏnga. *Kajok Iyaginŭn Ŏttŏke Mandŭrŏchinŭn'ga.* Ch'aeksesang Mun'go 4. Seoul: Ch'aeksesang, 2000.

Kwŏn, Myŏnga. "Mosŏngsinhwaŭikiwon, Kŭ P'asijŭmjŏk Hyŏngsigekwanhayŏ: 'Chŏnhu' Kyŏnghŏmgwa Mosŏngsinhwaŭi Hyŏngsŏnggwajŏng Yŏn'gu." *Wŏnuronjip* 30, no. 1 (1999): 37–60.

Kwŏn, Myŏnga. *Muhani Chŏngch'ijŏgin Oeroum: Han'guk Sahoeŭi Chŏngdongŭl Mutta.* Seoul: Kalmuri, 2012.

Kwŏn, Myŏnga. "Munyeyŏnghwawa Kongyukiŏk (Commemoration) Mandŭlgi: Han'gukchŏnjaengŭi Kyŏnghŏmgwa Yŏksaŭi Chaekusŏng." *Han'gukmunhwayŏngu* 26 (2003): 123–48.

Kwŏn, Myŏnga. *Ŭmnan'gwa Hyŏngmyŏng: P'unggimunnanŭi Kyebowa Chŏngnyŏmŭi Chŏngch'ihak.* Seoul: Ch'eksesang, 2013.

Kwŏn, Myŏnga. "Yŏsŏngsunansa Iyagi: Minjokkuka Mandŭlgiwa Yŏsŏngsŏngŭi Dongwŏn." *Yŏsŏngmunhagyŏn'gu*, no. 7 (2002): 105–34.
Kwŏn, Myŏnga. "Yŏsŏng·sunansa Iyagiŭi Yŏksajŏk Ch'ŭngwi." *Sanghŏhakpo*, no. 10 (2003): 149–76.
Kwŏn, T'aegyun. *Sajin'ga Im Ŭngsik k'ameraro Chinsirŭl Marhada*. Seoul: Namusup, 2006.
Lee, Hye-Kyung. "International Marriage and the State in South Korea: Focusing on Governmental Policy." *Citizenship Studies* 12, no. 1 (February 2008): 107–23.
Lee, Jin-kyung. *Service Economies: Militarism, Sex Work, and Migrant Labor in South Korea*. Minneapolis: University of Minnesota Press, 2010.
Lee, Jung Joon. "Envisioning Modernity, Practicing Desire: Baby and Family Photographic Portraiture in Korea." *History of Photography* 37, no. 3 (2013): 312–25.
Lee, Jung Joon. "1984: A Camptown Story." *photographies* 10, no. 3 (August 2017): 245–64.
Lee, Jung Joon. Review of *Korean War in Color: A Correspondent's Retrospective on a Forgotten War*, by John Rich, with Elizabeth Shim, Andrew Salmon, and Robert Koehler. *Trans-Asia Photography Review* 3, no. 1 (Fall 2012). http://hdl.handle.net/2027/spo.7977573.0003.114.
Lee, Kyu Sang, ed. *Han'guksajinŭi Chip'yŏng*. Seoul: Noonbit, 2001.
Lilley, James R. *China Hands: Nine Decades of Adventure, Espionage, and Diplomacy in Asia*. New York: Public Affairs, 2004.
Lim, Bliss Cua. *Translating Time: Cinema, the Fantastic, and Temporal Critique*. Durham, NC: Duke University Press, 2009.
Lim, Jie-Hyun. "Victimhood Nationalism in Contested Memories: National Mourning and Global Accountability." In *Memory in a Global Age: Discourses, Practices and Trajectories*, edited by A. Assmann and S. Conrad, 138–62. Basingstoke, UK: Palgrave Macmillan, 2010.
Liu, Lydia H. "The Eventfulness of Translation: Temporality, Difference, and Competing Universals." In *At Translation's Edge*, edited by Nataa Durovicova, Patrice Petro, and Lorena Terando, 13–30. New Brunswick, NJ: Rutgers University Press, 2019.
Lowe, Lisa. "Asian American Studies 101." Panel presented at the Hess Scholar in Residence Program, Brooklyn College, City University of New York, October 25, 2021.
Lowe, Lisa. *The Intimacies of Four Continents*. Durham, NC: Duke University Press, 2015.
Mbembe, Achille. *Necropolitics*. Translated by Steven Corcoran. Durham, NC: Duke University Press, 2019.
Marker, Chris. *Coreénnes*. Paris: Éditions du seuil, 1959.
Marker, Chris. *Puknyŏksaramdŭl (Coreénnes)*. Translated by Mukyŏng Kim. Seoul: Noonbit, 2008.
Martin, Bridget. "Base En/Closures: Development, Dispossession, and US Military Real Estate in Contemporary South Korea." Lecture presented at the SBS Seminar, hosted by the Korea Institute, Harvard University, December 2, 2021.
Martin, Bridget. "Field Notes from South Korea: Local Development in the Land of Securitized Peace." *California Geographer* 57 (2018): 227–43.

Martin, Bridget. "From Camp Town to International City: US Military Base Expansion and Local Development in Pyeongtaek, South Korea." *International Journal of Urban and Regional Research* 42, no. 6 (2018): 967–85.

May 18 Memorial Foundation, The. "5.18 Minjuhwaundong Kwannyŏn T'onggye (The May 18 Democratization Movement Statistics)." Accessed January 7, 2021. http://www.518.org/nsub.php?PID=010103.

Min, Pyŏnguk. "Kimjuyŏl Yŏlsa Pŏmgungminjang Masanhangsŏ Nunmul Sok Ŏmsu." Kyŏngnamdominilbo, April 11, 2010. http://www.idomin.com/news/articleView.html?idxno=314543.

Minjuhwaundongginyŏmsaŏphoe (Korea Democracy Foundation). *Han'gungminjuhwauntongsa*. Vol. 1. Paju: Tolbegae, 2008.

Mirinae, ed. *Pot'ongi Anin Naldŭl: Chaeiljosŏnin, p'ich'abyŏlburak, Ainu, Okinawa, Pillipin, Pet'ŭnam Yŏsŏngŭi Sam*. Translated by Chiyŏn Yang. Paju: Sakyejŏl, 2019.

Mookherjee, Nayanika. *The Spectral Wound: Sexual Violence, Public Memories, and the Bangladesh War of 1971*. Durham, NC: Duke University Press, 2015.

Moon, Katharine H. S. "Prostitute Bodies and Gendered States in US-Korea Relations." In *Dangerous Women: Gender and Korean Nationalism*. New York: Routledge, 1998.

Moon, Katharine H. S. "Resurrecting Prostitutes and Overturning Treaties: Gender Politics in the 'Anti-American' Movement in South Korea." *Journal of Asian Studies* 66, no. 1 (February 2007): 129–57.

Moon, Katharine H. S. "South Korean Movements against Militarized Sexual Labor." *Asian Survey* 39, no. 2 (April 1999): 310–27.

Moon, Katharine H. S. "Stars and Stripes and Sex: Nationalism and Globalization." In *The Gijichonin Women's History in Modern Korea*. Seoul: Seoul National University, 2004.

Moon, Seungsook. "Camptown Prostitution and the Imperial SOFA: Abuse and Violence against Transnational Camptown Women in South Korea." In *Over There: Living with the U.S. Military Empire from World War Two to the Present*, edited by Maria Höhn and Seungsook Moon, 337–65. Durham, NC: Duke University Press, 2010.

Moon, Seungsook. "Regulating Desire, Managing the Empire: U.S. Military Prostitution in South Korea, 1945–1970." In *Over There: Living with the U.S. Military Empire from World War Two to the Present*, edited by Maria Hörn and Seungsook Moon, 39–77. Durham, NC: Duke University Press, 2010.

Moon, Young Min. "Kim Yongt'aeŭi <DMZ>-Chŏngch'ijŏk Hwalddongŭrosŏui Yesul." *Minjogmihak* 13, no. 1 (2014): 236–40.

Moon, Young Min. "Report from the Underside: Dongducheon." *Trans-Asia Photography Review* 3, no. 1 (Fall 2012). http://hdl.handle.net/2027/spo.7977573.0003.110.

Moon, Young Min. "The Souvenir Photographs from the Military Camptown in South Korea, circa 1980." Korean Photography in Global Scene panel, hosted by Center for Creative Photography, Arizona, February 26, 2022.

Morris, Rosalind C. "Theses on the New 'Öffentlichkeit.'" *Grey Room*, no. 51 (Spring 2013): 94–111.

Morrison, Toni. *Home*. New York: Alfred A. Knopf, 2012.

Moten, Fred. *In the Break: The Aesthetics of the Black Radical Tradition*. Minneapolis: University of Minnesota Press, 2003.

Mroué, Rabih. "The Pixelated Revolution." Translated by Ziad Nawfal. *TDR: The Drama Review* 56, no. 3 (Fall 2012): 18–35.

Muñoz, José Esteban. *The Sense of Brown*. Durham, NC: Duke University Press, 2020.

Na, Myŏngsu, and Sujin Kim. "Int'ŏnet Kwangjangesŏ t'aorŭnŭn Ch'otpul Iyagi Agorawa 82cook (p'arik'uk) Net'ijŭni Malhada." *Ch'angjakkwa pip'yŏng (Creation and Criticism)* 36, no. 3 (September 2008): 94–107.

Na, Yŏnggyun. *Ilchesitae, Uri Kajogŭn: Ŏnŭ Kajogŭi Salmŭl t'onghae Pon Singminji Han'guk Chisigin Sahoeŭi p'unggyŏng*. Seoul: Hwangsojari, 2004.

Naing, Min Ma. "Beyond Burmese Esthetics." Presented at the Global Cornell Visual Culture Colloquium, Cornell University, September 14, 2021.

Nash, Jennifer C. *Black Feminism Reimagined: After Intersectionality*. Durham, NC: Duke University Press, 2019.

NationMaster. "GDP Growth Annual % Statistics—Countries Compared." Accessed September 15, 2011. https://www.nationmaster.com/country-info/stats/Economy/GDP.

Nelson, Kim Park. *Invisible Asians: Korean American Adoptees, Asian American Experiences, and Racial Exceptionalism*. New Brunswick, NJ: Rutgers University Press, 2016.

Neyra, Ren Ellis. *The Cry of the Senses: Listening to Latinx and Caribbean Poetics*. Durham, NC: Duke University Press, 2020.

Nguyen, Mimi Thi. *The Gift of Freedom: War, Debt, and Other Refugee Passages*. Durham, NC: Duke University Press, 2012.

Noh, Suntag. *Noh Suntag: State of Emergency (Pisang Kukka)*. Edited by Iris Dressler and Hans Christ. Berlin: Hatje Cantz, 2009.

Noh, Suntag. *Pisang Kukka: Che 4ŭi Pyŏk (State of Emergency II: The 4th Wall)*. Seoul: Art Sonje Center, 2017.

Nyong'o, Tavia. "Habeas Ficta: Fictive Ethnicity, Affecting Representations, and Slaves on Screen." In *Migrating the Black Body: The African Diaspora and Visual Culture*, edited by Leigh Raiford and Heike Raphael-Hernadez, 287–305. Seattle: University of Washington Press, 2017.

OECD. "Earnings and Wages—Gender Wage Gap." OECD Data, 2020. Accessed June 4, 2020. http://data.oecd.org/earnwage/gender-wage-gap.htm.

OECD. "Employment—Hours Worked." OECD Data, 2020. Accessed June 4, 2020. http://data.oecd.org/emp/hours-worked.htm.

Oh, Arissa. "From War Waif to Ideal Immigrant: The Cold War Transformation of the Korean Orphan." *Journal of American Ethnic History* 31, no. 4 (Summer 2012): 34–55.

Oh, Arissa. "A New Kind of Missionary Work: Christians, Christian Americanists, and the Adoption of Korean GI Babies, 1955–1961." *Women's Studies Quarterly* 33 (2005): 161–88.

Oh, Hye-ri. "Translating 'Photography': The Migration of the Concept of *Sajin* from Portraiture to Photography." *History of Photography* 39, no. 4 (November 2015): 366–89.

Oh, Hye-ri. "Photography, Technology, and Realism in 1950s Korea." In *Future Yet to Come: Sociotechnical Imaginaries in Modern Korea*, 177–203. Honolulu: University of Hawai'i Press, 2021.

Oh, Hyŏnju, *Kkumŭl Tchiknŭn Sŭtyudio*. Seoul: Noonbit, 2010.

Olin, Margaret. *Touching Photographs*. Chicago: University of Chicago Press, 2012.

Ŏm, Miok. "Kajoksajin Kŭrigo Mainŏriti Yŏsŏng Chŭngŏnŭi Sŏsa, Ch'abyŏlgwa p'yŏnkyŏne Chŏhanghako Sot'onggwa Yŏndaerŭl Mosaekhanda: Pot'ongi Anin Naldŭl." *Asiayŏsŏngyŏnku (Journal of Asian Women)* 58, no. 1 (April 2019): 121–31. https://doi.org/10.14431/jaw.2019.4.58.1.121.

Paek, Chihye. *Sŭwit'ŭ Homŭi Kiwŏn*. Sallim Chisik Ch'ongsŏ 152. Seoul: Sallim Buksŭ, 2005.

Pak, Ch'ankyŏng, "Ripaiŏtŏn—Maehyangni." In *Maehyangni P'unggyŏng*, 5–10. Seoul: Noonbit, 1999.

Pak, Chŏngmi. "Han'guk Kijich'on Sŏngmaemaechŏngch'aegŭi Yoksasahoehak, 1953–1995: Naengjŏn'gi Saengmyŏngjŏngch'i, Yewoesangt'ae, Kŭrigo Chukkwŏnŭi Yŏksŏl (A Historical Sociology of the Korean Governments Policies on Military Prostitution in U.S. Camptowns, 1953–1995: Biopolitics, State of Exception, and the Paradox of Sovereignty under the Cold War)." *Han'guksahoehak (Korean Journal of Sociology)* 49, no. 2 (April 2015): 1–33.

Pak, Kilsŏng, Myŏnggu Kang, and Jonggu Yi. *1960nyŏndae Sahoebyŏnhwa Yŏn'gu: 1963–1970*. Seoul: Paeksansŏdang, 1999.

Pak, P'yŏngjong. *Han'guksajinŭi Chasengnyŏk*. Seoul: Noonbit, 2010.

Pak, P'yŏngjong. "Multilateral View on Reality of Division: From Dongducheon Commemorative Photographs to Korean War Monuments." In *Kang Yong Suk*, 4–9. Harongni, Gangwondo: Donggang Museum of Photography, 2010.

Pak, P'yŏngjong. *Han'guksajinŭi Sŏn'gujatŭl*. Seoul: Noonbit, 2007.

Pak, To, ed. *Chiulsuŏmnŭn Imigi 3: Han'gukchŏnjaengi Namgin'gŏttŭl (The Indelible Image 3: The Photographs of the Korean War from National Archives and Records Administration in the United States of America)*. Vol. 3. Seoul: Noonbit, 2007.

Pak, Yŏngt'aek. *Kajogŭl Kŭrita: Kŭrim sokŭro tŭrŏon kajogŭi ŏlguldŭl*. Seoul: Pada, 2009.

Park, Hansol, Yun Seungyong, and Kyungjin Zoh. "The Characteristics of Minbuk Village in DMZ Border Area as Living Heritage: With Case Study on Igil-Ri and Yugok-Ri in Cheorwon." *Journal of the Urban Design Institute of Korea* 21, no. 6 (December 2020): 89–104.

Park, Jong Hyun. "A Study on the Expression and Thinking Method of Digital Photo Image with Emphasis on the Environmental Change in Media and the Meaning of Art Works." MA thesis, Pusan National University, 2009.

Park, Jongwoo. "Park Jongwoo: *DMZ Pimujangjitae (Inside DMZ-Guard Posts)*." Echo Photo Archive. Accessed February 27, 2022. https://ecophotoarchive.org/photographer/9/175.

Park, Ju Suk. *Han'guksajinsa*. Seoul: Munhaktongne, 2021.

Park, Ju Suk. "Han'guksajinŭi Doip Kwajŏng Sŏlmyŏnggwa Chŏng Haech'ang Sajinŭi Haesŏge Nat'anan Munjechŏm Koch'al." In *Han'guksajinŭi Chip'yŏng*, 103–19. Seoul: Noonbit, 2001.

Park, Myoung-Kyu. "Pundanch'eje, Segyehwa, Kŭrigo p'yŏnghwaminjokchuŭi (Regime of National Division, Globalization, and Peace Nationalism)." *Simin'gwa Segye* 8 (February 2006): 416–30.

Park, Sang Mi. "The Paradox of Postcolonial Korean Nationalism: State-Sponsored Cultural Policy in South Korea, 1965–Present." *Journal of Korean Studies* 15, no. 1 (Fall 2010): 67–93.

Pate, SooJin. *From Orphan to Adoptee: U.S. Empire and Genealogies of Korean Adoption*. Minneapolis: University of Minnesota Press, 2014.

Perry, Samuel. *A Century of Queer Korean Fiction*. New York: Modern Language Association of America, forthcoming.

Phu, Thy. "Diasporic Vietnamese Family Photographs, Orphan Images, and the Art of Recollection." *Trans-Asia Photography Review* 5, no. 1 (Fall 2014). http://hdl.handle.net/2027/spo.7977573.0005.102.

Phu, Thy. *Picturing Model Citizens: Civility in Asian American Visual Culture*. Philadelphia: Temple University Press, 2012.

Phu, Thy. "Reenactment and Remembrance: An-My Lê's *Small Wars*." Global Photography: Out of Time panel, sponsored by the University of New Mexico Art Museum, September 9, 2021.

Pinney, Christopher. *Camera Indica: The Social Life of Indian Photographs*. Chicago: University of Chicago Press, 1997.

Pinney, Christopher. "Locating Photography." In *A Companion to Photography*, 29–47. Hoboken, NJ: John Wiley, 2020.

Pinney, Christopher. "Troubled by Photography: Contingencies of the Image in South Asia." Global Photography: Across Space panel, hosted by the School of Art and Design and the Krannert Art Museum at the University of Illinois, September 10, 2021.

Puar, Jasbir K. "'I Would Rather Be a Cyborg than a Goddess': Becoming-Intersectional in Assemblage Theory." *PhiloSOPHIA* 2, no. 1 (2012): 49–66.

Puar, Jasbir K. "Queer Times, Queer Assemblages," *Social Text* 23, no. 3–4 (Fall–Winter 2005): 121–39.

Rai, Amit S. *Rule of Sympathy: Sentiment, Race, and Power, 1750–1850*. New York: Palgrave, 2002.

Raiford, Leigh. *Imprisoned in a Luminous Glare: Photography and the African American Freedom Struggle*. Chapel Hill: University of North Carolina Press, 2013.

Raiford, Leigh. "When Home Is a Photograph: Kathleen Cleaver's Albums of Exile." Global Photography: Across Space panel, hosted by the School of Art and Design and the Krannert Art Museum at the University of Illinois, September 10, 2021.

Rancière, Jacques. *The Emancipated Spectator*. London: Verso, 2009.

"REAL DMZ PROJECT." Accessed April 19, 2022. http://www.realdmz.org/.

Ribbat, Christoph. "Queer and Straight Photography." *Amerikastudien/American Studies* 46, no. 1 (2001): 27–39.

Rich, John. *Korean War in Color: A Correspondent's Retrospective on a Forgotten War*. Seoul: Seoul Selection, 2010.

Ryu, Youngju, ed. *Cultures of Yushin: South Korea in the 1970s*. Ann Arbor: University of Michigan Press, 2018.

Ryzova, Lucie. "Nostalgia for the Modern: Archive Fever in Egypt in the Age of Post-Photography." In *Photo Archives and the Idea of Nation*, edited by Costanza Caraffa and Tiziana Serena. Berlin: De Gruyter, 2015.

Sakai, Naoki. "Translation and Image: On the Schematism of Co-Figuration." In *At Translation's Edge*, edited by Nataa Durovicova, Patrice Petro, and Lorena Terando, 79–97. New Brunswick, NJ: Rutgers University Press, 2019.

Sarri, Rosemary, Yenoak Baik, and Marti Bombyk. "Goal Displacement and Dependency in South Korean-United States Intercountry Adoption." *Child and Youth Service Review* 20, no. 1/2 (1998): 87–114.

Seo, Young Chae. "The Birth of an Ethical Subject: The 1980s and South Korean Literature." In *Beyond Death: The Politics of Suicide and Martyrdom in Korea*, translated by Youngju Ryu, 260–86. Seattle: University of Washington Press, 2019.

Seoul Museum of Art. *Kangbak² (Compulsion to Repeat)*. Seoul: Seoul Museum of Art, 2019.

Shin, Gi-Wook. *Ethnic Nationalism in Korea: Genealogy, Politics, and Legacy*. Stanford: Stanford University Press, 2006.

Shin, Hye Sun. "Family Photo." Photographs: Shin Hye Sun. Accessed May 23, 2020. http://www.shinhyesun.com/family.htm.

Shorter, Edward. *The Making of the Modern Family*. New York: Basic Books, 1975.

Sim, Kyusŏn. "[Sim Kyusŏn taekijaŭi 人(in)] muchŏng 100nyŏn . . . Ch'unwŏnmunhak kwan, motmandŭnŭn'gŏn'ga anmandŭnŭn'gŏn'ga." *Dong-a Ilbo*. www.donga.com, October 1, 2016. https://www.donga.com/news/article/all/20161001/80573730/1.

Sin, Pokchin. *Kwangjunŭn Marhanda Ŏnŭ Sajin'gichakapon 5.18(Oilpal)Hangjaenggwa 6(Yu)Wŏl Hangjaeng: Sin Pokchin Sajinjip*. Seoul: Noonbit, 2006.

Sin, Kyŏnga. "Sanŏphwaihu Il-Kajok Munjeŭi Tamnonjŏk Chihyŏnggwa Pyŏnhwa." In *Il·kajok·jendŏ: Han'gukŭi Sanŏphwawa Il-Kajok Tillema*, 83–125. Paju, South Korea: Hanulak'ademi, 2009.

Sin, Sŭngho. "Kyŏngch'aresŏ Chosa Pattŏn Taehaksaeng 'Shokŭsa.'" *Joong-Ang Ilbo*, January 15, 1987, sec. Sahoemyŏn.

Sin'i. "D-Story 123: Sitaerŭl apsŏgan yŏkijatŭl(2) Hŏ Yŏngsuk." *Tongne: Tongamidiagŭrup kongsik bŭlogŭ* (blog), October 28, 2011. http://dongne.donga.com/2011/10/28/d-story-123-시대를-앞서-간-여기자들2-허영숙/.

Smith, Shawn Michelle. "The Afterimages of Emmett Till." *American Art* 29, no. 1 (Spring 2015): 22–27.

Smith, Shawn Michelle. *At the Edge of Sight: Photography and the Unseen*. Durham, NC: Duke University Press, 2013.

Smith, Shawn Michelle. "'Baby's Picture Is Always Treasured': Eugenics and the Reproduction of Whiteness in the Family Photograph Album." In *The Nineteenth Century Visual Culture Reader*, edited by Vanessa R. Schwartz and Jeannene M. Przyblyski, 358–70. New York: Routledge, 2004.

Smith, Shawn Michelle. *Photographic Returns: Racial Justice and the Time of Photography*. Durham, NC: Duke University Press, 2020.

Smith, Shawn Michelle, and Sharon Sliwinski, eds. *Photography and the Optical Unconscious*. Durham, NC: Duke University Press, 2017.

Sŏ, Kyŏngsik. "Wan'gohan Madadŭl-Chŏngyŏndu." *Hwanghae Review* 78 (March 2013): 319–44.

Sŏng, Tukyŏng. *Tasitorawapon Sŏul Sŏng Tukyŏng Sajinjip*. Seoul: Noonbit, 1994.

Sŏuldaehakkyo kyoyugyŏn'guwŏn. *(2002 Wŏldŭk'ŏp Ihuŭi) Munhwasimin'undongbalchŏnbangan Simp'osiŏm*. Seoul: Seoul National University Education Research Institute, 2003.

Strassler, Karen. *Demanding Images: Democracy, Mediation, and the Image-Event in Indonesia*. Durham, NC: Duke University Press, 2020.

Strassler, Karen. *Refracted Visions: Popular Photography and National Modernity in Java*. Durham, NC: Duke University Press, 2010.

Suh, Serk-Bae. "A False Martyr's Wager: Yi Kwangsu and Colonial Collaboration." In *Beyond Death: The Politics of Suicide and Martyrdom in Korea*, edited by Charles R. Kim, Jungwon Kim, Hwasook Nam, and Serk-Bae Suh, 115–41. Seattle: University of Washington Press, 2019.

Suh, Yehre. "Korean Borders: Real to Imagined." In *Crow's Eye View: The Korean Peninsula*, edited by Minsuk Cho and Hyungmin Pai, 181–92. Seoul: Achilife, 2014.

Supreme Court of Korea. "Potocharyo/Ŏnnonjaryohaemyŏng." News release, September 29, 2022. https://www.scourt.go.kr/news/NewsViewAction2.work?pageIndex=9&searchWord=&searchOption=&seqnum=1252&gubun=702.

Takemoto, Tina. "Drawing Complaint: Orientalism, Disidentification, and Performance." *Asian Diasporic Visual Cultures and the Americas* 1, no. 1 (2015): 84–107.

Tamunhwakachokkwa, Yŏsŏngkachokpu. "Kukchekyŏron Hyŏnhwang." e-Narachip'yo, July 22, 2020. http://www.index.go.kr/potal/main/EachDtlPageDetail.do?idx_cd=2430.

Tan'guktaehakkyo pusŏl tongyanghak yŏn'guso. *Ilsangsaenghwalgwa Kŭndaekyŏrhonjedo: Chapchip'yŏn*. Han'gukmunhwacharyoch'ongsŏ 37. Seoul: Minsokwŏn, 2010.

Tsai, Ming-liang, dir. *What Time Is It There?* Winstar Cinema, 2001. 116 min.

Ŭn, Sumi. "Ch'otpulgwa Han'guksahoe Chungsanch'ŭngŭi Chahwasang." In *Kŭtaenŭn Wae Ch'otpurŭl Kkŭsyŏtnayo*, edited by Tongjin Sŏ, Yunhyŏng Han, Sŭnguk Paek, T'aekkwang Yi, Yŏngju Yu, Sanggil Yi, Yongt'aek Chŏng, et al., 215–33. Seoul: Sanch'aekja, 2009.

Uroskie, Andrew V. "Far Above the Madding Crowds: The Spatial Rhetoric of Mass Representation." In *Crowds*, edited by Jeffrey T. Schnapp and Matthew Tiews, 307–34. Stanford: Stanford University Press.

Veterans of Foreign Wars. *Kŭtŭripon Han'gukchŏnjaeng 2: Mikun'gwa Yuenkun 1945–1950 (The Korean War as They Have Seen 2: The U.S. Army and the UN Force, 1945–1950)*. Translated by Chuyŏng Yi and Tongch'an Pak. Vol. 2. Seoul: Noonbit, 2005.

Virno, Paolo. *A Grammar of the Multitude: For an Analysis of Contemporary Forms of Life*. Los Angeles: Semiotext(e), 2004.

Watson, Iain. "Multiculturalism in South Korea: A Critical Assessment." *Journal of Contemporary Asia* 40, no. 2 (May 2010): 337–46. https://doi.org/10.1080/00472331003600549.

Westing, Arthur H. "Towards Environmental Sustainability and Reduced Tensions on the Korean Peninsula." *Environment* 52, no. 1 (February 2010): 20–23.

Wilderson Frank B., III. "Afropessimism and the Ruse of Analogy: Violence, Freedom, Struggle, and the Death of Black Desire." In *Antiblackness*, edited by Moon-kie Jung and João H. Costa Vargas, 37–59. Durham, NC: Duke University Press, 2021.

Wisch-Ray, Sharon. "Dallas Doings: Kasten's Photos Displayed Prominently." *Texas Jewish Post*, August 9, 2012. http://tjpnews.com/?p=5536.

Yang, Gyi-young. "Characteristics of Digital Culture in Candle Rallies." MA thesis, Jeonbuk University, 2008.

Yapp, Hentyle. *Minor China: Method, Materialisms, and the Aesthetic*. Durham, NC: Duke University Press, 2021.

Yea, Sallie. "Everyday Spaces of Human Trafficking: (In)Visibility and Agency Among Trafficked Women in U.S. Military-Oriented Clubs in South Korea." *Annals of the American Association of Geographers* 106, no. 4 (July 2016): 957–73.

Yi, Kwangsu. "Minjok Kaejoron." *Kaepyŏk* (May 1922).

Yi, Hyŏngnok. *Yi Hyŏngnok Sajinjip*. Seoul: Noonbit, 2009.

Yi, Hyŏn'u. "Chŏngch'ich'amyŏ Yuhyŏngŭrossŏŭi Ch'otpuljiphoe: Tap'yŏsŏngŭi Pyŏnhwa." In *Han'gukkukchechŏngch'ihakhoe Haksuldaehoe Palp'yŏ Nonmunjip*, 7–26. Seoul: Han'gukkukchechŏngch'ihakhoe, 2008.

Yi, Ilgyun. "'Ch'oerut'an Pakhin Kim Chuyŏl' Sekyee Allyŏttŏn Hŏ Chongssi Pyŏlse." *Kyŏngnamdominilbo*, March 23, 2011. http://www.idomin.com/news/articleView.html?idxno=248275.

Yi, Kihun, Hyejin O, T'aehun Yi, Hyeryŏng Yi, Hyein Yi, Hyŏnggŭn Cho, Chŏnghwan Ch'ŏn, and Chonguk Hong. "Chwadam: Singminjikŭntaessŏngnonŭi Yokssawa Hyŏnjae." *Yŏksapip'yŏng (Critical Review of History)*, no. 136 (August 2021): 10–53.

Yi, Kyŏngmin. *Han'guk Kŭntae Yesulsajin Akaibŭ (1910–1945) K'ameradanggwa Yesulsajinsitae*. Seoul: Akaibŭbuksŭ, 2010.

Yi, Kyŏngmo. *Kyŏktonggiŭi Hyŏnjang Yi Kyŏngmo Sajinjip*. Seoul: Noonbit, 2010.

Yi, Minchŏng. "'Kunin Hyutaep'on Sayongsigan Churyŏdalla' Kangwŏn Chumin Hosohan Iyu." Accessed November 3, 2019. https://news.joins.com/article/23566868.

Yi, Nayŏng. "Kijich'on Hyŏngsŏng Kwachŏnggwa Yŏsŏngdŭrŭi Chŏhang." *Yŏsŏnggwa p'yŏnghwa*, no. 5 (December 2010): 170–97.

Yi, Nayŏng. "Kijich'on Yŏsongŭi Kyŏnghŏmgwa Yunnichŏk Chaehyŏnŭi Pul/Kanŭngsŏng: T'alsingminjuŭi p'eminisŭt'ŭ Yŏksassŭki." *Yŏsŏnghagnonjip* 28, no. 1 (2011): 79–120.

Yi, Nayŏng. "T'alsingminjuŭi p'eminisŭt'ŭ Yilkki-Kijich'on Sŏngmaemae Yŏsŏnggwa Sŏngbyŏlhwatwaen Minjokchuŭi, Chaehyŏnŭi Chŏngch'ihak (Postcolonial Reading on Military Prostitutes in South Korea: Gendered Nationalism and Politics of Representation)." *Han'gukyŏsŏnghak (Journal of Korean Women's Studies)* 24, no. 3 (September 2008): 77–209.

Yi, Pongbŏm. "1980nyŏndae Kyŏmyŏlgwa Chetochŏk Minjuhwa." *Kubohakpo*, no. 20 (2018): 153–210.

Yi, Sŏku, and Siyŏng Pak. "'Hwachangp'um, Ttŏkpokkito Kwangupyŏng Wihŏm' Chŏndanji Ppuryŏ." *Chosun Ilbo*, May 3, 2008.

Yi, Tongyŏn. "Pulgŭnangmawa Chuch'ehyŏngsŏng: Naesyŏnŏllijŭmin'ga Sŭt'ailŭi Ch'wihyangin'ga." *Munhwakwahak* 31 (2002).

Yi, Wanbŏm. "Han'guk chŏnjaengŭi chŏngch'ichŏk yŏnghyang." In *Chiulsuŏmnŭn Imigi 3: Han'gukchŏnjaengi Namgin'gŏttŭl* (The Indelible Image 3: The Photographs of the Korean War from National Archives and Records Administration in the United States of America). Vol. 3. Edited by Pak To, 5–11. Seoul: Noonbit, 2007.

Yoneyama, Lisa. *Cold War Ruins: Transpacific Critique of American Justice and Japanese War Crimes*. Durham, NC: Duke University Press, 2016.

Yoo, Hyejong. "The Candlelight Girls' Playground: Nationalism as Art of Dialogy, the 2008 Candlelight Vigil Protests in South Korea." *Invisible Culture* 15 (Fall 2010): 40–78.

Yuh, Ji-Yeon. "Out of the Shadows: Camptown Women, Military Brides, and Korean (American) Communities." In *Asian American Studies Now: A Critical Reader*, edited by Jean Yu-wen Shen Wu and Thomas C. Chen, 239–55. New Brunswick, NJ: Rutgers University Press, 2010.

Yun, Hyeseon. "Minjuhwaundong Sajin DB Kuch'uk: Chŏng T'aewŏn k'oleksyŏn Sarye (Building Database of Korean Democratization Movements: Case of Tony Chung Collection)." *Journal of Korean Society of Archives and Records Management* 21, no. 1 (February 2021): 249–55.

Žižek, Slavoj. *Hyŏngmyŏngi Takaonda: Lenine Taehan Yolsekaji Yŏnku*. Translated by Sŏwon Yi. Seoul: Kil, 2006.

Zolghadr, Tirdad. "Them and Us: More Than a Feeling." *Frieze* 96 (January–February 2006). https://web.archive.org/web/20071118100528/http://www.frieze.com/issue/article/them_and_us/.

INDEX

Photo plate images are indicated with p1–p16.